Papers of the Forty-Eighth Algonquian Conference

Actes du quarante-huitième Congrès des Algonquinistes

PAPERS OF THE ALGONQUIAN CONFERENCES
ACTES DU CONGRÈS DES ALGONQUINISTES

Papers of the Forty-Eighth Algonquian Conference

Actes du quarante-huitième Congrès des Algonquinistes

EDITED BY Monica Macaulay and Margaret Noodin

MICHIGAN STATE UNIVERSITY PRESS | EAST LANSING

♾ The paper used in this publication meets the minimum requirements of ANSI/NISO Z39.48-1992 (R 1997) (Permanence of Paper).

Michigan State University Press
East Lansing, Michigan 48823-5245

Printed and bound in the United States of America.

28 27 26 25 24 23 22 21 20 19 1 2 3 4 5 6 7 8 9 10

ISBN 978-1-61186-306-2 (paperback)
ISBN 978-1-60917-585-6 (PDF)

Book design by Charlie Sharp, Sharp DesIgns, East Lansing, Michigan
Cover design by Erin Kirk New
Cover detail of a quill box is used courtesy of Julie L. Loehr

Michigan State University Press is a member of the Green Press Initiative and is committed to developing and encouraging ecologically responsible publishing practices. For more information about the Green Press Initiative and the use of recycled paper in book publishing, please visit *www.greenpressinitiative.org*.

Visit Michigan State University Press at *www.msupress.org*

CONTENTS

PREFACE

The Forty-Eighth Algonquian Conference was held in Milwaukee, Wisconsin, October 13–16, 2016. It was organized by Margaret Noodin and Maurina Paradise of the Electa Quinney Institute for American Indian Education at the University of Wisconsin–Milwaukee. The organizers are grateful to the Milwaukee Indian Community School for allowing attendees to spend time touring and dining at the campus where students and teachers work to use and preserve several of the heritage languages of the area including: Anishinaabemowin, Potawatomi, Menominee, Oneida, and Ho-Chunk. Organizers would also like to thank Jim Oskineegish for the use of his powerful painting of an Underwater Panther on conference materials.

In addition to the papers published here, the following papers were presented at the conference:

Steve Abney (University of Michigan): CLD: Software for Analysis of Anishinaabemowin Texts and Recordings

Sarah Acton (Eastern Michigan University): Learning About Cultural Priorities for Child Language Development in a First Nation: Qualitative Interviews with James Bay Cree Parents and Elders

Joey Awonohopay and Ron Corn Jr. (Menominee Indian Tribe of Wisconsin): Menominee Revitalization

Daryl Baldwin (Miami Tribe of Oklahoma), Michael Sullivan (College of St. Scholastica), Ron Corn Jr. (Menominee Indian Tribe of Wisconsin), and Jimena Terraza (Université du Québec à Montreal): Linguistics in Revitalization Panel

Heather Bliss (University of Victoria): The Robustness of Blackfoot's Proximate and Obviative Inflection

Nathon Breu (University of Wisconsin–Milwaukee), Susan Wade (University of Wisconsin–Milwaukee), Monea Warrington (University of Wisconsin–Milwaukee), and Mark Langenfeld (University of Wisconsin–Milwaukee): Interdisciplinary Studies in Anishinaabemowin at UW–Milwaukee

Chantale Cenerini (University of Manitoba): Towards a Renewed Understanding of Cree-Innu-Naskapi Dialectology: An Analysis of Phonological, Lexical, and Grammatical Isoglosses in the Algonquian Linguistic Atlas

Brendan Fairbanks (University of Minnesota Twin Cities): Realis and Irrealis Constructions in Ojibwe

Ashley Glassburn Falzetti (Eastern Michigan University) and Sara Acton (Eastern Michigan University): Finding Better Ways to Teach Grammar: A Community-Linguist Partnership in the Miami Nation

Michael Hamilton (Florida Atlantic University) and Miloje Despič (Cornell University): Theme Signs and Multiple Argument Indexing

Atticus G. Harrigan (University of Alberta), Katherine Schmirler (University of Alberta), and Antti Arppe (University of Alberta): Lexical Subtypes in a Plains Cree Corpus

Heather A. Howard (Michigan State University): "The Community—Our Extended Family": Relationality at the Intersection of Healing and Research in Indigenous Social and Health Services in Toronto

Norma Jean Jancewicz (SIL International): Exploring the Relevance of English Language Methodology to Naskapi L1 Teaching

Marie-Odile Junker (Carleton College), Conor Quinn (University of Southern Maine), and Rand Valentine (University of Wisconsin–Madison): Evidentiality and Epistemic Modality in Algonquian

Philip LeSourd (Indiana University Bloomington) and Steven Knipp (Indiana University Bloomington): Pitch Accent in Maliseet-Passamaquoddy: An Instrumental Study

Carol-Rose Little (Cornell University): On the Morphophonology of Mi'gmaq Subject Agreement

Monty McGahey II (Chippewas of the Thames First Nation): Comparing Dialectal Differences of Anishinaabemowin from Southern/Central Ontario from a Learner's Perspective

Taylor Miller (University of Delaware): Reexamining the Front Vowels in Saulteaux Ojibwe: The Case for the Short /e/

Sarah Murray (Cornell University): Mass and Count Nouns in Cheyenne

Mary Ann Naokwegijig-Corbiere (University of Sudbury): Nishnaabemwin Revitalization through a Cultural Studies Lens

Mathieu Paillé (University of Winnipeg): Discursive Uses of Main-Clause Conjunct Verbs in Ojibwe

David H. Pentland (University of Manitoba): The Origins of the Algonquian Impersonal ("Passive") Inflections

Kai Pyle (University of Minnesota Twin Cities): How Do You Say "Two-Spirit" in Algonquian?

Conor Quinn (University of Southern Maine), Andrea Bear Nicholas (St. Thomas University), Gabriel Paul (Penobscot Nation Department of Cultural and Historic Preservation), and Alwyn Jeddore (Membertou/Eskasoni/CBU): Reducing Anxiety, Increasing Core Competence: A Practical Program for Beginner Adult Heritage Learners of Eastern Algonquian Languages

Richard Rhodes (University of California, Berkeley): Peter Jones's Genesis

Daniel Stoltzfus (Université du Québec à Chicoutimi) and Aubrée Boissard (Université Laval): Lexical Patterning in Michif: Reconsidering the Role of French

Lucy Thomason (Smithsonian Institution): Postposed Preverbs and Prenouns in Meskwaki

Jan P. van Eijk (First Nations University of Canada): Cree Animacy-Inanimacy Hierarchy: A Conspectus

Natalie Weber (University of British Columbia): Blackfoot Reflexes of Proto-Algonquian Clusters in *ʔ and *h

Yadong Xu (University of Manitoba): Subject Preference and Object Attraction in Conjunct Central Agreement

Insights from Computational Modeling of the Derivational Structure of Plains Cree Stems

Antti Arppe, Katherine Schmirler, Miikka Silfverberg, Mans Hulden, and Arok Wolvengrey

The complex inflectional and derivational morphology of Plains Cree and other Algonquian languages has long been considered from both a synchronic and diachronic perspective (e.g., Bloomfield 1946; Goddard 1974; Oxford 2014). While the composition of some modern Plains Cree stems has been obscured by sound change, they can often still be identified by linguists, and for speakers, many morphemes are available to freely derive new stems. Unlike derivational morphology, the inflectional morphology of Cree is quite regular and lends itself to straightforward description, and this has translated to a computational model that can analyze inflected forms of Plains Cree lemmata (e.g., Harrigan et al. 2017; Snoek et al. 2014). Though the derivational morphology poses more challenges to model, lists of existing derivational morphemes can be extracted from existing sources, and various morphophonological rules have been described (Cook and Muehlbauer 2010; Wolfart 1996; Wolvengrey 2001). However, we can make use of the derivational model to assess how well the rules and morphemes given for Plains Cree apply when tested against lemmas included in available dictionaries. This approach, following Karttunen (2006), allows us to test theoretical descriptions against larger data sets than those used to produce the rules: where the human mind can only make sense of so much data at once, a quantitative approach can take thousands of words into account.

In this article, we present the first version of a computational model for Plains Cree derivational morphology, using a weighted finite-state transducer, and discuss its development, testing, strengths, and shortcomings. Our model is constructed using the morphological breakdowns of the stems given by Wolvengrey (2001) and documented morphophonological rules for Plains Cree (e.g., Wolfart 1996). While the concatenation of existing morphemes is straightforward, and most of the relevant morphophonological changes have been documented, the efficacy of the model is hindered by several factors, such as idiosyncrasies due to obscured sound changes, borrowings, and underdocumentation of morphemes and morphophonological rules. We consider the extent to which documented rules and morphemes are sufficient for the computational modeling of Plains Cree derivation.

Background

Plains Cree

Plains Cree is an Algonquian language spoken in western Canada with several thousands of speakers. The language is still learned by children in many communities, and it is used in many everyday contexts, such as in homes, in television and radio broadcasts, and in books and other written materials. Plains Cree is a member of the Cree-Montagnais-Naskapi dialect continuum; various language revitalization efforts have been undertaken for members of this continuum, such as textbooks or grammars (e.g., Ahenakew 1987; Okimâsis 2004; Wolfart 1973, 1996 for Plains Cree; Ellis 2000 for Swampy and Moose Cree), children's books (e.g., Ahenakew 1988; Lavallee and Silverthorne 2014), and morphological analyzers (e.g., Harrigan et al. 2017; Snoek et al. 2014). While existing computational analyzers focus primarily on inflectional morphology, Algonquian languages also display considerable derivational morphology. Cognate derivational morphemes are apparent across a number of Algonquian languages, and many of these are still productive in modern Algonquian languages. In the following subsection, we look at nominal and verbal derivational elements and derivational processes in Plains Cree.

Derivation

Derivation in Cree makes use of three types of morphemes: roots or initials, medials, and finals. All stems in Cree contain at least one root and one final, though phonetically null finals have been posited to maintain this structure; medials are generally optional in the derivation process. Roots are the initial elements of stems and carry considerable semantic content, but are generally free to occur across stem classes (nouns, verbs, and particles), as in (1) (Wolfart 1973:65–66). However, where nouns are formed through a process called primary derivation (see below), they generally occur with roots specific to nouns, rather than with those that can occur across word classes (Bloomfield 1946); see examples in (2).[1]

(1) *Root morphemes across stem classes* (Wolvengrey 2001)

a. /wâp-/ 'light, bright'

i.	wâpi-	'see, have vision'	VAI
ii.	wâpahta-	'see s.t.'	VTI
iii.	wâpam-	'see s.o.'	VTA
iv.	wâpastim	'white dog/horse'	NA

b. /âw-/ 'carry'

i.	âwacikan	'wheelbarrow'	NI
ii.	âwacikê-	'haul things'	VAI
iii.	âwah-	'haul s.o.'	VTA

c. /âyît-/ 'firm, tight'

i.	âyîci-	'firmly, tightly'	preverb
ii.	âyîtina-	'hold firmly to s.t.'	VTI

(2) *Nominal stems with zero finals* (Wolvengrey 2001)[2]

a. atim

atimw—'dog'

b. maskwa

maskw—'bear'

Medials occur between root and final morphemes, though they are not required in derivation. Like general roots, their occurrence is relatively unrestricted across stem classes. They also tend to have fairly concrete meanings. They may also be derived from other stem classes, such as in forms in (3). Dependent nouns (inalienably possessed body parts, kin terms) are considered medials that occur with zero roots, though body part medials may also occur in verbs, as in (4). Many medials fall into the subclass of classificatory medials, such as those in (5), which serve to denote not a stem class, but a semantic class. Finally, many medials have shorter and longer variants; the latter are known as extended medials (Wolfart 1973:66–68).[3]

(3) *Roots ~ derived medials*

a. /atimw-/ ~ /-astimw-/ 'dog'

b. /masin-/-ah-/ ~ /-asinah-/ 'mark, write'

c. /pâhpih-/ ~ /-âhpih-/ 'laugh at s.o.'

(4) *Body part medials*

a. ni**hcikwân** 'my knee' ~ kaski**hcikwân**êhw- 'break s.o.'s knee by shot'

b. ni**cihciy** 'my hand' ~ saki**cihc**ên- 'seize s.o. by the hand'

(5) *Classificatory medials*

a. /-âpisk(w)-/ 'stone, metal' > pîw**âpiskw**- 'piece of metal' (NA)

b. /-âpêk-/ 'rope' > it**âpêk**in- 'hold s.o. thus on a rope' (VTA)

Final morphemes are required for derivation, though they are often phonetically null. Some finals determine the stem class: noun, verb, or particle, and, within verbs, determine the subclass (transitivity and animacy) as well. They are often either more concrete or more abstract; concrete finals carry easily identifiable semantic information along with stem class information, while abstract finals contain only stem class information (Wolfart 1973:68–75). Examples of nominal and verbal finals, both with more concrete and more abstract semantics, can be seen in (6) and (7), respectively.

(6) *Nominal finals*

a. *Concrete*

i. /-âhtikw/ 'tree': ayôskanâhtikw- 'raspberry bush' (NA)

ii. /-âpoy/ 'liquid': maskihkîwâpoy 'tea' (NI)

b. *Abstract*

iii. /-win/ abstract noun: âcimowin 'story' (NI)

iv. /-n/ instrument, product: kistikân 'grain, wheat' (NA)

(7) *Verbal finals*

a. *Concrete*

v. /-(i)sw/ 'by heat': kîsisw- 'cook s.o.' (VTA)

vi. /-(i)n/ 'by hand': itin- 'move s.o. thus by hand' (VTA)

b. *Abstract*

vii. /-(i)kê/ general object: nôcihcikê- 'hunt things' (VAI)

viii. /-h/ causative: cîsih- 'mislead s.o.' (VTA)

Medials and finals are suffixed to roots in primary derivation, to form primary stems. Primary stems may then undergo further derivation with an optional medial and required final, forming a secondary stem. Secondary derivation may occur several times, forming morphologically quite complex stems, as in (8).

(8) *Complex derived forms*

a. *Verb*

ayamihcikêstamâso—/ayam-/	/-i/	/-htâ/	/-ikê/	/-stamaw/	/-iso/
ROOT	FINAL	FINAL	FINAL	FINAL	FINAL

'read to oneself'

b. *Noun*

matwêkahikêwin

/matwê-/	/-ikah/	/-ikê/	/-win/
ROOT	FINAL	FINAL	FINAL

'sound of chopping heard in the distance'

Alongside stem derivation, forms can also be derived through compounding. Noun compounds contain a noun with a prefixed particle or other noun, while verb compounds contain a preverb and a verb stem. Within noun compounds, the prefixed noun generally takes the suffix *-i*, formally identical to the particle final; the same form may occur as a particle, a prenoun, and a preverb (Bloomfield 1946; Wolfart 1973:75–78). Examples of compounds are given in (9).

(9) *Compounds*

a. *Nominal*

paskwâwi-mostos

paskwâw	mostos
prairie	cow

'buffalo'

b. *Verbal*

kâmwâci-pimâtisi-

kâmwâci	pimâtisi-
quiet	live

'live quietly'

In creating a derivational model for Plains Cree, we must recognize both stem derivation and compounding processes, as well as any derivation within the initial members of compounds or unfamiliar preverbs. We offer a brief description of a finite state transducer and how this has been applied to the inflectional morphology of Plains Cree and the recognition rate of the inflectional analyzer.

The Derivational Model

As the formalism in our computational modeling of Plains Cree derivational word formation, we make use of finite state transducer (FST) tools as described in, e.g., Beesley and Karttunen (2003), and in particular the Helsinki Finite-State Transducer (HFST) software technology suite (Lindén et al. 2011), since it allows for the weighting of the model, the details and benefits of which we will discuss further. The HFST compiler provides two subformalisms that we use: (1) LEXC, which allows us to specify how morphemes are concatenated, and (2) XFSCRIPT regular expressions, which enable us to define a cascade of ordered SPE-style rewrite rules for implementing the various morphophonological processes, typically occurring at morpheme junctures, but possibly across an entire stem (such as palatalization in conjunction with the diminutive morphemes *-is*, *-isis*, and *-si*). Previously, we have also made use of FST technology to build a computational inflectional model for Plains Cree (e.g., Harrigan et al. 2017; Snoek et al. 2014), which analyzes verbal and nominal inflection, such as person, number, tense, possession, etc.[4]

Constructing the Model

To analyze the derivational elements of Plains Cree stems, we first determined which morphemes are analyzed in Plains Cree stems. These were drawn from the database underlying Wolvengrey's (2001) Plains Cree dictionary, which contains a morphological breakdown of each recorded stem, noting the overt[5] roots or initials, medials, and finals for each. While there is some homophony in medials and finals, the total number of individual morphemes in the database is 2,550. Of these, there are 1,784 roots, 308 medials, and 547 finals, which are coded appropriately in a morpheme lexicon to which the FST can refer.

The morphological model to concatenate these morphemes is extremely simple. Using the LEXC formalism, we describe the concatenation of initial, medial, and final morphemes in various combinations. In Figure 1, the black arrows indicate the simplest paths of concatenation, initial+(medial)+final. The gray arrows indicate paths of possible recursion.[6]

FIGURE 1. The General Derivational Model.

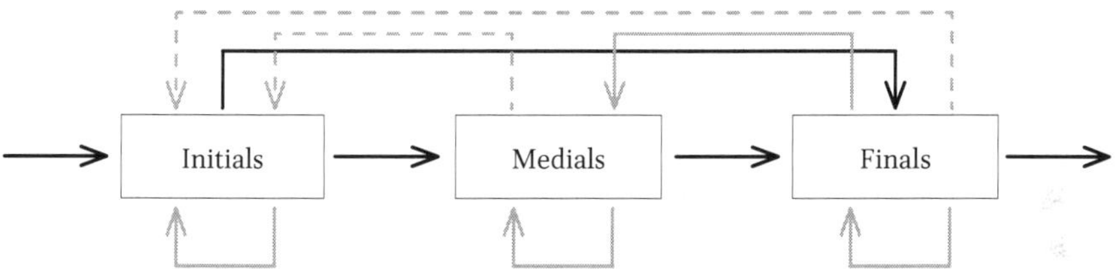

As presented, this model clearly does not accurately represent Plains Cree stem derivation: we have allowed for infinite initials, medials, and finals in any order, while in practice Cree demonstrates [[[initial + (medial) + final] + (medial) + final] . . .]. If we wanted to generate Plains Cree stems, this model would generate far more impossible stems than possible ones. However, the practical goal of such a model is to analyze existing stem forms, both known and unknown, and so the resulting analyses become problematic only in the case of homophonous medials and finals. Furthermore, this design has two main advantages. One, by allowing recursion in the medials and finals, we avoid the need for zero morphemes in the model. Two, if we allow for recursion from medials or finals back to initials, we can allow for compounding of preverbal or prenominal elements with the particle final *-i* followed by the initial morpheme of another stem: e.g., [[root/stem + *-i*] +

[root + (medial) + final]]. Moreover, we expect that the weighting of this simple morpheme concatenation model will be able to order the potentially large numbers of resultant analyses so that the most likely ones will be ranked first.

Alongside the morpheme concatenation model, we must also implement the relevant morphophonological rules. Since many of the morphophonological elements are no longer productive, we must both make reference to obsolete sounds and allow for the rules to be optional. As noted earlier for the morpheme concatenation, this does not accurately represent the morphophonology of Cree stems and is not restrictive for the analysis of unknown stems. However, this method is more likely to produce at least one analysis for any given stem, which can then be confirmed as a likely analysis by researchers or speakers when combined with a translation or other contextual information. For the ordered list of rules in (10), we have specified a morphophonological component in the computational derivational model, representing the resulting possible changes, using the XFSCRIPT regular expression formalism for implementing SPE-style rewrite rules.

(10) Morphophonological rules[7]

a. t → c / _ $ [is | isis | si] $ (nominal and verbal diminutives)

b. ê → â / $ _ $ n $

c. Palatalization rules

  i. T → t | s / _ $ i | î

  ii. t → t | c / _ $ i | î

  iii. T | t → t / _ $ *e

d. *e → i

e. Ø → i / C $ _ C[8]

f. Vowel-glide-*i* rules[9]

  i. [a | â] [w | y | ý[10]] $ i → â

  ii. ê [w | y | ý] $ i → ê

  iii. [i | î] [w | y | ý] $ [i | î] → î

  iv. [o | ô] [w | y | ý] $ i → ô

g. V-V rules[11]

  i. [a | â] $ [a | â] → â

  ii. [ê] $ [ê] → ê

  iii. [i | î] $ [i | î] → î

  iv. [o | ô] $ [o | ô] → ô

h. w $ i → o / C _ C
i. w $ o → [o | ô] / C _
j. w $ w → [w | ow] / C _ V
k. [m | n] $ → h / _ [p | t | k | c]

These rules are ordered to allow for the best possible recognition rates at this time, though further development may result in changes to their order. Many of these rules are straightforward, though some require further comment. First, note the use of <T> and <e>, which refer to the Proto-Algonquian reconstructions *θ and **e* (which have fallen together with *t* and *i*, respectively). While these sounds no longer occur in Plains Cree, they have left their marks in palatalization rules and are coded where possible in the lexicon.[12] However, they do not consistently palatalize as expected, and so the rules must still be optional. Second, we have sets of rules that can easily be summarized into single rules, but for the sake of the model must be written more specifically. These include the vowel-glide-*i* rules, which we must specify for each vowel, but can be stated as simply as "any vowel followed by a glide and short *i* will collapse to a long vowel of the same quality." Similarly, when vowels of the same quality meet at a morpheme boundary, regardless of length, they become a single long vowel; again, we must write four separate rules for each vowel quality. Further development may allow for many of these rules to be streamlined, as well as for the addition of rules that are known but not yet implemented, such as the hiatus of vowels of different qualities and morpheme-specific rules.

Training the Model

The combination of the morpheme concatenation and morphophonological rule components described earlier provides us with our basic computational derivational model. Since there are few restrictions on how the multiple morphemes may combine, and there are several single-character morphemes that can combine quite freely with the rest, for almost any stem this results in a large number of structurally possible but for the most part pragmatically improbable, if not entirely impossible, analyses. For instance, the VTA verb *nîhciwêpin-* 's/he throws s.o. down, off' is given altogether six derivational analyses, presented in (11), of which the fourth, (11d) /nîht-/wêp-/-n/,[13] is the correct one ('down', 'throw', 'by hand (VTA)').[14]

(11) Unweighted analyses

a. /niy-/iht-/wêp-/-n/ 0.000000[15]

b. /niy-/iht-/wêp-/-i/-n/ 0.000000

c. /niy-/iht-/wêp-/-in/ 0.000000

d. /nîht-/wêp-/-n/ 0.000000

e. /nîht-/wêp-/-i/-n/ 0.000000

f. /nîht-/wêp-/-in/ 0.000000

For the noncompound stems in Wolvengrey (2001), the basic derivational analyzer can provide for a single form anywhere from 1 up to as many as 51,092 alternative analyses, with a median number of analyses being 217. To impose some order into this thicket, weighting the morpheme transitions in the computational derivational model allows us to rank the multitude of structurally possible analyses, so that the most likely ones will be provided first. We make use of the substantial number of already attested forms and their derivational decompositions in Wolvengrey (2001), starting with the 11,614 noncompounding stems in that resource, to determine which morpheme sequences are most likely. In order to create such a weighted version of the basic derivational FST model (e.g., Mohri 1997; Pirinen 2014), we learn the transducer weights from the aforementioned list of string pairs, consisting of (a) realized stems and (b) corresponding derivational breakdowns, using a simple procedure: we (1) traverse the states and transitions of the unweighted FST using each string pair in turn, while keeping track of the number of times each transition was used; (2) normalize these counts (after *add-1 smoothing*) of outgoing transitions in each state to a proper probability distribution; and (3) convert the probabilities to penalty weights, which are the negated logarithms of the overall probabilities of the derivational analyses for a stem.[16] The resulting weighted derivational model can then rank the analyses for, e.g., *nîhciwêpin-* (11), as shown in (12). The smaller the weight is, the more likely the analysis is considered. Now, the correct, expected analysis, /nîht-/wêp-/-n/, receives the smallest weight of 14.08, and is thus also the best-ranked one.[17]

(12) Weighted analyses

a. /nîht-/wêp-/-n/ 14.082328

b. /nîht-/wêp-/-in/ 16.578869

c. /nîht-/wêp-/-i/-n/ 20.568705

d. /niy-/iht-/wêp-/-n/ 34.791088

TABLE 1. Proportions of rankings for the correct derivational decompositional analysis among all analyses for stems in the evaluation (= training) data

RANK(S)	PROPORTION (%)	CUMULATIVE (%)	COUNT
1	76.7	76.7	7,205
2	13.8	90.5	1,296
3	4.0	94.6	378
4	2.0	96.5	185
5	0.9	97.4	83
6	0.5	97.9	43
7	0.4	98.3	35
8	0.4	98.7	38
9	0.2	98.8	18
10	0.2	99.1	23
11–43	0.6	100.0	88

e. /niy-/iht-/wêp-/-in/ 38.455750

f. /niy-/iht-/wêp-/-i/-n/ 38.871815

Testing the Model

We next tested the weighted derivational model using the same set of 11,614 noncompounding stems and their derivational analyses from Wolvengrey (2001) that had been used to train the model. In terms of assessing the performance quantitatively, we first observed how many stems received a correct derivational analysis, or none at all, and second, and even more important, how the correct derivational analyses were ranked in terms of their weights.

Taking into account documented morphemes and the majority of documented phonological rules, this current derivational model was able to provide the correct morphological decomposition, among often a plethora of more or less likely analyses, for 80.9 percent (n = 9,392) of the 11,614 stems analyzed in the database underlying Wolvengrey (2001). Focusing on these 9,392 stems receiving the correct derivational decomposition, for 76.7 percent this was the top-most ranked analysis, and for 96.2 percent among the top four ranked analyses (Table 1). Moreover, the poorest ranking for any correct analysis was 43rd, and the median ranking was 1st.

For the 2,222 stems (19.1 percent) that did not receive a single correct analysis corresponding with the one provided by a linguist, the breakdowns that the weighted derivational model nevertheless produces allow us to determine where further modifications and extensions to the morpheme set and the morphophonological rules may be needed to improve the model's performance with respect to the training data, and, by extension, unknown stems in general. Of course, when applying this model to unknown stems, the recognition rate would drop considerably.

Discussion

Where this computational derivational model works, it works very well and would be an excellent tool in determining potential compositions of an unknown stem. However, this model still only holds for four-fifths of the data on which it was trained, and so further development is necessary.

Various issues that have resulted in nonrecognition can be identified in both the model and the test data. In the model, two main issues are apparent. First, the required morphemes may not be represented in our morpheme lexicon, and so will not be found in test analyses. Second, and perhaps foremost, our morphophonological rules are not yet exhaustive and display some issues with respect to rule ordering that affects their application. Unlike inflectional analysis, the morphophonological rules for derivational morphemes also do not apply as regularly, and several possibilities may present themselves where any two sounds meet. For example, . . . *Cw-w* . . . (where the hyphen represents a morpheme break) may become either *Cow* or *Cw*, and there is no wider phonological context that influences which surface form occurs. Similarly, where two vowels meet, various changes may take place based on the qualities and quantities of the vowels in question. While many of these rules are documented (e.g., Wolfart 1973, 1996), they still do not necessarily apply categorically, and further scrutiny of the data and rules is required.

Such morphophonological inconsistencies are often the cause of identifiable issues in our results, namely, that some forms are simply synchronically idiosyncratic. While historically we may be able to identify why a stem has a certain shape, we are not able to identify these contexts from synchronic stems. For example, the stem *apîst-* 'to sit near something' is composed of *api-* and *-st*, with no synchronic motivation for the lengthening of the vowel; this is simply a fact of the morpheme *-st* (Wolfart 1973:74–75). However, as such morpheme-specific rules are not yet implemented, this stem would not be recognized. Idiosyncrasies involving particular sounds also occur; for instance, palatalization rules in the literature generally refer to *i*, but we see instances of *t>s* before *o*, or of palatalization not occurring where the context indicates we would expect it. Historical motivations are sometimes identifiable on a case-by-case basis, which could in principle be modeled with morpheme-specific or sequence-specific morphophonological rules, but this would come with the cost of losing generality of application beyond the current morpheme set and training data, and would in practice run the risk of quickly inflating the rule set so that it could become unwieldy to maintain. For example, we can specify that our *Cw-w>Cow* rule always applies for the sequence *-amw-win*, but can vary with the *Cw-w>Cw* rule in other contexts. Occasionally, stems are idiosyncratic not because of obscured phonological context, but due to lexical semantics. For example, the form *apiscawâsis* 'small child', from the elements *apist-* and *awâsis*, would not be recognized (even if compounding were implemented satisfactorily) because there is no phonological context (i.e., *i*) or morphological context (i.e., a diminutive suffix) to trigger the palatalization of *t* to *c*.[18] However, this is a case of diminutive palatalization, because *awâsis* 'child' refers to a small person, and therefore frequently occurs with diminutive palatalization, even where an overt suffix is not present. Though idiosyncrasies are unavoidable as languages change, these will always be problematic for derivational recognition of unknown stems.

Conclusion

As a first attempt at modeling the derivational morphology of Plains Cree, the model we have presented in this article has been shown to be a good start for further development and understanding of Plains Cree derivation. Though we are able to return correct analyses for more than four-fifths of the training data, we are still left with many avenues for further development, in both the morpheme concatenation and morphophonological rules we have devised. We have noted a set of morphemes that need to be added to our lexicon to improve recognition, and we have different options for modeling the morphophonemic rules, which may yield improved results. Furthermore, our model sheds light on the documentation of morphemes and morphophonological rules in Plains Cree: while they have served as an excellent starting point for a derivational model, the variation that has arisen over time due to sound change and other idiosyncrasies that may occur cannot be handled by such a model. The model allows us to test quantitatively how much of the derivational morphology can indeed be modeled by a set of relatively general rules, and how much remains idiosyncratic. In the current instance, it appears that this ratio of regularity vs. irregularity/idiosyncrasy is approximately 4/5 vs. 1/5. However, with the results of the model available, we can begin to make improvements, which will allow us to examine and describe, and perhaps even model, more of the derivational morphology of Plains Cree. In the realm of Algonquian linguistics, where the corpora available to us are relatively limited and cannot thus be an extensive source for extracting a comprehensive lexicon of a language, a well-developed derivational model for Plains Cree morphology would complement the existing inflectional model, allowing us to identify the possible morphemes underlying unknown stems in our analyses, which would improve overall recognition rates not just in current corpora of Plains Cree but newly created texts as well, and can offer previously undocumented stems to add to dictionaries, teaching materials, and online language-learning tools.

NOTES

1. Abbreviations: VAI = animate intransitive verb, VTI = transitive inanimate verb, VTA = transitive animate verb, NA = animate noun, NI = inanimate noun.
2. These stems both end in *Cw* clusters, which are resolved in two ways. For *atim*, the *w* is deleted; however, for *maskwa*, a final *-a* is suffixed. This is an obsolete animate singular marker that is retained here to avoid a monosyllabic noun. As *atimw-* is disyllabic, this *-a* is not retained; the cluster simplification applies instead.
3. As all types of stem morphemes—initials, medials, and finals—can carry considerable semantic content; we may even deviate from traditional terminology and recognize that any of these categories can, in some way, contain rootlike morphemes. For instance, when we see derived medials, body part medials, and nominal finals, these can also be considered bound roots that require further morphological material to be used as free forms.
4. This inflectional model has been used to analyze a corpus of Plains Cree (Ahenakew 2000; Bear et al. 1992; Kâ-Nîpitêhtêw 1998; Masuskapoe 2010; Minde 1997; Vandall and Douquette 1987; Whitecalf 1993). Further development of the derivational analyzer can be used to improve analyses of unknown forms in the corpus.
5. Recall that zero finals are structurally posited (e.g., Bloomfield 1946).
6. The dotted lines in Figure 1 represent pathways that are necessary to the modeling of

Plains Cree, but are not yet fully implemented in the model tested in this article.

7. In this formalism, $ refers to a morpheme boundary, and | separates different possible contexts.
8. For the sake of simplicity, we use C here to represent any consonant, though this is represented in the actual formalism as [c | h | k | m | n | p | s | t | w | y | ý].
9. However, there are restrictions on the application of these rules, such as in particle/preverb constructions, e.g. /nitaw-/ + -i > *nitawi-* (never *nitâ-), and for certain stems, e.g. *mow-*.
10. The symbol *ý* is used by Wolvengrey (2001) to represent reflex of Proto-Algonquian *l or *r, which occurs as *y* in Plains Cree, but varies in closely related dialects and allows the dictionary to be used by speakers of these dialects.
11. However, two adjacent LONG vowels do not contract to a single long vowel. Instead, they are always kept separate, generally by epenthesizing [h] or [y].
12. As this coding for **e* vs. *i* is not yet exhaustive, and perhaps cannot be due to homophony or lack of evidence, these rules contribute to the model but do not apply perfectly.
13. The notation used in our derivational FST uses the slash '/' to indicate a morpheme boundary, so in the analysis /nîht-/wêp-/-n/ the model posits three morphemes.
14. Though not the primary focus of this paper, one can also use the computational derivational model in the inverse direction to provide expected realizations of a sequence of morphemes, taking into account the known morphophonological rules. In the case of */nîht-/wêp-/-n/*, this generates two alternative stems, *nîhciwêpin-* and *nîhtiwêpin-*.
15. A weight of 0.0 provided by an HFST analyzer indicates that the FST is not weighted. When weighting does not occur, there is no systematicity to the order in which analyses are presented.
16. These negated logarithms of probabilities, i.e., *-log*(*p*), are known in computational linguistics as *tropical weights*. These can be interpreted as penalties because a large *-log*(*p*) indicates a small probability, *p*. Additionally, if the computational model were nondeterministic, we would need a tropical semiring to approximate the actual probability, but that does not apply for our model as it is deterministic.
17. Similar to what was noted earlier in conjunction with the unweighted basic derivational model, the weighted computational model can just as well also be used in the inverse direction to produce realizations of stems resulting from morpheme sequences, taking into account the morphophonological rules (and their occurrences in the training data). For /nîht-/wêp-/-n/, the two possible stems are weighted as *nîhciwêpin-* (14,08) and *nîhtiwêpin-* (16,92), suggesting that the palatalization *t*>*c* is slightly more likely.

18. However, technically there is in fact a diminutive suffix in *awâsis-*, though it has historically fused. This becomes apparent in the possessive form *awâsimis-* (< *awâs-* + *-im* + *-is*). Alternatively, this could be interpreted as a case of semantic diminutivization.

REFERENCES

Ahenakew, Alice. 2000. *âh-âyîtaw isi ê-kî-kiskêyihtahkik maskihkiy / They Knew Both Sides of Medicine: Cree Tales of Curing and Cursing Told by Alice Ahenakew*, ed. by H. Christoph Wolfart. Winnipeg: University of Manitoba Press.

Ahenakew, Freda. 1987. *Cree Language Structures: A Cree Approach*. Winnipeg: Pemmican Publications.

———. 1988. *wîsahkêcâhk êkwa waskwayak: âtayohkêwin*. [Cree-only edition]. Saskatoon: Saskatchewan Indian Cultural Centre.

Bear, Glecia, Minnie Fraser, Irene Calliou, Mary Wells, Alpha Lafond, and Rita Longneck. 1992. *kôhkominawak otâcimowiniwâwa / Our Grandmothers' Lives as Told in Their Own Words*, ed. by Freda Ahenakew and H. Christoph Wolfart. Regina: Canadian Plains Research Center.

Beesley, Kenneth R. and Lauri Karttunen. 2003. *Finite State Morphology*. Stanford, CA: CSLI Publications.

Bloomfield, Leonard. 1946. Algonquian. *Linguistic Structures of Native America*, ed. by Harry Hoijer et al., pp. 85–129. Viking Fund Publications in Anthropology, vol. 6. New York.

Cook, Clare and Jeffrey Muehlbauer. 2010. A Morpheme Index of Plains Cree. Unpublished manuscript, University of Manitoba, Winnipeg. http://www.academia.edu/304874/A_morpheme_index_of_Plains_Cree.

Ellis, C. Douglas. 2000. *Spoken Cree, Level I*. 2nd ed. Edmonton: University of Alberta Press.

Goddard, Ives. 1974. Remarks on the Algonquian Independent Indicative. *International Journal of American Linguistics* 40(4):317–327.

Harrigan, Atticus, Katherine Schmirler, Antti Arppe, Lene Antonsen, Sjur Moshagen, and Trond Trosterud. 2017. Learning from the computational modeling of Plains Cree verbs. *Morphology* 27(4):565–598.

Hulden, Mans. 2009. Foma: A Finite-State Compiler and Library. *Proceedings of the Twelfth Conference of the European Chapter of the Association for Computational Linguistics*, ed. by Joakim Nivre and Claire Gardent, pp. 29–32. Stroudsburg, PA: Association for Computational Linguistics.

Kâ-Nîpitêhtêw, Jim. 1998. *ana kâ-pimwêwêhahk okakêskihkêmowina / The Counselling Speeches of Jim Kâ-Nîpitêhtêw*, ed. by Freda Ahenakew and H. Christoph Wolfart. Winnipeg:

University of Manitoba Press.

Karttunen, Lauri. 2006. The Insufficiency of Paper-and-Pencil Linguistics: The Case of Finnish Prosody. *Intelligent Linguistic Architectures: Variations on Themes by Ronald M. Kaplan*, ed. by Miriam Butt and Tracy Holloway King, pp. 287–300. Stanford, CA: CSLI Publications.

Lavallee, Ray and Judith Silverthorne. 2014. *Honouring the Buffalo: A Plains Cree Legend.* Regina: Your Nickel's Worth Publishing.

Lindén, Krister, Erik Axelson, Sam Hardwick, Tommi A. Pirinen, and Miikka Silfverberg. 2011. HFST—Framework for Compiling and Applying Morphologies. *Systems and Frameworks for Computational Morphology* (SFCM), ed. by Cerstin Mahlow and Michael Piotrowski, pp. 37–85. New York: Springer.

Masuskapoe, Cecilia. 2010. *piko kîkway ê-nakacihtât: kêkêk otâcimowina ê-nêhiawastêki*, ed. by H. Christoph Wolfart and Freda Ahenakew. Winnipeg: Algonquian and Iroquoian Linguistics.

Minde, Emma. 1997. *kwayask ê-kî-pê-kiskinowâpatihicik / Their Example Showed Me the Way: A Cree Woman's Life Shaped by Two Cultures*, ed. by Freda Ahenakew and H. Christoph Wolfart. Edmonton: University of Alberta Press.

Mohri, Mehryar. 1997. Finite-State Transducers in Language and Speech Processing. *Computational Linguistics* 23:269–311.

Okimâsis, Jean. 2004. *Cree, Language of the Plains*. Regina: University of Regina Press.

Oxford, William R. 2014. Microparameters of Agreement: A Diachronic Perspective on Algonquian Verb Inflection. PhD thesis, University of Toronto.

Pirinen, Tommi. 2014. Weighted Finite-State Methods for Spell-Checking and Correction. PhD thesis, University of Helsinki.

Snoek, Conor, Dorothy Thunder, Kaidi Lõo, Antti Arppe, Jordan Lachler, Sjur Moshagen, and Trond Trosterud. 2014. Modeling the Noun Morphology of Plains Cree. *Proceedings of ComputEL: Workshop on the use of computational methods in the study of endangered languages*, 52nd Annual Meeting of the Association for Computational Linguistics, Baltimore, Maryland, 26 June 2014, pp. 34–42. ACL Anthology.

Vandall, Peter and Joe Douquette. 1987. *wâskahikaniwiyiniw-âcimowina / Stories of the House People, Told by Peter Vandall and Joe Douquette*, ed. by Freda Ahenakew. Winnipeg: University of Manitoba Press.

Whitecalf, Sarah. 1993. *kinêhiyawiwininaw nêhiyawêwin / The Cree Language Is Our Identity: The La Ronge Lectures of Sarah Whitecalf*, ed. by H. Christoph Wolfart and Freda Ahenakew. Winnipeg: University of Manitoba Press.

Wolfart, H. Christoph. 1973. *Plains Cree: A Grammatical Study*. Transactions of the American Philosophical Society, n.s., vol. 63, part 5. Philadelphia.

———. 1996. Sketch of Cree, an Algonquian Language. *Handbook of North American Indians*. vol. 17, *Languages*, ed. by Ives Goddard, pp. 390–439. Washington, DC: Smithsonian Institution.

Wolvengrey, Arok. 2001. *nêhiyawêwin: itwêwina / Cree: Words*. Regina: University of Regina Press.

Semantic and Aspectual Considerations on Transitive Passives in Innu

Aubrée Boissard

Voice phenomena have received wide syntactic and cross-linguistic documentation by modern linguists.[1] Among them, passive constructions benefit from being the subject of much theorization, which has led to numerous descriptions, including descriptions of the passive voice in Algonquian languages. Indeed, within Algonquian languages, passive structures of transitive verbs have been documented in Plains Cree (Wolfart 1991; Dahlstrom 1991) and in Ojibwa (Rhodes 1991; Valentine 2001). More recently, passive constructions have been documented in Innu (Drapeau 2012), including descriptions of the passive forms of intransitive verbs, as well as medio-passives and lexical passives. Just as in other Algonquian languages, the passive voice of transitive verbs in Innu is formed by the addition of a passive suffix to the verb stem, along with the suppression of the Agent (Dahlstrom 1991; Rhodes 1991; Wolfart 1991; Valentine 2001; Drapeau 2012, 2014). The Patient is therefore the unique indexed argument, and the valence of the verb is reduced.

Despite this level of detail, very few semantic descriptions have investigated aspectual considerations in these languages (Denny 1978 for Ojibway, 1984 for Plains Cree; Cyr 1990, 1991 for Innu). As pointed out by Cyr (1991:58), at the time of Bloomfield the category of aspect "was poorly understood," and since then, given the strong tendency among Algonquian languages to agglutination, scholars have paid much more attention to the morphosyntactic relations between the different components.

This paper investigates the semantic and aspectual properties of transitive passive forms in Innu. It has been argued that Innu transitive passive forms are dynamic despite the capacity to change valency (Drapeau 2012). In contrast, here it will be shown that transitive passive verbs can bear stative/resultative semantics. Moreover, it will be argued, following Cyr, that the aspectual properties of transitive passive verbal forms in Innu must be deduced from context, since the opposition between the aspectual values of perfective and imperfective in this language has been neutralized (Cyr 1990, 1991).

Aspect and Voice in Innu

Aspectual Morphosyntax

The Innu language is an Algonquian language spoken by about 10,000 speakers in Québec, spread over eight communities along the North Shore and one community in Labrador. Innu people have French as a second language, except on the Lower North Shore and in Labrador, where it is English. According to Cyr (1990:67), aspectology in the Algonquian tradition has been practically nonexistent due, quite simply, to a lack of interest in this category from its earliest scholars. However, there has been some limited engagement with the subject. For example, Drapeau (2014:169–170) argues that the encoding of aspect and tense in Innu is simple, while mood and modalities are grammatically complex.

Aspect is generally understood as the internal temporal structure of an event (Comrie 1976; Smith 1991). In other words, Cyr (1991:62) describes it as "the way a process is represented by a speaker, that is by having an internal constituency (imperfective) or as not having such a constituency (perfective)." For Innu, Cyr (1990, 1991) claims that the opposition between perfective and imperfective is neutralized and that these aspectual values must be therefore deduced from nonlinguistic context. Thus, it is possible to bring out a double aspectual value in present, past, and future tenses in Innu, depending on the context. As present verbal forms from the independent order are neither marked with tense nor with aspect, they have an ambiguous semantics, but it can nevertheless be deduced from context, as illustrated by the following example in the active voice (Cyr 1990:68):[2]

(1) Nipaiu piǹeua
nipai-u piǹeu-a
kill.TA-3 partridge.AN-OBV
'Il/elle tue une perdrix.'
'S/he kills a partridge.' [author's translation]

This sentence can either mean 'S/he is killing the partridge' (imperfective) or 'S/he has killed the partridge' (perfective), since it does not bear any tense marking.

Passive of Transitives: Relevant Issues in Drapeau (2012)

In Innu, passives of transitive animate verbs and passives of transitive inanimate verbs are productive passives (Drapeau 2012). They are created via morphological derivation by adding a suffix to their stem. The choice of the passive suffix depends on the morphology of the verb rather than on the syntactic transitivity of the clause. Moreover, this type of passive does not specify the highest semantic role, but preserves an implicit Agent. This allows one to think of Innu passives as "unspecified Agent constructions" (Drapeau 2012:199). Thus, the Innu language does not display the equivalent encoding to express sentences like *the sand is blown by the wind* or *the camp was destroyed by the fire*. Indeed, the language does not allow an inanimate agent as a syntactic argument, when both the Agent and the Patient are inanimate, as in those instances. In Innu, Agents should always be animate entities (Drapeau 2012). Passives of transitive animate or inanimate verbs are characterized by the absence of any Agent argument, but by the unique Patient argument. In fact, they are Agentless in all Cree dialects (Dahlstrom 1991; Wolfart 1991; Drapeau 2012).

Passives of transitive animate verbs are derived by adding the suffix *-akani* to the TA verb stem when the Patient is third person. This suffix uses the morpheme *-akan* "which forms deverbal Patientive nouns and the abstract final *-i* found in many Animate Intransitive verb stems" (Drapeau 2012:182–183). When the Patient is first or second person, that is, when it is a speech-act participant, the suffix *-ikaw* is added to the verb stem. Likewise, passives of transitive inanimate verbs are formed by adding the suffix *-kani* to the TI verb stem, as illustrated in (3).

(2) cəpîm škwâtêm-ilu[3]
cipaym-w iškâtêm-ilu
close.TI-3 door.IN-OBV
'S/he closes the door.'

(3) cəpîkənu škwâtêm
cipay-kani-w îškwâtêm
close.TI-PT-3 door.IN
'The door is closed.' (Drapeau 2012:181)

Since passives of TA and TI verbs involve the suppression of the logical subject, they are Agentless in that the verb cannot index any Agent argument. Moreover, they are II verbs, because they are morphologically and syntactically intransitive.

According to Drapeau (2012:194), passives of TA and TI verbs are "not aspectually stative but eventive and dynamic." Despite the change in valency, they remain dynamic. Furthermore, as an implicit Agent remains in the conceptual frame, passives of transitives do not modify the aspectual category of the verb stem (Drapeau 2012:199). Thus, passives of transitives are semantically dynamic, in that they have an imperfective aspectual value.

Toward an Analysis of the Data

The Experiment

In order to focus on the linguistic encoding of certain types of situations, namely states and actions, an experiment was carried out with the help of images as illustrations of situations that could be interpreted with a passive meaning.[4] In that way, it was inspired by the work of Tomlin (1995) on focal attention, voice, and word order. The study involved three types of tasks. It is important to note that they have not been conducted one after the other. This tripartite procedure was designed to examine linguistic encoding from different points of view and by slightly different means. The goal was also to vary the tasks.

First, the participant was randomly presented images representing either an action (Figure 1) or a state/result (Figure 2).

He was asked to describe them in different ways in order to create spontaneous speech. He had then to write down the possible appropriate sentences in Innu and

iStock.com/kajakiki

FIGURE 1. Image representing an action.

iStock.com/icetocker

FIGURE 2. Image representing a state.

translate them afterward into French. Each produced sentence was discussed with the participant at the time of the answer. For this first task, it was expected that the consultant would produce active sentences to describe both actions and states/results, namely using transitive verbs to describe an action, like 'She cuts the meat', and using intransitive verbs with stative/resultative semantics for states/results, like 'The potatoes are peeled'.

Second, the participant was simultaneously shown two images, one illustrating an action and the other a state, along with a verbal constraint (see Figure 3 for an example). That way, he was asked to choose the image that would best illustrate the imposed verbal form. The verbal constraints were all in the passive voice, retrieved from the online Innu dictionary.[5]

The native speaker consultant was also asked to produce a complete sentence from the given verb form and the image and to write it down, before translating it into French.[6] Images of the first task were not necessarily presented in the second task. Actually, the second task was not dedicated to the verification of the first

Nutenakanu

iStock.com/Kritchanut

iStock.com/Vachom

FIGURE 3. Action and state with a verbal constraint.

Pimaueu

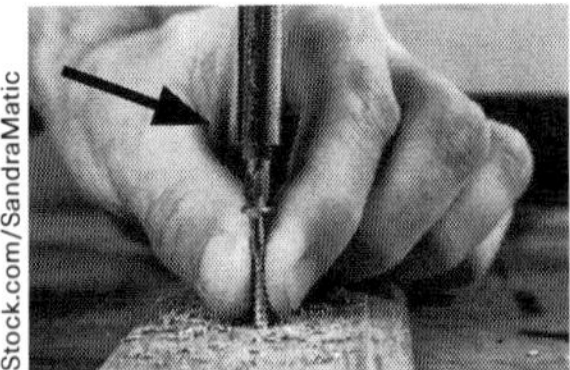

iStock.com/SandraMatic iStock.com/RonOrmanJr

FIGURE 4. Images with constraints of verb and focus.

one, as mentioned earlier. In the second task, as all verb forms were in the passive voice, it was conceivable to expect the participant to select an image representing a process involving two entities, that is to say an Agent and a Patient, where the latter appears to be the logical subject of the clause. So, in that case, the illustration of a processual action was expected to be chosen.

The third and final task involved in this procedure was the description of related images along with constraints of both verb and focus. "Constraint of focus" here means a constraint of focal attention, similar to Tomlin's (1995) use of the phrase. In other words, the participant was asked to describe the images with a specific verb giving special attention to the entity pointed at with an arrow (see Figure 4).[7]

Tomlin (1995) suggests that directing attention to a particular entity makes the participant more likely to produce an utterance in which the entity is going to be the logical subject. The goal of this task was to introduce verbal and focus constraints to limit the number of possible interpretations while ensuring the use of passive and active voices. Again, the participant was invited to write his answers down in a full sentence, before translating them into French. This third task was expected to make active as well as passive sentences emerge—namely, active clauses with transitive verbs when Agent focused, passive clauses with intransitive verbs when Patient focused, and last, active sentences with intransitive verbs when state focused.

This experiment gathered around 50 passivized transitive verb forms in the independent order, and each answer for each task was written down in Innu (the target language) and then translated into French (the task and communication language) for the sake of the analysis. This inverse elicitation constitutes a verification mode (Grinevald 2010), which accounts for the importance of the linguistic encoding pattern of action and state by a young native speaker of Innu.

Data Analysis

From a general point of view, results appeared to agree with the expected encoding of actions, but they proved to be quite different from the other predictions. For each task, the encoding of states differed from the expectations in about twenty cases. In this way, the experiment revealed the possibility of referring to a state/result by means of passives of transitives, namely by the *-(a)kanu* and *-(a)kanipan* passive verbal forms. The aspectual value of these passives of transitives is examined according to two "situation types" that arose from the experiment—namely, either "Accomplishment" or "Achievement" (Smith 1991). *-(a)kanu* passive verbal forms with stative/resultative semantics are classified as Accomplishments, and *-(a)kanipan* passive verbal forms with stative/resultative semantics are analyzed as Achievements. The following subsections are devoted to the evidence for this assertion.

Accomplishments

Smith (1991) defines an Accomplishment as a process that results in a change in state. This basic situation type has an inherent end. As mentioned earlier, the encoding of states/results varied from the expected results. The experiment revealed that the simple passive *-(a)kanu* verb forms could be used to denote a state/result. In other words, these passivized verb forms could get a stative/resultative meaning, although the processual meaning (imperfective aspect) of these passivized verb forms was also conceived by the speaker. Example (4) illustrates the verb used spontaneously to encode Figure 5.

iStock.com/tomap49

FIGURE 5. Image representing a state/result.

TABLE 1. Accomplishments

ACCOMPLISHMENTS	ENGLISH TRANSLATIONS
Pimaikanu	'It is screwed.'
Mamatshekenu	'It is sliced, cut into many pieces.'
Stakanu	'It is placed, put, set'; 'it (coffin) is placed in the ground.'
Munaikanu	'It is dug.'
Shenekanu	'It is open.'
Nutenakanu	'It is (half) open.'
Tshipaikanu	'It is blocked/closed.'
Atsheikaikanu	'It is locked.'
Atatsheikanu	'It is fenced.'
Atshekuakanu	'It is put in an enclosure.'
Tshetemuanu	'It is completely eaten or drunk.'

(4) Shene**kanu** shkuatem[8]
shena-**kani**-w ishkuatem
open.TI-PT-3.IND door.IN
'La porte est ouverte.'
'The door is open.'

In (4), we would expect an active verbal form. Rather, the use in this context of a transitive passive form to denote a state/result raises questions about the semantic and aspectual value of this form. Here, the sentence does not have an imperfective value ('The door is being opened.') and is thus not dynamic, since it does not denote an action. Likewise, a number of *-(a)kanu* transitive passives appeared in the experiment to be used with a stative/resultative meaning. Table 1 draws up a list of the main results.[9]

Although passives of transitives always bear dynamic semantics and therefore an imperfective value, the examples in Table 1 emerged with ambiguous semantics. Indeed, the speaker used them to denote a state/result as well. Thus, events that are conceived of as Accomplishments and encoded by an *-(a)kanu* transitive passive verbal form can either be semantically dynamic and imperfective or stative/resultative and perfective.

Achievements

An achievement is defined as an instantaneous event that involves a change of state (Smith 1991). The verb 'to break' is, for example, a typical Achievement. The experiment showed that a state/result can be encoded by an *-(a)kanu* transitive passive, when the event is perceived as an Accomplishment. Nonetheless, in my data, when the event is conceptualized as an Achievement, it is encoded by an *-(a)kanipan* transitive passive form, as illustrated in (5).

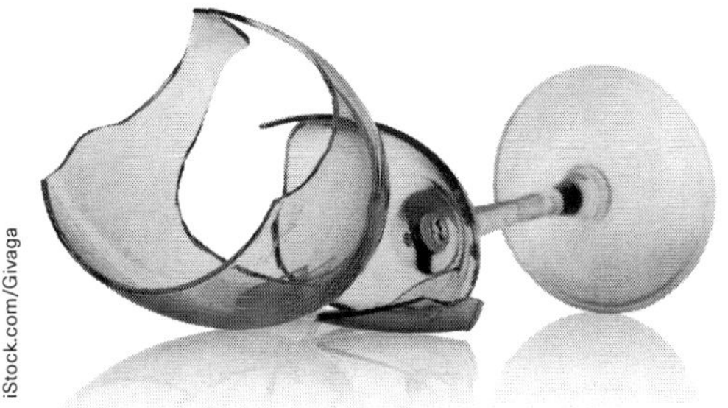

iStock.com/Givaga

FIGURE 6. Image representing a state.

(5) Pashtetanipem menan.
pashtititau-**kani**-pan minakan
break.AI-PT.IND-PRT glass.IN
'Le verre a été cases.'
'The glass has been broken.'

Here, the fact that the glass has been broken is considered as the resultant state of an instantaneous event, and not as a past process ('the glass was broken'). In other words, the semantics of the verb is stative/resultative, and it has a perfective interpretation, because the event here is conceptualized as an Achievement. Table 2 gathers verbs that operated similarly during the experiment.[10]

However, according to this semantic analysis, certain verbs can be classified either as an Accomplishment or as an Achievement, since the event or action they denote can be conceptualized slightly differently. For example, verbs like 'to open,' 'to close,' 'to pierce,' etc. can be seen either as processes or instantaneous events. In this way, Figure 5 was also described as (6):

TABLE 2. Achievements

ACHIEVEMENTS	ENGLISH TRANSLATIONS
Pashtetanipem	'It has been broken.'
Ashtueikanipem	'It has been extinguished.'
Shkuashitshanipem	'It has been lighted up.'
Takutastanipem	'It has been placed on a surface.'
Pikunakanipem	'It has been damaged.'
Kuapauakanipem	'It has been taken out of the water.'
Nashkuetakanipem	'It has been re-covered with fir branches.'

(6) Shenekanipem shkuatem

shena-**kani**-pan ishkuatem

open.TI-PT.IND-PRT door.IN

'La porte a été ouverte.'

'The door has been opened.'

Here, the fact of opening the door is conceived of as an instantaneous event that has taken place at a precise moment in the past, namely before the time of speech.

Discussion

As shown in Tables 1 and 2, some passives of transitives (*-(a)kanu* and *-(a)kanipan* verbal forms) emerged with stative/resultative semantics, along with dynamic semantics. These results therefore challenge Drapeau's (2012) claim that passives of transitive verbs in Innu are dynamic. As passives in Innu do not linguistically encode any obvious Agent, a passive-meaning sentence without any overt Agent involves semantic ambiguity. It is noteworthy that, from a cross-linguistic perspective, passive-meaning sentences without an overt Agent in English or in French are therefore also ambiguous. For example, the sentence *la viande est coupée* can mean both 'the meat is chopped' or 'the meat is being chopped.' One can ask if that sentence has a stative or a processual meaning, although it needs an overt Agent to be understood as a process, with an imperfective aspectual value. Indeed, the role of the main adstrate, namely French, should perhaps be taken into account to explain this. It would be interesting to explore to what extent the French language has had an effect on this semantic ambiguity in Innu. All these considerations need further investigation, in collaboration with other Innu native speakers from different ages and from different communities.

Furthermore, as certain passives of transitives in Innu can describe an ongoing process and/or an accomplished action, they can bear dynamic and/or stative/resultative semantics. Consequently, the aspectual value of the latter can be analyzed as perfective. Context-dependant double aspectual values, as highlighted by Cyr (1990), are thus also valid regarding the passives of transitives in Innu shown in Table 1. Boissard (2017) claims that this double value is explained by the morphology of the passive suffix *-akani*. The latter combines the suffix *-akan*, which forms deverbal nouns, and the abstract final (AF) *-i* (Drapeau 2012). According to Denny (1984), within the Cree dialects, the AF *-i* denotes a process. This analysis seems in agreement with the dynamic semantics generally associated to the passive voice. But the deverbal suffix *-akan* serves to derive a noun from a verb, and a noun is hardly conceivable as semantically dynamic. Thus, the passive suffix *-(a)kani* yields an ambiguous semantics to the verb stem it attaches to. Furthermore, according to Denny et al. (1984), there is no abstract final marking Accomplishments within the Cree-Innu continuum. They are therefore considered activities (processes). Indeed, activity verbs marked with the AF *-i* can refer either to an activity or to an Accomplishment (Denny et al. 1984:39). This study suggests then that this works similarly for the passive constructions in Innu. In this respect, it is interesting to look at Nishnaabemwin (Valentine 2001:337):

> Nishnaabemwin, in keeping with other dialects of Ojibwe, does not usually make a distinction between the onset and progress of an event and its resultant state. . . . [T]he two aspects of a verb reflecting a state or the shift into it are not typically morphologically distinguished, and the meaning of such verbs is ambiguous, resolved only on the basis of how the word is used in a particular context.

Given the linguistic proximity of this language, the same can be argued for Innu. Moreover, this quote agrees with Cyr's (1990, 1991) assertion that the aspectual value of the verbs in Innu must be deduced from the context.

Additionally, the passives of transitives classified as Achievements (Table 2) in the present paper have been systematically translated with a perfective value. Although Cyr (1990, 1991) analyzes the suffix *-pan* as the past morpheme, it is consequently considered as the preterit mark. In addition, these passive forms can be considered as perfect constructions, in that they refer to a situation that precedes the time of reference; they have a resultative semantics, and they assign a special property to the grammatical subject, due to its involvement in the situation described (Smith 1991).

Conclusion

This paper reported on the semantic and aspectual value of passives of transitives in Innu. The case study revealed the possibility of encoding a stative/resultative situation by means of passive constructions. This result calls into question the exclusive dynamicity of the passive of transitive verbs in Innu argued for by Drapeau (2012). *-(a)kanu* passive forms that appeared with stative/resultative semantics and perfective value were classified as encoding Accomplishments. Moreover, the fact that passives of transitives in Innu can have either dynamic semantics or stative/resultative semantics provides evidence for Cyr (1990, 1991), in that they can have a double aspectual value. Furthermore, these results support Denny et al. (1984), because the abstract final *-i* marks activity verbs as well as Accomplishments.

Finally, *-(a)kanipan* passive forms that emerged systematically with resultative semantics and a perfective value were classified as denoting Achievements. They were also analyzed as perfect constructions.

NOTES

1. This case study presents the preliminary analysis of my MA thesis. The preliminary results of this research were formerly presented at WSCLA 21. I thank the audience for helpful comments, as well as my supervisor, Manuel Español-Echevarría, for his support. A special thanks goes also to my main consultant, Patrice Bellefleur, without whom this research would not have been possible. Any errors are mine.
2. All examples in this paper are glossed using the following abbreviations: 3 = third person, AN = animate, AI = animate intransitive, IN = inanimate, IND = independent order, II = inanimate intransitive, OBV = obviative, PRT = preterit, PT = passive of transitive, TA = transitive animate, TI = transitive inanimate.
3. The orthography of examples (2) and (3) has been faithfully retranscribed from Drapeau (2012:181).
4. I am unable to reproduce the precise pictures used in the experiment due to their image quality. The figures shown in this paper are close approximations to the ones used. A

complete and detailed description of the experiment is provided in Boissard (2017).

5. http://www.innu-aimun.ca/dictionary/Words.
6. *Nutenakanu*, II : 'something (IN) is open'.
7. *Pimaueu*, TA: 's/he screws something (AN)'.
8. All the examples from the experiment are first transcribed in the way the speaker wrote them down.
9. The verbs are presented following the orthography of the speaker.
10. Again, the verbs are presented following the orthography of the speaker.

REFERENCES

Boissard, Aubrée. 2017. Voix passive et passif lexical en innu: une analyse aspectuelle et sémantique. MA thesis, Université Laval.

Comrie, Bernard. 1976. *Aspect: An Introduction to the Study of Verbal Aspect and Related Problems*. New York: Cambridge University Press.

Cyr, Danielle. 1990. Approche typologique du système aspectuel montagnais de la morphologie à la pragmatique. PhD thesis, Université Laval.

———. 1991. Algonquian Orders as Aspectual Markers: Some Typological Evidence and Pragmatic Considerations. *Papers of the Twenty-Second Algonquian Conference*, ed. by William Cowan, pp. 58–88. Ottawa: Carleton University.

Dahlstrom, Amy. 1991. *Plains Cree Morphosyntax*. New York: Garland.

Denny, J. Peter. 1978. Verb Class Meanings of the Abstract Finals in Ojibway Inanimate Intransitive Verbs. *International Journal of American Linguistics* 44(4):294–322.

———. 1984. Semantic Verb Classes and Abstract Finals. *Papers of the Fifteenth Algonquian Conference*, ed. by William Cowan, pp. 241–272. Ottawa: Carleton University.

Denny, J. Peter, Marion Johnson, and Mary Elizabeth O'Neil. 1984. Le concept d'accomplissement dans les langues et les cultures amérindiennes. *Recherches amérindiennes au Québec* 14(4):36–41.

Drapeau, Lynn. 2012. Passives in Innu. *International Journal of American Linguistics* 78(2):175–201.

———. 2014. *La grammaire de la langue innue*. Québec: Presses de l'Université du Québec.

Grinevald, Colette. 2010. Linguistique de terrain: locuteurs et méthodes. *Linguistique de terrain sur langues en danger: locuteurs et linguistes*, ed. by Colette Grinevald and Michel Bert, pp. 133–177. Paris: Ophrys.

Rhodes, Richard A. 1991. On the Passive in Ojibwa. *Papers of the Twenty-Second Algonquian Conference*, ed. by William Cowan, pp. 307–319. Ottawa: Carleton University.

Smith, Carlota S. 1991. *The Parameter of Aspect*. Dordrecht: Kluwer Academic Publishers.

Tomlin, S. Russell. 1995. Focal Attention, Voice and Word Order: An Experimental, Cross-linguistic Study. *Word Order in Discourse*, ed. by Pamela Downing and Michael Noonan, pp. 517–554. Philadelphia: J. Benjamins.

Valentine, J. Randolph. 2001. *Nishnaabemwin Reference Grammar*. Toronto: University of Toronto Press.

Wolfart, H. Christoph. 1991. Passives with and without Agents. *Linguistic Studies Presented to John L. Finlay*, ed. by H. Christoph Wolfart, pp. 171–190. Winnipeg: Algonquian and Iroquoian Linguistics.

Paradigm Leveling in South East Cree Verbal Inflections

Vincent Collette

Wolfart (1973:57) stated 45 years ago that the grammatical morphology of the transitive animate verbs of Plains Cree was "in a state of considerable fluctuation." This observation applies also for South East Cree (SEC hereafter), where we find two synonymous paradigms for the transitive animate verbs of the conjunct order. The "archaic" paradigm, which reflects Proto-Algonquian forms, displays fusional and opaque morphology, while the "innovative" paradigm has an agglutinative and transparent morphology that results from the overgeneralization of common grammatical morphemes. In this paper I present new SEC data that indicate that the actual shift from the archaic paradigm to the innovative one is age-graded: older monolingual speakers almost exclusively use the archaic inflections; middle-aged speakers use a combination of archaic and innovative inflections; and younger speakers almost exclusively use the innovative inflections. Although the aim of this study is descriptive and philological in nature, I offer potential avenues of inquiry concerning the causes of this linguistic change in progress.

South East Cree Transitive Animate Conjunct Paradigms

SEC is an Algonquian language belonging to the Cree-Innu-Naskapi-Atikamekw continuum. While being a subdialect of East Cree (along with North East Cree), SEC also splits into two local variants: SEC COASTAL is spoken in Waskaganish, Eastmain, and Washaw-Sibi, while SEC INLAND is used in Mistissini, Ouje-bougoumou, Waswanipi, and Nemaska (see MacKenzie 1980).

Verbs are inflected for PERSON/NUMBER, OBVIATION, DIRECTION, TENSE, and MOOD, the morphology of which differs according to verbal "orders."[1] In this paper I am concerned with the grammatical morphology of transitive animate (TA) verbs like *sâcihew* 's/he loves him/her', which encodes the person and number of two animate participants (in bold). In Algonquian languages participants are ranked according to the following person hierarchy: 2/1 > X > 3 > 3' > 0 (X 'unspecified actor', 3' 'animate obviative', 0 'inanimate proximate'). If a high-ranking participant is subject and a low-ranking one object, a DIRECT theme sign (like *-â-* 'third object') is used, but if the hierarchy is violated, as when a lower-ranking participant acts upon a higher-ranking one, then an INVERSE marker (like *-iku-* 'third subject') is used, as in example (1a–b).[2]

(1) a. ni-t-ashim-**â**-nân
1-*t*-feed.NA-DIR.3SG.OBJ-1PE
'we feed him/her' (TA)

b. ni-t-ashim-**iku**-nân
1-*t*-feed.NA-INV.3SG.SUBJ-1PE
's/he feeds us' (TA)

This neat process of morpheme alignment applies much better to the independent order than the conjunct one since in the latter the grammatical categories of person, number, and direction are expressed via a single opaque and fusional suffix, as in (2a–b):

(2) a. e-ashim-**ak**
CPL-feed.NA-DIR.1SG>3SG
'as I feed him/her' (TA)

b. e-ashim-**iyamiht**
CPL-feed.NA-INV.1PE<3SG
'as s/he feeds us' (TA)

Linguists working on SEC have documented the use of the archaic core TA conjunct inflections (see MacKenzie 1980; Junker et al. 2015). However, since the 1970s the TA conjunct paradigms of the *mixed set* (i.e., action involving a plural speech act participant [SAP] and a third person, like *-iyamiht* earlier) have gradually

TABLE 1. South East Cree core TA conjunct paradigms (mixed set)

	DIRECT			INVERSE	
	ARCHAIC			ARCHAIC	
1>3	-ak		1<3	-at	
2>3	-it		2<3	-isk	
3>3'	-**ât**		3<3'	-**ikut**	
	ARCHAIC	INNOVATIVE		ARCHAIC	INNOVATIVE
1PE>3	-aciht	-**âyâhc**	1PE<3	-iyamiht	-**ikuyâhch**
1PI>3	-ahk^{w}	-(**ây**)ahk^{w}	1PI<3	-itahk^{w}	-**ikuyahk^{w}**
2PL>3	-ek^{w}	-(**ây**)ek^{w}	2PL<3	-itâk^{w}	-**ikuyek^{w}**
1PE>3PL	-acihtwâw	-**âyâhc**(ic)	1PE<3PL	-iyamihtwâw	-**ikuyâhc**(ic)
1PI>3PL	-ahkuc	-**ây**ahku(c)	1PI<3PL	-itahkuc	-**ikuyahku**(c)
2PL>3PL	-ekuc	-**ây**eku(c)	2PL<3PL	-itâkuc	-**ikuyeku**(c)

been leveled out through overgeneralization of common grammatical suffixes, so much so that in synchrony one can find two synonymous sets of inflections, as displayed in Table 1.[3]

Paradigm leveling in the TA conjunct is common and has been reported for some dialects of Ojibwa (Valentine 1994:360), Moose Cree (Brousseau et al. 2015:450 et seq.), and Plains Cree (Dahlstrom 1989). By comparing Plains Cree liturgical material, Dahlstrom (1989) showed that the change from archaic to innovative TA conjunct mixed plural inflections occurred between 1855 and 1904, and that it happened in the inverse paradigm first. According to Dahlstrom (1989:67–69), the paradigmatic leveling of Plains Cree TA conjunct mixed plural inflections occurred in two stages:

> i) In the first stage, the ordering of the inverse theme sign *-iku-* 'third subject' and the person/number of the independent TA was extended to the core TA conjunct (i.e. rule reordering) on the model of the TA inanimate actor which requires *-iku-* 'third subject' and the common SAP morphemes: *-(y)âhk* '1PE', *-(y)ahk^{w}* '1PE', *-(y)ek^{w}* '2PL' (the semi-vowel /y/ is epenthetic);
>
> ii) In the second stage, the direct set was created by analogy with the inverse set, that is, the direct theme sign *-â-* 'third object' and the common SAP morphemes were extended to the direct mixed plural forms of the core TA conjunct.

While in Plains Cree the change is now complete, in SEC the archaic and innovative paradigms occur in synchrony, and their distribution provides important cues as to the mechanics of paradigm leveling in Algonquian languages. In the following section, I present SEC data that point to a correlation between the age of the speaker, the level of acculturation, and the use of archaic and innovative inflections. I then review the SEC literature to seek clues as to when paradigm leveling may have started, and in the penultimate section I present external and internal hypotheses concerning the cause(s) of this change.

Age-Graded Distribution of the Transitive Animate Conjunct (Mixed Set)

My working hypothesis stems from discussions with SEC speakers who stated that the distribution of the archaic and innovative paradigms was conditioned by age and exposure to traditional education and language. In what follows, I document the distribution of the TA conjunct forms of the mixed plural paradigms (i.e., action of plural SAP on non-SAP) for three age groups. The data stem from four sources: paradigm elicitation with 12 speakers, using translations of English interrogative sentences (since in this morphosyntactic context the main verb has to be in the conjunct order);[4] anthropological interviews conducted in 2009–2010 by the author for the Income Security Program of the Cree hunters and trappers; local radio broadcasts; and field notes.

Elderly Speakers

I conducted three paradigm elicitation sessions with elderly speakers born before 1945. The forms obtained are identical to the archaic ones presented in Table 1. The examples presented in this section are excerpts stemming from anthropological interviews where the age and years of residential schooling (if any) were provided by the informant.

(3)	Awâshsh-ic	kiyâ	mihcetuw-ic	e-kanaweyim-**iyamiht**-wâw.
child.NA-PL	EMP	many.AI-PL	CPL-watch.TA-1PE<3-PL

'And there were many children looking after us.' (OJB-013-21:40; woman, 67 years old in 2009; never attended school; monolingual)

(4) [. . .] meshikum-upîsim-ah ce-miskuw-**aciht** kiyâ.
every-month.NI-PL CJ.PROS-find.TA-1PE>3 of course
'[. . .] we will receive it (find it) (money NA) every month of course.' (SEN-002-4:59; woman, 67 years old in 2009; never attended school; monolingual)

(5) Ni-cisceyihte-n ce-cî âyimûm-**ahk**^{w} James.
1-think.TI-SG CJ.PROS-POT talk.about.TA-1PI>3 James
'I think we should talk about James.' (Field notes; man, 68 years old in 2009; attended school in Ontario for six years; bilingual)

During one of the paradigm elicitation sessions an elderly speaker provided all the archaic inflections of the mixed sets. Interestingly, however, she alternates between archaic (*-aciht-* '1PE>3') and innovative forms (*-iku-yâhc* '1PE<3'; *-â-yâhc* '1PE>3') in her children's books (6). (Due to the sensitivity of the topic I have withheld the reference for this excerpt.)

(6) Shâsh chî-iskwâ piminuw-e-w ni-kâwî. Ekuh mâk
now PERF-after cook.TA-DIR.3>3'-SG 1-mother.NAD then COOR

ce-ashim-**âkuyâhch**. Ce-muw-**aciht** namesh-h
CJ.PROS-feed.TA-1PE>3 CJ.PROS-eat.TA-1PE>3 fish.NA-3'

kâ-pitahay-**âyâhc**.
CJ.REL-caught.in.a.net.TA-1PE>3
'Then after that my mom cooked them. We were fed (with it). We would eat the fish we caught in the net.' (Woman, 70 years old in 2009; attended school for six years in Moose Factory; bilingual)

(7) Ekut ûtih âskiw e-kanaweyim-**âyâhc** ni-kâwiy ûtih û
right here sometimes CPL-look.after.TA-1PE>3 1-mother.NAD here DEM.SG

meskinaw [. . .] Ekuteh ây, iskîtiw e-ayâpacih-**âyâhc**.
road.NI right HES snowmobile.NA CPL-use.it.TA-1PE>3
'Right here sometimes we look after my mother, here on the road (pointing on the map) [. . .] Right here euh, we use a snowmobile.' (NSK-002-3:40; woman, 69 years old in 2009; attended school; bilingual)

Although it could be an error, the use of *-aciht-* and *-âyâhc* '1PE > 3' (in 6) in the same sentence seems to indicate that the standard archaic forms are more prestigious but that children may not understand them. Since other elderly speakers use innovative forms too (7), even though *-âyâhc* is considered by many as "sloppy Cree," I consider the spread of the innovative direct *-âyâhc-* as a case of hypocorrection, where older speakers adopt innovative forms in order to level their speech with that of younger speakers.[5] In sum, speakers born before 1945 predominantly use archaic inflections only or the innovative ones when addressing younger speakers.

Middle-Aged Speakers

I conducted five paradigm elicitation sessions along with participant observation with speakers born between 1945 and 1970. The examples presented here are taken from interviews I recorded in 2009 and local radio broadcasts. I have also included biographical details when available. The general tendency with this age group is to use the innovative form *-ikuyâhc-* instead of *-iyamiht-* '1PE<3' but to keep the direct archaic counterpart *-aciht-* '1PE>3'.

(8) Chibougamou-hc ekuth kâ-wâpam-**aciht**.
Chibougamau-LOC that's.where CJ.PERF-see.TA-1PE>3
'In Chibougamau, that's where we saw him/her.' (Field notes; man, 60 years old in 2016, attended high school in Chibougamau, Quebec; bilingual)

(9) Ek^w ni-mâmâ-m kâ-kanaweyim-**ikuyâhc**. Namuy nâsht
so 1-mother.NAD-POS CJ.PERF-watching.TA-1PE<3 NEG really
uhci minihkwe-w.
GEN drink.AI-3SG
'So my mother was taking care of us. She did not really drink.' (TIP-008-0:24; woman, 56 years old in 2004; attended residential school; bilingual)

TABLE 2. Mixed (archaic and innovative) core TA conjunct paradigms

	DIRECT ARCHAIC		INVERSE INNOVATIVE
1PE>3	-aciht	1PE<3	-ikuyâhc
1PI>3	-ahk^{w}	1PI<3	-ikuyahk^{w}
2PL>3	-ek^{w}	2PL<3	-ikuyek^{w}
1PE>3PL	-acihtwâw	1PE<3PL	-ikuyâhc(ic)
1PI>3PL	-ahkuc	1PI<3PL	-ikuyahku(c)
2PL>3PL	-ekuc	2PL<3PL	-ikuyeku(c)

(10) Mistahiy ni-nanaskum-iti-nâ-wâw misiwe kiyâh awen-icî
alot 1-thank.TA-1>2-SG-PL all EMP people.NA-PL

kiye aniteh ây along the coast aniteh e-uhcî-twâw
and there HES along the coast there CPL-live.AI-3PL

e-peci-masinahamuw-**ikuyâhc** kiyâ ây on the Facebook
CPL-toward.SPEAKER-write.TA-1PE<3 and HES on Facebook

e-peci-textiwih-**ikuyâhc-ic**
CPL-toward.SPEAKER-text.TA-1PE<3-PL
'I really thank all the people, and also those who lived along the coast, to have written to us euh on Facebook and to have texted us.' (RAD-2016-08-03-6:01; man, 66 years old in 2016; attended residential school for six years; bilingual)

(11) N-îtiskwew kâk û-cî ni-boy-im-ish-ic kâcî-wîcim-**ikuyâhc**
1-wife.NAD and DEM.NA-PL 1-son.NAD-POS-DIM-PL CJ.PERF-live.with.TA-1PE<3
'My wife and my sons live with us.' (MIS-020-4:23; man, 59 years old in 2010, never attended school; monolingual)

Table 2 displays the combination of forms representative of this age group—i.e., archaic (direct) and innovative (inverse) inflections. The combination corresponds to the first stage of paradigm leveling reported for Plains Cree (Dahlstrom 1989:62).

As can be seen in Table 2, plural agreement *-(i)c* in the inverse set is optional for some speakers. When prompted to give a literal translation of an English sentence that includes a plural third person subject, some speakers will add the plural morpheme *-(i)c* on the innovative inverse forms, but in general it does not come naturally for many speakers, as can be seen in (10) and (11). Syncretism in plural marking of non-SAP subject is also found in Moose Cree (see Brousseau et al. 2015:450 et seq.).

Younger Speakers

With younger speakers (born between 1970 and 2005) I conducted four paradigm elicitation sessions along with participant observation. One respondent was monolingual, while others made heavy use of Creenglish (mixing Cree verbal inflections with English roots as shown in (12)). As with the other age groups, the data presented here come from interviews done in 2009, local radio broadcasts, and field notes. The tendency with this age group is toward a full replacement of archaic forms by innovative ones.

(12) [. . .] just to let her know   kiyâ   that we   e-supportiwi-h-**âyâhc**.
                                                       EMP   CPL-support-TA-1PE>3
‘[. . .] just to let her know of course that we support her.’ (RAD-2016-08-08-25:30; woman, around 40–45 years old in 2016; bilingual)

(13) Ekuth   kâ-mûs   ciskutimaw-**ikuyâhc**   ni-pâpâ-m.
that.is   CJ.REL-always   teach.TA-1PE<3   1-father.NAD-POS
‘That is what my father always taught us.’ (MIS-006-9:36; 32 years old in 2009; attended local school; bilingual)

(14) Ni-cî-âyim-ih-iku-nân   e-nipah-**âyâhc**   mahcesuw.
1-PERF-to.have.problems-CAUS.TA-<3-1PE   CPL-kill.TA-1PE>3   fox.NA
‘We had problems killing the fox.’ (Field notes; boy, 10 years old in 2007; attended local school; monolingual)

(15) Wâpam-**âyahkw**-e   mahcesuw   cika-nipah-ânuw.
see.TA-1PI>3-SUBJ   fox.NA   2.PROS-kill.TA-1PI>3
‘If we see a fox we’ll kill him.’ (Field notes; boy, 10 years old in 2007; attended local school; monolingual)

TABLE 3. Mixed plural (archaic and innovative) core TA paradigms

	DIRECT INNOVATIVE/ARCHAIC		INVERSE INNOVATIVE
1PE>3(PL)	-âyâhc(ic)	1PE<3(PL)	-ikuyâhc(ic)
1PI>3(PL)	-âyahku(c) ~ -ahku(c)	1PI<3(PL)	-ikuyahku(c)
2PL>3(PL)	-âyeku(c) ~ -eku(c)	2PL<3(PL)	-ikuyeku(c)

For the younger age group there are two patterns: use of innovative forms only, and use of innovative forms only except for -*(ây)ahk*^{w} '1PI>3' and -*(ây)ek*^{w} '2PL>3'. As indicated in Table 3, the change seems to have started with the ousting of the exclusive plural -*aciht*—the most opaque form of the direct set—and is extending gradually to the other two forms.

The direct innovative paradigm is highly criticized by elderly and middle-aged speakers as well as by Cree language teachers. Metalinguistic comments are important because they suggest that the TA conjunct innovative inverse inflections (e.g., -*ikuyâhc*) are now acceptable SEC forms, while this is not yet the case for the direct innovative inflections (e.g., -*âyâhc*). The awareness of some of my SEC interlocutors concerning the innovative direct is clearly a synchronic indicator of a change in progress. In the next section, I survey the available literature in SEC as to when, or with which generation, the change started.

Tracing Paradigm Leveling in South East Cree Literature

The main difficulty in tracing the appearance of the first stage of paradigm leveling in SEC comes from the paucity of written sources. To my knowledge, the oldest SEC written document is a handwritten map that illustrates the locations of beaver reserves in Fort Rupert (now called Waskaganish).[6] This single-page document—which is kept at the Ânischâukamikw Cree Cultural Institute in Ouje-Bougoumou (Quebec)—has a short syllabic text written in SEC (coastal) that contains archaic TA conjunct (mixed plural SAP/THIRD) inflections only.

Other sources like Rogers (1960) do not have innovative mixed plural SAP/THIRD conjunct inflections. However, Marguerite MacKenzie (1971:52), who worked with a former residential school student, documented the use of innovative inverse inflections (along with the archaic direct ones). This is probably the oldest source confirming the first stage of paradigm leveling in SEC. In the course of the 1970s, a group of young Cree collected, transcribed, and published a series of booklets. The language used in these publications is that of proficient speakers. It contains no innovative TA conjunct inflections and has many occurrences of the dubitative preterit and independent subjective paradigms, which are now rarely heard and unknown to the younger generations of speakers.

Interestingly, in the editor's note and acknowledgments of some of these books, the young editors (Mary Ann Coon-Come and Clara Copper) used the combination of inflections that is typical of the middle-aged group, as seen in the 'Middle-Aged Speakers section—that is, use of the innovative inverse (*-ikuyâhc*) and the archaic direct (*-aciht*) inflections, and omission of plural number agreement, which is compensated by NP morphology and independent order inflections (underlined in the next examples).

(16)	Kaye	ni-nâskum-ânân-ic	an-icî	kâ-awih-**ikuyâhc**
	and	1-thank.TA-13>3-PL	DEM-NA.PL	CJ.REL-lend.TA-1PE<3

masinâpiskahikan(-ah) [. . .]	Peyakw	mâk	cekwân	ni-mihcîwesi-n
picture.NI.PL	one	COOR	thing.NI	1-sorry.AI-SG

ewikw	kâ-waniciscihitutâ-wâhce	cecî-wîh-**aciht**
it's those	CJ.REL-forget.TA-DUB.1PE>3	CJ.PROS-name.TA-1PE>3

'And I thank those who have lent us the pictures [. . .] I am also sorry for one thing is for those whose names we may have forgotten (to write).' (Coon-Come 1982:49; editor's note)

(17)	Ni-wî	na-nâskum-ânân-ic	û-cî	awen-icî	kâ-peci wîcih-**ikuyâhc**.
	1-VOL	REDUP-thank.TA-1PE>3-PL	DEM-NA.PL	person.NA-PL	CJ.REL-GEN help.TA-1PE<3

'We want to thank those who have helped us.' (Cooper 1981:iv; editor's note)

The same pattern—especially (i) earlier—appears again in child literature translated from English by SEC (coastal) speakers (18), and confirms that the inverse innovative inflections are now acceptable forms that are used with younger addressees/readers.

(18) Mâmâ peci wâpahtam-uy-**ikuyâhc**, wâpushu-me-yiw [. . .]
mom (CPL-)GEN see-CAUS.TA-1PE<3 rabbit.NA-way-0'SG

wiyâpam-**aciht** kâkw-Ø e-akusî-t mishtiku-hc.
IC.see.TA-1PE>3 porcupine.NA-SG CPL-perched.AI-3 tree.NA-LOC
'Mom showed us the rabbit way [. . .] we saw a porcupine siting on a tree.'
(Keeshig-Tobias 1993:10, 12; translation in SEC (coastal) by Whiskeychan and Salt)

In sum, oral and written data suggest that the first stage of paradigm leveling (archaic direct/innovative inverse) had been reached by the mid-1970s. The second stage (all innovative forms) is characteristic of younger speakers (born after 1970), but the innovative direct forms are not yet considered acceptable inflections.

External and Internal Factors of Paradigm Leveling

In this section I explore external and internal hypotheses concerning paradigm leveling. Although I am unable to engage in an in-depth discussion given space constraints, the ideas contained in this section are intended to serve as working hypotheses for future research on the topic.

In the previous section I showed that the first stage of paradigm leveling started with speakers born between 1945 and 1970. Since they belong to the same generation of children who attended residential schools in Ontario or Quebec between 1955 and 1975, language attrition would seem to be a likely cause of paradigm leveling. The psychological impact of residential schooling on SEC teenagers belonging to the Mistissini and Waswanipi bands has been studied in detail by a team of psychologists in the 1960s. Wintrob and Sindell (1968) showed that formal education[7] had considerable and dramatic effects on the student's cultural values, attitude, and self-esteem in two ways: increased bilingualism, and disruption of Cree language transmission.[8] Since the Mistissini and Waswanipi teenagers studied by Wintrob and Sindell at the end of the 1960s belong to the same age group as our middle-aged group, I claim that the first stage of paradigm leveling (e.g., mix of archaic direct and innovative inverse forms) is a reflection of discontinuity in language and cultural transmission. This was probably reinforced by increased peer-group identification that contrasted dramatically with traditional (i.e., intergenerational) patterns of interaction.

The data provided in the preceding section seem to concord with research on paradigm leveling. According to Vago (1991), language-external factors like bilingualism, intergenerational gaps in language transmission, and domain loss (L1 used in fewer domains than L2) can trigger or accelerate paradigm leveling. He states that paradigm leveling is part of internally induced changes where overgeneralization of common grammatical morphemes results in reduced allomorphic variation (loss of opaque inflections) and maximization of paradigm regularity (Vago 1991:241).

Even though the correlation between age, degree of acculturation, and the distribution of the archaic and innovative TA paradigms is strong, one should not exclude internally motivated forces like structural imbalances, universal tendencies, or pattern pressure (Thomason 2008:47) to account for paradigm leveling. In order to see how exactly pattern pressure works, let us consider two other types of TA verbs—the TA inanimate actor and the TA unspecified actor, which are similar semantically, morphosyntacticly, and phonologically. The TA inanimate actor is built by adding the inverse *-iku-* on a AI or a TI stem plus *-(i)h-* 'TA transitivizer'. The TA inanimate actor inflects for the gender and number of the subject/patient, and the inanimate actor is always expressed by a pronoun, a conjunct clause (see 14), or an external NP, as in the following example:

(19) Tân eteyihtam-ih-**iku**-yan û cekwân-Ø?
WHAT IC.think.TI-CAUS.TA-NI.ACTOR-2SG DEM.SG thing.NI-SG
'What do you think about that thing? ' (lit. what does it make you think of?) (Field notes; boy, 10 years old in 2007)

The TA unspecified actor form (which is often analyzed as an animate intransitive passive verb by some authors) is obtained by suffixing *-ikaw-i-* (first, second person of independent order) ~ *-iku-* (SAP plural forms of independent and all SAP forms of the conjunct order) or *-kan-i-* (third person, both orders) on a TA stem (*-i-* is an animate intransitive final). In this type of TA the unspecified actor is doing something to an animate subject/patient, but the person, gender, and number of the former are formally unspecified. In standard SEC an external NP or a pronoun referring to the unspecified actor cannot be expressed externally, as indicated in (20b).

TABLE 4. TA paradigms

PERSON AND NUMBER	CONJUNCT TA INVERSE (INNOVATIVE)	CONJUNCT TA INANIMATE ACTOR	CONJUNCT TA UNSPECIFIED ACTOR	INDEPENDENT TA UNSPECIFIED ACTOR
1	. . . -it	. . . -ikuyân	. . . -ikuyân	ni- . . . -ikawin
2	. . . -isk	. . . -ikuyan	. . . -ikuyan	ci- . . . -ikawin
1PE	. . . -ikuyâhc	. . . -ikuyâhc	. . . -ikuyâhc	ni- . . . -ikunân
1PI	. . . -ikuyahk^{w}	. . . -ikuyahk^{w}	. . . -ikuyahk^{w}	ci- . . . -ikunânuw
2PL	. . . -ikuyek^{w}	. . . -ikuyek^{w}	. . . -ikuyek^{w}	ci- . . . -ikunawâw
3	. . . -ikut	. . . -ikut	. . . -âkanit	. . . -âkaniw
3PL	. . . -ikutwâw	. . . -ikutwâw	. . . -âkanitwâw	. . . -âkaniwac

(20) a. Ni-mîy-**ikawi**-n û kiyâ.
1-give.it.to.him/her.TA-UNSPECIFIED.ACTOR-SG DEM.SG EMP
'That is given to me of course.' (NSK-002-7:50; woman, 69 years old in 2009)

b. *Ni-mîy-**ikawi**-n û kiyâ ni-kâwiy- Ø.
1-give.it.to.him/her.TA-UNSPECIFIED.ACTOR-SG DEM.SG EMP 1-mother.NAD-SG
'That is given to me by my mother of course.'

There are salient morphosyntactic and semantic parallels between core TA (2 arguments), TA unspecified actor, and TA inanimate actor forms (1 argument). First, core TA and TA unspecified actor are built from simple TA stems (*mîy-*), while the TA inanimate actor is built on a TI stem plus the -(*i*)*h*- 'TA transitivizer' (*iteyihtamih-*). Second, the external arguments of the core TA may surface but this is not obligatory; the actor of the TA unspecified is never expressed, while the inanimate actor is always expressed externally. Thus, the core TA and TA unspecified actor have similar argument structure—since the core TA always has a grammatically and semantically animate subject/agent marked by the inflection—while the TA unspecified actor has an animate subject/patient marked by the inflection but a referential animate agent only. In other words, in a TA unspecified actor verb like *niwâpamikawin* "I am seen/one sees me" the entity doing the seeing is always a referentially animate one, even though it is not specified linguistically. Strikingly similar forms for the core TA conjunct, TA inanimate actor, and TA unspecified actor (conjunct and independent orders) are presented in Table 4.

In what follows I try to substantiate the hypothesis that the remodeling of core TA conjunct inflections is based on the TA unspecified actor (see Jacques and

TABLE 5. Morphophonemics of some conjunct TA inflections

PHONOLOGICAL RULES	/EMI:YIKAWIYAKW/	/ETEYIHTAMIHIKUYAHKW/
1) iy > i:y	e:m**i:y**ikaw**i:y**ahkw	e:te:yihtamihi:kuyahkw
2) Cuy > Cwi:y	e:mi:yikawi:yahkw	e:te:yihtamihi:**kwi:y**ahkw
3) syncope of short unstressed vowels	e:mi:ykwi:yhkw	e:te:yhtamhi:kwi:yhkw
4) syncope of y / i:yC	[e:mi:ˈ**kwi:hkw**] 'as one gives it to us'	[e:te:yhtamhi:ˈ**kwi:hkw**] 'as it makes us think of it'

Antonov 2015:20–21) and not directly on the TA inanimate actor as proposed by Dahlstrom (1989:68). My argumentation stems from phonology and morphosyntactic reanalysis.

First, short/lax vowels (/ɪ/, /ʊ/, /a/) and semivowels (/w/, /y/) undergo phonological rules that affect greatly the morphophonemics of TA conjunct forms.[9] As shown in Table 4, the historical long form *-ikawi-* 'unspecified actor' appears only in the first and second person forms of the independent order; elsewhere, *-ikawi-* is contracted in [-(ɪ)gʊ] and identical with the inverse *-iku-* of the other paradigms, a situation that leads to formal homonymy between the conjunct TA inanimate and unspecified actor forms. These rules are illustrated in Table 5 for a TA unspecified actor and a TA inanimate actor verb of the conjunct order.[10]

Given the formal homonymy between these similar verb types, it is highly plausible that the argument structure of the TA inanimate actor (VERB + external NI actor) was extended to that of the TA unspecified actor. The syntax of the latter came to be reanalyzed as VERB + externally "specified" animate actor, in addition to the original TA unspecified actor reading. In sum, the valency of TA unspecified actor was modified by the addition of a "specified" animate actor argument and became nearly identical to that of core TA verbs. The reanalysis of TA unspecified is at play in (21) where, instead of using core TA conjunct forms like the inverse *-it* '1<3', the speaker employs a TA unspecified actor form *-ikuyân* specified by an NP (underlined),[11] a construction that is considered ungrammatical in standard SEC but not in English. The same phenomenon has also been reported for North East Cree child language acquisition, and both examples point to a third stage of paradigm leveling (i.e., with SAP singular forms).

TABLE 6. Stages of paradigm leveling in the conjunct order

CORE TA (INVERSE)	TA UNSPECIFIED ACTOR (X)	TA INANIMATE ACTOR	STAGES
-it '1<3' *-iyimiht* '13<3' (+ ext. argument(s))	*-ikawiyân* '1<X' *-ikawiyâhc* '13<X' *ext. NA actor	*-ikuyân* '1<NI' *-ikuyâhc* '13<NI' + ext. NI actor	Archaic forms
-it *-iyimiht* (+ ext. argument(s))	*-ikuyân* *-ikuyâhc* *ext. NA actor	*-ikuyân* *-ikuyâhc* + ext. NI actor	Morphophonological rules lead to formal homonymy between TA X and TA NI
-it *-iyimiht* (+ ext. argument(s))	*-ikuyân* *-ikuyâhc* (+ ext. NA "specified" actor)	*-ikuyân* *-ikuyâhc* + ext. NI actor	Misassignment of constituent structure (i.e., + NA "specified" actor) leads to similar argument structure between core TA and TA X
-it *-ikuyân* *-ikuyâhc* (+ ext. argument(s) or ext. NA "specified" actor)		*-ikuyân* *-ikuyâhc* + ext. NI actor	Paradigm leveling in plural SAP forms (first and second stages)
-ikuyân *-ikuyâhc* (+ ext. argument(s) or ext. NA "specified" actor)		*-ikuyân* *-ikuyâhc* + ext. NI actor	Paradigm leveling in singular SAP forms (third stage); maximization of paradigm regularities

(21) [. . .] kâk <u>my uncle</u> after kâ-teachiwih-**ikuyân**
and CJ.PERF-teach.TA-1SG<3

ekutih wiyeš 1990's ni-cî-iskûliwih-**ikawi**-n
right.then around 1-PERF-go.to.school-TA.UNSPEC.ACTOR-SG

'[. . .] and after that, my uncle taught me" or "and after that, I was taught by my uncle [. . .] then around 1990's I was schooled.' (CBJ-012-3:55; man, 37 years old in 2010; | went to local school)

(22) Susie â-ihtâ-t ni-chî-iti-**kiwi**-n ni-kâwiy.
Susie CPL-be.there.AI-3SG 1-PERF-tell-TA.UNSPEC.ACTOR-SG 1-mother.NAD
[(name) o-jtat ni-tsta-n-ʧi**təkʊn** nɪ-kawi]
'Susie's place, she told me, my mother.' (or "Susie's place I was told by my mother" VC)
(Johansson 2012:82; North East Cree, 5-year-old speaker)

Table 6 summarizes the findings of this paper (the parentheses indicate optionality of externally expressed arguments/actors, and * indicates ungrammaticality).

Data on the reanalysis of the TA unspecified form provide strong evidence of what Parker (1976:450) calls "mis-assignment of constituent structure," a situation where different speakers assign different constituent structures, or syntactic properties, to the same verb form. If the deviant or misassigned structure (i.e., TA unspecified actor + "specified" NP) is internalized by a group of speakers and spreads in the speech community (as with younger bilingual Cree speakers), part of the morphosyntactic structure of the language may start to change and lead to maximization of paradigm regularities, which results in the ousting of irregular inflections and functionally identical forms.

Conclusion

In this paper I show that the mixed inflections (i.e., action involving a plural SAP on a non-SAP one) of the core TA conjunct are in a state of great fluctuation in SEC. The correlation stemming from natural and textual data indicates that the first stage of paradigm leveling of core TA conjunct inverse happened with speakers born between 1945 and 1970. The second stage, which is characterized by the analogical extension of the direct theme sign *-â-* 'third object' to the mixed plural forms, is actually taking place with speakers born after 1970. Finally, some younger speakers have leveled out singular SAP object forms, and this constitutes the final stage of paradigm leveling since all TA conjunct forms (i.e., inverse core TA, unspecified actor, and inanimate actor) are morphologically identical. Although more work is needed to clarify the effects of external factors of language changes, a probable scenario is that external factors outlined earlier advanced the drive for paradigm leveling, and that the exact phonological and morphological shape of the paradigms followed factors internal to the language (i.e., phonological rules and morphosyntactic reanalysis). One of the main challenges for future investigations will be to articulate external and internal factors of language change along with findings on Cree language acquisition and especially on the acquisition of passive voice. One crucial question for future research is whether paradigm leveling is an irreversible process due to language attrition or just a stage of language acquisition, unique to children and early teenagers, which is later corrected.

NOTES

1. Generally speaking, the inflections of the INDEPENDENT ORDER are used in independent clauses (***mîcisuwac*** "they eat/they are eating"), as well as in main clauses (***cisceyimâwac*** *tâniteh kâ-ihtâyic* "They know where s/he was."). Those of the CONJUNCT ORDER are used in independent interrogative sentences (*tâniteh kâ-ihtâ****twâw*** "Where were they?") as well as in dependent clauses (*nicisceyimâwac tâniteh kâ-ihtâ****twâw*** "I know where they were."). Finally, the inflections of the IMPERATIVE ORDER are used in independent clauses to give orders or commands (*nipâ****hk***^{w} "All of you sleep!").
2. The abbreviations used are as follows: AI = intransitive animate verb, CAUS = causative, CJ = conjunct order, COOR = coordinator, CPL = complementizer, DEM = demonstrative, DIM = diminutive, DIR = direct marker, DUB = dubitative mood, EMP = emphatic particle, GEN = genitive, towards speaker, IC = initial change, INV = inverse marker, LOC = locative, NA = animate noun, NI = animate noun, NAD = dependent animate noun, NEG = negative preverb, NI = inanimate noun, NID = dependent inanimate noun, NP = noun phrase, NSK = Nemaska, OBV = obviative, PE = exclusive plural, PERF = perfective aspect, PI = inclusive plural, PL = plural, POS = possessive suffix, POT = potential preverb, PROS = prospective aspect, RAD = radio broadcast, (CJ)REL = relative conjunct clause, SAP = speech act participant, SEC = South East Cree, SG = singular, SUBJ = subjunctive mood, TA = transitive animate verb, TI = transitive inanimate verb, VOL = volition preverb, 1 = first person, 3 = animate third person, 3' = animate third person obviative, 0'SG = inanimate obviative singular. In this paper I have kept the roman orthography used by the Cree School Board except for long and tensed vowels such as *aa*, which I have replaced with *â*, as well as *ch*, which I have replaced with *c*.
3. In fact, not all inflections presented in Table 1 are truly fusional and opaque, like *-aciht* '1PE>3' (< PA **-akenči*) (PA forms taken from Jacques and Aronov 2015). Others, like *-(y)ahk*^{w} '1PI>3' (< PA **-ankwe*) and *-(y)ek*^{w} '2PL' (< PA **-ekwe*), are inflections common to AI/TI and TA verbs. The inverse inflections are built with inverse markers, which indicate that a SAP participant is object. For instance, *-itahk*^{w} is formed of *-it-* 'second object' (< PA **-eθ-*) and the general inflection *-ahk*^{w} '1PI'; *-itâk*^{w} is formed of *-it-* 'second object'

and a suffix *-âk*^{w}, which occurs nowhere else in the language. Finally, *-iyamiht* '1PE<3' is formed of *-i(y)-* 'first object' (< PA **-iy-*) and *-amiht-* (< PA **-ament-* '1PE<3'); however, this inflection is considered opaque since *-amiht-* is a "cranberry" morph in synchrony. Quite unsurprisingly, then, the data presented in the following sections indicate that paradigm leveling is first triggered on the two most opaque forms, *-aciht-* and *-iyamiht-*, and is extended later to the other members of the paradigm that are more agglutinative and transparent.

4. Speakers had to translate English interrogative sentences and provide metalinguistic comments about the innovative inflections. This method has obvious flaws since it does not account for stylistic variations and pragmatic factors (e.g., level of fluency of one's addressee, copresence of an elder, etc.). For instance, some middle-aged speakers stated that they used the archaic direct inflections with elderly speakers but innovative ones with their children. To avoid these issues, I rely mostly on naturally occurring speech to document the actual use of the inflections.
5. Bill Jancewicz (personal communication, 2016) reports that similar pragmatic factors (e.g., presence of an elder; age of the addressee) condition the use of archaic TA inflections among younger speakers of Naskapi.
6. A handwritten note indicates that it was found by Donald E. Denmark, who was manager of the beaver reserve at Rupert House in 1941. I want to thank John Bishop and Kevin Brousseau, who brought to my attention the existence of this map.
7. Formal schooling in eastern James Bay began in the 1940s when a small number of children from the Mistissini and Waswanipi bands were sent to an Anglian residential school in Chapleau (Ontario). Later in the 1950s other small contingents attended residential schools in Moose Factory, Sault Ste. Marie, Brantford (Ontario), and La Tuque (Quebec) (Morantz 2002:212–220)
8. Wintrob and Sindell (1968:24–25) write that "Most parents say that children who have gone away to school for several years come back during the summer unable to speak Cree adequately. . . . After several years in school children do have great difficulty in speaking Cree and find it hard to communicate meaningfully with their parents or older kin. Older students almost invariably speak English (mixed with Cree) with their peers and siblings."
9. See MacKenzie (1980:253 et seq.) for further details on the phonology of SEC.
10. I want to thank Kevin Brousseau, who provided many useful comments about SEC phonological rules.
11. Paradigm leveling in the mixed singular SAP set is often the first answer provided in elicitation with younger speakers.

REFERENCES

Brousseau, Kevin, Susan Cheechoo, Vincent Collette, and Jimena Terraza. 2015. An Introduction to Cree Grammar. *Ililîmôwasinahikan: A Dictionary of Moose Cree, Cree/English*, ed. by Kevin Brousseau, pp. 375–469. Oujé-Bougoumou, QC, and Moose Factory, ON: Moose Cree First Nation/Cree Nation Government.

Coon-Come, Mary Ann (ed.). 1982. *Canoe Brigades from Mistassini*. Mistassini, QC: Cree Publications.

Cooper, Clara (ed.). 1981. *Iskweuch kaaisi-nachiskahko ewaapamaausuto*. Mistissini Lake, QC: Cree Publications.

Dahlstrom, Amy. 1989. Morphological Change in Plains Cree Verb Inflection. *Folia Linguistica Historica* 9(2):59–71.

Jacques, Guillaume and Antov Antonov. 2015. The Directionality of Analogical Change in Direct/Inverse Systems. Unpublished manuscript. https://hal.archives-ouvertes.fr/hal-01386721/document.

Johansson, Sara. 2012. Acquiring Northern East Cree Verbal Morphology: Evidence from Inchoative Verbs. PhD thesis, Memorial University.

Junker, Marie-Odile, Louise Blacksmith, and Marguerite MacKenzie. 2015. East Cree Verbs (Southern Dialect). [Revised and expanded from 2006 original and 2013 revised edition.] In *The Interactive East Cree Reference Grammar*. http://verbs.eastcree.org/?11.

Keeshig-Tobias, Lenore. 1993. *Kaa kaskamemuuch meskanu*, trans. by Annie Whiskeychan and Ruth Salt. Markham, ON: Fitzhenry and Whiteside.

MacKenzie, Marguerite. 1971. The Eastern (Mistissini) Cree Verb: Derivational Morphology. MA thesis, McGill University.

———. 1980. Towards a Dialectology of Cree-Montagnais-Naskapi. PhD thesis, University of Toronto.

Morantz, Toby. 2002. *The White Man's Gonna Getcha: The Colonial Challenge to the Crees in Québec*. Montreal-Queen: McGill-Queen's University Press.

Parker, Frank. 1976. Language Change and the Passive Voice. *Language* 52(2):449–460.

Rogers, Jean H. 1960. *Notes on Mistissini Phonemics and Morphology*, vol. 167. Ottawa: National Museum of Canada.

Thomason, Sarah. 2008. Social and Linguistic Factors as Predictors of Contact-Induced Change. *Journal of Language Contact* THEMA 2:42–56.

Vago, Robert M. 1991. Paradigmatic Regularity in First Language Acquisition. *First Language Acquisition*, ed. by Herbert W. Seliger and Robert M. Vago, pp. 241–251. Cambridge: Cambridge University Press.

Valentine, J. Randolph. 1994. Ojibwa Dialect Relationships. PhD thesis, University of Texas.

Wintrob, Ronald M. and Peter S. Sindell. 1968. *Education and Identity Conflict among Cree Indian Youth: A Preliminary Report.* Montreal: McGill University, Department of Forestry and Rural Development.

Wolfart, H. Christoph. 1973. *Plains Cree: A Grammatical Study.* Transactions of the American Philosophical Society, n.s., vol. 63, part 5. Philadelphia.

Rounding Dissimilation in Miami-Illinois

David J. Costa

'Rounding dissimilation' is the name for a sound change in Miami-Illinois, which is already evident in the late seventeenth-century records of the language.[1] This is a process whereby Proto-Algonquian **o* and **wa* change to Miami-Illinois *a* in weak syllables preceding the labial consonants *p*, *m*, and *w*, or *Cw* clusters, or *ko* sequences. Weak syllables are defined in terms of the Miami-Illinois Strong Syllable Rule (see Costa 2003:98–102), an iambic metrical rule that states that odd-numbered syllables are weak and even-numbered syllables are strong. For the purposes of this rule, long vowels are always strong; thus, the syllable count is always restarted after long vowels, and short vowels immediately after long vowels are always weak.[2]

The following Miami-Illinois words are straightforward examples where Proto-Algonquian **o* and **wa* have been reduced to Miami-Illinois *a* in weak syllables before *m*, *p*, and *w*:

(1) *mihtekamini* 'acorn' (Gr ‹mitegamini›, LB ‹mittegamini›, Gt ‹mtäkámini›, D ‹m'täkamĭni›), < PA **meʔtekomini*; cf. Kickapoo *mehtekomini*

(2) *niwiihka̲maa* 'I call him, summon him' (Gr/LB ‹ni8icama›, Gt ‹niwixkáma›, D ‹niwĭkáma›); < PA stem **wi·hkom-* (Costa 2003:61)

(3) *wiika̲pi* 'basswood inner bark' (Gr/LB ‹8icapi›, Gt ‹wikápi›)

(4) *wiika̲pimiši* 'basswood tree' (Gt ‹wíkapimízhi›, D ‹wikápĭmĭ́njĭ›); cf. Meskwaki *wi·kopi*, *wi·kopimiši*

(5) *eeka̲mi* 'each, every' (P ‹égami›, LB/Gr ‹egami›, Gt/D ‹äkámi›); < older **eekwami*; cf. Kickapoo *akwami-*, Potawatomi *egmə-* 'each, every'[3]

(6) *alaaka̲we* 'yesterday' (Gr /P ‹araga8e›, LB ‹araca8e›); cf. Meskwaki *ana·kowe* 'yesterday'[4]

The following examples show that rounding dissimilation is blocked when the *o* is in a strong syllable:

(7) *ašaahšiko̲pa* 'slippery elm' (Gt ‹ashaxshíkopa›, D ‹cacĭ́kopa›); cf. Ojibwe *ožaašigob*; for the same final, cf. 'basswood' (3–4)

(8) *mahko̲miši* 'sumac' (Gt ‹m'kumĭ́ži›, D ‹mŭkkomĭ́njĭ›); cf. Meskwaki *mahkomiši*

(9) *pinko̲mini*, pl. *pinko̲mina* 'blueberry, huckleberry' (D ‹pĭ́ngōmini›, LB ‹pincomin›, Gr ‹ping8mina›); cf. Meskwaki *pekomini* 'currant'

The effects of rounding dissimilation are also evident in reflexes of the phonologically similar Proto-Algonquian finals **a·towe* 'language' and **a·rowe* 'tail', which appear in Miami-Illinois as *aata̲we* and *aala̲we*, respectively (see Costa 2003:146–147):

(10) 'language'

a. independent *ilaata̲weewa* 'he speaks a particular language' (Gr ‹irata8e8a›)

b. the corresponding conjunct *iilaata̲weeci* (Gt ‹ilatawä́dshi›, D ‹ĭ́latáwätc›); < PA stem **eθa·towe·*; cf. Meskwaki *ina·towe·wa* 'he speaks such a language'

c. participle *peewaaliaata̲weeta* 'he speaks Peoria' (Gt ‹päwaliatáwäta›)

d. Illinois *nimpeewaareewaata̲wee* 'I speak Peoria' (P ‹nipe8are8ata8e›); cf. Shawnee *nipeewaaleewaatowe* 'I speak Peoria'

(11) 'tail'

a. *kiinwaala̲weeta* 'he has a long tail' (Gr ‹kin8ara8eta›, Gt ‹kinwalawắta›, D ‹kinwalauwäta›); < PA **kenwa·rowe·-*; cf. Meskwaki *kenwa·nowe·wa* 'he has a long tail'

b. *waapaala̲weeta* 'he has a white tail' (Gr ‹8abara8eta›, Gt ‹wápaláweta›); < PA **wa·pa·rowe·-*; cf. Ojibwe *waabaanowed*

In the words for 'buffalo' and 'rabbit' (12–13), the Proto-Algonquian final *-*oswa* (see Goddard 2002:59) appears as Miami-Illinois -*answa*.[5] In 'buffalo', the prenasalization of the sibilant can be explained as deriving from regular phonological rule, given the Miami-Illinois process whereby plain sibilants become prenasalized (and voiced) after sequences of nasal consonants plus vowels (see Costa 2003:71–73). However, no such phonological rule can explain the prenasalization of the sibilant in 'rabbit', where it is presumably generalized from 'buffalo' (perhaps reinforced also by Illinois *moonswa* 'deer'):[6]

(12) *waapa̲nswa* 'rabbit' (Gr ‹8abans8a›, Gt ‹wapá^{n}swa›, Mc ‹wâpá^{n}zwa'›); < PA **wa·poswa* (Goddard 2002:59)

(13) a. old Illinois *irena̲nswa* 'buffalo'[7] (Gr ‹irenans8a›, P/LB ‹irenans8o›)

b. modern Miami-Illinois *alena̲nswa* 'buffalo, cow' (Hk ‹lenãnswa›, Tr ‹ulaanāūzwau›, D ‹länánzwa›); < PA **erenoswa* (Goddard 2002:59)

One can find a handful of nouns with stems historically ending in **kw* where the possessed theme sign *-*em* contracts with the preceding **kw* as -*kam* in weak syllables:

(14) a. *ninciihciika̲ma* 'my wart' (Gr ‹nitchitchigama›, D ‹n'djı̆́tcĭkáma›)

b. *ciihciika̲ma* 'wart' (Gt ‹tchixtchikáma›); cf. Meskwaki *či·hči·koma*

(15) *nincihciika̲ma* 'my soul, shadow, echo' (Gr/LB ‹nitchitchigama›, Gt ‹nintshixtchikáma›; cf. Ojibwe *ninjičaag* and Munsee *nčíhča·kw* 'my soul'

(16) *nisehka̲mi* 'my spit, saliva' (Gr/LB ‹nisecami›, Gt ‹nisäxkámi›); < PA stem **sehkw*-; cf. Menominee *sɛhko·m* 'saliva', *nesɛ·hkom* 'my saliva'

Possessed forms of the Proto-Algonquian noun **ehkwa* 'louse' usually appear in

Miami-Illinois as the dependent noun stem *-tehka̱ma*. Moreover, Miami-Illinois also has the independent noun *atehkama* 'louse', backformed from the possessed forms (similar to contemporary Meskwaki):

(17) a. *nitehka̱ma* 'my louse' (Gr ‹nitescama›, ‹nit'ecama›)
 b. *atehka̱mali* 'his louse' (Gr ‹atecamari›, Gt ‹atäxkamali›)
 c. *atehka̱ma* 'a louse' (Gt ‹atäxkáma›, D ‹täkama›); < PA **netehkoma* 'my louse'; cf. Meskwaki *otehkoma* 'louse' (see Goddard 2002:71–72)

More commonly, however, rounding dissimilation FAILS to apply with stems ending in *Cw* when taking the possessed theme sign **-em*. In the following typical examples, the vowel *o* has been restored to the *-om* sequences, probably on analogy from nouns where the *o* is preserved in even-numbered syllables:

(18) *noohko̱ma* 'my grandmother, female ancestor' (Gr ‹n8c8ma›, LB ‹nohc8ma›, Mc ‹nṓ'koma^{n}›); < PA **no·hkoma*

(19) *nimehko̱ma* 'my vein, pulse' (Gr/LB ‹nimec8ma›, Gt ‹nimä'hkúma›); < PA **nemerkoma* 'my vein'[8]

(20) a. *niniihpikato̱mi* 'my blood' (Gr/LB ‹ninipigat8mi›, D ‹nĭnĭpĭ́katómĭ›)
 b. nonpossessed *niihpikatwi* 'blood' (Gt ‹ní'hpíkatwi›)[9]

(21) a. *alenko̱maawi* 'one's armpit' (Gr ‹aring8ma8i›)
 b. modern locative *alenko̱maanki* 'in one's armpit' (Gt ‹längumángi›); cf. *nilenkwi* 'my armpit' (Gr ‹niring8i›); cf. Kickapoo *nenekwi* 'my wing, armpit'

There is at least one noun with stem-final *kw* that varies in whether it combines with the possessed theme sign as *kam* or *kom*:

(22) a. old Illinois *nimelihtika̱ma* 'my snot, mucus' (Gr ‹nimeriticama›, LB ‹nimerittigama›)
 b. versus reanalyzed modern *nimelihtiko̱ma* (D ‹nimälĭtikóma›)
 c. cf. the simplex form *milihtikwa* 'snot, mucus' (Gr ‹miritic8a›, Gt ‹militígwa›, D ‹mĭlĭtĭkwa›)

Alternations

The fact that rounding dissimilation happens in weak syllables means that there are numerous alternations found with single Miami-Illinois morphemes where the rule variously applies or fails to apply, depending on syllable count. Rounding dissimilation alternations are found in adverbs with the 'day' final, *-okone*. This morpheme regularly appears as *-o̲kone* when the initial *o* of the final is in a strong syllable, but as dissimilated *-a̲kone* when it is in a weak syllable. Thus, *-okone* appears with the numbers three, five, six, and seven, while *-akone* appears with one, two, and four:

(23) *ninkota̲kone* 'one day' (Gr ‹nig8tag8ne›, D ‹n'gotakonä›); cf. Kickapoo *nekotokone*

(24) *niiša̲kone* 'two days' (Gr ‹ninchag8ne›, LB ‹ninchac8ne›, Gt ‹nīzhakonä›, D ‹nĭ^{n}jakonä›); cf. Kickapoo *niisokone*

(25) *nihso̲kone* 'three days' (Gr/LB ‹niss8g8ne›, Gt ‹nissókonä›, D ‹nĭssokonä›); cf. Kickapoo *neθokone*

(26) *niiya̲kone* 'four days' (Gt ‹níakunä›, D ‹niakonä›); cf. Meskwaki *nye·wokoni*, Ojibwe *niiyogon*

(27) *yaalano̲kone* 'five days' (D ‹yalanokonä›); cf. Kickapoo *niananokone*

(28) *kaakaathso̲kone* 'six days' (LB ‹cacats8gone›, D ‹kakátsokónä›)[10]

(29) *swaahteethso̲kone* 'seven days, week' (LB ‹s8atets8gone›)

Another common source of alternations are verb stems where underlying *o* unrounds to *a* when it is in a weak syllable, yet remains as *o* when initial change (or the lack of it) places the same syllable in a strong position:

(30) a. independent *kato̲nkwaamwa* 'he is sleepy' (Gr ‹gatt8ng8am8a›)
b. dissimilated participle *keeta̲nkwaanka* 'he is sleepy' (LB ‹ketang8anga›, Gt ‹ketángwanga›)

c. independent *ninkata̱nkwa(an)* 'I am sleepy' (P/LB ‹nigatang8an›, Gt ‹ngátangwa›); < stem *katonkwaam-*; cf. Kickapoo *katokwaamwa* 'he is sleepy' (see also Costa 2008:146)

(31) a. *isko̱hpweewa* 'he leaves him from eating' (Gr ‹esc8p8e8a›)
b. dissimilated *ninteska̱hpwaa* 'I leave him from eating' (Gr ‹nitescap8a›, LB ‹nintecap8o›)

As a verb initial, Miami-Illinois *nekotw-* 'one, single' consistently appears as *niko̱tw-* (modern *ninko̱tw-*) when word-initial, but as dissimilated *neka̱tw-* (modern *nenka̱tw-*) with a person prefix present, and as *neeka̱tw-* (modern *neenka̱tw-*) when the verb undergoes initial change, placing it in a weak syllable. The attested forms of the AI stem *nekotwaapahee-* 'have one child' show these alternations clearly:

(32) a. nondissimilated *niko̱twaapaheewa* '(s)he has only one child' (P ‹nig8tt8apahe8a›)
b. dissimilated *nineka̱twaapahee* 'I have only one child' (LB ‹ninegatt8apahe›)
c. changed participle *neeka̱twaapaheeta* '(s)he has only one child' (LB ‹negat8apaheta›); cf. Kickapoo *nekotwaapahee-* 'give birth once'

This alternation between *o* and *a* is very consistent for other verbs with the 'one' initial (see also Costa 2003:146):

(33) a. nondissimilated *niko̱tweewa* 'he speaks alone' (Gr ‹nig8t8e8a›)
b. dissimilated *nineka̱twee* 'I speak alone' (Gr ‹ninegat8e› 'je parle seul')

(34) a. nondissimilated *niko̱toopiwa* 'he is alone, sits alone' (Gr ‹nig8t8pi8a›)
b. dissimilated *nineka̱toopi* 'I sit alone' (LB ‹ninegatopi›, Gr ‹ninegat8pi› 'je suis seul')

Rounding dissimilation also explains the second-syllable vowel *a* in Illinois *neeka̱tokašiiwa~ neeka̱tokašia* 'horse' (literally 'single-claw, single-hoof'; Gr ‹negat8cachi8a›, LB ‹negatt8cachia›), which in turn was borrowed into Meskwaki as *ne·kato·škaše·ha* and *ne·kato·kaše·ha* (and other less common forms), and into Sauk as *ne·kato·škaša·ha* (see Costa 2013:199–200).

As mentioned in Costa (2003:365–366), another result of rounding dissimilation is that inanimate intransitive stems ending in underlying *-kwat* regularly take the ending *-katwi* in weak syllables in the independent order, yet retain the *wa* with the dependent ending *-kwahki*:[11]

(35) a. dissimilated *mihšahkatwi* 'it is clear weather' (Gr ‹michacat8i›, Gt ‹m'shakátwi›)
b. nondissimilated dependent *meehšahkwahki* (Gr ‹mechac8aki›, D ‹mäckwakĭ›); stem *mihšahkwat-*; cf. Ojibwe independent *mižakwad*, conjunct *mežakwak*

(36) a. dissimilated *išinaakatwi* 'it is thus, it is so, it happens that way' (LB ‹ichinagat8i›, D ‹ĭcĭ́nakátwĭ›)
b. nondissimilated dependent *iišinaakwahki* (LB ‹ichinag8ki›, Gt ‹ĭ́shinák^{8}gi›); stem *išinaakwat-*; cf. Ojibwe independent *ižinaagwad*, conjunct *ežinaagwak* 'it looks so'

(37) a. dissimilated *aahkatwi* 'it is important, difficult' (Gr ‹acat8i›, LB ‹ahcat8i›)
b. nondissimilated dependent *aahkwahki* (Gr ‹ac8aki›, LB ‹ac8ki›); stem *aahkwat-*; cf. Meskwaki *a·hkwatwi* 'it is dangerous, painful'

Likewise, when the 'wood, tree' medial *-aahkw-* combines with the inanimate intransitive final *-at*, the resultant ending appears as *-aahkwahki* in the dependent but as *aahkatwi* in the independent:

(38) a. dissimilated *kinwaahkatwi* 'it is long, of wood' (Gr/LB ‹kin8acat8i›)
b. dependent *kiinwaahkwahki* (Gr ‹kin8ac8ki›, Gt ‹kínwak^{8}gi›); cf. Ojibwe independent *ginwaakwad*, conjunct *genwaakwak* 'it is long (as something stick- or wood-like)'

(39) a. dissimilated *mihcaahkatwi* 'it is a big tree' (Gr/LB ‹mitchacat8i›, D ‹mitcakátwĭ›)
b. dependent *meehcaahkwahki* (LB ‹metchac8ki›, Gt ‹mätcá'kgi›, D ‹mätcákkĭ›); cf. Ojibwe independent *mičaakwad*, conjunct *mečaakwak* 'it is big (as something stick- or wood-like)'

The only known II stem where *-kwat* lands in a strong syllable is *aalahkwat-* 'be cloudy'. The great majority of the time, its *-kwat* sequence does NOT dissimilate to *kat* in the independent, precisely because the *-kwat* syllable is in an even-numbered position; thus, one almost always finds independent *aalahkwatwi* 'it is cloudy'. However, there are two stray instances in the records of apparent *aalahkatwi*, presumably by analogy with the far more numerous II stems where *-kwat* lands in a weak syllable:

(40) a. dependent *aalahkwahki* (Gt ‹alxkwaki› D ‹alakwaki›, P/H ‹ʔalxkwaxki›)
b. normal independent *aalahkwatwi* 'it is cloudy' (Gr/LB ‹arac8at8i›, WP ‹ʋlʋqʋtue›, Gt ‹álxkwatwi›, D ‹alkwatwĭ›)
c. reshaped independent *aalahkatwi* (LB ‹aroccat8i›,WP ‹ʋlkʋtue›); < PA **a·raskwatwi* 'it is a cloud, cloudy'; cf. Ojibwe *aanakwad, ayaanakwak* 'it is cloudy'

A few verbs whose stems would be expected to alternate by the rounding dissimilation rule have leveled out the alternation entirely. The TA stem *nahkom-* 'answer him, reply to him' always appears with second-syllable *o*, regardless of whether this syllable is in a weak or strong position:

(41) a. *nahkomi* 'answer him!' (P ‹nak8mi›)
b. *ninahkomaa* 'I answer him, reply to him' (Gr/LB ‹ninac8ma›)
c. changed participle *neehkomehka* 'he answers you, replies to you' (D ‹näkomäka›); cf. Meskwaki *nahkome·wa* 'he answers him, agrees with him'

More common than stems following the rounding dissimilation alternations exactly as expected or stems that have eliminated the alternation entirely are stems that do alternate, yet which show reshaping for some speakers or in certain time periods. Some of the most elaborate alternations seen with the rounding dissimilation rule are with the Miami-Illinois verbs for 'be heavy', as discussed in Costa (2008:146–147). The II for 'be heavy', underlyingly *kahcokwan-*, shows rounding dissimilation alternations in both its second and third syllables, varying between an independent stem *kahcokan-* versus a changed dependent allomorph *keehcakwan-*:

(42) a. *kahcokanwi* 'it is heavy' (Gr ‹catch8gan8i›, LB ‹ktch8can8i›, Gt ‹kaxtchukánwi›)
b. dependent *keehcakwanki* 'it is heavy' (Gr ‹ketchag8anghi›, Gt ‹kä'htchákwangi›, D ‹kätchákwangĭ›)

However, one can find forms where these alternations fail to appear in the 'correct' places; for example, the alternate (43a) has undone the rounding dissimilation in its third (weak) syllable, and is attested in at least four sources, while the dependent alternate (43b) has undone rounding dissimilation in its SECOND syllable, and is attested by Gatschet (n.d.) once:

(43) a. *kahcokwanwi* (Gr ‹catch8g8an8i›, V ‹ktchokouâné›, Tr ‹ketshoakwōnwaa›, D ‹k'tcokwánwĭ›)
b. *keehcokwanki* (Gt ‹kä'htchúkwangi›)

Likewise, the AI stem for 'be heavy', underlying *kahcokwal-*, normally shows rounding dissimilation in its second and third syllables as well, alternating between a stem shape *kVhcakwal-* seen in prefixed independent and changed dependent forms, versus a stem shape *kahcokal-* seen in unprefixed independent and unchanged dependent forms:

(44) *kVhcakwal—*
a. *ninkahcakwali* 'I am heavy' (Gr/LB ‹nicatchag8ari›)
b. *keehcakwalita* 'he is heavy' (D ‹kắtcakwalí́ta›)

(45) *kahcokal—*
a. *kahcokalwa* 'he is heavy' (Gr ‹catchagar8a›, LB ‹catch8car8a› 'il est pesant a marcher', Gt ‹kaxtchukálwa›)
b. *kahcokalooki* 'they are heavy' (Gt ‹kxtchukalōkí›)

A handful of verbs with stem-final *o(o)* show rounding dissimilation of the vowel in the preceding syllable, even without an intervening labial consonant. An especially clear example of this is the TI stem *akotoo-* 'hang it', where the second-syllable vowel is commonly reduced to *a* in weak syllables:

(46) a. *akotoolo* 'hang it up!' (LB ‹acot8ro›; P ak8t8ro›, D ‹akótoló›)
b. dissimilated *eekatoonki* 'one hangs it up' (Gr ‹ecat8nghi›)
c. first person *eekatwaani* 'I hang it up' (Gt ‹äkatuáni›, D ‹äkatwánĭ›); cf. Cree *akota·w* 'he hangs it'

However, paradigmatic leveling has considerably disturbed the results of this rule in that one often sees *a* generalized to strong syllables or, less often, *o* restored to weak syllables, even in the oldest Illinois records:

(47) a. expected *ako̲toowa* 'he hangs it up' (P ‹ak8t8a›, LB ‹ac8t8a›)
b. reanalyzed alternate *aka̲toowa* 'he hangs it up' (P ‹akat[8a]›, LB ‹acat8o›).

(48) a. expected *nintaka̲too(n)* 'I hang it up' (LB ‹nitacat8n›, P ‹nitakat8n›, Gt ‹ndákatû›, D ‹nĭndákató›)
b. reanalyzed *ninatko̲too(n)* (Gr ‹nit'ac8t8›, P ‹nitak8t8n›, D ‹nĭndakóto›)

The Proto-Algonquian final **-ton-* 'mouth' commonly appears as Miami-Illinois *-tan-* in weak syllables, especially in old Illinois:

(49) a. *ninkipito̲ne* 'I am mute, close my mouth' (Gr/LB ‹nikipit8ne›)
b. *kiipito̲nka* 'he is mute, shuts his mouth' (LB ‹kipit8nga›, Gt ‹kipítunga›)
c. dissimilated *kipeta̲nwa* 'he is mute, shuts his mouth' (Gr ‹kipetan8a); cf. Shawnee *kipitonwa* 'he is mute, has a stopped-up mouth'

However, just as often, the *a* of the 'mouth' final is generalized to strong syllable positions:

(50) a. expected *taawito̲nka* 'he is hare-lipped' (D ‹tawĭ́tonga›)
b. reanalyzed *taawita̲nwa* (LB ‹ta8itan8o› 'il a la levre fendue co[mm]e un lievre')

Sometimes one finds *o* restored to odd-numbered, weak syllables:

(51) a. expected *taawaleta̲nwa* 'he opens his mouth' (Gr/P ‹ta8aretan8a›)
b. reanalyzed *taawaleto̲nwa* (Gr ‹ta8aret8n8a›, LB ‹ta8ereton8o›)

Similarly, *-ahoko*, the AI 'float, be in water' final, regularly appears as *-aha̲ko-* when its second syllable is in a weak position:

(52) a. *nimpemaho̲ko* 'I float, float past, go along by water' (Gr ‹nipemah8g8›)
b. dissimilated *pimaha̲kowa* 'he floats, floats past, goes by water' (LB ‹pemahag8a›); cf. Meskwaki *pemahokowa* 'he swims past'

Though again, it is common to find examples where *-aha̲ko-* has been generalized to places where, based on syllable count, one would expect *-aho̲ko-*:

(53) a. expected *nintampaho̲ko*
b. reanalyzed *nintampaha̲ko* 'I float on the surface' (Gr ‹nitampah8g8›, LB ‹nitampahag8›)
c. *eempaha̲koka* 'he floats on the surface' (Gt ‹embahakúka›)

While there are not many examples, it appears that even though the Miami-Illinois 'saw' final was originally *-ihpo̲too-* (cf. Kickapoo *-ipotoo-*), it has generalized its second syllable vowel to *a* in almost all attested forms, regardless of syllable count, giving *-ihpa̲too-*:[12]

(54) a. nondissimilated *nikiiskihpo̲too* 'I saw it crosswise' (Gr ‹nikiskip8t8› 'je coupe en sciant, limant')
b. *kiihkihpo̲taakani* 'hand saw' (D ‹kĭkpótakánĭ›)
c. *keehkihpa̲twaani* 'I saw it crosswise' (Gt ‹käkpatuáni›, D ‹kä́kĭpatwánĭ›); cf. Kickapoo *kiiskipotoo-* 'saw it apart'

All attested forms of *pahsihpatoo-* 'saw it lengthwise' attest only *a*, even when this vowel is in an even-numbered syllable:

(55) a. *peehsihpa̲twaani* 'I saw it lengthwise' (Gt ‹pässpatwáni›, D ‹päsĭpatwánĭ›)
b. *peehsihpa̲toonki* 'it is split' (D ‹pä́spatúngĭ›)
c. *pahsihpa̲taakani* 'mill saw' (D ‹p'sĭpátakánĭ›); initial < PA **paʔs-* 'split'; cf. Menominee *paʔsepocekan* 'sawmill'

At least one alternation attributable to rounding dissimilation has become morphophonemically generalized in Miami-Illinois, regardless of syllable count: when TA stems ending in *Cw* take the theme 2 sign *-eko-*, the *Cw* + *-eko-* sequence always appears as *Ca̲ko*, with contraction of *w* + *e* to *a* rather than the expected **o* (as found in, e.g., Meskwaki).[13] In most of the following examples the dissimilated *a* is in fact in strong syllables:

(56) a. dissimilated *šeehšaha̲koci* 'he (obv.) stings him, burns him' (Gt ‹shäsháhakutch›, D ‹cäcáhakotc›, Mc ‹ceʻcä́ʻakutci›); < stem *šiihšahw-*
b. *nišiihšahwaa* 'I sting him, burn him' (Gr ‹nichichah8a› 'je le brusle'); cf. Meskwaki *ši·šahwe·wa* 'he pokes him with a burning stick'

(57) a. dissimilated *meešahakoci* 'he (obv.) spears him' (D ‹mänjahakotci›); < stem *mešahw-*
b. Illinois *nimešahwaa* 'I spear him' (Gr ‹nimechah8a› 'je le darde, le frap[p]e en dardant, en jettant')

(58) a. dissimilated *niweeweehseehakwa* 'he fans me' (Gt ‹niwäwäđähákwa›)
b. participial *weeweehseehakota* 'he (obv.) fans him' (Gt ‹wäwässahákuta›); < stem *weeweehseehw-*
c. *niweeweehseehwaa* 'I fan him' (Gr ‹ni8e8esseh8a›, Gt ‹niwäwäthä'hwá›); cf. Ojibwe *niwewese?waa* 'I fan him'

The following sentence from LeBoullenger's (n.d.) dictionary is an excellent example of rounding dissimilation with the theme 2 sign in old Illinois:

(59) *seehsinehkiipakota kineepikooli* 'a snake (obv.) bites him on the hand, he is bitten on the hand by a snake' (LB ‹sesinekipag8ta kinepic8ri› 'mordu a la main par un ser[pent]'); TA stem *siihsinehkiipw-* 'bite him on the hand', < underlying **siihs-inehkii-ipw-eko-ta* 'pinch-hand-by teeth-theme 2–3sg participle'

This unrounding also takes place when TA stems ending in long vowels + *w* take the theme 2 sign, along with a concomitant shift of the preceding *w* to *y*:

(60) a. participle *neeyakota* 'he (obv.) sees him' (Mc ‹nēyá̄kuta^{n}›)
b. independent *nineeyakwa* 'he sees me' (Gr ‹nineïag8a›, LB ‹nineiac8o›, D ‹ninä́yakwa›, Mc ‹ninäyākwa^{n}›)[14]; < stem *neew-* 'see him'
c. *nineewaa* 'I see him' (Gr/P ‹nine8a›, Mc ‹ninäwá'›)

Though there are not many examples, this morphophonemic rule also extends to *Cw-* and *V·w-* final stems when they take the local independent indefinite subject (passive) marker *-ekoo-*:

(61) *niweeweehseehakoo* 'I am fanned' (Gt ‹niwäwäthäháko›); < stem *weeweehseehw-*; see (58a–c)

(62) *nineeyakoo* 'I am seen' (Gr ‹nineïag8›); < stem *neew-*; see (60a–c)[15]

Conclusion

While rounding dissimilation in Miami-Illinois unquestionably began as a sound change, even by the old Illinois period it can no longer be described as a simple phonological rule. From the earliest records, its effects are already considerably disturbed by analogy, being reversed in some environments where it would be expected to apply or extended to forms where its phonological conditioning is absent. Its effects are unsurprisingly most regular in forms where it is immune to metrical alternations of any kind, such as in nouns immediately following long vowels and NOT following a morpheme boundary. However, there are numerous forms where the rounding dissimilation alternation is followed with total regularity, hinting that its effects have been morphologized for certain morphemes. The morphologization of rounding dissimilation is most thorough with the theme 2 and passive markers following *Cw* stems, where the change of *o* to *a* is obligatory regardless of metrical factors. Either way, rounding dissimilation is a splendid example of a sound change that does not submit to normal phonological description, and which cannot be accurately described ignoring morphology and its numerous analogies and irregularities.

NOTES

1. Miami-Illinois is an Algonquian language originally spoken primarily in what is now Illinois, northern Indiana, and western Ohio, and later in northern Indiana and northeastern Oklahoma. The name 'Miami-Illinois' is a cover term for a cluster of very closely related dialects, the primary ones being Miami (also known as Myaamia), Wea, Piankashaw, and Illinois, the main groups of the Illinois being the Peoria and Kaskaskia. In this paper, 'Illinois' is used to designate the language in the dialectally mixed French missionary materials of the late seventeenth and early eighteenth centuries, while 'modern Miami-Illinois' is used to refer to materials collected by various individuals (especially Albert Gatschet, Jacob Dunn, and Truman Michelson) in the late nineteenth and early twentieth centuries. I thank Ives Goddard and two anonymous reviewers for helpful comments and corrections.
2. I have dealt with Miami-Illinois rounding dissimilation in a piecemeal fashion in previous work (e.g., Costa 2003, 2008), but in the present work I discuss the phenomenon in a more systematic fashion, bringing more data under review, as well as examining the exceptions to the rule. The following abbreviations are used in this

paper: AI = animate intransitive, D = Jacob Dunn's notes on Miami-Illinois (Dunn n.d. (a); n.d. (b)), Gr = the Gravier/Largillier Illinois-French dictionary (Largillier n.d.), Gt = Albert Gatschet's notes on Miami-Illinois, Hk = Heckewelder's notes on Miami-Illinois, II = inanimate intransitive, LB = LeBoullenger's French-Illinois dictionary, Mc = Truman Michelson's (1916) notes on Peoria, P = Pinet's (n.d.) French-Illinois dictionary, PA = Proto-Algonquian, P/H = Hockett's Peoria field notes, TA = transitive animate, TI = transitive inanimate, Tr = Trowbridge's notes on Miami, V = Volney's (1857) Miami wordlist, WP = the 1837 Wea Primer (Anonymous 1837).

3. The Miami-Illinois and Potawatomi forms both appear to have obligatorily undergone initial change.
4. In modern Miami-Illinois, the final *-awe* in this word is reduced to *e* by normal sound law: *alaake* 'yesterday' (Hk ‹allake›, Tr ‹aulāūkyaa›, Gt ‹lákiä›); the palatalization of *k* to [k^y] before *e(e)* is regular (Costa 2003:198, n.38).
5. These are the only two words with this final that have been found in Miami-Illinois.
6. For Illinois 'deer', note Gr ‹m8ns8a› and LB ‹m8ns8o› (see Costa 2003:72). Strictly speaking, the *n* in *moonswa* is predictable by phonological rule, so this word could also be phonemicized as *mooswa*. By the 1790s, this word has been reshaped as *moohswa* (see Costa 2003:76).
7. This word could also be phonemicized as Illinois *irenaswa*, modern *alenaswa*.
8. Cf. Shawnee *nimhskoma* 'my vein', Unami *nəmó·kəmak* 'my veins' (Goddard 2015:354), and Arapaho *béʔib* 'vein' (animate). Proto-Algonquian **nemerkoma* 'my vein' is the animate analog of the far more widely attested inanimate PA **nemerkomi* 'my blood'.
9. The far more common simplex term for 'blood' is *niihpikanwi* (Gr/LB/P ‹nipigan8i›, Gt ‹ni'hpikanwi›, P/H ‹nixpikanwi›). However, possessed Miami-Illinois forms of 'blood' are always formed off *niihpikatwi* and never *niihpikanwi*.
10. The initial *o* of *-o̱kone* is in an even-numbered (strong) syllable in 'six days' and 'seven days' due to the former presence of a syncopated (and unattested) short vowel between the *t* and the *hs* in *kaakaathswi* 'six' and *swaahteethswi* 'seven'.
11. In the Illinois records, the sequence *kwahk* in weak syllables is usually written ‹c8k› or ‹g8k›, especially by Pinet and LeBoullenger. Given the handful of instances when this ending is actually written as ‹c8ak› (e.g., Gravier's ‹mechac8aki› for *meehšahkwahki* 'it is clear weather', 54–55), it is most likely that these ‹c8ki› and ‹g8ki› sequences represent phonetic [kw̥ḁk], with a rounded, entirely voiceless glide + vowel sequence. Dunn often writes these same sequences as ‹qk›, ‹kk›, or ‹k'k›, while Gatschet usually writes them as ‹kg›, ‹k^{8}k›, or ‹k^{8}g›, showing the common late-nineteenth century use of ‹8› and ‹^{8}› to represent voiceless lip rounding, for a sound along the lines of [ʍ].

12. The preaspirated *hp* of this final is unexpected on a comparative basis (cf. Kickapoo *-ipotoo-*, Ojibwe *-iboodoo-*), but seems certain based on transcriptions like Dunn's ‹kắkpatúngĭ› 'it is sawed' (*keehkihpatoonki*) and Gatschet's ‹pässpatwáni› 'I saw it, saw it lengthwise' (*peesihpatwaani*). This preaspiration also extends to its TA equivalent *-ihpal-*, which is implied by the detransitivized form *keehkihpašikwaani* 'I saw crosswise' (Gt ‹käkpashikwáni›; cf. Kickapoo *kiiskipon-* 'saw him apart').
13. For example, cf. Meskwaki *netepahokwa* 'he paid me', from the stem *tepahw-* (Goddard 2001:169).
14. Pinet attests contracted *nineekwa* 'he sees me' (P ‹nineg8a›), very likely an archaism; precisely the same contraction is seen in Massachusett ‹nunnogq› 'he sees me' (Eliot 1663, Numbers 22:33; phonemic **nənākʷ*). Cf. also Shawnee *ninookwa* and Fox *nene·wokwa* (see Goddard 2001:212–214).
15. Note also Illinois *neeyaawa* 'he is seen' (P ‹neïa8a›, LB ‹neia8a›), which shows that the *w* > *y* shift has been generalized to all persons in the passive. Additionally, Gatschet attests a form *neeyakosici* 'he appears, is seen, born' (‹neyakussítchi›), showing uncontraction and rounding dissimilation from the derived PA passive **no·kosi-* 'he is seen' (see Goddard 2001:213).

REFERENCES

Anonymous. 1837. *The Wea Primer, Wev Mvs Nv Kv Ne, to Teach the Wea Language.* Cherokee Nation: Mission Press.

Costa, David J. 2003. *The Miami-Illinois Language.* Lincoln: University of Nebraska Press.

———. 2008. New Notes on Miami-Illinois. *Papers of the Thirty-Ninth Algonquian Conference,* ed. by Karl S. Hele and Regna Darnell, pp. 123–165. London, ON: University of Western Ontario.

———. 2013. Borrowing in Southern Great Lakes Algonquian and the History of Potawatomi. *Anthropological Linguistics* 55(3):195–233.

Dunn, Jacob P. [n.d.]a. Miami Filecard Dictionary. Manuscript at the Indiana State Library, Indianapolis.

———. [n.d.]b. Various Notes on Miami. Manuscripts at the Indiana State Library, Indianapolis.

Eliot, John. 1663. *The Holy Bible. Containing the Old Testament and the New. Translated into the Indian Language and Ordered to be Printed by the Commissioners of the United Colonies in New England.* Cambridge, MA: Samuel Green and Marmaduke Johnson.

Gatschet, Albert. [n.d.] *Vocabulary and Text.* (Three original Miami and Peoria field notebooks.) Manuscript #236, National Anthropological Archives, Smithsonian Museum Support Center, Suitland, MD.

Goddard, Ives. 2001. Contraction in Fox (Meskwaki). *Papers of the Thirty-Second Algonquian Conference*, ed. by John Nichols, pp. 164–230. Winnipeg: University of Manitoba.

———. 2002. Explaining the Double Reflexes of Word-Initial High Short Vowels in Fox. *Diachronica* 19(1):43–80.

———. 2015. Arapaho Historical Morphology. *Anthropological Linguistics* 57:345–411.

Largillier, Jacques. [n.d.] [ca. 1700]. *Illinois–French Dictionary*. Manuscript in Watkinson Library, Trinity College, Hartford, CT. (Manuscript previously attributed to Jacques Gravier.)

LeBoullenger, Antoine-Robert, S.J. [n.d.] [ca. 1725]. *French and Miami–Illinois Dictionary*. Manuscript at the John Carter Brown Library, Brown University, Providence, RI.

Michelson, Truman. 1916. *Notes on Peoria*. Manuscript #2721, National Anthropological Archives, Smithsonian Museum Support Center, Suitland, MD.

Pinet, Pierre-François. [n.d.] [ca. 1702] *French-Miami-Illinois Dictionary*. Manuscript at the Archives des jésuites au Canada, Montreal.

Volney, Constantin F.C. de. 1857. *Œuvres Completes de Volney*. Paris: Chez Firmin Didot Frères, Fils et Cie.

Embedded Questions in Meskwaki: Syntax and Information Structure

Amy Dahlstrom

In descriptive and theoretical treatments of the syntax of Algonquian languages, there has been quite a bit of work done on the syntax of questions (cf. Johnson and Macaulay 2015 and the work cited there).[1] Less attention has been paid specifically to the syntax of embedded questions: that is, when a main verb like 'ask', 'wonder', or a negated main verb 'know' takes a complement clause that is in the form of a question. Perhaps the explanation for the relative neglect of embedded questions in Algonquian syntax is that many languages of the family employ strategies that seem to be identical to the formation of main clause questions. For example, consider the Plains Cree examples in (1–2):

(1) Plains Cree
tānisi kā-kī-isi-nikamoyan?
how CNJ-PAST-thus-sing.2
'How did you sing?' (Wolvengrey 2011:312)

(2) namōya kiskēyihtam ēkwa [**tānisi** kik-ēsi-kakēskimāwasot]
not know.3>0 now how CNJ-thus-counsel.one's.children.3
ayisiyiniw
person
'now people do not know [how to counsel their children]' (Wolvengrey 2011:232)

The question word *tānisi* is used to ask 'how?' in the main clause question in (1) and also in the embedded question in (2). In both instances, the question word appears at the left edge of its clause.

Anishinaabemowin (Ojibwe) and Menominee are similar to Plains Cree in that they also employ independent question words in an embedded question:

(3) Anishinaabemowin
Wa-nda-gkenim [**aaniin** naa endshiwaad giwi
go.and.find.out.2s>3 **how** as.many.as.they.were those
eyaajig wadi].
who.were.there there
'Go find out [how many of them there are over there].' (Valentine 2001:990)

(4) Menominee
'S aw-kocēmonakeh [**wāēkiq** cew-āwek eneh
AOR IRR-ask.TA.1PL>3CONJ **what** EPIS-be.II.0CONJ that.INAN
nayōhtah].
carry.on.back.TI.3>0CONJ
'We will ask him [what it is that he carries on his back].'
(Johnson and Macaulay 2015:369)

Meskwaki, however, exhibits a different pattern. Main clause questions contain independent question words, as in (5) with *kaši* 'how'. But the independent question words do not appear in embedded questions, as in (6).[2]

(5) Meskwaki
kašiča·hi išina·kosiwaki?
kaši=ča·hi išina·kosi-waki
how=so appear.thus-3P/IND.IND
'What did they look like?' W346P

(6) ni·hmawiča·hi –nana·tohtawa·waki e·ne·nemikwe·hiki
n-i·h-mawi–=ča·hi –nana·tohtaw-a·waki [IC-ine·nem-ikwe·hiki]
1-FUT-go.to–=SO –ask-1>3P/IND IC-think.thus.of-3P>1/INT.PART/OBL
'So I will go to ask them what they think of me.' W140GH

Meskwaki uses a special inflected form of the verb called the INTERROGATIVE PARTICIPLE to express embedded questions: the inflection on the verb itself indicates which argument of the verb is being questioned.

In this paper I demonstrate how the interrogative participles function to express embedded questions and show how they are related to formally similar evidentials and a subclass of relative clauses in Meskwaki. In the last section I raise some issues about the interaction of syntactic structure and information structure in embedded questions.

What Is a Participle?

Participles are verb forms used as nouns or modifiers of nouns. Meskwaki exhibits both conjunct participles and interrogative participles. That is, the portion of the inflectional morphology agreeing with the subject and object of the verb comes from the conjunct order for conjunct participles and from the interrogative order for interrogative participles.[3] Since conjunct participles are more common and have a wider distribution, I first illustrate participle formation with a conjunct participle.

(7) Template for participle formation:
Initial Change + Verb.stem + Subj.(&.Obj).Agr + Head.suffix

As seen in (7), participles are formed by applying the ablaut rule of Initial Change to the left edge of the verb stem and with suffixes that encode subject (and object) features of the lower verb, plus a final suffix that encodes features of the head of the relative clause.[4] The head suffixes are listed in (8):

(8) Head suffixes

a.	-a	anim. prox. sg.	(3)
b.	-iki	anim. prox. pl.	(3p)
c.	-ini	anim. obv. sg.	(3')
d.	-ihi	anim. obv. pl.	(3'p)
e.	-i	inan. sg.	(0)
f.	-ini	inan. pl.	(0p)
g.	-i	oblique head	(obl)

(9) contains a conjunct participle built from the stem *mahkate·wi·*- 'fast', which modifies the head noun *oškinawe·ha* 'young man'. The suffix *-t* indicates that the subject of 'fast' is third person singular; the head suffix *-a* indicates that the head of the relative clause is the third person singular argument, coreferential to the subject of 'fast' and to the head noun *oškinawe·ha* 'young man'.

(9) oškinawe·ha me·hkate·wi·ta

oškinawe·h-a IC-mahkate·wi·-ta

young.man-SG IC-fast-3/PART/3

'A young man who fasted' L.title

IC	+	*mahkate·wi*	+	*t*	+	*a*
		fast		3 (subject)		3 (head)

In (10) the head of the conjunct participle is third person obviative singular, coreferential to the object of the lower verb *nes-* 'kill', and to the demonstrative pronoun that is the head of noun phrase, *i·nini* 'that one (obv.)'.

(10) i·nini ne·sa·čini pačana

i·nini [IC-nes-a·čini pačan-a]

that.ANIM.OBV IC-kill-3>3'/PART/3' Lazybones-SG

'that one (obv) whom Lazybones (prox) killed' L306

IC	+	*nes*	+	*a·t*	+	*ini*
kill		3>3' (subj & obj)				3' (head)

(11) illustrates the formation of a participle whose head corresponds to an oblique argument of the lower clause. The verb stem *oči·*- 'be from' requires an oblique argument expressing source; a conjunct participle formed on the oblique argument has the gloss 'the place from which they came.'

(11) we·či·wa·či
IC-oči·-wa·či
IC-be.from-3P/PART/OBL
'the place from which they came' (Dahlstrom 2015:§152.11L)
IC + *oči·* + *wa·t* + *i*
be from | 3P (subject) | oblique (head)

Participles in which the head is an oblique argument expressing stationary location exhibit a slight irregularity in formation. Instead of Initial Change applying to the left edge of the verb, the aorist prefix is used instead:

(12) e·howi·kiwa·či
e·h-owi·ki-wa·či
AOR-dwell.there-3P/PART/LOC.OBL
'the place where they live'
AOR + *owi·ki* + *wa·t* + *i*
dwell (there) | 3P (subject) | oblique (head)

As stated earlier, (9–12) are examples of conjunct participles, where the suffixes indicating the subject (and object) of the lower verb are drawn from the conjunct order of inflection. Interrogative participles are formed using the same template given in (7), but the suffixes agreeing with the subject and object of the lower verb are taken from the interrogative order. Interrogative participles used as relative clauses either indicate that the existence of the referent is not presupposed or have an evidential function—that is, they explicitly mark something about the speaker's source of evidence. (13) illustrates a relative clause for which the existence of the referent is not presupposed:

(13) ne·sa·kwe·na
IC-nes-a·kwe·na
IC-kill-3>3'/INT.PART/3
'whoever kills him' [if anyone] L120
IC + *nes* + *a·kwe·n* + *a*
kill | 3>3' (subj & obj) | 3 (head)

Likewise, an interrogative participle is often found as the object of verbs like *natone·h-* 'search for', where the existence of the object need not be presupposed.

(14) e·hnatone·hamowa·čike·hi wi·hpwa·wi–taši–kemiya·nikwe·ni

e·h-natone·h-amowa·či=ke·hi IC-wi·h-pwa·wi–taši–kemiya·n-nikwe·ni

AOR-search.for-3P>0/AOR=and IC-FUT-not–there–rain-0'/INT.PART/OBL

'And they were looking for a place where it would not rain' R138.47

Interrogative participles used as relative clauses may also be used with an evidential function, to explicitly indicate the absence of direct, firsthand knowledge on the part of the speaker.[5] For example, (15) is an interrogative participle formed on the stem *omeso·ta·ni-* 'have (second object) as a parent'. Here the speaker, a young man, can surely assume that the addressee, an old woman, had parents; however, since he is too young to have known the parents personally, he uses an interrogative participle.

(15) we·meso·ta·niwane·hiki

IC-omeso·ta·ni-wane·hiki

IC-have.O2.as.parent-2/INT.PART/3P

'whoever your parents were' W19B

(16) is similar: here the interrogative participle with a stationary location as the head indicates that the speaker does not know where the other people are living.

(16) e·howi·kikwe·hikimekoho ma·hiye·ka mehtose·neniwaki

e·h-owi·ki-kwe·hiki=mekoho ma·hiye·ka

AOR-dwell.there-3P/INT.PART/LOC.OBL=EMPH these.ABSENT

mehtose·neniw-aki

person-PL

'wherever these (absent) people might be living' W108D

The two functions of interrogative participles display a clear connection: interrogative participles may be used if the speaker has no reason to assume the existence of any referent satisfying the description of the relative clause (examples (13–14)), or this type of participle may be used to explicitly distance the speaker from claiming firsthand knowledge of the existence of the referent.

Other Interrogative Order Paradigms: Plain Interrogative and Prioritive

The various verbal modes classified together as the interrogative order all exhibit suffixes containing a *-w*, which Goddard (2004:106) labels the irrealis *-w*, viewing the system from a diachronic perspective.[6] The Meskwaki irrealis *-w* ultimately derives from a Proto-Algonquian negative morpheme, as demonstrated in Goddard (2006b:189ff.). The link between interrogative order inflection and evidential functions can be seen most clearly in the verbal mode labeled the PLAIN INTERROGATIVE, in which there is no initial change applied to the left edge of the verb stem and which does not exhibit the variation in head suffixes seen earlier with the interrogative participles.[7] The plain interrogative is used as an evidential indicating that the speaker is deducing after the fact that an event occurred:

(17) nesekokwe·nima·hi·na mahkwani
nes-ekokwe·ni=ma·hi=i·na mahkw-ani
kill-3'>3/PLAIN.INTERR=after.all=that.ANIM bear-OBV
'A bear (obv) must have killed that guy (prox), after all.' L111

(18) aniwisa·hikwe·ni
aniwisa·hi-kwe·ni
run.fast.DIM-3/PLAIN.INTERR
'He must have run fast.' W1005

In (17) the speaker bases his comment on tracks in the snow and evidence of a struggle. (18) is from a long text about the culture hero Wisahkeha; the speakers are young women who failed to keep up with a no longer visible Wisahkeha. It may be noted that Meskwaki utterances containing the plain interrogative are specifically used for expressing inferred knowledge; a separate verb form, the DUBITATIVE mode of the independent order, is used for more general statements expressing what is probably true.

The relatively uncommon verbal mode of the PRIORITIVE is used to indicate that the action in the main clause occurred before the action in the adverbial clause:

(19) me·h–ki·ši–wi·seniwa·kwe
IC-me·h–ki·ši–wi·seni-wa·kwe
IC-before–PERF–eat-3P/PRIOR
'before they had finished eating, . . .' L161

In this context the irrealis *w* is motivated because the subjects had not in fact finished eating at the relevant moment reported here.

Main Clause Questions and Participles

Returning to the subject of questions, we saw earlier that main clause questions in Meskwaki contain an independent question word. Example (5) is repeated:

(5) kašiča·hi išina·kosiwaki?
kaši=ča·hi išina·kosi-waki
how=so appear.thus-3P/IND.IND
'What did they look like?' W346P

The verb in (5) is inflected in the independent indicative paradigm, typical of main clauses. This paradigm is used only with the three Meskwaki question words, which begin with *k* : *kaši* 'how?', *ke·swi* 'how many?', and *ke·senwi* 'how many times?'.

The other question words in Meskaki begin with *w* (*we·ne·ha* 'who?', *we·kone·hi* 'what?') or with *ta·* (e.g., *ta·ni* 'where?', *ta·tepi* 'whither?, whence?') and typically are found with conjunct participle inflection on their accompanying verb:

(20) we·ne·hča·hi i·ni e·ta?
we·ne·ha=ča·hi i·ni IC-i-ta
who=so that IC-say.thus-3/PART/3
'Who said that?' W156N

(21) ta·tepiya·pi we·či·yani?
ta·tepi=ya·pi IC-oči·-yani
whence=may.I.ask IC-be.from-2/PART/OBL
'Where did you come from?' W851

Though conjunct participles are the usual forms in such questions, it is also possible to use interrogative participle inflection in a main clause question:

(22) we·kone·hi wi·hmi·čiwa·ne·ni?
we·kone·hi IC-wi·h-mi·či-wa·ne·ni
what IC-FUT-eat-1>0/INT.PART/0
'What will I eat (if there is anything to eat)?' (Michelson 1937:§70.33–34)

Interrogative Participles in Embedded Questions

With this background we can now turn to the phenomenon of embedded questions. Embedded questions in Meskwaki differ from main clause questions in two ways. First, no independent question word is employed in the embedded question. Second, interrogative participles are rare and marked in main clause questions but required in embedded questions.

The examples that follow demonstrate how different types of arguments of the lower clause may be questioned in an embedded question. In (23) the subject is questioned:

(23) e·hwe·pi–nana·tohtawi·nameki . . . e·škike·hi–mi·čikwe·na
e·h-we·pi–nana·tohtaw-i·nameki . . .
AOR-begin–ask-X>1P/AOR

[IC-aški–=ke·hi–mi·či-kwe·na]
IC-first.time–=and –eat-3>0/INT.PART/3
'They (unspec) began to ask us . . . who ate it first.' W63MN

The object of the lower verb may be questioned:

(24) e·hpwa·wi–kehke·nema·či wi·hasemiha·kwe·hini
e·h-pwa·wi–kehke·nem-a·či [IC-wi·h-asemih-a·kwe·hini]
AOR-not–know-3>3'/AOR IC-FUT-help-3>3'/INT.PART/3'
'He (prox) didn't know whom (obv) he (prox) should help.'
(Michelson 1930:118)

(6) illustrates an oblique expressing manner being questioned:

(6) ni·hmawiča·hi –nana·tohtawa·waki e·ne·nemikwe·hiki

n-i·h-mawi–=ča·hi –nana·tohtaw-a·waki

1-FUT-go.to–=SO –ask-1>3P/IND.IND

[IC-ine·nem-ikwe·hiki]

IC-think.thus.of-3P>1/INT.PART/OBL

'So I will go to ask them what they think of me.' W140GH

(25–27) provide additional examples of an oblique in the lower clause being questioned: an oblique expressing stationary location in (25), one expressing source of motion in (26), and one expressing quantity in (27).

(25) e·hpwa·wi–kehke·nema·wa·či e·hawinikwe·ni oškinawe·hani

e·h-pwa·wi–kehke·nem-a·wa·či

AOR-not–know-3P>3'/AOR

[e·h-awi-nikwe·ni oškinawe·h-ani]

AOR-be.there-3'/INT.PART/LOC.OBL young.man-OBV

'They (prox) didn't know where the young man (obv) was.' J186.14

(26) e·hnana·tohtawoči we·či·kwe·ni

e·h-nana·tohtaw-eči [IC-oči·-kwe·ni]

AOR-ask-X>3/AOR IC-be.from-3/INT.PART/OBL

'She was asked where she came from.' W930

(27) e·hnana·toše·či še·škesi·hani e·tašinikwe·ni

e·h-nana·toše·-či [še·škesi·h-ani IC-taši-nikwe·ni]

AOR-ask-3/AOR young.woman-OBV IC-be.so.many-3'/INT.PART/OBL

'He (prox) asked how many young women (obv) there were.' J40.2

Embedded Yes-No Questions

Interrogative participles are also used if a yes-no question is embedded as a complement clause. In this construction a 'dummy' relative root preverb *iši–* is added to the lower verb, and the participle is formed on the expletive oblique associated with *iši–*.

(28) e·hnana·tohtawa·či e·ši–ki·yose·nikwe·ni. "ehe·he," e·hiniči . . .
e·h-nana·tohtaw-a·či [IC-iši–ki·yose·-nikwe·ni]
AOR-ask-3>3'/AOR IC-thus–walk.around-3'/INT.PART/OBL

"ehe·he," e·h-i-niči
yes AOR-say.thus-3'/AOR
'He (prox) asked him (obv) whether he (obv) had walked around.
"Yes," he (obv) said. . . .' (Michelson 1927:§44.10–11)

Since an embedded yes-no question requires the relative root preverb *iši–*, otherwise associated with obliques of manner or of goal of motion, a verb such as *e·ši–ki·yose·nikwe·ni* in (28) is ambiguous out of context. In a different context the same verb might mean 'how he (obviative) walked around.' In (28), however, the following line in which the obviative third person responds *ehe·he* 'yes' confirms that the construction is an embedded yes-no question.

Interrogative Complement Omitting the Main Verb

The association between interrogative participle inflection and embedded questions is so strong in Meskwaki that an interrogative participle may be used on its own, with no overt matrix verb, as if the participle is the complement of an understood main verb 'I wonder . . .'.

(29) e·šawikwe·niškwe nekwisa?
IC-išawi-kwe·ni=iškwe ne-kwis-a
IC-fare.thus-3/INT.PART/OBL=woman's.EXCLAM 1-son-SG
'I wonder how my son is doing?' R116.43

(30) e·hawiwe·kwe·ni, maneto·tike?
e·h-awi-we·kwe·ni maneto·tike
AOR-be.there-2P/INT.PART/LOC.OBL spirit.VOC.PL
'I wonder where you are, spirits?' R509.29

(31) we·yo·siwakwe·nani·hka, nesese?
IC-o·si-wakwe·na=ni·hka, nesese
IC-have.O2.as.father-21/INT.PART/3=man's.EXCLAM elder.brother.VOC
'I wonder who our father is, brother?' W276G

Although (29–31) resemble subordinate clauses with a 'missing' main verb, I do not want to claim that there is a covert, unpronounced main verb in these examples. Instead, I hypothesize that these are main verbs displaying an inflectional pattern that is more commonly found in embedded clauses.

Syntax and Information Structure

Examples (1–6) at the beginning of the paper contrasted two strategies for expressing embedded questions: the morphological strategy seen in Meskwaki versus employing a question word as a separate syntactic constituent (Plains Cree, Anishinaabemowin, and Menominee). We may note that both strategies are semantically identical: both clearly indicate that the complement clause is interrogative and identify the element being questioned. Comparing the two constructions, I conjecture that Meskwaki's morphological strategy is archaic. That is, loss of final vowels in the sister languages would entail that the distinctions encoded by the head suffix in final position of the participle would be obscured, favoring the spread of the main clause question formation strategy to embedded clauses as well.

Elsewhere (e.g., Dahlstrom 1993) I have proposed the template in (32) as accounting for much of the word order variation observed in Meskwaki main clauses:

(32) [$_{S'}$ TOPIC [$_{S}$ NEG FOCUS OBLIQUE V XP*]]
{SUBJ, OBJ, OBJ2, COMP}

The position dedicated to FOCUS (following a negative element, if any, and preceding any oblique argument) is where independent question words in main clauses appear.

Could we hypothesize that the focus position is not present in Meskwaki subordinate clauses? The answer to this question is no: other elements that typically appear in the main clause focus position also appear to the left of the verb in subordinate clauses, e.g., *ke·ko·hi* 'something' in (33) or the contrastive independent pronoun in (34):

(33) . . . e·hkaka·to·nena·ni ke·ko·hi wi·hnahihto·yani
e·h-kaka·to·n-ena·ni [**ke·ko·hi** wi·h-nahiht-o·yani]
AOR-urge-1>2/AOR something FUT-know.how.to.make-2>0/AOR
'. . . when I push you to learn to make something.' (Goddard 2006a:27)

(34) . . . wi·hanwa·či·yani ki·na·na i·ni wi·hišawiyakwe
wi·h-anwa·či·-yani [**ki·na·na** i·ni wi·h-išawi-yakwe]
FUT-consent-2/AOR we.inclusive that FUT-do.thus-21/AOR
'. . . you should consent for **us** to do that.' (Goddard 2006a:135)

The syntactic position labeled FOCUS thus seems to be available in Meskwaki for a lower question word, if the morphological strategy were not employed.

It is worth emphasizing that the position labeled FOCUS in (32) is a syntactic position: a syntactic position that is occupied by elements that typically bear the information structure relation of focus in the sense of Lambrecht (1996). This may be seen most clearly in a main clause question-word question, where the material following the question word is presupposed; the answer to the question word fills in the gap in the open proposition. Consider example (21):

(21) ta·tepiya·pi we·či·yani?
ta·tepi=ya·pi IC-oči·-yani
whence=may.I.ask IC-be.from-2/PART/OBL
'Where did you come from?' W851

The question in (21) presupposes 'you came from x-place', and the answer to (21) will identify the value of x.

An embedded question, on the other hand, has quite different information relations. An embedded question does not seek an answer to 'what is the value of x?'.

(26) e·hnana·tohtawoči we·či·kwe·ni
e·h-nana·tohtaw-eči [IC-oči·-kwe·ni]
AOR-ask-X>3/AOR IC-be.from-3/INT.PART/OBL
'She was asked where she came from.' W930

Rather, an embedded question like (26) is a report on an earlier speech event.

The difference between the information structure of (21) and that of (26) is important to keep in mind. Though space does not permit exploring this issue in depth in the current paper, consider the following example, offered in Fry and Mathieu (2017) as part of their arguments against explaining Long Distance Agreement in terms of the information structure relation topic:[8]

(35) Algonquin (Ojibwe)
ngikenmaa wegonesh gaa-zheshemgowang nen kwezhegaasan
ni-gikenim-aa wegonesh gaa-zheshemgow-ang
1-savoir.VTA-DIR.3(IND) qui wh.PASSÉ-voler-3PL(CONJ)

nen kwezhegaas-an
ces biscuit-PL
'Je sais qui a volé ces biscuits.' (Fry and Mathieu 2017, ex. 3)
(lit. 'I know **him** [who stole the cookies]')

In (35) the question word *wegonesh* 'who' in the lower clause triggers agreement on the higher verb.

Fry and Matheiu's argument runs as follows: question words bear focus; a single element cannot be both focus and topic; therefore (36) shows that topic is not the relevant notion for explaining Long Distance Agreement.[9] However, the discussion of examples (21) and (26) demonstrates that the premise that all question words bear the information structure relation of focus is not valid: the context in which a given question word is used must be taken into account. The fact that question words in main clauses bear the information structure relation of focus does not entail that a question word in an embedded question is also an instance of focus.

Conclusion

In this paper I have outlined the morphological strategy employed by Meskwaki to express embedded questions and contrasted this strategy with the more familiar syntactic strategy found in Plains Cree, Anishinaabemowin, and Menominee. Meskwaki embedded questions are expressed by interrogative participles: the details of participle formation for both conjunct and interrogative participles were presented, along with examples of main clause questions containing participles. Some formally similar other paradigms belonging to the interrogative order, all containing the irrealis suffix *-w*, were illustrated, providing a motivation for this morphological set to perform the function of expressing embedded questions. Examples of embedded questions questioning subject, object, and various types of oblique arguments were provided, and the strategy for expressing an embedded yes-no question explained. Finally, the relation between a syntactic position in which main clause questions typically appear and the information structure relation of focus was explored, showing that we cannot assume that embedded questions exhibit the same information structure relations as that of main clause questions.

NOTES

1. Many thanks to the audience at the Forty-Eighth Algonquian Conference for their comments.
2. Abbreviations in the Meskwaki examples: 1P = first person exclusive plural, 21 = first person inclusive plural, 3' = obviative, 0 = inanimate, 0' = inanimate obviative, ANIM = animate, AOR = aorist, DIM = diminutive, EMPH = emphatic, EXCLAM = exclamation, FUT = future, IC = Initial Change (ablaut rule), IND.IND = independent indicative, INT.PART = interrogative participle, LOC.OBL = oblique head of relative clause expressing stationary location, O2 = second object, OBL = oblique head of relative clause, OBV = obviative, PART = conjunct participle, PERF = perfective, PLAIN.INTERR = plain interrogative inflection, PL = plural, PRIOR = prioritive, SG = singular, VOC = vocative, X = unspecified subject. Sources for examples: J = Jones (1907), L = text in Dahlstrom (1996), R = Michelson (1925), W = Kiyana (1913).
3. See Goddard (1994:187–204) for a complete listing of the verbal morphology of the conjunct, interrogative, and other orders in Meskwaki.
4. The ablaut rule of Initial Change applies to the vowel of the first syllable of the verb stem

or compound verb. In Meskwaki, short *e, i, a* change to long *e·*; short *o* changes to *we·*; long vowels are not affected.

5. See Brugman and Macaulay (2015) for an extensive overview of evidentiality. The encoding of evidential functions in Meskwaki is the 'scattered' type (Brugman and Macaulay 2015:224) rather than occurring in a single paradigmatic slot: besides the evidential use of interrogative participles illustrated in (15) and (16) and the use of the plain interrogative exemplified in (17) and (18) for inferred knowledge, there is also a hearsay evidential second position enclitic *=ipi*, which is a grammaticalized verb form meaning 'people say'.
6. The irrealis *w* is not indicated as a separate morpheme in the interlinear glosses; instead, the complex of suffixes is glossed with the subject (and object) features that the complex encodes.
7. Another paradigm, the CHANGED INTERROGATIVE, is found in the protasis of conditional clauses, also reflecting the irrealis function of the *-w* suffix.
8. It is not clear that (36) should be analyzed as an embedded question; a negated main verb 'know' ('I don't know who stole the cookies') would strengthen the argument here.
9. See Dahlstrom (2016) for discussion of other arguments put forward by Fry and Mathieu (2017) on Long Distance Agreement.

REFERENCES

Brugman, Claudia and Monica Macaulay. 2015. Characterizing Evidentiality. *Linguistic Typology* 19(2):201–237.

Dahlstrom, Amy. 1993. The Syntax of Discourse Functions in Fox. *Berkeley Linguistics Society 19: Special Session on Syntactic Issues in Native American Languages*, ed. by David A. Peterson, pp. 11–21. Berkeley, CA: Berkeley Linguistics Society.

———. 1996. Narrative Structure of a Fox Text. *nikotwâsik iskwâhtêm, pâskihtêpayih! Studies in Honour of H.C. Wolfart*, ed. by J.D. Nichols and A.C. Ogg, pp. 113–162. Algonquian and Iroquoian Memoir 13. Winnipeg: Algonquian and Iroquoian Linguistics.

———. 2015. Highlighting Rhetorical Structure through Syntactic Analysis: An Illustrated Meskwaki Text by Alfred Kiyana. *New Voices for Old Words: Algonquian Oral Literatures*, ed. by David J. Costa, pp. 118–197. Lincoln: University of Nebraska Press.

———. 2016. On the Pragmatic Relationship Indexed by Long Distance Agreement in Meskwaki. Paper read at the 2016 SSILA meetings, Washington, DC.

Fry, Brandon and Éric Mathieu. 2017. La sémantique de l'accord à longue distance en Ojibwé Algonquin. *Papers of the Forty-Sixth Algonquian Conference*, ed. by Monica Macaulay and

Margaret Noodin, pp. 55–69. East Lansing: Michigan State University Press.

Goddard, Ives. 1994. *Leonard Bloomfield's Fox Lexicon: Critical Edition.* Algonquian and Iroquoian Linguistics Memoir 12. Winnipeg: Algonquian and Iroquoian Linguistics.

———. 2004. Meskwaki Verbal Affixes. *Papers of the Thirty-Fifth Algonquian Conference,* ed. by H.C. Wolfart, pp. 97–123. Winnipeg: University of Manitoba.

———. 2006a. *The Autobiography of a Meskwaki Woman.* Winnipeg: Algonquian and Iroquoian Linguistics.

———. 2006b. The Proto-Algonquian Negative and Its Descendants. *Papers of the Thirty-Seventh Algonquian Conference,* ed. by H.C. Wolfart, pp. 161–208. Winnipeg: University of Manitoba.

Johnson, Meredith and Monica Macaulay. 2015. A Monoclausal Analysis of Menominee Wh-Questions. *International Journal of American Linguistics* 81:337–377.

Jones, William. 1907. *Fox Texts.* American Ethnological Society Publications, vol. 1. Leiden.

Kiyana, Alfred. 1913. *wisakea osani okyeni osimeani okomeseani* [Wisahkeha, His Father, His Mother, His Younger Brother, His Grandmother]. Manuscript 2958-a in National Anthropological Archives, Smithsonian Institution, Washington, DC.

Lambrecht, Knud. 1996. *Information Structure and Sentence Form: Topic, Focus, and the Mental Representations of Discourse Referents.* Cambridge: Cambridge University Press.

Michelson, Truman. 1925. Accompanying Papers. *Annual Report of the Bureau of American Ethnology,* vol. 40, pp. 23–658. Washington, DC: G.P.O.

———. 1927. *Contributions to Fox Ethnology.* Bureau of American Ethnology Bulletin 85. Washington, DC: G.P.O.

———. 1930. *Contributions to Fox Ethnology II.* Bureau of American Ethnology Bulletin 95. Washington. DC: G.P.O.

———. 1937. *Fox Miscellany.* Bureau of American Ethnology Bulletin 114. Washington, DC: G.P.O.

Valentine, J. Randolph. 2001. *Nishnaabemwin Reference Grammar.* Toronto: University of Toronto Press.

Wolvengrey, Arok Elessar. 2011. *Semantic and Pragmatic Functions in Plains Cree Syntax.* Amsterdam: Amsterdam Center for Language and Communication.

The Kansas Unami Writings of Ira D. Blanchard, Pioneering Algonquian Linguist

Ives Goddard

Ira D. Blanchard was a schoolteacher in the Baptist Mission to the Delawares in Indian Territory (near present-day Kansas City, Kansas).[1] Arriving in 1831, he acquired a gradually increasing knowledge of Unami, and he published a series of now excessively rare books in the language on the press set up at the Shawnee Mission nearby: a twice-revised primer (Blanchard 1834a, 1834b, 1842), a hymnbook that survives only as reprinted (Blanchard 1836), and a 217-page translation of a Harmony of the Gospels that took nearly three years to complete (Blanchard 1837 [1839]). On the Unami title pages of the last two books to be printed he acknowledges, respectively, James Conner (1817–1872) as his assistant and Charles Journeycake (1817–1894) as his coauthor, both later prominent tribal leaders. Conner's father was William Conner, a white trader and interpreter, and Journeycake's mother, Sally, was an interpreter, HER mother having been a white captive.

The phonology of Unami (unm; Delaware, Lenape, Southern Unami; later, Oklahoma Delaware) presents some challenges (1).[2]

(1) Phonemes of Unami

voiceless stops and affricate	p	t	č	k		
voiceless long stops and affricate	p·	t·	č·	k·		
voiceless fricatives	s	š	x	h		
voiceless long fricatives	s·	š·	x·			
voiced nasals	m	n				
voiced approximants	w	l	y			
short vowels	i	e	a	ɔ	u	ə
long vowels	i·	e·	a·	ɔ·	o·	

There is also a stress accent marked by an acute. After a homorganic nasal, the plain stops and affricate are voiced (e.g., /nt/ is [nd]), and the phonemic long stops and affricate are short and voiceless (e.g., /nt·/ is [nt], [n$^{\text{n̥}}$t], [n̥t]). In the pronunciation that predominated in the twentieth century /Vns/ and /Vnš/ were [Ṽ·s] and [Ṽ·š] (with nasalized vowels conventionally written as phonemically long), but some speakers had an older pronunciation like that of the other nasal clusters, with short, oral vowels and voiced consonants (/Vns/ [V̆nz]; /Vnš/ [V̆nž]), and this is what Blanchard's spellings point to: e.g., ⟨Kxuns⟩ 'your older brother' (for /kxáns/, not the later /kxá·ns/ [kxã·s]). The primary clusters are *sk*, *sp*; *šk*; *xp*, *xk*; *mp*, *nt*, *nč*, *nk*, *ns*, *nš*; *hp*, *ht*, *hč*, *hk*, *hs*, *hš*. The secondary clusters (which always arise from the syncope of a short vowel) include the geminates *pp*, *tt*, *čč*, *kk*, *šš*, *hh*, *mm*, *nn*, *ww*, *ll*; except for *tt*, *čč*, *šš*, and *hh*, these may occur word-initially (where /pp-/ is [p:]; /kk-/ is [k:]). Length was not considered to be phonemic for the fricatives by Voegelin (1946; cf. Goddard 1979:22), but the contrast between /s/ and /s·/, for example, is clearly heard in *sa·sa·p·í·s·ak* 'fireflies', *hilo·sə́s·ak* 'old men', and *xa·wši·sə́sak* 'old women' as pronounced by Lucy Blalock (*Lenape Talking Dictionary* [www.talk-lenape.org]).

The alphabet used by Blanchard (2) was devised by the printer Jotham Meeker, who had learned some Potawatomi and even more Ottawa, and who developed a series of alphabets for Indian languages that assigned arbitrary values to unneeded letters (McCoy 1835:26; Pilling 1891:351–356; McMurtrie and Allen 1930; Walker 1996:168–169).

(2) Delaware alphabet used by Blanchard (and values as explained by English words)

a	[a]	h	[č]	r	[e(y)]
b	[yu(w)]	i	[ɪ]	u	[ʌ]
c	[ɛ]	j	[š]	v	[h]
e	[i(y)]	o	[o]	w	[u(w)] (also [w])
f	[ŋg] (also [ŋ])	q	[kw]	y	[ay]

k, l, m, n, p, s, t: used as in English.

x: /x/ ("a guttural sound peculiar to the Delaware, and . . . quite indescribable.")

The phoneme /x/ was generally kept distinct from /h/, and Blanchard was pretty successful at writing /h/ (⟨v⟩) before a consonant and often writes the generally nondistinctive word-final aspiration. Distinguishing the vowels was a problem, but he became more reliable and consistent over time. With rare exceptions, the long and geminate consonants are not distinguished from the plain consonants.

Changes in Transcription

There is a fair amount of variation in the spelling of sounds and words in Blanchard's books. Some of this must reflect variation in the speech community, but some is only apparent variation, which actually documents improvements in the accuracy of Blanchard's transcriptions. This improvement can sometimes be traced with some precision in the Harmony, for which there exists detailed information on the progress of the printing of the 14 signatures of the book from 1837 to 1839 (McMurtrie and Allen 1930:152–154). For example, *šúkw* 'only, but' is only ⟨jwk⟩ in the 1834 primers (61x), and this spelling is used throughout the Harmony (B1837:5–204 211x), but it appears only six times after page 81 (in signatures F–N), where the more precise spelling ⟨jwq⟩ predominates (B1837:81–220 401x). The 1842 primer has ⟨jwq⟩ throughout (32x), with a single relic of ⟨jwk⟩.

Another instructive example of improved transcription is in the spelling of *ləna·p·e·í·i* PN '(of) Delaware' in the titles of the three primers: ⟨Linapi'e⟩ (B1834a), ⟨Linapie⟩ (B1834b), ⟨Lunapre⟩ (B1842). This prenoun is derived from *ləná·p·e* 'a Delaware; the Delawares (collectively)' (pl. *ləna·p·é·ɔk*), and the earlier renditions are influenced by the spelling of this noun as ⟨Linapi⟩, explained as "properly Lin-nop-pe" (McCoy 1835:25).

In fact, Blanchard at first commonly wrote word-final /-e/ as ⟨-i⟩. Another example is Un *šá·e* 'immediately', which he wrote ⟨jayi⟩ and ⟨jyi⟩ (B1834a:19), then ⟨jai⟩ (B1834a:23, B1834b 1x, B1837:9–87 31x), and finally ⟨jac⟩ (B1837:35–218 37x, B1842 3x). Un *šá·e* (also the pronunciation heard in Oklahoma) matches Ill ⟨cha8e⟩ /ša·we/, Mah /šãwa/, and Loup ⟨sen8a⟩, all reflecting PA **ša·we·*. Blanchard's early spellings might appear to attest an old cognate of Mun *šá·wi* (found in several sources), but the fact that the spelling he eventually settled on has comparative support shows that the Munsee final *-i* is actually isolated and must be an innovation.

In some cases where Blanchard evidently records a variant that differs from what is found later, his is actually an earlier form, supported by other evidence. Speakers in the 1960s used Un *níke* 'at that time', and recordings show that Willie Longbone used this in the 1930s (not *nə́ke* [Voegelin 1945:113–115]), but Blanchard wrote this word as ⟨nrki⟩ (B1834a), then ⟨ncki⟩ (B1837:5–113), and finally ⟨nckc⟩ (B1837:37–218, B1842), all spelling *néke*. This matches Northern Unami ⟨néke⟩ (Zeisberger 1887:194) and EAb *nèke* 'that (inan. abs.); then, at that time' (< PEA **ənēkē*) (Goddard 2003:50, 53).

A more complicated case is presented by verbs with inflections corresponding to Mun *w(t)–á·wal* 3s–3′.IND. Blanchard has six spellings for the cognate of Mun *wtəlá·wal* 'he or she says {so} to him, her, them (obv.)', excluding misprints. For the older form Un *təlá·ɔl* (with the *-l* of the obviative suffix retained) there is ⟨tclawl⟩ (B1834b 5x; B1837:20–31 5x), ⟨tclaul⟩ (B1837:21–23, 4x), and ⟨tclaol⟩ (B1837:32–94, 19x); the first two variants are confined to signature B in the Harmony, while the third is found on the last page of B and in C–F. For the later form Un *təlá·ɔ* the Harmony has ⟨tclau⟩ (B1837 2x in C), ⟨tclao⟩ (B1837 191x in D–I), and ⟨tulao⟩ (B1837 181x in J–N; B1842 16x). In addition, this ending was at first spelled simply ⟨-a⟩, a seventh variant: e.g., ⟨wava⟩ *o·wa·há·ɔ* 'he knows them (obv.)' (B1834a:24). The early spellings ⟨-a⟩ and ⟨-au⟩ are reminiscent of the ending *-á·a* (presumably originally an allegro variant of *-á·ɔ*) that was predominant in the 1960s and had completely replaced *-á·ɔ* for some speakers, but they do not prove its existence, since Blanchard was not at first consistent in writing /ɔ/ with ⟨o⟩ and often used ⟨u⟩ for /ɔ/ as well as for /a/ and /ə/: ⟨takw kutu mexanalaeul⟩ *takó· kɔ́t-a-mi·x·ana·la·í·ɔl* 'he did not want to shame her' (B1837:9).

The /l/ of *-al* obv. and *-al* inan. pl. is more common the earlier the date, but it never disappears completely. For example, only *kkwí·s·al* ⟨qesul⟩ 'his or her son, his or her sons' is found in signatures A and B of the Harmony (B1837:8–31 19x), but even after *kkwi·s·a* ⟨qesu⟩ begins to be used (B1837:33–219 36x; misprinted ⟨quesu⟩ 1x), *kkwi·s·al* is found occasionally (B1837:33–217 11x; B1842 1x). The case is similar with *lə́nəwal* 'man, men (obv.)' (B1834b 2x; B1837:8, 193) and *lə́nəwa* (B1834b 3x; B1837:53–211 33x). Inanimate plurals also have both *-al* and *-a* throughout the Harmony, and both can even be found in a single sentence: *nɔ́xkal ɔ́·k wsí·t·al kaxpi·s·úwwa* 'his hands and his feet were tied' (B1837:143). In fact, when Trowbridge (2011) wrote his grammar in 1824 the situation was already in flux: he used *-al* ⟨-ul⟩ obv., but *-a* ⟨-au⟩ inan. pl. There is too much overlap between the variants of these suffixes with and without /l/ to ascribe them simply to, say, the usage of different interpreters; the evidence suggests rather that as the variants with /l/ went gradually out of use in the speech community some speakers used both.

Phonological Archaisms

Besides the archaic retention of *ns* and *nš* clusters and the suffix-variants with /-l/, there are other cases in which, despite the inadequacies of Blanchard's alphabet, his transcriptions provide evidence for phonological archaisms.

Blanchard has many third singular verb forms spelled with a final *-w*: e.g., *pé·w* ⟨prw⟩ 'he or she comes'; *kšəp·éhəle·w* ⟨kjwpcvulrw⟩ 'it flows'; ⟨*áhi-wəli·t·é·he·w* ⟨ave wletrvrw⟩ 'he was very good-hearted'; *ɔwəlá·məwe·w* ⟨owlamwrw⟩ 'he always told the truth'; *alə́mske·w* ⟨alumskrw⟩ 'he left'. The situation appears to have been about the same as what was recorded from Willie Longbone in the 1930s by Voegelin (1946:137, 146, 151), who describes the *-w* as "usually not heard." In the 1960s this *-w* had all but completely disappeared.

When the second person prefix |kə-| preceded /w/, the /ə/ was dropped, and the resulting /kw-/ was indistinguishable from a stem-initial /kw-/ in the speech of Willie Longbone (Voegelin 1946:141–142), though /kəw-/ (which always contains the prefix) was pronounced distinctly on at least some occasions in the 1960s by Ollie Anderson and Martha Ellis (as confirmed by sound recordings). Blanchard, however, distinguished /kəw-/ (as ⟨kw-⟩) from /kw-/ (⟨q-⟩) about three-quarters of the time in the Harmony: e.g., *kəwe·t·ənə́mən* 'you (sg.) take (or took) it' (Blanchard ⟨kwrtunimun⟩ 2x, ⟨kwrtunumun⟩ 1x; but Voegelin ⟨kwe·ᴛanə́mən⟩). It should be noted, though, that Blanchard also sometimes wrote ⟨q⟩ for medial /kəw/, which is always distinct from /kw/.

The negative suffix |-(ō)w(ī)| appeared word-finally as /-i/ in Willie Longbone's speech (Voegelin 1946:139), giving *-á·i, -é·i, -ɔ́·i, -ó·wi,* but in the 1960s these sequences had assimilated to *-á·a, -é·e, -ɔ́·ɔ, -ó·u* for most speakers. Blanchard has the unassimilated sequences in the Harmony (3a–d), except in three of the nine occurrences of one word (3e). This variant with assimilation appears to attest an allegro pronunciation that had already emerged in his day.

(3) Nonassimilation of /-i/ NEG after a long vowel
  a. *máta no·wa·há·i lə́nu* 'I know no man' (B1837:8)
  b. *máta nkak·əlo·né·i* 'I do not lie' (B1837:7)
  c. *tá=á· pahki·t·a·t·amaɔ́·i* 'he would not be forgiven' (B1837:70)
  d. *máta=č pəma·wsəwá·k·an ne·mó·wi* 'he will not see (eternal) life' (B1837:28)
  e. *wəli·x·ənó·wi* (B1837 6x) 'it is (not) lawful'; also *wəli·x·ənó·u* (B1837 3x)

The same assimilation also took place in some particles, but not in all of them.

(4) Retention and assimilation of /-i/ after a long vowel in particles
  a. *kahtəné·i* P 'year(s)' (B1834b 1x, B1837 9x, B1842 2x), *kahtəné·e* (1960s)
  b. *məsəč·é·i* P 'whole' (B1837 18x), *məsəč·é·e* (B1837 1x; 1960s)
  c. But: *mayá·i* P 'really, very' and *nahkɔ́·i* P 'any' (all periods)

The third person prefix |wə-| is realized as a |w| that metathesizes with a following consonant if the resulting sequence is permissible or if the |w| combines with |a| or |a·| as, respectively, /ɔ/ or /ɔ·/ (Goddard 1979: Foreword xvii, 24). The early pages of the Harmony, however, have many occurrences of unmetathesized /wt-/, /ws-/, /wš-/, and /wən-/ before /a/ and /a·/, sequences that are mostly replaced by /tɔ(·)-/, /sɔ(·)-/, /šɔ(·)-/, and /nɔ(·)-/ in later pages and for all twentieth-century speakers (5). In fact, the word for 'hand' has only unmetathesized forms in Blanchard, except for one with the archaic plural *-al* (5d). There is one occurrence of /wtɔ·-/ ⟨wto-⟩ (5a), which was also an extremely rare alternative in the 1960s.

(5) Unmetathesized |wə-| 3
  a. *wta·pto·ná·k·an* 'his word', loc. *wta·pto·ná·k·anink* (B1837:12, 14);
     wtɔ·pto·ná·k·an ⟨wtoptonakun⟩ (B1837:20);
     tɔ·pto·ná·k·an (and other forms; ⟨top-⟩, 1x ⟨tap-⟩; B1834b, B1837:6–214 31x)
  b. *wsa·k·i·ma·ɔ́·k·an* 'his kingdom', loc. *wsa·k·i·ma·ɔ́·k·anink* (B1837:8–76 6x);
     sɔ·k·i·ma·ɔ́·k·an, loc. *sɔ·k·i·ma·ɔ́·k·anink* (B1837:64–220 33x)
  c. *wša·khuk·wí·ɔno·p* 'he had a coat' (B1837:18);
     šɔ·khuk·wi·ɔnəwá·ɔ ⟨jokvwqeunwao⟩ 'their garments' (B1837:164)

d. *wənáxk* 'his hand', pl. *wənáxka*, loc. *wənáxkink* (B1837:10–217 12x);
wənaxkəwá·ink 'in their hands' (B1837:20, 67);
wənaxkí·li·t 'his or her (obv.) hand' (B1837:51–106 4x);
nɔ́xkal 'his hands' (⟨noxul⟩ B1837:143, for ⟨noxkul⟩)

In a metrically weak syllable, |a| is realized as /ah/ before a voiceless consonant other than /x/ or /h/, but the metrical template shifts when a prefix is added before a short-vowel syllable (Goddard 1979:Foreword xiv, 22). The resulting alternations between /a/ and /ah/ in different forms of a given stem are often eliminated by paradigmatic leveling, but Blanchard, despite some inconsistency in writing preconsonantal /h/, sometimes shows that this process had not progressed as far as in later materials.

(6) Unleveled weak /ah/ syllables (written ⟨av⟩ and ⟨uv⟩)
a. *lə*_**mátahpi**_ 'sit down (2 sg.)!' (B1837 ⟨lumutavpi⟩ 3x);
*wələ*_**mahtáp**_*·i·n* 'he or she sat (there, then)' (B1837 ⟨wlumuvtupen⟩ 3x, ⟨wulumuvtupen⟩ 1x; also ⟨wlumutupen⟩ 2x, ⟨wulumutupen⟩ 1x)
b. *lə*_**mátahpi**_ 'sit down (2 sg.)!';
*nlə*_**mátahpi**_ 'I sat down', *nlə*_**mátahpi**_*·n* 'I sat (there, then)' (1960s)

Morphology: Archaisms

Proto-Algonquian obviative subjects (and inverse objects) were marked on verbs with a suffix *-*ri* appearing before the third person suffixes *-*w*, *-*t*, and *-*k* (Bloomfield 1946:97, 101, 102; Goddard 1979:41–42, 92–94): PA **pya·*_**rite**_*·* 'if he or she (obv.) comes' > Mes *pya·*_**nite**_, Un *pa·*_**lí·t**_*·e* (B1837:120). There was a suffix PA *-*em* that marked obviative objects with first, second, and indefinite subjects (Bloomfield 1946:98, 102): PA **neʔ*_**remente**_*·* 'if (obv.) is killed' > Mes *nesemete*, Oj *nisimind*. Unami does not have a reflex of PA *-*em* but uses |-lī|, the reflex of PA *-*ri*, to mark an obviative object in independent TA passive and n-ending paradigms (TA+O and subordinative) and in the conjunct (Goddard 1979:94–95). After Blanchard only ME sometimes used |-lī| this way.

(7) Marking of obviative object with Un |-lī| OBV

a. *ko·wa·tələ́·li·n* 'you (sg.) let them (obv.) know it' (B1837:11)
(|kə–ān| 2s–3+0s.IND + |-lī| OBV, |wəwāhtəl-| TA+O 'cause to know')

b. *lí-=á· -kənte·ləmá·li·n* 'for him (obv.) to be condemned' (B1837:214)
(|–ān| X–3.SUBD + |-lī| OBV, |kənte·ləm-| TA 'condemn'; =*á·* POT)

c. *pe·š·əwa·línki* 'one (obv.) who was brought' (B1837:110)
(|IC–ālīnkī| X–3′(OBV).PPL < |-ā| TH1+ |-lī| OBV + |-ənk| X + |-ī| OBV [cf. |–ənt| X–3(ANsg).PPL], |pēšəw-| TA 'bring')

d. *e·lanko·ma·liénki* 'our people (obv.)' (lit., 'our relatives') (B1837:200)
(|IC–āləyēnkī| 1p–3′(OBV).PPL < |-ā| TH1+ |-lī| OBV + |-(y)ēnk| 1p + |-ī| OBV [cf. |–ēnk| 1p–3(ANsg).PPL], |əlankōm-| TA 'be related to ({so})')

Blanchard has a number of forms with a plural or obviative peripheral suffix after the second and third plural n-ending |-ənēwā(w-)| 2p,3p. These are not found in later materials.

(8) Peripheral suffixes after |-ənēwā(w-)| 2p,3p

a. *mwe·k·əne·ɔ́·i=č* 'they shall hand him (obv.) over' (B1837:144)
(|mēk-| AI+O 'give O2 (to someone)', |wə–ənēwāw-ī| 3p+3′.IND; =*č* FUT)

b. *o·lana·ke·ne·ɔ́·i* 'they spread them (inan.) down' (B1837:150)
(|wəlanāhkē-| AI+O 'spread (as on the ground)', |wə–ənēwāw-ī| 3p+0p.IND)

c. *aləwí·i ktəla·ɔhti·ne·ɔ́·i·k čo·ləntə́t·ak.* 'You (pl.) are more highly valued than the little birds.' (B1837:118) (*aləwí·i* 'more'; |əlāwatī-| AI 'be worth {so}', |kə(t)–ənēwāw-īk| 2p+3p.IND; *čo·ləntə́t·ak* 'small birds')
(The standard of comparison is an adjunct treated as a secondary object.)

d. *wwe·t·ənəməne·ɔ́·i né·l mɔ́nia* 'they took those coins (inan.)' (B1837:199)
(|wə–əmənēwāw-ī| 3p–0p.IND, |wētən-| TI(1b) 'take'; *né·l* 'those'; *mɔ́nia* 'coins')

The same inflections without these peripheral suffixes, the only ones used later, are also found in the Harmony.

Although the obviative category does not distinguish singular and plural, there is a suffix |-īna| (also |-īnay|) that explicitly marks an obviative noun as plural. Blanchard uses this several times (9a–d), but in the 1960s it was only heard from Martha Ellis (9e).

(9) Obviative plural suffix on nouns

a. *tɔ·ní·na* 'his daughters (obv. pl.)' (used as a vocative; B1837 1x)

b. *wti·la·yəmí·na* 'his officers (obv. pl.)' (B1837 1x)

c. *wi·mahtí·na* 'his brothers (obv. pl.)' (B1842 2x).

d. *wi·mahtí·nay* 'his brothers (obv. pl.)' (B1837 1x, B1842 1x)

e. *aesəs·í·na* 'animals (obv. pl.)' (ME); cf. *aésəs* 'animal', pl. *aesə́s·ak*

In this function Munsee has *-í·nay* plus *-al* obv.: *wi·mătəsí·nayal* 'his brothers'; this was not known to all speakers in the 1960s (Goddard 2013:94).

Blanchard commonly marks an obviative possessor with a suffix |-īlīt|, which is never followed by any further suffix, leaving obviative, plural, or locative unspecified.

(10) Obviative possessor

a. *wəškinkwí·****li·t*** 'his (obv.) eyes, their (obv.) eyes, his (obv.) face' (cf. *wə́škinkw* 'his eye, his face', *wəškínkɔ* 'his or her eyes')

b. *kɔhe·s·****í·li·t*** 'his (obv.) mother' (cf. *kɔhé·s·a* 'his or her mother')

The only example of this inflection after Blanchard is *wsəp·o·t·ií·li·t* '(in) his (obv.) rectum' (Voegelin 1945:107, 110 ⟨səPu·Ti·í·li·t⟩, incorrectly glossed "being where his anus is"). This suffix continues PA **-iriw-*, which is directly reflected in Cree, Ojibwe, and Arapaho (Goddard 2015:366), but has been partly assimilated to the obviative conjunct ending *-li·t* (as in Un *énta-kaí·li·t* 'as he, they (obv.) slept'). The forms with this suffix cannot be conjunct participles of verbs of possession, however, as such participles usually have initial change; often have the head marked by a peripheral suffix; and refer to the possessor, not to what is possessed: contrast *wəni·č·a·ní·li·t* 'her (obv.) foal' and (participle) *we·ni·č·a·ni·lí·č·i* 'his mother (obv.), his father (obv.)' (lit., 'the one (obv.) whose child he was'); and *wto·t·e·naí·li·t* 'their (obv.) town' and (participle) *we·t·o·t·e·naí·li·t* 'townspeople (obv.)' (13c; cf. *we·t·o·t·e·naí·č·i·k* 'townspeople'). In Shawnee this suffix is reshaped as in Unami (Goddard 2015:404, n.79).

Blanchard attests an almost complete set of forms for the future imperative (Goddard 1979:58, 191).

(11) Future imperative

a. *íka á·me* 'go there (you sg.) (then)' (B1837:44)

b. *íka a·mɔ́·e* 'go there (you pl.) (then)' (B1837:112)

The singular suffix Un *-me* has cognates in Mahican (/-mah/) and Innu (*-me*); the plural suffix Un *-mɔ́·e* (|-mwāwe|, with |-wāw| pl.) preserves an archaic shape that is eliminated in favor of the second plural conjunct suffix in these other two languages (Mah /-māk^w/, Innu *-mek^w*). The term "delayed imperative" sometimes used for similar categories is inappropriate for the Unami forms, which indicate commands that are contingent on a future condition ('if' or 'when' something) or apply generally ('always'). The cognate mode in Innu is called the "impératif indirecte" (Drapeau 2014:201, 515).

Morphology: Other Interesting Variants

When the inverse theme sign |-əkw| is followed by an n-ending (|-ən(ē-)| sg., |-ənēn(ān-)| 1p,12, |-ənēwā(w-)| 2p,3p), all speakers heard in the 1960s had /-k(·)o·ne·n(-)/ (with |ō|) in the first plural endings, but /-k(·)wən-/ (with |kwən|) in the endings /-k(·)wən/ sg. (when word-final) and /-k(·)wəné·ɔ/ 2p,3p. When |-əkw-ən| was followed by |-a| inan. pl., some speakers had /-k(·)wəna/ and others had /-k(·)o·na/. Blanchard, in contrast, has contraction in all these endings: /-k(·)o·n/ sg., /-k(·)o·ne·n/ 1p,12, /-k(·)o·né·ɔ/ 2p,3p, and these endings with further suffixes.

(12) Contraction of |-əkw| INV with n-endings

a. *wəni·skhá·lko·n* ⟨wneskvalkwn⟩ 'it defiles him' (1960s |-əkwən|)

b. *ntə́lko·n* ⟨ntclkwn⟩ 'he told me it' (1960s |-əkwən|)

c. *wəni·skha·lkó·na* ⟨wneskvalkwnu⟩ 'they (inan.) defile him' (1960s |-əkwəna| and |-əkōna|)

d. *ntəlkó·ne·n* ⟨ntclkwnrn⟩ 'it tells us' (1960s |-əkōnēn|)

e. *ktəlko·né·ɔ* ⟨ktclkwnru⟩ 'he tells you (pl.) it' (1960s |-əkwənēwā|)

Blanchard's completely consistent spelling with ⟨kwn⟩ shows that all these endings have contraction to /o·/; with a single exception, Blanchard always spells /k(·)wən/ in the Harmony with a ⟨q⟩: e.g., *ppo·**kwənə́mən*** ⟨pw**q**nimun⟩, ⟨pw**qu**nimun⟩ 'he breaks it'; *tə́nta-po·**kwənə́mən*** ⟨tuntu pw**qw**nimun⟩ 'he breaks it {smwh}' (B1837:42). The contraction that Blanchard and some later speakers had in the ending for inanimate plural subject (12c), like the contraction for all speakers in the first plural ending (12d), was presumably analogical to |-əkōnā(n-)|, the TA ending for first plural object: *ktahɔ·**lkó·na*** 'he loves us (inc.)' (B1837:50). This |-əkōnā(n-)|

has or is treated as having an old contraction of an underlying |-əkw-ə-**wənā(n-)**|, with the w-ending |-wənā(n-)| (of the TA paradigms) that appears on the surface in the corresponding direct form: *ktahɔ·lá·**wəna*** 'we (inc.) love him'. All sources and speakers show contraction in both Unami and Munsee in this ending. The contraction throughout the n-ending inverse paradigm that Blanchard attests (12a–e) was also heard in the speech of a Munsee speaker in the 1960s, but other Munsee speakers had all these endings with uncontracted |-əkwən| (Goddard 1979:107). The forms in Blanchard thus add importantly to the picture of dialectal variation in the Delaware languages.

Participles with an obviative head regularly have *-lí·č·i* (B1837:5–221 passim; 13a), which is |-əlī| obv. + |-t| 3 + |-ī| obv. (with |t| > /č·/), or if preterite *-li·tpáni*, with |-p(an-)| PRET (B1837:166–216 3x; 13b); these suffix complexes follow an AI stem or a TA or TI theme sign. But some forms that function as obviative participles lack |-ī| obv. (13c–d).

(13) Participles with obviative head

a. *pi·lsi·lí·č·i* '(who is) holy (obv.)' (B1837:70–175 4x)
ke·t·o·p·wi·lí·č·i 'those that are hungry (obv.)' (B1837:10)
pa·lsi·lí·č·i 'a sick person, sick people (obv.)' (B1837 17x)
ke·k·e·p·inkɔ·lí·č·i 'a blind person (obv.)' (B1837:46)
pe·š·əwa·lí·č·i 'those (obv.) that brought them (obv.)' (B1837:137)

b. *pehpalalo·ka·s·i·li·tpáni* 'ones (obv.) who had been criminals' (B1837:205)
né·tami-ne·ɔ·li·tpáni 'who (obv.) had first seen him (obv.)' (B1837:216)

c. *pi·lsí·li·t* '(who is) holy (obv.)' (B1837:7–92 6x):
pi·lsí·li·t či·čánkɔ 'Holy Spirit (obv.)' (4x), *pi·lsí·li·t či·čánkɔl* (1x)
pi·lsí·li·t či·čánkunk 'Holy Spirit (obv. loc.)' (B1837:19)
we·t·o·t·e·naí·li·t 'the people (obv.) of (*lit.*, who have) the towns' (B1837:65)
pa·tamwe·ɔ́·k·an ke·nahki·tó·li·t 'caretaker (obv.) of temple' (B1837:123, 195)

d. *enkələlí·t·əp* 'one (obv.) who had died' (B1837:132 2x)
a·mwi·lí·t·əp 'who (obv.) had risen (from the dead)' (B1837:149)
me·t·e·ləma·lí·t·əp 'who (obv.) had thought badly of them (obv.)' (B1837:136)

Although obviative participles without |-ī| obv. are somewhat more common toward the beginning of the Harmony, the number and variety of these forms suggest that they were true variants and not simply due to confusion with the inflection of other conjunct modes. This |-ī| obv. is also not used on some TA participles without |-əlī|

obv. (14), and in some of these, if taken out of context, the proximate argument could also be the head (14a–c).

(14) TA participles with obviative head not marked

a. *phɔthitehəmáɔ·t hwitaɔk·í·li·t* 'the one (obv.) whose ear he (prox.) chopped off' (B1837:197); cf. *ehɔ·lá·č·i* 'one (obv.) that he (prox.) loved' (B1837:50)

b. *ne·óhti·t* 'the one (obv.) they (prox.) saw' (B1837:109); cf. *e·k·e·ki·mahtí·č·i* 'ones (obv.) they (prox.) taught, their disciples' (B1837:160)

c. *pa·tamá·k·uk=č* 'the one (obv.) who will pray to him (prox.)' (B1837:30); cf. *wi·č·e·ykúk·i* 'those (obv.) that were with him (prox.)' (B1837 5x)

The failure to mark some obviative heads can be compared to what has happened in Cree and Menominee, where distinctly marked participles have disappeared completely. And in fact, a proximate participle is often used for an obviative in the Harmony (B1837:7–213). The situation is different with the two ostensible participles having *-lí·č·i·k* for obviative plural in the first two signatures of the Harmony (B1837:7, 26); the use of the proximate plural suffix |-īk| to pluralize an obviative would be inconsistent with what is otherwise known about Algonquian grammar, and these forms were presumably incorrectly constructed early in the task.

Morphology: Some Forms and Constructions

Blanchard attests some good examples of otherwise inanimate nouns used as animates, very much as in traditional texts in Menominee and Cree (Goddard 2002:202–204).

(15) Inanimates used as animates

a. *ahsə́n* IN 'stone': *šá·e=á·* ***ahsə́nak*** *kənčí·məwak* '**stones (anim.)** would immediately cry out' (B1837:151)

b. *ɔhčú* IN 'mountain' as object of |əl-| TA 'say {so} to':
lé·k·we=á· ***yó·ni*** *ɔhčú* 'if you (pl.) say to **this (inan.)** mountain' (B1837:107)
lé·k·we ***wáni*** *ɔhčú* 'if you (pl.) say to **this (anim.)** mountain' (B1837:156)

c. *ɔ́·k=č* ***sa·k·i·ma·ɔ́·k·anak*** *kahto·nalə́t·əwak* 'and **kingdoms (anim.)** shall attack each other' (B1837:168)

d. ***nči·ló·sələm*=*č** *tɔ·phiká·k·u ɓ·mánsa* '**Jerusalem (anim.)** will be trod down by the Romans (obv.)' (B1837:170) (NOTE: Phonemics of loanwords is conjectural.)
e. ***wáni*** *hák·i tɔmi·mə́nsəma* 'the children of **this (anim.)** earth' (B1837:131)
f. ***kəlo·ne·ɔ́·k·anak*** *o·x·əwá·ɔ* 'the father of **lies (anim.)**' (B1837:96)

The hesitation in the gender of the demonstrative in (15b) is notable and can be accepted as authentic; the same inconsistency is found in a Cree text (Goddard 2002:204). In (15d) Jerusalem is not only treated as animate, it is the proximate object of an inverse verb.

There are lexicalized participles that have a more nounlike inflection and make secondary derivatives and other forms like noun stems. The ostensible participle *ki·š·e·ləmúwe·t* 'God, *lit.*, the one who created people [with his mind]' has a regular participial obviative *ki·š·e·ləmawe·lí·č·i* 'God (obv.)' (B1837:13–54 5x), but also the innovative form *ki·š·e·ləmawé·č·i* 'God (obv.)' (B1837:6–14 4x), which lacks |-lī| obv. but still has the suffix *-i* obv. of a participle (instead of the noun suffix *-a*). The locative *ki·š·e·ləmawé·t·ink* 'God (loc.)' (B1837:5–35 4x), however, has the nominal suffix |-ənk|, which is not used on true participles. The synonymous *ke·tanət·ó·wi·t* (lit., 'he who is a great spirit') has only the participial obviative *ke·tanət·o·wi·lí·č·i* (B1837 42x, B1842 4x), but it makes a prenoun and a possessed form as if a noun: *ke·tanət·o·wi·t·í·i* PN 'of God' (B1837 4x), *kke·tanət·o·wí·t·əm* 'your (sg.) God' (B1842:11). And some participles are reinterpreted as nouns in secondary derivation (16a,b).

(16) Verbs of being made on inflected participles
a. *ki·š·e·ləmúk·ɔnkw* 'our (inc.) creator' (|(IC)–əkwankw| 3–12(ANsg).PPL); regular participial obviative *ki·š·e·ləmuk·ɔ́nkwi*:
ki·š·e·ləmuk·ɔnkw- 'God' + |-ī| AI,II 'be': *ki·š·e·ləmuk·ɔnkwi·-* II 'be God':
ki·š·e·ləmuk·ɔ́nko·p 'it was God' (B1837:5); ending |-w-əp| 0s.PRET
b. *memhálamunt* 'merchant, seller' (|IC+mih-mahlamaw-ənt| 'one bought from', with |mih-| HAB and |-ənt| X–3), pl. *memhalamúnči·k*:
memhalamúnči̲ 'merchant (obv.)' (lexicalized participle; cf. regular participle: 7c)
memhalamunt- 'merchant' + |-ī| AI,II 'be': *memhalamunti·-* AI 'be a merchant':
énta-memhalamuntíhti·t 'where they were merchants' (|-hətīt| 3p conj.)
énta-memhalamúntink 'in the market (*lit.*, where people are merchants)' (|-nk| X)

Neither of the words in (16) has been completely restructured or reinterpreted as a noun stem or is still just a participle.

New or Remarkable Words

Blanchard attests many words that have not been found in later sources or are otherwise worthy of note.

The Harmony attests some 16 enclitics, and these do not include the commonplace *=húnt* HRSY found later.

(17) Enclitics

a. *=á·* (*=á·m=*) POT, (with negative) FUT:

máta=á·. 'It shouldn't be so.' (B1837:10)

tá=á· ɔ·x·e·é·i. ⟨taa oxrri⟩ 'There will be no light.' (B1837:170)

b. *=č* FUT:

kkəptó·na=č 'you (sg.) will be mute' (B1837:7)

kpé·t·o·n=č wí·l. 'You (sg.) must bring his head.' (B1837:78)

c. *=ét* 'maybe, must, must have', (in questions) 'possibly' (evidential):

kpəč·e·ɔ́nkəl=ét. 'He must be out of his mind.' (B1837:69)

awé·n=ét=tá wá lɔ́nu? 'Who can this man be?' (B1837:53)

d. *=ɔ́nt* 'nevertheless':

sa·k·í·ma=ɔ́nt khák·ay? 'Are you nevertheless a king?' (B1837:200; KJV: "then")

e. *=háč* Q:

kí·=háč nčo·wí·i-sa·k·í·ma? 'Are you king of the Jews?' (B1837:200)

f. *=hánkw* 'always, usually, would' (general truth):

kkək·ɔ́·ni-=hánkw -pa·tamáhəmɔ 'you (pl.) always say long prayers' (B1837:164)

g. *=ínk, =nínk* Q (in rhetorical or exclamatory questions):

tá=háč=ínk=láh e·li·ná·kwsi·t 'what is (he) like?' (B1837:64)

tá=háč=ínk=láh ləkhíkwi-áhɔt 'how hard is it?' (B1837:139)

kéku=nínk=č=háč ntɔ́ləwe li·ná·k·ɔt? 'What shall I say it is like?' (B1837:124)

h. *=k* (*=ké=*) 'Well':

píši=k ktá 'Yes, indeed, in fact' (B1837:64)

yú=ké=č ntɔ́lsi·n. 'Well, this is what I'll do.' (B1837:119)

nɔ́=ké=x 'well, in fact it was (because . . .)' (B1837:141)

i. *=ksí* 'then, So, well (if you're saying THAT)' (question or imperative); also (17k):

ktaləwí·i-=ksí -lɔ́s·i·n 'Are you (sg.) then greater than . . . ?' (B1837:29)

kələstái·kw=ksí lahápa 'So, listen to me for a while . . . ' (B1842:18)

j. *=ktá* 'rather' (also *ktá*):

nó·x=ktá nəmax·inkwé·ləmukw. 'It is rather my father that thinks highly of me.' (B1837:97)

k. =*láh* (in rhetorical questions and mirative statements); also (17g):
awé·n=ksí=láh? i·láyas=háč khák·ay? 'Who, then? Are you Elias?' (B1837:21)

l. =*máh* PAST:
ná=máh nčí·sas tələwe·n 'then Jesus said' (B1837:65)

m. =*néh* 'possibly?' (in skeptical questions)
né·k·a=háč, ší=néh kwi·kayó·yəma? 'Was it him, or possibly his parents?' (B1837:97)

n. =*tá* FOC; also (17c):
ní·=tá. 'It's me.' (B1837:80, 98) (KJV: "It is I."; "I am he.")

o. =*x* 'in fact':
nə=ké=x 'well, in fact it was (because . . .)' (B1837:141)

p. =*xán* 'however, although' (also *xánne·*):
nčó·=xán khák·ay 'Even though you are a Jew . . . ' (B1837:28)

The enclitics generally do not directly translate specific English words, and they are often combined idiomatically: *awé·n=néh=á·m=ét káski- íka -pé·?* 'Who would possibly be able to get there?' (KJV: "Who then can be saved?" Mark 10:26). Several are cognate with enclitics in Munsee (Goddard 2013:95–96), Mahican (Goddard 2008:263), and Western Abenaki (LeSourd 2015), and Un =*ksí* (17i) appears to be cognate with Mun *ksí* 'you (sg.) say {so}'.

The Harmony preserves several old words that pertain to watercraft and fishing. Un *wtenka·lté·e* ⟨wtifaltri⟩ 'in the stern of the boat' is *wtenk-* 'behind' + |-ālətēw| 'boat' (which can be regularly derived from an earlier **wārətēw* 'dugout', with virtual PEA **wār-* 'hole, hollow' + **-ətē* 'by burning'). The expected particle final would be Un *-e* after a medial, and Blanchard's ⟨-i⟩ must be a hypercorrection influenced by cases of /-é·e/ as the allegro pronunciation of /-é·i/ (4b). Un *wi·kwé·link* 'outside the (door [i.e., at the end] of the) house' was presumably earlier used for 'at the bow of the canoe', as it evidently consists of *wi·kwe·-* 'end' and a final PA **-weθ* 'canoe', seen with contraction also in Sh *holake·ši* 'boat' (stem *holake·l-*), but with leveling of the mutation and no contraction in Mes *anake·weni* 'bark canoe'. Un *lílahta·* 'goes {to smwh} by boat' is used with no word for boat: *íka lilahtá·ɔk* 'they went there by boat' (B1837:218). There are two words for 'fishing net', used interchangeably: *anshí·k·an* and *ahkɔ·ní·k·an*; the first was presumably originally 'dip net' (from *ansh-* TI(1a) 'dip up'). The second (and Mu *ăkwa·ní·kan* 'fishing net') must have the original meaning (PEA **akwā-n-* would be 'take out of water'); the glosses "fish Dam" and "Bush-Net" (Zeisberger 1776:36, 1887:30, 75) refer to the method of taking shad by using a suspended screen of branches to drive them downstream into a large box placed at the narrow opening of a weir (Loskiel 1794, 1:95).

The word *me·ya·wxwé·e·kw* 'you guides' (B1837:164, 165) must have originally meant 'you warparty leaders'. It is cognate with early Munsee *me·yá·wə̆xe·t,* used for 'leader' or "Captain" in a hymn that uses martial metaphors (Goddard 2013:112–113), and with Mes *me·ya·wosa·ta* 'warparty leader'.

Biblical references to the processing of wheat are sometimes transformed into references to maize. English "fan" (for winnowing chaff from grain) is translated *paɔle·tí·k·an,* which must be the word for the winnowing basket, matching Mun *pawalehtí·kan* 'fanning mill' (its modern replacement). The reference to two women "grinding together" (Luke 17:35) is rendered *ɔ́·k=č ní·š·a xkwé·ɔk níši-kɔhɔ·k·é·ɔk* 'And two women will be pounding corn in a mortar together', evoking what would have been the familiar scene of two women, standing on opposite sides of a log mortar, striking downwards with their long pestles alternately to crush the dried corn.

The Harmony uses a presentational deictic that is not found later or apparently in other languages: *nánal* (accent conjectured) 'he, she, it (is)' (*nanáli* obv., inan. pl.; *nanáli·k* anim. pl.); there are also short forms with *nál*(-).

(18) Presentational deictic

a. *nánal ná mahtánt·u* '. . . , that is the devil.' (B1837:75)

b. *nánal yó·ni nahtuhé·p·i* 'This is my body . . . ' (B1837:183)

c. *nanáli·k né·k ni·mahtə́s·ak* 'they are my brothers' (B1837:72)

d. *nanáli yó·l ní·š·a tahpantəwá·k·ana* 'it is these two commandments' (B1837:162)

Blanchard attests an objurgative (Miller 1996:236; Goddard 1997:80; LeSourd and Quinn 2009), perhaps not recognized as such: *me·x·alé·t·ia·t* 'glutton' (lit. 'damn big-butt'). This has the medial |-alē-| 'penis' preceding the medial |-təy-| 'rear end', a violation in expressive language of the usual constraint against having two successive medials in the surface constituent structure of a stem (Goddard 1990:452, 462–469).

Beside Un *sa·k·í·ma* 'chief' (< PEA **sākīmāw,* with cognates in Meskwaki and Ojibwe; used for 'king, prince'), Blanchard attests the verb *sa·k·i·ma·-* AI 'be king': *sa·k·i·má·t·e* 'when he was king'. Un *sa·k·i·ma·ɔ́·k·an* 'kingdom' must also be derived from this verb, since |-wākan| NF makes a noun from an AI verb but not directly from a noun.

Blanchard has Un *wəlúnkwink* 'in the fold of his robe', i.e., in the pouch created above the belt, which must have originally meant *'under his arm', locative to *wəlúnkwi < PA *oθenkwiyi (> Oj *oninkwi* 'his armpit', Ar *hiθéʔ* 'wing'). This agrees with the locative Mun *wə̆lónkwi·nk* 'his side (loc.)' in the Prayer Book, which survived in the 1960s in the archaic expression Mun *é·kwi· wə̆lónkwi·nk* 'under his wing'. This word was otherwise reshaped to Un *wəlúnkɔn*, Mun *wə̆lónkwan* 'wing'.

Conclusion

The examination of Blanchard's publications reveals, once again, how wrong and unfortunate was the blanket judgment of Truman Michelson (1912:290) when he wrote: "It is simply a waste of time to attempt to unravel the vagaries of the orthography of the older writers in the case of dialects existing to-day." Not surprisingly, Blanchard preserves many significant facts about the Unami language, but also evident is his increasing competence in Delaware and, in effect, his development as a linguist. He merits being added to the list of pioneer Algonquianists.

NOTES

1. ACKNOWLEDGMENTS: I am grateful to the Bartlesville Public Library for permitting the photocopying of their copy of Blanchard (1837) many years ago, and to Jim Rementer and Todd Thompson for copies of Blanchard's primers and of the English translation of the Harmony of the Gospels that Blanchard used. I also thank two reviewers for their helpful comments. And above all I remember with gratitude the patient help that so many speakers of Lenape gave me in the years 1966 to 1970.
2. ABBREVIATIONS AND CONVENTIONS: abs. = absentative, AI = animate intransitive, AI+O = AI used with a second object, AN, anim. = animate, Ar = Arapaho, B (+ date) = Blanchard, conj. = conjunct, exc. = exclusive, FOC = focus, FUT = future, HAB = habitual, HRSY = hearsay, IC = initial change (ablaut), II = inanimate intransitive, Ill = Illinois, IN, inan. = inanimate, inc. = inclusive, IND = independent indicative, KJV = King James Bible, loc. = locative, Mah = Mahican, ME = Martha Ellis, Mes = Meskwaki, Mun = Munsee, NEG = negative, NF = noun final, OBV, obv. = obviative, Oj = Ojibwe, O2 = second object, p, pl. = plural, PA = Proto-Algonquian, POT = potential, PPL = participle, PRET = preterite, prox. = proximate (non-obviative), Q = question marker, s, sg. = singular, smwh = somewhere, TA = transitive animate, TH1 = theme 1, TI = transitive inanimate, Un = Unami.

   1 = first person, 1p = exclusive, 12 = inclusive, 2 = second person, 3 = third person

animate, 3′ = third person animate obviative, 0 = third person inanimate, X = indefinite person, 3s–3′ = third singular animate acting on obviative, +3p = animate plural second object, +0s = inanimate singular second object, (ANsg) = animate singular head of participle, (OBV) = obviative head of participle.

Italics = standardized phonemic transcription, ⟨ . . . ⟩ = exact transliteration of source, / . . . / = conjectural phonemicization or individual phoneme, [. . .] = narrow or broad phonetic transcription, { . . . }= abstract gloss (of relative root).

In the Unami examples a hyphen links or flags components of a compound stem (one consisting of more than one phonological word); if the components are discontinuous, words that are not part of the compound are set off by spaces following or preceding these hyphens. Textual examples and their English translations are punctuated as sentences if they are complete sentences, or complete except for the omission of syntactically insignificant words at the end (indicated by suspension dots). English glosses of words and phrases are capitalized to indicate that the use as a word-initial discourse marker is the one intended.

Munsee /ə̆/ and /ă/ are extrashort vowels, which are pronounced with breathy voice before voiceless consonants.

REFERENCES

Blanchard, Ira D. 1834a. *Linapi'e Lrkvekun*. Shawnee Mission: J. Meeker.

———. 1834b. *Linapie Lrkvekun, Ave Apwatuk*. Shawannoe Mission: J. Meeker.

———. 1836. [Delaware Hymns.] (Reprinted: *Hymns in the Delaware Language*. Wyandott, KS, 1875, and Coffeyville, KS, 1894.)

Blanchard, Ira D. [and James Conner]. 1837 [1839]. *The History of our Lord and Saviour Jesus Christ*. Shawanoe Baptist Mission: J. Meeker [and John G. Pratt]. (Reprinted: *The History of our Lord and Savior Jesus Christ*. Bartlesville, I.T., 1906. http://www.kansasmemory.org/item/211693/page/4.)

Blanchard, Ira D. [and Charles Journeycake]. 1842. *The Delaware First Book*, 2nd ed. Shawanoe Baptist Mission Press: J.G. Pratt.

Bloomfield, Leonard. 1946. Algonquian. *Linguistic Structures of Native America*, pp. 85–129. Viking Fund Publications in Anthropology, vol. 6. New York.

Drapeau, Lynn. 2014. *Grammaire de la langue Innue*. Québec: Presses de l'Université du Québec.

Goddard, Ives. 1979. *Delaware Verbal Morphology: A Descriptive and Comparative Study*. New York: Garland Publishing.

———. 1990. Primary and Secondary Derivation in Algonquian. *International Journal of American Linguistics* 56:449–483.

———. 1997. Pidgin Delaware. *Contact Languages: A Wider Perspective*, ed. by Sarah G. Thomason, pp. 43–98. Amsterdam: John Benjamins.

———. 2002. Grammatical Gender in Algonquian. *Papers of the Thirty-Third Algonquian Conference*, ed. by H.C. Wolfart, pp. 195–231. Winnipeg: University of Manitoba.

———. 2003. Reconstructing the History of the Demonstrative Pronouns of Algonquian. *Essays in Algonquian, Catawban, and Siouan Linguistics in Memory of Frank T. Siebert, Jr.*, ed. by Blair A. Rudes and David L. Costa, pp. 41–113. Winnipeg: University of Manitoba.

———. 2008. Notes on Mahican: Dialects, Sources, Phonemes, Enclitics, and Analogies. *Papers of the Thirty-Ninth Algonquian Conference*, ed. by Karl S. Hele and Regna Darnell, pp. 246–315. London, ON: University of Western Ontario.

———. 2013. The Munsee of Charles Halfmoon's Translations. *Papers of the Forty-First Algonquian Conference*, ed. by Karl S. Hele and J. Randolph Valentine, pp. 81–119. Albany, NY: SUNY Press.

———. 2015. Arapaho Historical Morphology. *Anthropological Linguistics* 57(4):345–411.

LeSourd, Philip S. 2015. Enclitic Particles in Western Abenaki: Form and Function. *International Journal of American Linguistics* 81:301–335.

LeSourd, Philip S. and Conor M. Quinn. 2009. How to Swear in Maliseet-Passamaquoddy and Penobscot. *Anthropological Linguistics* 51:1–37.

Loskiel, George Henry. 1794. *History of the Mission of the United Brethren among the Indians in North America.* Translated by Christian Ignatius La Trobe. London.

McCoy, Isaac. 1835. *Annual Register of Indian Affairs within the Indian (or Western) Territory.* [No. 1.] Shawanoe Mission.

McMurtrie, Douglas C. and Albert H. Allen. 1930. *Jotham Meeker, Pioneer Printer of Kansas.* Chicago: Eyncourt Press.

Michelson, Truman. 1912. Preliminary Report on the Linguistic Classification of the Algonquian Tribes. *Twenty-Eighth Annual Report of the Bureau of American Ethnology (1906–1907)*, pp. 221–290b. Washington, DC: G.P.O.

Miller, Wick R. 1996. The Ethnography of Speaking. *Handbook of North American Indians*, vol. 17, *Languages*, ed. by Ives Goddard, pp. 222–243. Washington, DC: Smithsonian Institution.

Pilling, James C. 1891. *Bibliography of the Algonquian Languages.* Bureau of [American] Ethnology Bulletin 13. Washington, DC: G.P.O.

Trowbridge, C.C. 2011. *Delaware Indian Language of 1824*, ed. by James A. Rementer. Merchantville, NJ: Evolution Publishing.

Voegelin, Carl F. 1945. Delaware Texts. *International Journal of American Linguistics* 11(2):105–119.

———. 1946. Delaware, an Eastern Algonquian Language. *Linguistic Structures of Native America*, by Harry Hoijer et al., pp. 130–157. Viking Fund Publications in Anthropology, vol. 6. New York.

Walker, Willard B. 1996. Native Writing Systems. *Handbook of North American Indians*, vol. 17, *Languages*, ed. by Ives Goddard, pp. 158–184. Washington, DC: Smithsonian Institution.

Zeisberger, David. 1776. *Essay of a Delaware-Indian and English Spelling-Book.* Philadelphia: Henry Miller. [Facsimile edition: Arthur W. McGraw 1991.]

Zeisberger, David. 1887. *Zeisberger's Indian Dictionary*, ed. by Eben Norton Horsford. Cambridge: John Wilson and Son, University Press.

Second-Position Enclitics Occur within Constituents in Maliseet-Passamaquoddy

Philip S. LeSourd

Like many languages of the Algonquian family, Maliseet-Passamaquoddy (MP, New Brunswick and Maine) has a set of enclitic particles that are usually stationed in second position in a clause: they follow the first word of the clause or, less often, the first phrase.[1] There are thirteen of these enclitics in MP, plus two conjunctions that appear either initially in the clause or in second position. Included among the enclitics are future and conditional markers, a reportative particle, several adverbials, and particles indicating contrast and emphasis. Seven of these particles figure in the examples in this paper: *=al* 'uncertain', =(*ŏ*)*lu* 'but, however', =(*ŏ*)*na* 'also', *=op* 'would' (conditional), *=tahk* 'surprisingly' (mirative), *=yaka* 'afterward, furthermore', and *=yaq* 'it is said, they say' (reportative).[2]

The examples in (1) and (2) illustrate the two modes of second-position placement that are characteristic of MP enclitics.[3]

(1a) [$_{\text{AdvP}}$ Kàt=ŏ**na** qìn] cipŏk-elt-ùwĭ-yil pskihq-ís-ol.
not=also really intense-be.much-(3)-NEG-IN.PL grass-DIM-IN.PL
'There is also not really a whole lot of grass.' (Mal., Paul 1963, no. 26)

(1b) [$_{\text{AdvP}}$ Kàt qìn]=**yaq**=**ŏna** nokŏm-okil-ù.
notreally=REPORT=also fairly-be.size-(3)-NEG
'And he was not really very big, they say.' (Mal., LeSourd 2007:4)

(2a) [$_{\text{NP}}$ Malíyan=**yaq** mihtáqs-ol] kìs api–punáwe.
Mary.Ann=REPORT (3)-father-OBV.SG already go–set.traps-(3)
'Mary Ann's father, they say, had already gone out to set traps.' (Pass., Socobasin 1979:40)

(2b) [$_{\text{NP}}$ Wásis wilítpan]=**yaka**=**yaq** pson-íkon etucéyi-t kamáhcin.
child (3)-brain=after=REPORT full-grow-(3) be.so.old-3AN six
'A child's brain will reach its full size, they say, when he or she is six.' (Pass., Francis and Leavitt 2008:606)

In both examples in (1), the constituent negator *kàt* modifies the adverb *qìn* 'really'. (Sentence negation is usually expressed by *kŏtáma* 'not', or a reduced variant of this.) The enclitic =(*ŏ*)*na* has been positioned after the first word of the clause in (1a), while both =*yaq* and =(*ŏ*)*na* have been placed after the entire clause-initial constituent in (1b). The reportative enclitic =*yaq* follows the first word of the clause in (2a), with the result that it separates the possessor from the possessed noun in the expression 'Mary Ann's father'. In (2b), =*yaka* 'afterward' and =*yaq* appear together after the initial constituent of the clause, which again consists of a possessor and a possessed noun, 'a child's brain'.

In (1a) and (2a), second-position enclitics appear to occur within constituents. Johnson and Rosen (2015) analyze comparable examples in several Algonquian languages as involving discontinuous constituents with enclitics attached to an independent initial segment, thus avoiding having to postulate enclitics that actually interrupt constituents. My purpose in this paper is to show that an analysis along these lines cannot be carried out in general in MP.

Enclitics Interrupting Constituents

Second-position particles freely occur between the words of constituents. An Adverb Phrase (AdvP) is interrupted in this fashion in (1a) and a Noun Phrase (NP) in (2a). Additional examples illustrating NPs interrupted by enclitics are given in

(3a) and (3b), while (3c) illustrates the same situation in the case of a Prepositional Phrase (PP). (For the structure of the PP, see LeSourd 2014. Note that the emphatic enclitic *=ŏte* in (3c) is not restricted to second position.)

(3a) [$_{\text{NP}}$ Yùkk=**yaq**=ŏlu kótŏk-ik kukéc-ok]
these.PROX=REPORT=but other-PROX.PL game.warden-PROX.PL

etuci–palitahas-ultí-hti-t nemiy-á-hti-t
to.extent–be.pleased-MPL-PROX.PL-3AN see-DIR-PROX.PL-3AN
w-itapé-wa-l . . .
3-friend-PROX.PL-OBV.SG
'But, they say, these other game wardens were so happy when they saw their friend . . . ' (Pass., W. Newell 1974:8)

(3b) Yùt=tahk=yaq éhtek mihkután-is qahqŏlunsq-èy,
here=MIRATIVE=REPORT be.located-3IN knife-DIM clay-NF

[$_{\text{NP}}$ 'tomákon=**na** qahqŏlunsq-èy].
pipe=also clay-NF
'Sitting here was a clay knife, and there was a clay pipe as well.' (Mal., Polchies et al. 2013:§11.14)

(3c) Am=ŏte, [$_{\text{PP}}$ tètt=ŏna olŏqìw Wahsipekùsk]
finally=EMPH that.way=also toward St.Lawrence.LOC

olŏq-apasi-htì-t naci–qilŭwaht-à-q wèn salawèy,
toward-pl.walk-PROX.PL-3AN go–look.for-TH-3AN someone salt

on Muhàks matŏn-okù-nĭ-ya . . .
and Mohawk-(OBV.PL) (3)-fight-INV-N-PROX.PL
'And in the end, if they traveled over to the St. Lawrence country so that someone could look for salt, then the Mohawks would fight them . . . ' (Mal., LeSourd 2007:128)

The material that precedes an enclitic or enclitic sequence in an interrupted phrase may bear any kind of structural relationship to the remainder of the phrase. Thus, the enclitics in (3a) follow the initial demonstrative *yùkk* ‘these (prox.)’ in the NP ‘these other game wardens’, which consists of this demonstrative, a modifier, and a head noun. In (2a), the enclitic separates the possessor ‘Mary Ann’ from the possessed head ‘her father’. But in (3b), the head noun *’tomákon* ‘pipe’ is initial in the bracketed NP, so the second-position enclitic *=na* ‘also’ is stationed between this head noun and the following modifier, *qahqŏlunsqèy* ‘made of clay’.

Discontinuous Constituents

Like many other Algonquian languages, MP permits discontinuous expression for a variety of types of constituents. When it is initial in a clause, the first segment of a discontinuous constituent may host a second-position enclitic. The examples in (4) illustrate. (Subscripts “a” and “b” indicate the segments of the discontinuous NPs.)

(4a) [$_{\text{NPa}}$ **Wòt**]=ŏlu wŏlíku [$_{\text{NPb}}$ yùt olŏqì tol-èy pilsqéhsis].
this.PROX=but be.pretty-(3) here toward location-NF girl
‘But the girl from over this way was pretty.’ (Mal., LeSourd 2007:80)

(4b) [$_{\text{NPa}}$ **Psì=na** **yùkt**] pehkì kisac-ultú-w-ok
all=also these.PROX completely be.ready-MPL-3-PROX.PL

[$_{\text{NPb}}$ somakŏnóss-ok] weci–peskhik-hotí-hti-t psì wiwŏnìw.
soldier-PROX.PL so.that–shoot-MPL-PROX.PL-3AN all around
‘And all these soldiers were fully prepared to shoot, all around (the church).’ (Mal., LeSourd 2007:118)

In (4a), the demonstrative *wòt* ‘this (prox.)’ is the first segment of the discontinuous NP *wòt . . . yùt olŏqì tolèy pilsqéhsis* ‘the girl from over this way’; the verb *wŏlíku* ‘she is pretty’ intervenes between the segments of this NP. Note that the first segment of the NP serves as the host for the second-position enclitic =ŏlu ‘but’. In (4b), the second-position enclitic *=na* ‘also’ follows the first word of *psì yùkt . . .* ‘all these (prox.)’, the first segment of the discontinuous NP *psì yùkt . . . somakŏnóssok* ‘all these soldiers’.

Johnson and Rosen (2015) analyze constituents that include second-position clitics in Menominee and several other Algonquian languages. They propose that all examples in which an enclitic appears to interrupt a constituent in fact involve discontinuous phrases, with the enclitic attached to the first segment of the phrase.

They take NPs involved in this construction to be uniformly either topics or foci. On their account, these NPs become discontinuous through a sequence of movement operations that target the positions of functional heads in the hierarchical structure of the left periphery of the clause. This structure may contain more than one instance of Topic Phrase (TopP) or Focus Phrase (FocP) nodes. For example, structures along the lines of (5) are permitted. (I omit labeling for potentially distinct categories such as External Topic Phrase and Internal Topic Phrase.)

(5) [TopP . . . [FocP . . . [TopP . . .]]]

The derivations of discontinuous NPs proceed in steps. First, either Topic or Focus Movement fronts an NP into the position of Specifier (Spec) of TopP or FocP. Then a second application of the same type of movement operation fronts just an initial segment of the NP into the Spec position of a second, higher TopP or FocP. The result for a Menominee sentence like (6) is a structure like (7), adapting Johnson and Rosen's example (18) (2015:145). (I have added marking of the clitic boundary before =*taeh* 'and'.)

(6) **Ayom=taeh** **owōhnemaw** 's oseēqtahnacen
this.AN=and father AOR prepare.3/3OBV.CONJ

onīcianaesan 's maek-mesāhkataewā̄enet . . .
his.child.OBV AOR while.fast.3OBV.CONJ
'And as this father prepared for his child's fast . . . ' (Menominee)

(7) [$_{\text{TopP}}$ [$_{\text{D}}$ **Ayom**] [$_{\text{Top°}}$ [$_{\&}$ **=taeh**]] [$_{\text{FocP}}$ [$_{\text{Foc°}}$ ∅] [$_{\text{NP}}$ [$_{\text{D}}$ t_{ayom}] **owōhnemaw**] [$_{\text{Top°}}$ ∅]
this.AN and father

[$_{\&\text{P}}$ [$_{\&}$ t_{tach}] [$_{\text{TP}}$'s oseēqtahnacen
AOR prepare.3/3OBV.CONJ

onīcianaesan 's maek-mesāhkataewā̄enet]]] . . .
his.child.OBV AOR while.fast.3OBV.CONJ
'And as this father prepared for his child's fast . . . ' (Menominee)

The second-position enclitic =*taeh* 'and' is assumed to be generated at the outset as the head of a Conjunction Phrase (&P) in a position below TopP and FocP. It is raised from there to the head of the upper TopP: this places it in second position in the clause as a whole. The clause-initial position is filled by the demonstrative segment of the NP *ayom owōhnemaw* 'this father': first this NP is moved as a unit to the Spec position within the lower TopP, then *ayom* 'this' is moved by itself into the Spec position in the upper TopP.

Whatever the merits of this analysis may be for Menominee, I argue in the sections that follow that an analogous treatment for MP finds no support. I conclude instead that enclitics that interrupt constituents are located exactly where they appear to be: in the interior of those constituents.

Against the Movement Analysis for MP: Coordinate Structures

Examples involving coordinate structures provide evidence against a movement analysis for MP of the kind that Johnson and Rosen (2015) have proposed for Menominee. Consider in this connection the examples in (8). Moving the element that bears the enclitic in these examples into a Spec position in a superordinate TopP or FocP would require violating the Coordinate Structure Constraint of Ross (1967).

(8a)	[$_{NP}$ [$_{NP}$	Éhpit=ŏlu]	naka	[$_{NP}$	skitàp]]	nis-ikapŭwú-w-ok.
		woman=but	and		man	together-stand-3-PROX.PL

'But a woman and a man are standing together.' (Mal., Paul 1963, no. 8)

(8b)	[$_{NP}$ [$_{NP}$	**Wòt=yaq**	*mahtoqèhs*]	*naka*	[$_{NP}$	*cŏqóls*]]	*tamà=al*[4]
		this.PROX=REPORT	rabbit	and		frog	somewhere=UNCERTAIN

kcíhk-uk	etŏl-akŏnutŏmá-hti-t.
forest-LOC	ongoing-tell.stories-PROX.PL-3AN

'This rabbit and a frog, they say, were telling stories somewhere in the woods.' (Pass., E. Newell 1974:1)

To see what is at issue here, we need to consider just how the Coordinate Structure Constraint works. The formulation of the Coordinate Structure Constraint given in (9) is due to Pollard and Sag (1994:201). The principle has two parts: the Conjunct Constraint (9a) and the Element Constraint (9b), cf. Grosu 1973.

(9) Coordinate Structure Constraint
In a coordinate structure,
a. no conjunct may be moved,
b. nor may any element contained in a conjunct be moved out of that conjunct.

The Conjunct Constraint (9a) appears to hold of extraction operations across languages without exception (although we will see in the following section that MP in fact allows coordinate structures, like other phrases, to be discontinuously expressed).[5] The Element Constraint (9b), on the other hand, is known to permit certain types of exceptions in cases involving extraction (Goldsmith 1985; Lakoff 1986), such as the acceptable extraction out of just one of two coordinated Verb Phrases (VPs) seen in (10).[6]

(10) How many lakes can we [destroy ___ and not arouse public antipathy]?
(Pollard and Sag 1994:201)

Such exceptions have been attributed to semantic and pragmatic factors that do not seem relevant to our MP examples, such as the degree to which conjoined VPs like those in (10) jointly constitute a narrative structure (Deane 1991).

An analysis of MP enclitics along the lines proposed by Johnson and Rosen (2015) will yield violations of both the Conjunct Constraint and the Element Constraint in the examples in (8). In (8a), *éhpit* 'woman' is conjoined with *skitàp* 'man'. To move *éhpit* to the left out of the coordinate structure and into Spec of TopP (or FocP) in order to make it the host of the clitic *=ŏlu* 'but', assumed to be in the head position in such a projection, will violate the Conjunct Constraint. In (8b), movement of *wòt* 'this' leftward out of *wòt mahtoqèhs* 'this rabbit' so that *wòt* can pick up the enclitic *=yaq* will violate the Element Constraint, since *wòt mahtoqèhs* is conjoined with *cŏqóls* 'frog'. I conclude that a movement analysis of examples in which an enclitic interrupts a constituent is not viable in general for MP.

More on Coordination

The argument just advanced against a movement account of MP clitic placement relies on the claim that the Coordinate Structure Constraint is applicable in this language. It should be noted, however, that coordinate NPs formed with *naka* 'and', like that in (11a), may receive discontinuous expression. A discontinuously expressed conjoined subject in which both conjuncts are singular may trigger plural agreement, as in (11b). Alternatively, agreement may be singular, as in (11c), which I take to reflect agreement with the first conjunct alone. First conjunct agreement with a nonsingular NP is seen in (12c).[7]

(11a) Mecimí=te **Píyel** **naka** **Máli** pŏm-íh-hik.
always=EMPH Peter and Mary along-go-(3)-PROX.PL
'Peter and Mary are always on the go.' (Pass.)

(11b) Mecimí=te **Píyel** pŏm-íh-hik **naka** **Máli.**
always=EMPH Peter along-go-(3)-PROX.PL and Mary
'Peter and Mary are always on the go.' (Pass.)

(11c) Mecimí=te **Píyel** pŏm-íye **naka** **Máli.**
always=EMPH Peter along-go-(3) and Mary
'Peter and Mary are (lit., is) always on the go.' (Pass.)

The two discontinuous constructions are distinguished by their treatment in extraction, as shown in (12).

(12a) Wèn macáha-t naka Píyel?
who leave-3AN and Peter
'Who is leaving with Peter?' (lit., 'Who is leaving and Peter?') (Pass.)

(12b) *Wèn macahá-hti-t naka Píyel?
who leave-PROX.PL-3AN and Peter
'Who (sg.) are leaving and Peter?' (Pass.)

(12c) Wén-ik macahá-hti-t naka Píyel?
who-PROX.PL leave-PROX.PL-3AN and Peter
'Who (pl.) are leaving with Peter?' (Pass.)

In (12a), the verb *macáhat* 'he or she leaves' agrees only with the first of the two NPs that are understood as constituting its subject: this is the question word *wèn* 'who'. In this case, it seems reasonable to suppose that *naka Píyel* 'and Peter' is actually an independent phrase, rather than a true part of a conjunction structure. If this hypothesis is correct, then the extraction of *wèn* in this example (by *Wh*-Movement) does not violate the Coordinate Structure Constraint.

In (12b), on the other hand, agreement is with the two conjuncts together, showing that they constitute a unified conjunction structure. In this case, extracting *wèn* yields an ungrammatical sentence. This result follows if the Coordinate Structure Constraint—in particular the Conjunct Constraint (9a)—is applicable in MP, as expected. Compare (12c), where the apparent first conjunct is *wénik* 'who (pl.)', which can control plural agreement on the verb on its own. Extraction proceeds without obstacle in this case, since *naka Píyel* can once again be analyzed as an independent phrase.

I conclude that the segments of a discontinuously expressed conjunction structure with *naka* 'and' may jointly form a constituent. When they do, they also jointly control subject agreement in examples like (11b). The Coordinate Structure Constraint is obeyed in such structures, because they are true coordinate structures.

As a final point, the fact that the Coordinate Structure Constraint holds in MP strongly suggests that the discontinuous expression of conjunction structures (and, by extension, other NPs) is not achieved through the application of one or more movement operations, since any such process would have to violate this constraint. An alternative approach to the derivation of discontinuous constituents is the linearization theory of Head-Driven Phrase Structure Grammar (HPSG). Donohue and Sag (1999) provide a nonmovement analysis of discontinuous NPs in Warlpiri (Pama-Nyungan, Australia) in this framework that may offer an instructive model.

Against the Movement Analysis for MP: Clitics in Two Positions

We observed at the outset of this discussion that second-position enclitics in MP may follow either the first word in a clause or the first constituent phrase in a clause. In fact, both modes of clitic placement may obtain in the same structure. The examples in (13) illustrate.

(13a) [$_{NP}$ Yùkt=ŏlu wasís-ok]=**yaq** 'totŏli–tokŏm-á-wa-l.
these.PROX=but child-PROX.PL=REPORT (3)-ongoing–hit-DIR-PROX.PL-OBV.SG
'But the children, they say, were hitting him.' (Mal., Polchies et al. 2013:§10.16)

(13b) [$_{NP}$ Wòt=ŏlu mihkomŭwèhs]=**yaq** sŏlahkiw unakéssi-n.
this.PROX=but little.person=REPORT suddenly (3)-stand.up-N
'But the little person, they say, suddenly stood up.' (Mal., Polchies et al. 2013:§ 10.17)

The fact that the reportative particle =*yaq* has been positioned after the bracketed expressions in these examples shows that these are phrases, namely NPs. Only clitic placement after a clause-initial constituent can account for the fact that =*yaq* does not occur together with =*ŏlu* 'but' after the clause-initial word in these examples.

Since the bracketed expressions in (13) are thus shown to be intact constituents, it follows that =*ŏlu* can only be located within an NP in each example, not between the segments of a discontinuous phrase. I conclude that second-position particles can and do quite literally interrupt phrases in MP. When they do, their location is internal to the phrases in question.

Penn (1999) and Diesing and Zec (2017) have reached a similar conclusion in analyzing second-position enclitics in Serbian and Croatian.[8] Like MP enclitics, these may either follow the first word of a clause ("second word placement") or follow the first constituent ("second daughter placement"). The cited works demonstrate in detail that second word placement is determined by prosodic structure: a second-word clitic is attached to the first prosodic word within the domain of clitic placement (usually the clause), which may include a proclitic preposition. Because second word placement is determined by prosodic structure, rather than syntactic constituency, it may station an enclitic within a phrase.[9] Second daughter placement, by contrast, is determined by syntactic constituent structure and places an enclitic at a phrase boundary.

An analysis of clitic placement in MP along the same lines appears promising. In particular, there is evidence that second word enclitics in MP are placed after the first prosodic word in a clause, rather than after the first syntactic word. These conditions diverge in the case of certain idiosyncratic expressions that themselves include clitics that are not part of an ordinary clitic sequence. Two such expressions are *tàn=op=al* 'would somehow; how would?' and *mèc=op=al* 'please; would it be possible?' These are based on the independently occurring adverbs *tàn* 'how' and *mèc* 'still'. Both expressions include the enclitics =*op* 'would' and =*al* 'uncertain'. Examples are given in (14).

(14a) Tàn=**op**=al kt-oli=kis-ŏnúh-m-on?
how=COND=UNC 2-thus=able-buy-TH-N
'How can you (sg.) possibly buy it?' (Mal., LeSourd 2007:112)

(14b) Mèc=**op**=al k-kisi–anku-hqè-p kekèsk?
still=COND=UNC 2-able–farther-body-sit a.little
'Can you please move over a little?' (Pass., Francis et al. 2016, v. *ankuhqepu* 'he or she moves over')

What makes these expressions unusual is the fact that the conditional clitic *=op* may be repeated after them, doubling the occurrence of this clitic that forms part of the item, as shown in (15), where the symbol "ω" indicates a prosodic word.

(15) [$_{\omega}$ [$_{\omega}$ Tàn=**op**=al]=**op**=ŏlu] 't-oli=kisi='sotŭw-á-nĭ-ya
how=COND=UNC=COND=but 3-thus=able=understand-DIR-N-PROX.PL

kecciya-lí-c-il skicinúw-ol?
be.pure-OBV-3AN-OBV.SG Indian-OBV.SG
'But how could they determine what a full-blooded Indian is?' (Pass., Francis and Leavitt 2008:160)

(15b) [$_{\omega}$ [$_{\omega}$ Mèc=**op**=al]=**op**] nt-api–wikŭwamkóm-a-n n-uhkomoss-òn?
still=COND=UNC=COND 1-go–visit-DIR-N 1-grandmother-1PL
'Could we please go see our grandmother?' (Pass., Francis et al. 2016, v. api- 'go and return')

This property, together with the idiosyncratic sense of *mèc=op=al* as 'please', suggests that we are dealing here with idioms, that is, with lexically listed expressions that include enclitics in their basic forms. These idiomatic enclitics form a prosodic word with their hosts. The ordinary clitic sequences *=op=ŏlu* in (15a) and *=op* in (15b) are stationed after the whole idiomatic expression in each of these examples, not after its initial word. This is expected if clitics are positioned with respect to prosodic, rather than syntactic words, since the base for the insertion of the productively placed clitics will naturally include the whole lexically specified prosodic word that appears in first position in each clause in the examples, as indicated by the bracketing. If we were to suppose instead that clitic sequences are positioned after the first syntactic word in a clause, we would expect the productively added enclitics to intervene between the base word of the idiom in each example and its lexically specified enclitics.

Conclusion

The evidence reviewed here suggests that second-position enclitics in MP that appear to have been stationed within a constituent are in fact so located, contrary to the claims of Johnson and Rosen (2015), who have analyzed examples of this kind in several Algonquian languages as involving the attachment of enclitics to the first segment of a discontinuous phrase.

Clitic placement after the first word of a clause is plausibly analyzed in MP in prosodic terms. Note further that this analysis provides a clear rationale for analyzing the second-position particles of MP as enclitics in the first place, that is, as components of a single prosodic word with their hosts.

We are left with a picture of clitic placement in MP as a dual process: part prosodically based and part syntactically based, just as in Serbian and Croatian. Given that second word placement is stated in terms of prosodic structure, the conclusion that clitics may occur within syntactic constituents in MP is unsurprising: second word clitics are stationed without regard to phrase boundaries because their position is not determined on the basis of syntactic structure.

NOTES

1. The comments of two reviewers and the editors of these *Papers*, as well as the questions of members of the audience at the conference, have been invaluable in helping me to sharpen and clarify the ideas presented in this paper. Naturally, remaining errors are my own.
2. The practical orthography used here employs the following conventions: <c> is /č/, <q> is /kʷ/, <o> is /ə/, and a word-initial /h/ before a consonant is written as an apostrophe <'>. Acute and grave accents mark distinctively high- and low-pitched stressed syllables, respectively. The breve <˘> marks phonologically "weak" vowels, which are ignored in stress assignment (which yields nondistinctive alternating stress to the left of the distinctively accented syllable). The double hyphen (=) marks the boundary between an enclitic and its host. The boundary between a preverb (prior member in a verbal

compound) and the verb or compound that it modifies is indicated by a dash (–).

3. The following abbreviations are used in glosses: 1 = first person, 2 = second person, 3 = third person, AN = animate, AOR = aorist, COND = conditional, CONJ = conjunct, DIM = diminutive, DIR = direct, EMPH = emphasis, IN = inanimate, INV = inverse, LOC = locative, Mal. = Maliseet, MPL = multi-plural (the subject of the verb refers to three or more individuals), N = suffix -*(ŏ)n(e)*- (with several functions), NEG = negative, NF = noun final (noun-forming suffix), OBV = obviative, Pass. = Passamaquoddy, PL = plural, PROX = proximate, REPORT = reportative, SG = singular, TH = thematic suffix, UNC = uncertain. Glosses are given in parentheses for morphemes that have no surface segmental shape.
4. The enclitic =*al* 'uncertain' is added to indefinite pronouns to indicate approximation. In this use, the enclitic is not restricted to second position.
5. See Stjepanović (2013) for some potentially problematic cases in Serbian and Croatian.
6. See Postal (1998:51–95) for an attempt to provide syntactic analyses for cases of extraction out of apparent coordinate structures in English that would make it unnecessary to recognize exceptions to the Element Constraint.
7. Recall that the emphatic clitic =*(ŏ)te* is not restricted to second position.
8. There is an extensive literature on clitic placement in Serbian and Croatian; see Bošković (2001) for a good overview. Both Bošković (2001) and Diesing and Zec (2017) analyze clitic placement in terms of movement operations. Penn (1999), on the other hand, develops a nonmovement analysis in the HPSG framework.
9. Penn (1999:3) and Diesing and Zec (2017:13–14) report that a second-position enclitic may be stationed after the prosodic unit formed by a proclitic preposition and an attributive modifier of a following noun, even where these do not form a syntactic constituent together. Diesing and Zec (2017:10–11) also note that it is possible to place a second-position enclitic after the first of two conjoined predicate nouns or adjectives. As in comparable cases in MP, the clitic host in such examples cannot have been separated from the remainder of the conjunction structure without violating the Coordinate Structure Constraint.

REFERENCES

Bošković, Željko. 2001. *On the Nature of the Syntax-Phonology Interface: Cliticization and Related Phenomena.* Amsterdam: Elsevier.

Deane, Paul D. 1991. Limits to Attention: A Cognitive Theory of Island Constraints. *Cognitive Linguistics* 2:1–63.

Diesing, Molly and Draga Zec. 2017. Getting in the First Word: Prosody and Predicate Initial

Sentences in Serbian. *Glossa: A Journal of General Linguistics* 2:1–25.

Donohue, Cathryn and Ivan A. Sag. 1999. Domains in Warlpiri. Paper read at the Sixth International Conference on Head-Driven Phrase Structure Grammar, Edinburgh, August 4–6. http://www.cs.toronto.edu/~gpenn/csc2517/donohue-sag99.pdf.

Francis, David A. and Robert M. Leavitt. 2008. *Peskotomuhkati Wolastoqewi Latuwewakon / A Passamaquoddy-Maliseet Dictionary*. Orono: University of Maine Press.

Francis, David A., Robert M. Leavitt, and Margaret Apt. 2016. *Passamaquoddy-Maliseet Language Portal*. Fredericton: University of New Brunswick. http://pmportal.org/.

Goldsmith, John J. 1985. A Principled Exception to the Coordinate Structure Constraint. *Papers from the Twenty-First Regional Meeting of the Chicago Linguistic Society*, ed. by William Eilfort, Paul Kroeber, and Karen Peterson, pp. 133–143. Chicago: Chicago Linguistic Society.

Grosu, Alexander. 1973. On the Nonunitary Nature of the Coordinate Structure Constraint. *Linguistic Inquiry* 4:88–92.

Johnson, Meredith and Bryan Rosen. 2015. The Syntax of Discontinuous Noun Phrases in Algonquian Languages: Left Branch Extractions and Focus Movements. *Papers of the Forty-Third Algonquian Conference*, ed. by Monica Macaulay and J. Randolph Valentine, pp. 135–153. Albany, NY: SUNY Press.

Lakoff, George. 1986. Frame Semantic Control of the Coordinate Structure Constraint. *Chicago Linguistic Society 22: Parasession on Pragmatics and Grammatical Theory*, ed. by Anne M. Farley, Peter T. Farley, and Karl-Erik McCullough, pp. 152–167. Chicago: Chicago Linguistic Society.

LeSourd, Philip S. 2007. *Tales from Maliseet Country: The Maliseet Texts of Karl V. Teeter*. Lincoln: University of Nebraska Press.

———. 2014. Prepositional Phrases in Maliseet-Passamaquoddy. *International Journal of American Linguistics* 80:209–240.

[Newell, Elizabeth.] 1974. *Mahtoqehs naka Malsom* [Rabbit and Wolf]. Indian Township, ME: Wabnaki Bilingual Education Program.

[Newell, Wayne.] 1974. *Kukec* [Game warden]. Indian Township, ME: Wabnaki Bilingual Education Program.

Paul, Peter. 1963. Text Number 1, Maliseet Texts 1963. Audiotaped interview with Karl V. Teeter, Woodstock, NB. [Original tape is deposited with the Papers of Karl V. Teeter in the Harvard University Archives, Cambridge, MA.]

Penn, Gerald. 1999. A Generalized-Domain-Based Approach to Serbo-Croatian Second-Position Clitic Placement. *Constraints and Resources in Natural Language Syntax and Semantics*, ed. by Gosse Bouma, pp. 119–136. Stanford, CA: CSLI.

Polchies, Margaret, Archie Polchies, Madeleine Tomah, and John Sacoby. 2013. *Kəloskapeyal naka Kansohseyal Atkohkakənəl* [Stories of Koluskap and Ancient Things]. Fredericton, NB: St. Thomas University.

Pollard, Carl and Ivan A. Sag. 1994. *Head-Driven Phrase Structure Grammar.* Chicago: University of Chicago Press.

Postal, Paul M. 1998. *Three Investigations of Extraction.* Cambridge, MA: MIT Press.

Ross, John R. 1967. Constraints on Variables in Syntax. PhD thesis, Massachusetts Institute of Technology.

Socobasin, Mary Ellen. 1979. *Maliyan / Mary Ann.* Indian Township, ME: Wabnaki Bilingual Education Program.

Stjepanović, Sandra. 2013. Left-Branch Extraction and the Coordinate Structure Constraint. *Proceedings of Forty-Fourth Annual Meeting of the North East Linguistic Society*, vol. 2, ed. by Jyoti Iyer and Leland Kusmer, pp. 157–170. Amherst, MA: Graduate Linguistic Student Association.

Theme Signs in Potawatomi as Object Agreement and the Inverse

Robert E. Lewis Jr.

The suffix that occurs immediately after the transitive verb stem in Potawatomi, as in other Algonquian languages, is called the theme sign.[1] The exact nature of this theme sign has been the subject of debate out of which three clear approaches have taken shape: the theme sign is sensitive to a person hierarchy (Fabri 1996); the theme sign is partial object agreement (McGinnis 1999:9; Goddard 1979:82); and the theme sign is full object agreement (Rhodes 1994; Oxford 2014). Due to complications with the first two approaches, this paper follows the third approach and gives a Distributed Morphology (Halle and Marantz 1993) analysis of Potawatomi's theme signs as full object agreement with the inverse marker superimposed. To accomplish this task, I implement an analysis that makes use of privative feature geometries (Harley and Ritter 2002; Béjar and Rezac 2009) and two probe heads whose lexical insertion rules are contextualized to each other, following Oxford (2014) for Proto-Algonquian. These contextualized insertion rules with the use of privative feature geometries create the direct/inverse pattern.

This paper is organized as follows: In the first section, I present complications for the "sensitive to a person hierarchy" and "partial object agreement" approaches to theme signs and sketch an alternative approach that relies on full object agreement. In the second section, I present a morphosyntactic analysis of the theme signs as full object agreement that goes beyond Oxford (2014). I generalize how agreement works on the higher head (Infl^{0}), finding that it always agrees with two arguments and that it creates two types of spell-out: object agreement and the inverse. I also account for the first person inclusive with equally articulated first and second person feature geometries. Last, I capture the fact that the distribution of the inverse theme sign varies by verbal order with contextual rule ordering. In the third section, I address a few phonologically opaque rules and briefly reply to concerns about the spell-out of the inner suffix.

Person Hierarchy

In Potawatomi, the form of the theme signs given in (1) has been argued to vary according to the rank of the subject and object on the person hierarchy in (2) (see Macaulay 2009 for a typological study of this hierarchy). Note the third person prefix /w-/ deletes before a [w], but I have kept it for illustrative purposes. The inverse marker is phonemically /-əgw/. Its final glide either deletes or changes to an [o] when followed by the obviative marker.[2]

(1)
a. n-wabm-a
   1-see.TA-DIR
   'I see him/her'
b. g-wabm-a
   2-see.TA-DIR
   'you see him/her'
c. w-wabm-a-n
   3-see.TA-DIR-OBV
   'she sees her (OBV)'
d. n-wabm-əg
   1-see.TA-INV
   'she/he sees me'
e. g-wab-əg
   2-see.TA-INV
   'she/he sees you'
f. w-wabm-əgo-n
   3-see.TA-INV-OBV
   'she (OBV) sees her'

When the subject is higher ranked on the hierarchy the direct *-a* surfaces, while when the object is higher ranked, the inverse /-əgw/ surfaces.

(2) SAP > 3PROX > 3OBV

Complications

The claim that the theme signs are read off a person hierarchy is complicated by the theme signs that surface in combinations of first and second person. This is shown in (3a) and (3b) where the theme signs *-ən* and *-ə* surface, respectively.

(3) a. g-wabm-ən-mən
2-see.TA-INV-1p
'we see you (s/p)'

b. g-wabm-ə-ymən
2-see.TA-DIR-1p
'you see us'

Some authors claim that examples like those in (3) illustrate a need for the hierarchy in (2) to be further unpacked as the person hierarchy in (4), where SAP is replaced by second person ranked above first person (see Wolfart 1973; Béjar and Rezac 2009; among others). In effect, these authors claim that *-ə* is another direct theme sign and *-ən* is another inverse theme sign.

(4) 2 > 1 > 3PROX > 3OBV

However, the theme signs *-ə*/*-ən* are also used in the conjunct order with a third person subject and a first/second person object. The theme signs *-ə* and *-ən* are given alongside *-a* and /-əgw/ in (5). Assuming that the theme signs that appear in the independent and conjunct orders are the same theme signs, the appearance of the theme signs *-ə* and *-ən* in the conjunct order in (5b) and (5c) defies predictions made by a person hierarchy, and therefore makes a person hierarchy approach appear suspect.

(5) a. wabm-a-d
see.TA-TS-3s
'she/he sees her/him (obv)'

b. wabm-ə-d
see.TA-TS-3s/1s
'she/he sees me'

c. wabm-ən-ag
see.TA-TS-3(s)/2p
'she/he/they see(s) you all'

d. wabm-əgo-d
see.TA-TS-3s
'she (obv) sees her'

TABLE 1. Potawatomi TA theme signs

INDEPENDENT ORDER				CONJUNCT ORDER			
-əgw (INV)	-a (DIR)	-ə	-ən	-əgw (INV)	-a (DIR)	-ə	-ən
3-1	1-3				1-3	3-1	3-2
3-2	2-3	2-1	1-2		2-3	2-1	1-2
4-3	3-4			4-3	3-4		

Object Agreement

As has been pointed out for other Algonquian languages (Rhodes 1976; LeSourd 1976; Oxford 2014; among others), the theme sign pattern seen in (5) does indicate object agreement. That is, the expansion of the theme signs in the conjunct order is easily understood through the lens of object agreement with an inverse system superimposed on it. This means if we set the inverse theme sign aside, the other theme signs signal the person feature of the object, as shown in (6), where regardless of verbal order (independent left column, conjunct right column), the theme signs correlate with the person of the object. Note that the theme signs do not include specification for number.

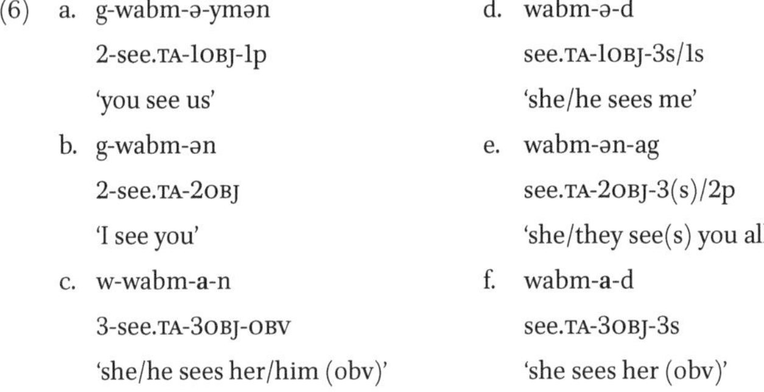

(6) a. g-wabm-ə-ymən
2-see.TA-1OBJ-1p
'you see us'

b. g-wabm-ən
2-see.TA-2OBJ
'I see you'

c. w-wabm-a-n
3-see.TA-3OBJ-OBV
'she/he sees her/him (obv)'

d. wabm-ə-d
see.TA-1OBJ-3s/1s
'she/he sees me'

e. wabm-ən-ag
see.TA-2OBJ-3(s)/2p
'she/they see(s) you all'

f. wabm-a-d
see.TA-3OBJ-3s
'she sees her (obv)'

In (6), the theme sign *-ə* is used with a first person object; the theme sign *-ən* is used with a second person object; the theme sign *-a* is used with a third person object. A complete list of theme signs is summarized in Table 1.

I pause here to take stock of a few important generalizations about the data just presented. First, the theme signs (minus the inverse) look like object agreement. Second, the inverse and object agreement are not distributed in parallel across orders. The inverse surfaces in the independent order any time a third person acts on a SAP, otherwise object agreement surfaces. In the conjunct order, however, the inverse surfaces any time a third person obviative acts on a third person proximate; otherwise object agreement surfaces. In the next section, I address how to account for these facts. I also show how such an account can capture the first person inclusive, which has eluded some previous analyses of object agreement (Oxford 2014).

Object Agreement and the Inverse

This section provides an object agreement analysis of the Potawatomi theme signs. In the first part of this section, I provide privative feature geometries for persons. In the second part of this section, I explicate how these person features coupled with a multiple probe agreement system spell out the appropriate theme sign. I also show that the first person inclusive easily fits into this object agreement approach. In the third part of this section, a high-ranked contextualized insertion rule is introduced to account for differences in the inverse/theme signs across verbal orders.

Person Features

I treat persons as privative feature geometries that have hierarchy effects following Oxford (2014). In other words, one person geometry entails another, so a third person proximate is made up of a third person obviative, as shown in (7). Note these person geometries do not necessarily reflect morphological markedness. That is, the obviative has an overt suffix, while the proximate does not. I treat semantic markedness and morphological markedness as two distinct systems of markedness. Furthermore, I assume first and second persons are equally (semantically) marked, as shown in (7) following Harley and Ritter (2002) and contra Béjar and Rezac (2009) and Oxford (2014). This equal markedness plays a key role in the analysis that follows.

(7) Figure 1. *π features*

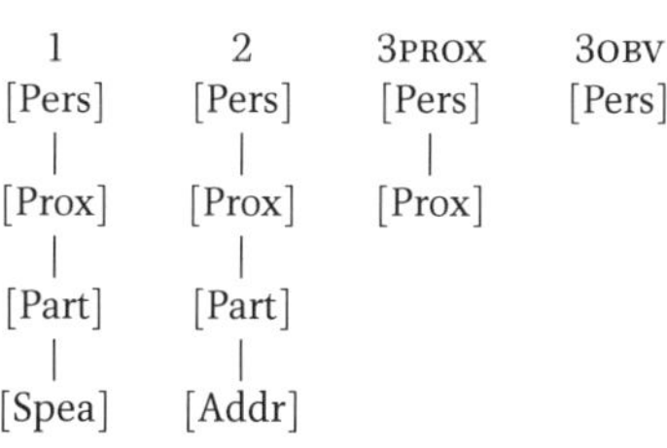

Agreement and Spell-out

I use derivations of combinations of first and third persons to illustrate how agreement and spell-out work. I start with the independent order in this second part of the section and then extend the analysis to the conjunct order in the third part of this section. The relevant examples are given in (8a) and (8b).

(8) a. n-wabm-a
1-see.TA-3OBJ
'I see him/her'

b. n-wabm-əg
1-see.TA-INV
'she/he sees me'

The tree structure in (9) is given for (8a) with a first person subject whose person features are more articulated than those of a third person object. The structural gist of the tree structure in (9) is that in transitive verbs the object is introduced by *v* and the subject is introduced by Voice^0, which has a π:[_] probe and an [EPP] feature that attracts the object to its specifier position. Last, Infl^0 is introduced with a π:[_] probe.

(9) Tree 1.

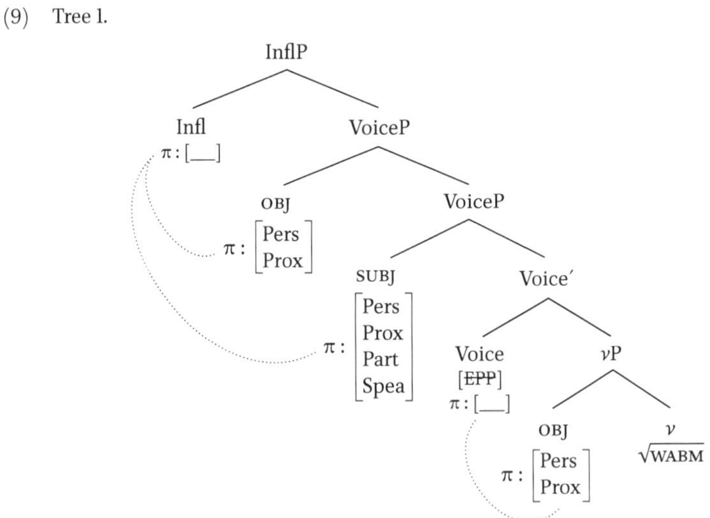

Take note of the two probes in (9) that mirror Oxford (2014). Both probes work the same way; following Chomsky (2000), they agree with the closest argument that they c-command. Voice^0 probes and agrees with the object in person. The object moves to the specifier of VoiceP via an [EPP] feature and Infl^0 probes and agrees with both the object and the subject because they are both specifiers of VoiceP; they are both the closest argument to Infl^0 following Béjar and Rezac (2009) and Oxford (2014). Even though Infl^0 agrees with two arguments, it only has one feature geometry, not two. The verb next raises to Voice^0 and then to Infl^0 to form the complex head v-Voice^0-Infl^0. This ordering of heads is predicted by Baker's (1985) Mirror Principle and Travis's (1984) Head Movement Constraint. The complex head formed by head movement in the structure in (9) is given in (10a), and the complex head for (8b) is given in (10b). The tree structure before head movement for (8b) is omitted due to space restrictions.

(10) a. Tree 2. b. Tree 3.

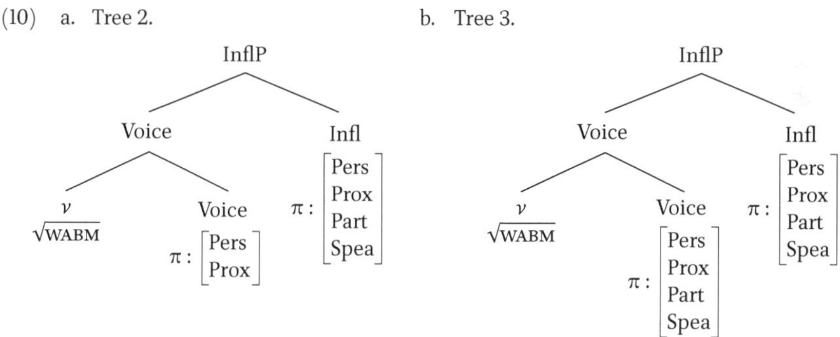

Given these complex heads let us now take a look at how spell-out works. Note that the person feature geometries, not the lexical insertion rules in this section, are novel. The lexical insertion rules closely follow Oxford (2014). The lexical insertion rules for agreement in Voice^0 are:

(11) *Spell-out rules in Voice^0*

Rule 1.

a. Voice^0[π:α] ⟷ -∅ / ____ Infl^0[π:α]

b. Voice^0[Pers, Prox, Part, Addr] ⟷ -ən

c. Voice^0[Pers, Prox, Part] ⟷ -ɔ

d. Voice^0[Pers] ⟷ -a

There is a complementarity problem in (11). The rule in (11a) is equally as likely to apply as the rules in (11b–d). To resolve this complementarity problem, the lexical insertion rule in (11a) must be ordered before the rest of the rules in this set by stipulation. The elsewhere condition will not do. The rule in (11d) will then apply to the structure in (10a) because Voice^0 and Infl^0 have different sets of person features, which results in object agreement surfacing, while the rule in (11a) will apply to the structure in (10b) because Voice^0 and Infl^0 have the same person features. The lexical insertion rules in Infl^0 are:

(12) *Spell-out rules in Infl^0*

Rule 2.

a. Infl^0 $\leftrightarrow$ -əgw / -∅ _____

b. Infl^0 $\leftrightarrow$ -∅

The rule in (12b) will apply to the structure in (10a). On the other hand, the rule in (12a) will apply to the structure in (10b) obtaining the inverse suffix.

Before we move on, note that the use of a null head here was inspired by Merchant (2011), but one could rewrite the rule in (11a) so that the inverse theme sign /-əgw / was spelled-out in Voice^0 and replace (12) with a single rule that would spell out a null morpheme in Infl^0. This would work for Potawatomi, but would not generalize to those Algonquian languages that spell out some theme signs to the right of a diminutive suffix and others to the left (see Oxford 2014:65 for further discussion of this asymmetry).

Abstracting away, these person features coupled with the multiple probe agreement system form two types of agreement. In the inverse cases (13), Voice^0 agrees with the object (which has a more articulated feature geometry than the subject), and Infl^0 agrees with both the subject and the object, which in the inverse always has the same feature set as the object.

(13) *Inverse*

Figure 2.

$$\begin{array}{ccccc} \textbf{Infl} & \text{OBJ} & \text{SUBJ} & \textbf{Voice} & \text{OBJ} \\ \pi:\begin{bmatrix} x \\ y \\ z \end{bmatrix} & \pi:\begin{bmatrix} x \\ y \\ z \end{bmatrix} & \pi:\begin{bmatrix} x \\ y \end{bmatrix} & \pi:\begin{bmatrix} x \\ y \\ z \end{bmatrix} & \pi:\begin{bmatrix} x \\ y \\ z \end{bmatrix} \end{array}$$

The lexical insertion rules for Voice^0 would be:

(14) *Spell-out rules in Voice^0*

Rule 3.

a. Voice$^0[\pi{:}\alpha]$ $\leftrightarrow$ -∅ / _____ Infl$^0[\pi{:}\alpha]$

b. Voice^0[x, y, z] $\leftrightarrow$ -ən

c. Voice^0[x, y] $\leftrightarrow$ -ə

d. Voice^0[x] $\leftrightarrow$ -a

The π features of Voice^0 will match those of Infl^0, so I predict that the rule in (14a) will apply to Voice^0, and it will be spelled out as -Ø. The lexical insertion rules for Infl^0 are:

(15) *Spell-out rules in Infl^0*

Rule 4.

a. Infl^0 $\leftrightarrow$ -əgw / -∅ _____

b. Infl^0 $\leftrightarrow$ -∅

There is a null suffix in Voice^0, so I predict that the rule in (15a) will apply in Infl^0 and the inverse theme sign /-əgw/ will be spelled-out.[3]

In the non-inverse cases Voice^0 agrees with the object and Infl^0 agrees with both the subject (which has a richer set of features) and the object. This pattern will always result in Infl^0 having a richer set of features than Voice^0.

(16) *Object agreement*

a. *direct*

Figure 3.

Infl	OBJ	SUBJ	**Voice**	OBJ
$\pi: \begin{bmatrix} x \\ y \\ z/u \end{bmatrix}$	$\pi: \begin{bmatrix} x \\ y \end{bmatrix}$	$\pi: \begin{bmatrix} x \\ y \\ z/u \end{bmatrix}$	$\pi: \begin{bmatrix} x \\ y \end{bmatrix}$	$\pi: \begin{bmatrix} x \\ y \end{bmatrix}$

b. *you-and-me*

Figure 4.

Infl	OBJ	SUBJ	**Voice**	OBJ
$\pi: \begin{bmatrix} x \\ y \\ z\ u \end{bmatrix}$	$\pi: \begin{bmatrix} x \\ y \\ z \end{bmatrix}$	$\pi: \begin{bmatrix} x \\ y \\ u \end{bmatrix}$	$\pi: \begin{bmatrix} x \\ y \\ z \end{bmatrix}$	$\pi: \begin{bmatrix} x \\ y \\ z \end{bmatrix}$

This system ensures that the lexical insertion rule in (14a) will never obtain, correctly predicting that the relevant object agreement suffix will be used instead (14b–c). The feature combination for (14d) is not shown. Likewise, this system ensures that the first lexical insertion rule in Infl^0 never obtains, correctly predicting that the inverse theme sign is not used in these cases. The application of these lexical insertion rules is straightforward in most cases; I turn next to the more difficult situation when one of the arguments is a first person inclusive.

First Person Inclusive

When it comes to accounting for the first person inclusive, if we indicate that the second person is richer than the first person or vice versa, we will always make the wrong predictions about the form of the theme sign that will surface. This means, for instance, if the second person were richer than the first person, we would expect the inverse theme sign to show up with a first person subject and a second person object, contrary to fact.

(17) *1–2 where second person is richer than first person*

Figure 5.

$$\begin{array}{ccccc} \textbf{Infl} & 2\text{OBJ} & 1\text{SUBJ} & \textbf{Voice} & 2\text{OBJ} \\ \pi:\begin{bmatrix} x \\ y \\ z \end{bmatrix} & \pi:\begin{bmatrix} x \\ y \\ z \end{bmatrix} & \pi:\begin{bmatrix} x \\ y \end{bmatrix} & \pi:\begin{bmatrix} x \\ y \\ z \end{bmatrix} & \pi:\begin{bmatrix} x \\ y \\ z \end{bmatrix} \end{array} \rightarrow \ {}^{*}\text{Inv}$$

In (17), Voice^0 copies the features from the object and Infl^0 copies the features from the subject and the object. Crucially, the object has a richer feature set than the subject; therefore, Infl^0 will have the same feature set as Voice^0. This incorrectly predicts that the inverse theme sign will be inserted via the lexical insertion rules in (14a) and (15a). Likewise, the critical case to show that a treatment of the first person as richer than the second person is wrong would be a combination of a second person subject and first person object, which I leave up to readers to work out on their own.

There is a simple solution to this problem. I specify first person with the [Spea] feature, second person with the [Addr] feature (contra Oxford 2014, who does not address the first person inclusive form), and first person inclusive with both the [Spea] and [Addr] features. These person features are presented in (18).

(18) *π features*

Figure 6.

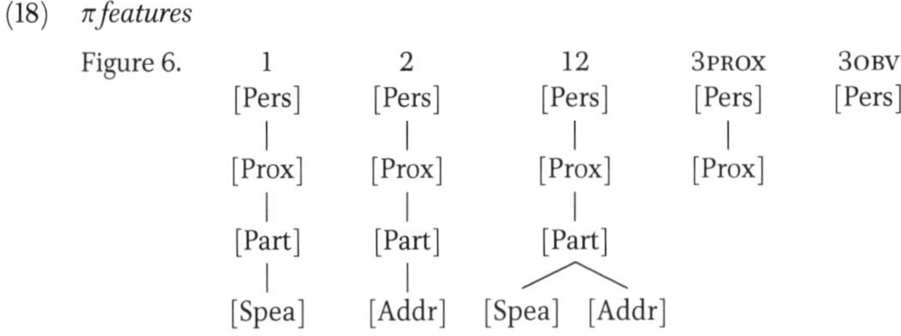

Furthermore, these person features allow us to capture the fact that the first person inclusive is treated the same as a second person form in the grammar. Notice that in (19), the theme sign used with a first person inclusive object is the same one that is used with the second person object (*-ən*).

TABLE 2. Potawatomi TA theme signs (with emphasis)

INDEPENDENT ORDER				CONJUNCT ORDER			
-əgw (INV)	-a (DIR)	-ə	-ən	-əgw (INV)	-a (DIR)	-ə	-ən
3-1	1-3				1-3	**3-1**	**3-2**
3-2	2-3	2-1	1-2		2-3	2-1	1-2
4-3	3-4			4-3	3-4		

(19) a. wabm-**ən**-əg
see.TA-12OBJ-3s/12
'she/he sees us (incl)'

b. wabm-**ən**-ag
see.TA-2OBJ-3(s)/2p
'she/they see(s) you all'

Thus, the mechanism for spelling out a common theme sign for second person objects and first person inclusive objects is a lexical insertion rule that tracks the [Addr] feature present in both forms. The rule is Voice^0[Pers, Prox, Part, Addr] ←→ *-ən,* which was given in (11b). This fills out my discussion of the independent order; I turn next to the conjunct order.

Conjunct Order Agreement and Spell-out

The distribution of inverse theme signs in the conjunct order highlights an important difference in its use across verbal orders. In the conjunct order, the inverse theme sign /-əgw/ is used in fewer contexts than in the independent order. This shows us that the way in which the lexical insertion rules were written in (11) incorrectly inserts the inverse theme sign in too many contexts. Following the lexical insertion rule in (11), the inverse theme sign would be inserted for 3–1 and 3–2 forms in the conjunct order contrary to fact as illustrated in Table 2.

My answer to this problem differs significantly from that in Oxford (2014). Whereas Oxford points to the presence of an unchecked feature in the higher probe as the answer, I argue that the answer to this problem in Potawatomi is a contextualized rule. That is, given that lexical insertion rules are contextually conditioned by adjacent heads, negation is the triggering context for the inverse theme sign since negation immediately follows Infl^0 only in the independent order. Consider the independent order in (20a) and the conjunct order in (20b).

(20) a. **jo** w-gi-gəkenm-əg-**si**-n
NEG 3-PST-know.TA-INV-NEG-OBV
'she/he (OBV) did not know her/him (PROX)'
b. e-gi-**bwa**-gkenm-a-d
FCT-PST-IRR-know.TA-3OBJ-3/3OBV
'[as/when] she/he (PROX) did not know her/him (OBV)'

Unlike other Algonquian languages, Potawatomi does not always suffix negation with either *-s* or *-w* (see Goddard 2006 for a discussion on this point). Therefore, the difference between the independent and the conjunct in terms of negation is clearly distinguished by the structural position of the negative head. Negation is above Infl^0 in the independent order while negation is absent in the conjunct order where the irrealis marker *bwa* is used instead. The verb does not move to the head containing the irrealis marker in the conjunct order. This can be seen where an independent word may surface between *bwa* and the rest of the verb stem as shown in (21) from Hockett (1940:37); also see Johnson (2012) and Lewis (2016), who treat *bwa* as negation.

(21) e-wi-bwa minə gego dodwəd
FCT-FUT-IRR again something do.to.TA.2s/3s
'you will not do anything to him/her again'

Furthermore, negation is housed in a head called Pol^0, which is always present regardless of the independent order clause's polarity. Pol^0 is present in the independent order but is absent in the conjunct order.[4]

I give two derivations to show the difference between the independent and conjunct orders. Compare the form of the theme sign for a third person subject with a first person object in the independent (22a) and conjunct (22b) orders.

(22) a. n-wabm-əg
1-see.TA-INV
'she/he sees me'

b. wabm-ə-d
see.TA-1OBJ-3s/1s
'she/he sees me'

The structural position of Pol^0 is illustrated in (23) with a third person subject and a first person object. (23) is the tree for (22a) as Pol^0 is only present in the independent order, and shows that in transitive verbs, the object is introduced by *v* and the subject is introduced by Voice^0, which has a π:[ ] probe and an [EPP] feature that attracts the object to its specifier position. These features are left out of the tree in (23), but their effects are shown in (24a) and (24b). Next, Infl^0 is introduced with a π:[ ] probe. Lastly, Pol^0 is introduced.

(23) Tree 4.

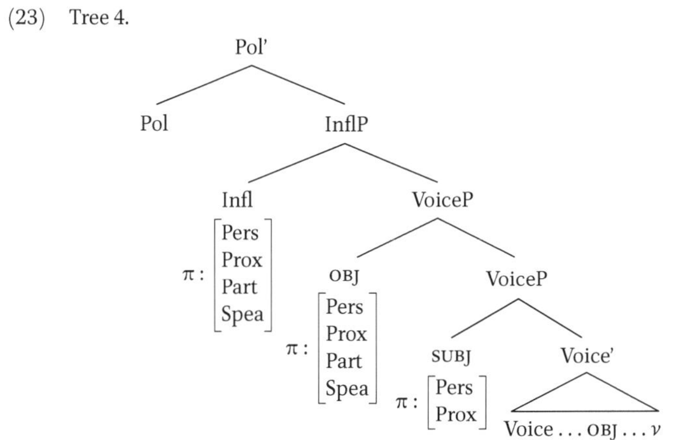

The verb undergoes head-movement to Pol^0 moving through v, Voice^0, and Infl^0 in the independent order, but only to Infl^0 in the conjunct order. The complex head from this head movement of the structure in (23) is given in (24a), and the complex head from this head movement for (22b) is given in (24b). The tree structure before head movement for (22b) is omitted due to space restrictions.

(24) a. *Independent* b. *Conjunct*

Tree 5. Tree 6.

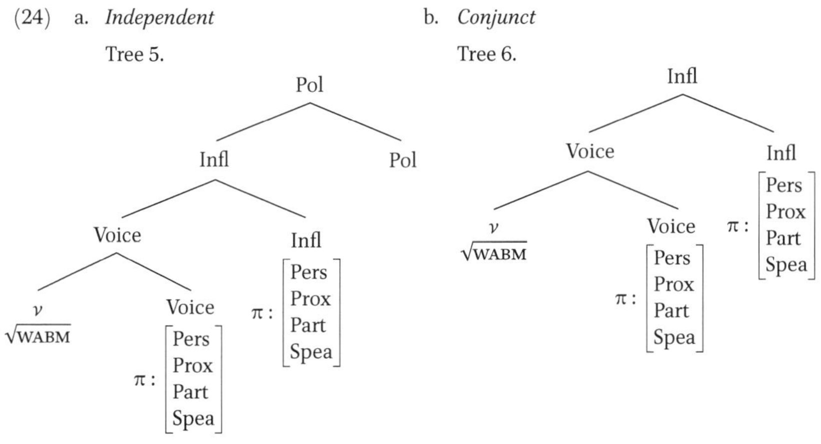

I add a spell-out rule to Voice^0 that is span-conditioned not only by the feature in Infl^0 but also by the feature(s) of the immediately adjacent head Pol^0 (see Merchant 2015 for another use of span-conditioned rules). I also assume the following rule ordering:

(25) *Spell-out rules in Voice^0 (Final Version)*

Rule 5.

a. Voice^0[π:α] ↔ -∅ / _____ Infl^0[π:α]Pol^0

b. Voice^0[Pers, Prox, Part, Addr] ↔ -ən

c. Voice^0[Pers, Prox, Part] ↔ -ə

d. Voice^0[π:α] ↔ -∅ / _____ Infl^0[π:α]

e. Voice^0[Pers, Prox] ↔ -a

It is the ordering of (25a) over all the other rules that correctly accounts for the wide application of the inverse in the independent order. The rule in (25a) will apply to the structure in (24a) because Infl^0 and Voice^0 have the same feature sets with a Pol^0 present, so a null head is inserted. The rule in (25a) will not apply, however, to the structure in (24b) because the rule only applies in the independent order. As the rules in (25) are ordered as given, (25c) will apply to the structure in (24b). This is because even though Voice^0 and Infl^0 have the same person features, conjunct order clauses lack a Pol^0. So, without a Pol^0 to trigger (25a), object agreement is inserted via (25c).

The lexical insertion rules in Infl^0 given for the independent order where we insert the inverse theme sign when it is adjacent to a null suffix obtains the correct surface forms in the conjunct order, so no updating of these previous rules is needed.

(26) *Spell-out rules in Infl^0 (Final Version)*

Rule 6.

a. Infl^0 ↔ -əgw / -∅ _____

b. Infl^0 ↔ -∅

The rule in (26a) will apply to the structure in (24a). Since there is a null suffix in Voice^0, we correctly predict that the inverse theme sign will be inserted in Infl^0. On the other hand, the rule in (26b) will apply to the structure in (24b). Since there is an overt suffix in Voice^0, we correctly predict that a null suffix will be inserted in Infl^0.

Opaque Phonological Rules and Spell-out

There are two issues that still need to be addressed. The first part takes up three opaque phonological rules that affect the shape/presence of the theme sign. Note these are not phonological readjustment rules, but, rather, general phonological rules present elsewhere in the language. The second part briefly addresses some concerns about the extendibility of my analysis to the inner suffix.

Opaque Phonological Rules

There are a few opaque phonological rules that predict the absence or mutation of the theme signs. The first is a word-final schwa deletion rule given in (27b). The effects of this rule are seen in a combination of a singular second person subject and a singular first person object, as shown in (27a). In addition to this rule, there are metrical processes that are at play to shape the verb form; see Lockwood (2012) for a discussion of the metrical structure of Potawatomi.

(27) a. g-wabəm
gə-wabəm-ə
2-see.TA-1OBJ

b. *Word final schwa deletion*:
Rule 7.
$ə \rightarrow \varnothing \ / \ \_\_\_ \ ]_{\omega>}$

The second is a nasal consonant deletion rule in consonant clusters given in (28c). The [n] in the theme sign *-ən* is absent in combinations of third person subjects and second person objects in the conjunct as shown in (28a) and (28b). Compare combinations of a third person singular/plural subject and a second person singular object to combinations of a third person singular/plural subject and a second person plural or a first person inclusive object in (19). This rule will not apply to the first person prefix as it is restricted to syllable final consonant clusters.

TABLE 3. Conjunct indicative

	STEM	TS	SFX
1s-3s	wabm	/a/	-əg
1s-3p	wabm	/a/	-əgwa
1p-3s	wabm	/a/	-əgo
12-3s	wabm	/a/	-ad
2s-3s	wabm	/a/	-əd
2s-3p	wabm	/a/	-ədwa
2p-3s	wabm	/a/	-əg
2p-3p	wabm	/a/	-əgwa

(28) a. wabməg

wabm-ən-g

see.TA-2OBJ-3s/2s

b. wabməkwa

wabm-ən-kwa

see.TA-2OBJ-3p/2s

c. *Pre-consonantal nasal deletion*:

Rule 8.

n → ∅ / ____ + C $]_\sigma$

The third is a vowel hiatus rule given in (29).

(29) *Vowel hiatus*:

Rule 9.

-a → ∅ / ____ + V

The theme sign *-a* used with the third person object in the independent order is absent in the conjunct order when the subject is a SAP and the object is a third person singular/plural. That is, *-a* before a vowel initial suffix deletes. Oxford (2014) notes that this rule cannot be all that is going on, but since I am restricting myself to the theme signs, I will not pursue this further. Forward slashes indicate underlying Potawatomi forms in Table 3.

Spell-out of the Inner Suffix

The inner suffix is an independent order suffix that immediately follows the theme sign of the verb stem in positive sentences and immediately follows the negative suffix in negative sentences. In combinations of first and second person plurals, the first person plural suffix (*-mən*) is always spelled out. Several conference participants pointed out that it looked like this was a problem for my analysis because the spell-out rule for the second person theme sign tracks the [Addr] feature, and not the [Spea] feature. Thus, it looks like it would not spell out the correct inner suffix. I briefly address this concern.

While Macaulay (2009) points out that there are at least three hierarchy effects present in the Algonquian verb—the prefix, the theme sign, and the suffix—the goal of this paper is only to analyze the theme sign. Nevertheless, the person feature geometries that I give can also account for the plural suffix. This is because in a Distributed Morphology framework each node has its own set of spell-out rules, and the features that one spell-out rule tracks are independent of the features that another spell-out rule tracks. In other words, while the second person theme sign tracks the [Addr] feature, the first person plural inner suffix may simply track the [Spea] feature. Given that the first and second person feature geometries put forward in this paper are equally as marked as the other, it allows the hierarchy effects for the theme sign and the inner suffix to be simultaneously at play.

Conclusion

I have given a Distributed Morphology analysis of Potawatomi's theme signs as object agreement with an inverse marker. To account for the direct/inverse pattern, in the second section I used privative person feature geometries (Harley and Ritter 2002; Béjar and Rezac 2009; Oxford 2014) and two probe heads whose lexical insertion rules are contextualized to each other following Oxford (2014) for Proto-Algonquian. I refined Oxford's (2014) analysis in several ways. I generalized how agreement works on the higher head (Infl^0), finding that it always agrees with two arguments. That is, importantly the higher head agrees with both a subject and an object (not only in combinations of first/second persons, i.e., 'you-and-me' forms). I also accounted for the first person inclusive form, which is problematic for any analysis that represents a second person as more articulated than a first person. I argued instead that the first person inclusive has both first and second person features. Last, the restricted use of the inverse theme sign in the conjunct order shows that there is a high-ranked lexical insertion rule for the inverse that is only applicable in the independent order, while a more general lower ranked rule applies for the conjunct order. In the third section, I finished out the analysis by addressing opaque phonological rules affecting the theme signs and addressed the spell-out of the inner suffix.

NOTES

1. I am grateful for comments from Karlos Arregi, Amy Dahlstrom, Jason Merchant, participants at the Morphology and Syntax Workshop at the University of Chicago, participants at the Forty-Eighth Algonquian Conference, and reviewers for this paper.
2. The data is taken from Hockett (1940, 1948a, 1948b, 1966). I use the following abbreviations: 1 = first person, 2 = second person, 3 = third person, 4 = obviative third person, AN = animate, DIR = direct, FCT = factive, FUT = future, INV = inverse, IRR = irrealis, NEG = negative, OBJ = object, OBV = obviative, p = plural, PST = past, PROX = proximate, s = singular, TA = transitive animate, TS = theme sign.
3. This analysis may seem similar to Anderson's principle of Layering (1992, ch. 4 and 160). This is to be expected given that his analysis is also in a realizational theory of morphology.
4. Note I opt to not keep Pol^0 present across the independent and conjunct orders because its presence in both orders would erase the context for applying the spell-out rules in (27), which are central to account for the different theme signs across orders. An approach that follows Johnson's (2012) approach to negation and head-movement could also work, but would need different spell-out rules than those given in (27).

REFERENCES

Anderson, Stephen R. 1992. *A-Morphous Morphology*. Cambridge: Cambridge University Press.

Baker, Mark. 1985. The Mirror Principle and Morphosyntactic Explanations. *Linguistic Inquiry* 16(3):373–415.

Béjar, Susana and Milan Rezac. 2009. Cyclic Agree. *Linguistic Inquiry* 40(1):35–73.

Chomsky, Noam. 2000. Minimalist Inquires: The Framework. *Step by Step: Essays on Minimalism in Honor of Howard Lasnik*, ed. by Roger Martin, David Michaels, and Juan Uriagereka, pp. 89–155. Cambridge, MA: MIT Press.

Fabri, Ray. 1996. The Inverse Morphology of Plains Cree (Algonquian). *Yearbook of Morphology 1995*, ed. by Geert Booij and Jaap van Marle, pp. 17–41. Dordrecht: Kluwer.

Goddard, Ives. 1979. *Delaware Verbal Morphology: A Descriptive and Comparative Study*. New York: Garland.

———. 2006. The Proto-Algonquian Negative and Its Descendants. *Actes du trente-septième Congrès des Algonquinistes*, ed. by H.C. Wolfart, pp. 161–208. Winnipeg: University of Manitoba.

Halle, Morris and Alec Marantz. 1993. Distributed Morphology and the Pieces of Inflection. *The View from Building 20: Essays in Linguistics in Honor of Sylvain Bromberger*, ed. by Kenneth L. Hale and Samuel Jay Keyser, pp. 111–176. Cambridge, MA: MIT Press.

Harley, Heidi and Elizabeth Ritter. 2002. Person and Number in Pronouns: A Feature-Geometric Analysis. *Language* 78(3):482–526.

Hockett, Charles F. 1940. Hockett Potawatomi field notebook III. Unpublished field notebook, Welcher.002.003, Survey of California and Other Indian Languages, University of California, Berkeley, CA.

———. 1948a. Potawatomi III: The Verb Complex. *International Journal of American Linguistics* 14(3):139–149.

———. 1948b. Potawatomi IV: Particles and Sample Texts. *International Journal of American Linguistics* 14(4):213–225.

———. 1966. What Algonquian Is Really Like. *International Journal of American Linguistics* 32(1):59–73.

Johnson, Meredith. 2012. New Arguments for the Position of the Verb in Potawatomi. *Papers of the Forty-Fourth Algonquian Conference*, ed. by Monica Macaulay, Margaret Noodin, and J. Randolph Valentine, pp. 157–173. Albany, NY: SUNY Press.

LeSourd, Philip. 1976. Verb Agreement in Fox. *Harvard Studies in Syntax and Semantics*, vol. 2, ed. by Jorge Hankamer and Judith Aissen, pp. 445–528. Cambridge, MA: Department of Linguistics, Harvard University.

Lewis, Robert E., Jr. 2016. Information Structure Conditioned Word Order in Potawatomi. Paper read at the Forty-Second Society for the Study of the Indigenous Language of the Americas, Washington, DC.

Lockwood, Hunter Thompson. 2012. Revisiting Potawatomi Syncope. Paper read at the Forty-Fourth Algonquian Conference, University of Chicago.

Macaulay, Monica. 2009. On Prominence Hierarchies: Evidence from Algonquian. *Linguistic Typology* 13:357–389.

McGinnis, Martha. 1999. Is There Syntactic Inversion in Ojibwa? In *Papers from the Workshop on Structure & Constituency in Native American Languages*, ed. by L. Bar-el, Rose-Marie

D'echaine, and C. Reinholtz, pp. 101–118. MIT Occasional Papers in Linguistics, vol. 17. Cambridge, MA.

Merchant, Jason. 2011. Aleut Case Matters. *Pragmatics and Autolexical Grammar: In Honor of Jerry Sadock*, ed. by Etsuyo Yuasa, Tista Bagchi, and Katharine P. Beals, pp. 382–411. Amsterdam: John Benjamins.

———. 2015. How Much Context Is Enough? Two Cases of Span-Conditioned Stem Allomorphy. *Linguistic Inquiry* 46(2):273–303.

Oxford, Will. 2014. Microparameters of Agreement: A Diachronic Perspective on Algonquian Verb Inflection. PhD thesis, University of Toronto.

Rhodes, Richard A. 1976. The Morphosyntax of the Central Ojibwa Verb. PhD thesis, University of Michigan.

———. 1994. Agency, Inversion, and Thematic Alignment in Ojibwe. *Proceedings of the Twelfth Annual Meeting of the Berkeley Linguistics Society: General Session Dedicated to the Contributions of Charles J. Fillmore*, pp. 431–446. Berkeley: University of California, Berkeley.

Travis, Lisa. 1984. Parameters and Effects of Word Order Variation. PhD thesis, Massachusetts Institute of Technology.

Wolfart, H.C. 1973. Plains Cree: A Grammatical Study. *Transactions of the American Philosophical Society* 63(5):1–90.

Revisiting the Position of Potawatomi in (Central) Algonquian

Hunter Thompson Lockwood

It is now widely accepted that Potawatomi and Ojibwe form a genetic subgroup (Oxford 2015:325; Costa 2013:197–198, 204–218; Goddard 1994:196–197, 204; Valentine 1994:100–102).[1] However, this is contrary to the view presented by Hockett (1943; PPCA hereafter) in the last detailed comparative study of Potawatomi. In this paper, I revisit the claims laid out in PPCA, showing how the arguments presented there actually argue in favor of a Potawatomi-Ojibwe genetic subgroup, contrary to Hockett's intentions.

The section that follows includes a bit of brief background on PPCA. In the following three sections, I discuss the sound inventory of Potawatomi, critiquing and contextualizing Hockett's presentation of it. In the section following that, I discuss some inflectional facts that Hockett glosses over but which were sufficient to convince Michelson (1912). In the final section, I summarize my proposal, which I perceive as the standard view among Algonquianists.

On PPCA

Hockett's PPCA does not appear to have been a widely read piece, even in its time. It is a short paper (six pages) that was delivered to a nonspecialist, probably nonlinguist audience at the Michigan Academy of Science, Arts, and Letters, and only appears published in the conference proceedings.

The paper is based on the data and analyses from Hockett's (1939) dissertation. Both his dissertation and PPCA lean heavily on early versions of Bloomfield (1946; cited in PPCA:537 n.2 as "Algonquian Sketch, c.1939"). In it, Hockett provides 44 reconstructions of PCA forms alongside Potawatomi examples; comparison forms to the other languages are not provided. The focus of the piece is entirely on the phoneme inventory and phonology except for a brief mention of inflectional morphology in the final paragraphs.

Note that Hockett's paper was explicitly about how Potawatomi fits into *Central* Algonquian; Central Algonquian is no longer recognized as a valid subgroup, and the goal of this paper is not to attempt to resurrect it. Conversely, changes in the Algonquianist consensus spurred by new information about Algonquian linguistic history have necessitated a reinterpretation of Hockett's conclusions.

Sound Inventory

Hockett's descriptions of Potawatomi in his dissertation (1939) and the series of articles derived from it (1948a, 1948b, 1948c, 1948d) are foundational texts in the study of Potawatomi; unsurprisingly, these texts form the basis of his claims in PPCA, and much of what he wrote in those pieces is not debated here.

Hockett's phoneme inventory is given here; in the sections that follow, I demonstrate that some adjustments are necessary.

(1) Consonants: /m, n, w, j, ʔ, p, b, t, d, ʧ, ʤ, k, g, s, z, ʃ, ʒ/

(2) Vowels: /a, ɛ, i, o, ə/

For the vowels, Proto-Algonquian *i and *e merged into Oji-Pot *i. Oji-Pot *i and *a merged into Potawatomi /ə/. The long vowels *e·, *a·, and *i· continue. Contra Hockett, Oji-Pot *o and *o· did not merge in Potawatomi, or at least did not merge completely, as Potawatomi retains crucial elements of the long and short distinction in the rounded vowels. For the consonants, Proto-Algonquian plain consonants continue into Oji-Pot and Potawatomi as lenis consonants, contrasting with fortis consonants derived from Proto-Algonquian consonant clusters. Ojibwe lost *y following consonants, generally with coalescence of the following vowel (e.g., *Cye· > Ci·).

Consonants and Clusters

Hockett describes five non-obstruents in Potawatomi that "occur freely in all positions" (PPCA 538). These are /m, n, w, j, and ʔ/, and examples of each follow.

(3) *pemwehθe·wa 'he walks by' (Goddard 1994:194) P bmosé /bəmosɛ:/

(4) *nye·wi 'four' (Goddard 1994:196) P nyéw /njɛ:w/

(5) *elenyiwa 'man' (Goddard 1994:196) P nene /ənənəw/

(6) *aθemwa 'dog' (Bloomfield 1946:86) P nemosh /ənəmoʃ/

Some of these classifications could be problematic from the perspective of today's linguistic theories; /m/ and /n/ are frequently categorized as stops, for instance. Nothing in this paper hinges on this.

However, the inclusion of the glottal stop /ʔ/ as a non-obstruent is especially puzzling. Hockett describes /ʔ/ as a merger of PA *h and *ʔ "if indeed they were distinct in PCA" (PPCA 540). In a footnote, he adds that "Bloomfield now believes that of these two only a single phoneme existed in PCA." This may be a relic of an early draft of Bloomfield (1946); the Sketch only uses the word "glottal" once in the sound section, and that is to describe the Ojibwe reflex of PA *h. In current spoken Potawatomi, both /ʔ/ and /h/ appear, though while /ʔ/ is relatively abundant, /h/ is limited to interjections (with perhaps a few other exceptions).

Hockett characterizes Potawatomi as having six obstruents, which appear in fortis-lenis pairs (perhaps why Hockett was reluctant to classify the glottal stop as an obstruent). I list them here, with the fortis first and lenis second, by place and manner of articulation.

(7) a. Labial stops: /p, b/
b. Alveolar stops: /t, d/
c. Alveolar fricatives: /s, z/
d. Palatal stops: /k, g/
e. Palatal fricatives: /ʃ, ʒ/
f. Affricates: /ʧ, ʤ/

For reasons of space, I do not present examples of every consonant; representative examples are:

(8) *pa·hpiwa 'he laughs' (Costa 1991:376) P bape 's/he laughs' O baapi

(9) *ato·xpoweni 'table' (Bloomfield 1946:91) P dopwen 'table' O adoopowin

(10) *weθkweni 'liver' (Goddard 1991:58) P kwen[2] O okon

(11) *axkyi 'land, soil' (Goddard 1994:194) P ke

(12) *keʔči 'big, much' (Bloomfield 1946) P gche /gəʧə/ O gichi

In Potawatomi, as in Ojibwe, fortis consonants are a reflex of a subset of PA primary consonant clusters, while lenis consonants continue PA consonants. Though Hockett acknowledges the similarity of Potawatomi and Ojibwe phonology and phoneme inventories (PPCA 541–542), he also has several caveats.

On Fortis Stops

Proto-Algonquian had only a voiceless series of stop consonants, so the fact that both Ojibwe and Potawatomi share a fortis/lenis contrast is significant. Hockett notes this fact, but downplays the connection with several observations that can be called into question. First, Hockett notes that "fortis stops are not found in phrase-initial nor in phrase-final" (PPCA 538). He later walks back this claim; after reviewing data from WNALP (the Wisconsin Native American Languages Project), he remarks, "in this case I am more inclined to the simple explanation that [Mary Daniels, a fluent speaker] heard right and I did not" (Hockett 1992:508–509).

On the surface, fortis stops appear both initially and finally. In modern Potawatomi, there is a robust word-final fortition rule (*mtek* 'tree' but *mtegok* 'trees') much like Ojibwe (see also Gathercole 1978:23). So, in fact the opposite of what Hockett said is true in that regard; lenis stops are not found word-finally. Fortis stops are found in initial position in several contexts, some derived but others apparently underlying. In the following examples, word-initial fortis is attested in the following contexts: when an initial vowel is syncopated, as in (13); in cases of regressive/anticipatory assimilation, as in (14); when two lenis consonants come together, as in (15); in loans like (16); and haphazardly elsewhere, as in (17).

(13) P pabwé 's/he adds (sth) to the cooking pot as flavor', O apaabowe 's/he flavors, seasons soup'

(14) P pkan 'different', O bakaan 'different'

(15) P pamadze 's/he travels/lives here and there', O babaamaadizi 's/he travels/lives about'

(16) P pay 'pie', English pie

(17) P papasé 'woodpecker', O baapaase 'woodpecker'

There are a few genuine examples of word-initial fortition like (17). In cases like these, Welcher (1998) and previous researchers consistently report initial lenis consonants, while records from 2010 to the present inconsistently report the quality of the initial consonant.

Second, of the fortis/lenis consonants, Hockett remarks that "in Potawatomi the 'longs' are phonemically segmental phone plus accent, whereas in Ojibwa they are geminates." This criticism can also be discarded in light of more recent work on Ojibwe dialectology. Valentine (1994:122) notes that, in different dialects of Ojibwe, the fortis/lenis distinction surfaces in a number of different ways, including voicing, aspiration, and length. Gathercole's phonetic work shows that length is "a significant articulatory correlate" (1978:22–24) of the fortis/lenis contrast, though he does not report on aspiration or voicing.

Hockett's Objections: Nasals and Glides

Toward the end of PPCA, Hockett raises a few objections against placing Potawatomi under an Ojibwe-Potawatomi subgroup. He notes that Potawatomi, though it resembles Ojibwe in many important ways, also resembles Fox and Shawnee. He notes two specific objections (PPCA 542): "the dropping, without trace, of the nasal of PCA nasal clusters" and "the retention of interconsonantal **yee*." More generally, we now have a much better understanding of the extent of borrowing from Fox to Potawatomi (Costa 2013:204–223), and in this specific case, research after Hockett's revealed both of these noted resemblances are areal features that spread through borrowing (Goddard 1994:196–197, 1973:6).

First, consider the deletion of nasals in nasal clusters. Goddard (1973:6) concludes that "the loss of the nasal must be an areal innovation that spread over languages that were already differentiated" (see also Goddard 1981:280). Note also that, contra Hockett, some dialects of Ojibwe do in fact lose nasals, and they do so in the exact same context as Potawatomi (cf. Valentine 1994:131–132).[3] For example, Potawatomi retains the nasal in the morpheme *-end* 'act by thought on it; perceive it by thought'.

(18) P nmenwéndan 'I like it', O nminwendaan, Nipissing niminwenindaan 'I enjoy it'

This is originally from /enim-d/, as evidenced by the Nipissing variety.

As an aside, there are NC/C doublets; i.e., the Potawatomi data reveals examples where a word with a historical nasal cluster can occur both with and without the nasal. For example, the examples have two different versions of the medial meaning 'face'.

(19) nshkaj**igwé**gabo 's/he stands with a mad face' with expected /-i:gwɛ:-/

(20) nshkaj**ingwé**be 's/he sits with a mad face' with /-i:ngwɛ:-/

This process must have occurred sometime in the 1800s; a brief eighteenth-century Potawatomi vocabulary given by Barton (1798; Costa, personal communication, 2016) shows nasal clusters where Bourassa 50 years later did not find any.

(21) <anung> 'star' (Barton 1798:57) P negos O anang EOj/Ot nangoons (Rhodes 1993), but Bourassa <nug>

(22) <neninch> 'hand' (Barton 1798:41) P nnech O nininj, but Bourassa <onihj>

Next, we consider the glides. The loss of *y following a consonant in Ojibwe is generally seen as a change that diffused from Cree. Goddard (1994:196–197), for example, argues that the word for 'five' "[in Cree] must have been borrowed from Pre-Ojibwa, or Common Ojibwa-Potawatomi, at a time when Cree had lost post-consonantal *y but pre-Ojibwa still retained it." Goddard then gives the following example, one of vanishingly few reconstructed forms of "Common Ojibwa-Potawatomi" (the parent language of both Ojibwe and Potawatomi) in the literature.

(23) PA *nya·θanwi 'five' > Oji-Pot *nya·ran > O naanan, P nyanen

Vowels

Hockett posits a five-vowel system: /a, ɛ, i, o, ə/. In PPCA, he does not allude to a length or strength contrast; in his other work, he argues that all the vowels are STRONG except /o/ (sometimes) and /ə/ (which can strengthen to /ɛ/, /a/, or even /i/ in different morphophonological contexts), which are WEAK. Some sources use the terms LONG and SHORT instead of STRONG and WEAK, aligning with Gathercole (1978:21–22), who showed that the Potawatomi weak vowels are half the duration of the strong vowels. Synchronically, I argue that Potawatomi is actually a six vowel system: /a:, ɛ:, i:, o:, ə, o/. This is essentially Hayes's (1995:221) analysis, based on his interpretation of Hockett's work. This is still an impoverished length contrast (with only roundness contrasting in the short vowels), but less so than Hockett's (and thus less typologically curious).

Several lines of evidence converge to demonstrate that Potawatomi retains a length contrast in the rounded vowels. First, note that some (morpho)phonological rules only target short vowels; long vowels are immune. Hockett's own formulation of the syncope rules (a major focus of his work on Potawatomi) requires recognizing a distinction between /o/ and /o:/ at an underlying level of representation. To put it simply and gloss over the details, Potawatomi constructs iambic feet from left to right. There are three acceptable feet, with the bolded syllable being strong: (weak, **weak**), (weak, **strong**), and (**strong**). As is common in iambic languages, weak (short) vowels in stressed positions undergo vowel lengthening, as do vowels word-finally (see Gathercole 1978:25). Weak vowels in a weak position are reduced, but more often lost entirely.

Consider the following near-minimal pair.

(24) bmosé
/bəmosɛ:-w/
'S/he walks along'

(25) bmodé
/bəmo:dɛ:-w/
'S/he crawls along'

(26) mbemsé
/nə-bəmosɛ:/
'I walk along'

(27) mbemodé
/nə-bəmo:dɛ:/
'I crawl along'

In (26) and (27), the rounded vowel is in a metrically weak position; the addition of the person prefix has triggered its deletion in (26), but it remains in (27). Because weak vowels lengthen in a strong position, the distinction is neutralized on the surface, but it remains at an underlying level of representation.

As another example, short vowels at the end of animate intransitive verb stems are deleted by apocope, even if they occupy a strong position. In (28), for instance, the underlying /o/ is in a strong position, but deletes anyway.

(28) nnegem
/nə-nəgəmo/
'I sing' (O ninagam)

(29) ngemo
/nəgəmo-w/
'S/he sings' (O nagamo)

In (30), though, the final /o:/ is not subject to apocope because it is long at an underlying level of representation. If it were short, it would be occupying a metrically weak position (and thus vulnerable to deletion by syncope in addition to apocope).

(30) mbembeto
/nə-bəməbəto:/
'I run along' (O nibimibatoo/nimbimibatoo)

(31) bmepto
/bəməbəto:-w/
'S/he runs' (O bimibatoo)

Evidence for a Pre-Potawatomi Vowel System

Regardless of the analysis of the synchronic vowel system, there is evidence that the Pre-Potawatomi vowel system would have had seven vowels, exactly as attested in modern Ojibwe: *a·, *e·, *i·, *o·, a, i, o. Here I discuss four sources of evidence for this: two cases of irregular inflectional facts, palatalization, and older records of Potawatomi.

Irregular noun and verb inflections run rampant in Potawatomi; these provide hints of the older vowel system. In the following example, we would describe the synchronic pattern as /ə/ alternating with /i:/ in the first person possessive.

(32) nene 'man' (O inini)

(33) ndennim 'my man' (O indininiim)

In Ojibwe, which is generally the more conservative variety, the addition of the possessive suffix triggers a straightforward vowel lengthening rule. However, in Potawatomi, short /i/ merged with the other short vowels to erase that distinction, rendering the synchronic rule more opaque.

Another inflectional irregularity showing the older system involves transitive inanimate verb inflection; first person forms show a long /a:/ while conjunct forms show /ə/ in the same position.

(34) P nwagnan 'I bend it (by hand)' /nə-wa:g-ən-əm-n/

(35) O niwaaginaan /ni-wa:g-in-am-n/

(36) P wagnek 'that s/he bends it (by hand)' /wa:g-ən-əm-k/

(37) O waaginang /wa:g-in-am-g/

Again, in Ojibwe, this is a straightforward compensatory lengthening rule. In Potawatomi, because of the change in the Potawatomi vowel system, it looks like suppletion.

Palatalization can show that PA *i and *e merged in Ojibwe, because in the modern language some cases of short /i/ trigger palatalization while others fail to (cf. Valentine 2001:88, 338). The Potawatomi facts mirror the pattern in Ojibwe, but because of the additional subsequent vowel mergers, the case is less clear. Still, consider the following cases of palatalization in primary derivation. In each pair of examples, in the first one /ə/ triggers palatalization, while in the second, it does not (the initial and vowel providing the palatalizing environment are bolded).

(38) zhenkazo
/əNənəka:zo/
'it (an.) is named thus' (O izhinikaazo)

(39) netagwet
/əNəta:gwəd/
'it (in.) sounds a certain way' (O initaagod 'it (in.) is heard, understood a certain way')

(40) wzhegé
/**oN**ə.gɛ:/
's/he builds a house' (O ozhige)

(41) ndewnekwna
/ . . . **oN**ə**kon** . . . /
'I carve it (an.)' (O indoonikonaa 'I cut it (an.) to shape')

(42) najmijmé
/**na:d**-ə-mi:jəm-ɛ:/
's/he shops for groceries' (O naajimiijime 's/he goes to get food')

(43) nnaden
/nə**na:d**ən/
'I fetch it (in.)' (O ninaadin)

In each case, modern Potawatomi /ə/ corresponds to Ojibwe /i/. The same logic that points toward the Ojibwe merger of PA *i and *e can be extended to Potawatomi.

Finally, note that older records of Potawatomi provide evidence of older pronunciations and a vowel system that is no longer in existence. The following examples from Bourassa (1843) are typical.

(44) <onihj> 'hand' (modern P wnech 'his hand', O oninj)

(45) <odib> 'head' (modern P wdep 'his head', O ondib)

(46) <onug gizh> 'guts' (modern P wnegesh 'his guts', O onagizh)

In these examples, those cases of modern Potawatomi /ə/ that correlate with Ojibwe /i/ are recorded with <ih> or <i>, while the cases of modern Potawatomi /ə/ that correlate with Ojibwe /a/ are recorded as <u>. Note that this pattern is not completely consistent in the older materials, probably reflecting the shifting nature of the pronunciation of the short vowels that ultimately led to their loss in Potawatomi. However, instrumental phonetic work on Potawatomi vowels in all their contexts is overdue.

Inflection

For over a hundred years, the inflectional facts have been used as a strong argument in support of an Ojibwe-Potawatomi subgroup. After reviewing Gailland's manuscripts, Truman Michelson reaffirmed his earlier stance (1912:262, 267 et passim) that "Potawatomi belonged to the Ojibwa group" (1915:450). His overview remains the core of the argument that Potawatomi and Ojibwe form a subgroup. The evidence that convinced him is summarized (for reasons of space), following Michelson (1915:451–452):

(47) negative in the independent mode is formed with a *-ssi* suffix (cf. Goddard 2006)

(48) sibilant is retained before *p*

(49) inflectional morphology (summarized below)

To Michelson, the similarity of Ojibwe and Potawatomi inflectional morphology was "decisive," and "thus far the most satisfactory classificatory criteria."

Note that Michelson's reasoning in this case seems prescient, but in other cases led him astray. Based also on the negative, for example, he argued that Peoria also "belongs to the Ojibwa group" (Michelson 1912:270) though "somewhat removed" (Michelson 1915:450). This is no longer thought to be the case. Also, the retention of sibilants before bilabial stops is not sufficient; Bloomfield's work a decade later and his later work would clarify Algonquian primary clusters.

Hockett characterizes Michelson (1912) as arguing "that Potawatomi is simply a divergent Ojibwa dialect." He rejects this characterization, claiming to have demonstrated that the two are separate languages, though "Potawatomi is closer to Ojibwa than any other language now spoken." Hockett does not publish a serious comparison of Potawatomi and Ojibwe inflectional morphology, mentioning inflection only briefly in his comparative works. Still, Hockett recognizes inflectional morphology as one of the ways that Potawatomi "resembles" Ojibwe (PPCA 541–542). He marks three specifically:

(50) a. "the endings of the independent mode of transitive verbs"
b. "the development of the dubitative mode"
c. "the development of a second obviative by superadding the obviative suffix to the form which already has it"

The latter two "resemblances" are unimportant. In and of itself, the development of a dubitative mode would be convincing evidence if it were unique to Ojibwe and Potawatomi, but Bloomfield (1946:99) notes the existence of a dubitative mode also in Cree and Fox. The "further obviative" or "second obviative" Hockett sees in Potawatomi probably never existed (see Buszard 2003:157–158).

The first resemblance Hockett notes, however, deserves a principled explanation, which Hockett does not provide. As noted earlier, Michelson (1915—which Hockett does not cite) had already made the connection between Ojibwe and Potawatomi transitive verb inflection. While for Michelson this was "decisive," for Hockett it receives only a brief mention. In a footnote to a later work, Hockett would walk back his argument that Potawatomi is a separate language that ought not be grouped with Ojibwe (Hockett 1992:507 n.10). Here, Hockett clarified that his hesitation was primarily due to the Potawatomi treatment of nasals in nasal clusters (dealt with in the previous section) and acknowledged the significance of the inflectional facts.

Since Hockett's work made Potawatomi more accessible to scholars, authors have noted the deep inflectional similarities between Potawatomi and various dialects of Ojibwe (Costa 2013:197–198 and sources cited there; Valentine 1994:329).

(51)
a. Second person plural suffix on intransitive verbs (*-m*)
b. First person plural suffix on transitive verbs with inanimate objects (*-min/-mən*)
c. First person plural suffix on verbs with second person subject (*-min/-mən*)
d. Suffix on verbs meaning "we do something to you" (*-nimin, -inmin/-ənəmən*)[4]
e. Lack of separate suffix for obviative plural
f. Suffix on conjunct verbs meaning "he does something to us (excl.)" contains *m*[5]
g Unique pejorative suffixes (*-sh/-sh*)
h. Unique form of the imperative (*-ish/-əsh*)

Conclusion

Most experts, both linguists and native speakers, already consider Potawatomi and the dialects of Ojibwe to be sister languages, forming a genetic subgroup. In this paper, I have shown why that is the case: Hockett's objections to this idea were entirely phonological, and research since his time has shown that his objections can be safely ignored. But most important, after controlling for these sound changes, Potawatomi and Ojibwe can be shown to have a largely shared vocabulary as well as important, unique inflections seen nowhere else in the family. This is emphatically not to say that Potawatomi is a dialect of Ojibwe; rather, as Goddard showed in 1994, there existed a "Common Ojibwa-Potawatomi" (196–197) language that both Ojibwe and Potawatomi descend from.

NOTES

1. Thanks to Monica Macaulay, David Costa, Lindsay Marean, Thomas Loftis, Bill Daniels Jr., Jim Thunder, two anonymous reviewers, and innumerable others. Needless to say, any errors are solely mine. This material is based upon work supported by the National Science Foundation under Grants No. 1562774 and 1263888. Forms with an asterisk denote a reconstructed form. Abbreviations used in this paper include: EOj = Eastern Ojibwe, F = Fox (Meskwaki), sometimes used as a cover term for Sauk-Fox-Kickapoo, LBW = form citing Laura Welcher's data, M = Menominee, O = Ojibwe, Ot = Ottawa, P = Potawatomi, PA = Proto-Algonquian, PCA = Proto Central Algonquian, PPCA = The Position of Potawatomi in Central Algonquian (Hockett 1943). All Ojibwe data is from the *Ojibwe People's Dictionary* (2015) and all Fox data from Goddard and Thomason (2014) unless otherwise noted.
2. *kwen* 'liver' is one of a number of dependent body part nouns that have become independent. Older records show the formerly obligatory person prefix and /o/ in the second syllable (Bourassa <okon>, LBW wkon).
3. Hockett notes this in his review of Nichols 1988 (Hockett 1992:510).
4. The Ojibwe forms given here are from Odawa (Valentine 2001:287).
5. Compare Potawatomi *-eymet* (Welcher 1998; Hockett 1948c:148) with Ojibwe *-iyamingid* (Valentine 2001:295).

REFERENCES

Barton, Benjamin Smith. 1798. *New Views of the Origin of the Tribes and Nations of America.* Philadelphia: John Bioren.

Bloomfield, Leonard. 1924. On the Sound System of Central Algonkian. *Language* 1:130–156.

———. 1946. Algonquian. *Linguistic Structures of Native America,* ed. by Cornelius Osgood and Harry Hoijer, pp. 85–129. Viking Fund Publications in Anthropology, vol. 6. New York.

Bourassa, Joseph. 1843. A Vocabulary of the Po-da-wahd-mih Language. Manuscript, Smithsonian Institution.

Buszard, Laura Ann. 2003. Constructional Polysemy and Mental Spaces in Potawatomi

Discourse. PhD thesis, University of California, Berkeley.

Costa, David. 1991. The Historical Phonology of Miami-Illinois Consonants. *International Journal of American Linguistics* 57(3):365–393.

———. 2013. Borrowing in Southern Great Lakes Algonquian and the History of Potawatomi. *Anthropological Linguistics* 55(3):195–233.

Gathercole, Geoff. 1978. Instrumental Phonetic Studies and Linguistic Analysis: The Case of Kansas Potawatomi. *Kansas Working Papers in Linguistics* 3:20–33.

Goddard, Ives. 1973. Proto-Algonquian *nl and *nθ. *International Journal of American Linguistics* 39(1):1–6.

———. 1981. Against the Linguistic Evidence Claimed for Some Algonquian Dialectal Relationships. *Anthropological Linguistics* 23(7):271–297.

———. 1991. Algonquian Linguistic Change and Reconstruction. *Patterns of Change, Change in Patterns: Linguistic Change and Reconstruction Methodology*, ed. by Philip Baldi, pp. 99–114. Berlin: Mouton de Gruyter.

———. 1994. The West-to-East Cline in Algonquian Dialectology. *Papers of the Twenty-Fifth Algonquian Conference*, ed. by William Cowan, pp. 187–211. Ottawa: Carleton University.

———. 2006. The Proto-Algonquian Negative and Its Descendants. *Papers of the Thirty-Seventh Algonquian Conference*, ed. by H.C. Wolfart, pp. 161–208. Winnipeg: University of Manitoba.

Goddard, Ives and Lucy Thomason. 2014. *A Meskwaki-English and English-Meskwaki Dictionary Based on Early Twentieth-Century Writings by Native Speakers.* Petoskey, MI: Mundart Press.

Hayes, Bruce. 1995. *Metrical Stress Theory: Principles and Case Studies*. Chicago: University of Chicago Press.

Hockett, Charles F. 1939. The Potawatomi Language. PhD thesis, Yale University.

———. 1943. The Position of Potawatomi in Central Algonkian. *Papers of the Michigan Academy of Science, Arts, and Letters* 38:537–542 (for 1942).

———. 1948a. Potawatomi I: Phonemics, Morphophonemics, and Morphological Survey. *International Journal of American Linguistics* 14(1):1–10.

———. 1948b. Potawatomi II: Derivation, Personal Prefixes, and Nouns. *International Journal of American Linguistics* 14(2):63–73.

———. 1948c. Potawatomi III: The Verb Complex. *International Journal of American Linguistics* 14(3):139–149.

———. 1948d. Potawatomi IV: Particles and Sample Texts. *International Journal of American Linguistics* 14(4):213–225.

———. 1992. Review of *An Ojibwe Text Anthology* (John Nichols, ed.). *International Journal of*

American Linguistics 58(4):502–512.

Michelson, Truman. 1912. Preliminary Report on the Linguistic Classification of Algonquian Tribes. Twenty-Eighth Annual Report of the Bureau of American Ethnologists. Washington, DC: Smithsonian Institution.

———. 1915. The Linguistic Classification of Potawatomi. *Proceedings of the National Science Academy of the United States of America* 1(8):450–452.

Nichols, John D. (ed.). 2015. *Ojibwe People's Dictionary*. http://ojibwe.lib.umn.edu/.

Nichols, John, Billy Daniels, Mary Daniels, Ramona Sandoval, Roger Philbrick, and Mabel Deverney. 1981. *Potawatomi Language Manual: Resource Materials and Training Exercises.* Milwaukee: Bureau for Special Education Programming, Division for Instructional Services, Wisconsin Department of Public Instruction.

Oxford, Will. 2015. Patterns of Contrast in Phonological Change: Evidence from Algonquian Vowel Systems. *Language* 91(2):308–357.

Rhodes, Richard A. 1993. *Eastern Ojibwa-Chippewa-Ottawa Dictionary*. Berlin: Mouton de Gruyter.

Valentine, J. Randolph. 1994. Ojibwe Dialect Relationships. PhD thesis, University of Texas at Austin.

———. 2001. *Nishnaabemwin Reference Grammar*. Toronto: University of Toronto Press.

Welcher, Laura. 1998. Topics in Potawatomi Grammar. Manuscript, University of California, Berkeley.

The Status of Classifying Morphemes in Ojibwe

Cherry Meyer

In Ojibwe, certain morphemes are said to have a classifying function (Baraga 1878:311–314; Valentine 2001:572, 883–884), i.e., they denote a specific property of a referent.[1] Their position in the word structure is as medials, and their semantic parameters are based on physical properties including shape, e.g., *-minag* 'round'; material, e.g. *-aabik* 'mineral'; inherent nature, e.g., *-oonag* 'boat, vessel'; arrangement, e.g., *-wewaan* 'pair'; and quanta, e.g., *-naagaans* 'cupful'; or possibly a combination of these such as shape and material, e.g., *-aatig* 'stick, wooden pole'. The same classifying morphemes may occur in multiple environments, including numerals (1), verbs (2), and nouns (3).[2]

(1) Classifying morphemes in numeral

a. ningodw-aabik
one-mineral.CL
'one metal/glass/stone (object)'

b. ningodw-eg
one-cloth.CL
'one cloth (object)'

(2) Classifying morphemes in verb

a. ginw-aabik-ad
long-mineral.CL-be.VII
'IN (metal/stone/glass object) is long'

b. ginw-eg-ad
long-cloth.CL-be. VII
'IN (cloth object) is long'

(3) Classifying morphemes in noun

a. waasechigan-aabik
window-mineral.CL
'window pane'

b. waasechigan-iig-in
window-cloth.CL-NOM
'curtain'

However, it is not necessarily the case that these morphemes serve as classifiers proper in all environments. I argue that classifying morphemes occurring in numerals and verbs are classifiers, thus Ojibwe may be labeled a multiple classifier language (Aikhenvald 2000:205). In contrast, these morphemes are not classifiers when occurring in nouns; rather, they are simply lexical morphemes.

The data for this study come from the Southwestern, Eastern, and Odawa dialects, as found in Valentine's *Nishnaabemwin Reference Grammar* (2001) and the online *Ojibwe People's Dictionary* (OPD). I first provide a general definition of classifiers and a description of the numeral and verbal classifiers found in Ojibwe, before moving on to the question of how to label these morphemes as they occur in nouns. Three potential labels for classifying morphemes in nouns are explored, including noun classifiers, class terms, and lexical morphemes.

Defining Classifiers

Classifiers may be described as free or bound morphemes denoting a particular property of the referent of a nominal that occur in specifiable morphosyntactic units (Aikhenvald 2000:13). They usually have a clear lexical origin (Grinevald 2000:61). Classifiers individuate, i.e., to make countable a noun that is unspecified for shape (aka mass, ensemble, or concept nouns; see Rijkhoff 1991, 2010; Dik 1989:123), or to highlight some particular aspect of a referent, supplementing nouns with highly generalized meanings. This allows a structured mechanism, based on the available classifier semantics, to avoid enlarging the lexicon. This derivational use is illustrated in (4) with an example of numeral classifiers from Yucatec Maya (Lucy 2000:329).

TABLE 1. Degrees of grammaticalization between noun categorization systems

GENDER–NOUN CLASS SYSTEMS	CLASSIFIER SYSTEMS
Classify all nouns	Do not classify all nouns
Noun belongs to single gender/class	Noun may occur w/multiple classifiers
Obligatory	Potentially dependent on discourse factors
Smaller inventory (of values/classes)	Larger inventory (of classifiers)
Closed system	Open system
May be marked on noun	Not affixed to noun
Realized in agreement patterns	Marked once

Adapted from Grinevald 2000:62.

(4) Derivational Use of Numeral Classifiers with Single Noun

a. 'un-tz'íit há'as
one-1.dimensional.CL banana
'one banana fruit'

b. 'un-wáal há'as
one-2.dimensional.CL banana
'one banana leaf'

c. 'un-kúul há'as
one-planted.CL banana
'one banana tree'

The last portion of this definition referring to "specifiable morphosyntactic units" is important because the current classifier typology relies on identifying the locus of classifiers. They may occur within the noun phrase, e.g., numeral classifiers and noun classifiers, or outside of it, e.g., verbal classifiers. Some languages even have distinct sets of classifiers that occur in separate areas of the clause.

Classifiers form a system of nominal classification that is distinguished from gender and noun classes in that grammaticalization remains incomplete (Grinevald 2000:61). For illustration, some of the PROTOTYPICAL differences are shown in Table 1, though we should keep in mind that there is a certain amount of variation for certain characteristics across classifier languages.

Now that a general understanding of classifiers has been established, the next section offers a more detailed account of the Ojibwe classifying morphemes as they occur in numerals and verbs. It is shown that the data align with current definitions of numeral and verbal classifiers.

Ojibwe Classifiers

Numeral Classifiers

Numeral classifiers occur in contexts of quantification (Aikhenvald 2000:98). In Ojibwe, classifying morphemes are suffixed to numeral roots to create a classifier-specific numeral (Valentine 2001:883), meeting the criterion for numeral classifiers.

(5) Numeral Classifiers

a.	ningodw-aatig one-stick/wooden/pole.CL	b.	ningodw-eg one-cloth.CL
c.	ningodw-aabik one-mineral.CL	d.	ningodw-aabiig one-string/row.CL
e.	ningodw-minag one-round.CL	f.	ningodw-oonag one-boat/canoe/vessel.CL
g.	ningodw-ewaan one-pair.CL	h.	ningodo-zid one-foot.CL
i.	ningodo-naagaans one-cupful.CL	j.	ningod-ooshkin one-bagful/pailful.CL

(Baraga 1878:311–314; Rhodes 1985; Valentine 2001:883–884)

The following textual examples show the use of numeral classifiers with overt nouns.[3] Valentine (2001:572) remarks that the use of the wooden classifier in (6), translated as 'bottle', evokes the past use of wooden containers to store liquor.

(6)

Mii	dash	iw	niibwa	gii-nangdaaso,	bezhig	baashkzigan
And	so	that.IN.SG	lots	PST-charge.VAI.IND.3SG	one	rifle.IN.SG

miinwaa	**bezhgw-aatig**	**wiishkii** . . .
and	one-wooden.CL	whiskey

'And he charged a lot, one gun and one bottle of whiskey . . . ' (Nichols 1988:95)

(7)

. . . miinwaa	**ngodw-ewaan**	wgii-miinaan	**niw**	**mkiznan**.
and	one-pair.CL	3.PST-give.VTA.IND.3'	those.IN.PL	shoe.IN.PL

'. . . and she gave her one pair of shoes.' (Valentine 2001:884(56))

In her classifier typology, Aikhenvald (2000:99) states that the existence of numeral classifiers in a language "presupposes that numerals are a special word class." This is in contrast to languages that have an extremely small inventory of numbers, perhaps limited to 'one', 'two', 'three', and 'many'. Ojibwe has an extensive inventory of numerals, certainly garnering designation as a special class. Baraga (1878:306) identifies no less than five distinct types of numerals, including, among others, distributive and multiplicative types. Given the large inventory of numerals and the ability of classifying morphemes in numerals to occur with overt nouns, it is appropriate to apply the label of numeral classifier to classifying morphemes in this environment.

Verbal Classifiers

Verbal classifiers occur in verbs and categorize a property of the referent of one of its arguments. In Ojibwe, either the subject of an intransitive or the (first or second) object of a transitive verb is categorized (Denny 1978).[4]

It is necessary to clarify which type of verbal classifiers are found most commonly in Ojibwe, as they have been mislabeled in the recent literature. Aikhenvald (2000:149–171) distinguishes three types of verbal classifiers: classificatory noun incorporation, classificatory verbal affixes, and suppletive classificatory verbs. Verbal classifiers in Ojibwe are erroneously labeled (Aikhenvald 2000:154–155) as suppletive classificatory verbs based on Denny's (1979:106–107) discussion, when they should be labeled as classificatory verbal affixes for several reasons. First and most important, it is the choice of the classifying morpheme and not the verb root that is determined by properties of the nominal referent. This is illustrated with the root /*gizh-*/ 'hot', which can optionally take a classifier with no suppletion.

(8) a. **gizh**-izan
hot-act.on.it.by.heat.VTI
'heat it'

b. **gizh**-aabik-izan
hot-mineral.CL-act.on.it.by.heat.VTI
'heat it (mineral)'

Second, as noted by Conathan (2004:23–24), the label of suppletive classificatory verbs misses the fact that the classifying morphemes are the same in numerals as in verbs. Last, there are several examples of suppletive classificatory verbs in Ojibwe. Rhodes (1981) notes that certain verbs of breaking are associated with specific classes of objects, e.g., the stem /*bookw-*/ with two-dimensional objects, and /*baashk-*/ with three-dimensional objects.[5] Examples include VTI *bookbidoon* 'break X (of sticks)' and VTI *baashka'an* 'break open X with something (of something three-dimensional)'. Note that these do not include any discernible classifiers.

(9) Ojibwe suppletive classificatory verbs

a. book-bid-oon
break-use.hands.on.it-VTI
'break it using the hands (of sticks)' (Valentine 2001:440)[6]

b. baashk-a'-an
break.open-with.tool/medium-VTI
'break open X using something (of something three-dimensional)'
(Nichols and Nyholm 1995:29)

There are various kinds of verbs that classifiers may occur with, including verbs of counting (Valentine 2001:883–886), attributive verbs (Valentine 2001:342–347), verbs of physical location and motion (Valentine 2001:347–348), goal focus verbs (Valentine 2001:349–354), causatives (Valentine 2001:433–442), and benefactives (Valentine 2001:463–465). Examples (10) and (11) show verbal classifiers co-occurring with overt nouns.

(10)

Ikw-**eg**-in-an	iwe	gibiiga'igan.
higher-cloth.CL-act.on.it.by.hand.VTI-2.SG>0.IMP	that.INAN.SG	curtain.INAN.SG

'Put the curtain up out of the way.' (OPD)

Example (11) is particularly interesting because it shows repetition of the same classifying morpheme, /-aabik-/, in the verb and the noun.

(11)

150 degrees piit-**aabk**-ibdoon	**gzhaabkizgan** . . .
150 degrees to.a.certain.degree-mineral.CL-VTI.2SG>0SG	stove. INAN.SG

'Set the stove to 150 degrees . . . ' (Valentine 2001:898)

So far, it has been shown that there are clearly numeral and verbal classifiers in Ojibwe. Numeral classifiers occur suffixed to numerals. The same morphemes occur in verbs, as classificatory verbal affixes. What is less obvious, and the topic of the next section, is the status of these classifying morphemes when they occur inside of nouns.

How to Label Ojibwe Classifying Morphemes in Nouns

As seen in (11), the same classifying morphemes found in numerals and verbs can also occur in nouns, illustrated with further examples:

(12) a. waasechgan-**iig**-in
window-cloth-NOM
'curtain'

b. waasechgan-**aabik**
window-glass
'window pane'

(13) kikw-**aabik**
kettle-mineral
'tin can' (Valentine 2001:499)

(14) ookwe-**min**
maggot-berry
'black cherry'

(15) naba**gisag**-o-jiimaan[7]
board-linking.vowel-boat
'wooden boat'

(16) mazin-**aabik**-iwebin-igan
figured.image-mineral-fling.by.hand-NOM
'typewriter, computer'

In contrast to numeral and verbal classifiers, the definitions of which seem relatively straightforward, the label of noun classifier is not as easily applied to these morphemes. I examine three potential labels for these classifying morphemes occurring in nouns: noun classifiers, class terms, and lexical morphemes.

Noun Classifiers

Noun classifiers characterize the noun and co-occur with it in the noun phrase. They are distinguished from other types of classifiers in that they occur independently of other operations such as quantification or possession (Grinevald 2000:64). They have been most thoroughly documented in Australian (Dixon 1982) and Mesoamerican languages (Craig 1986, 1992).

Selection of a particular noun classifier is dependent on semantics; the same noun may often be used with different noun classifiers in order to highlight certain properties of the referent of the noun, effecting a change in meaning as shown in example (17) from Murrinhpatha (Southern Daly family of Australia).

(17) Noun Classifiers in Murrinhpatha

a.	nanthi kamarl	b.	kura kamarl
	generic.CL eye		aquatic.CL eye
	'eye/face'		'water hole'
c.	kardu kamarl	d.	mi kamarl
	human.CL eye		vegetable.CL eye
	'sweetheart'		'seed'

(Walsh 1997:275, as cited in Aikhenvald 2000:84)

Crucially, in all languages attested to have noun classifiers, the noun classifier is a free morpheme, not a bound one (Grinevald 2000:64). Further, the relationship between the noun classifier and the noun is usually one of generic-specific, where the classifier signals a more general category of which the noun is a member. This description of noun classifiers does not fit the use of classifying morphemes in Ojibwe nouns.

Class Terms

Class terms are derivational components that function as the head of compounds that are exemplars of the category labeled by the class term (Haas 1964; DeLancey 1986:438). Class terms may be semantically akin to noun classifiers, but crucially, they are limited to a small number of semantic fields in a language, such as flora and fauna. Class terms may occur in languages with and without classifiers, and they have at times been mislabeled as classifiers (Grinevald 2000:62). Indeed,

Grinevald applies the label of class terms to English because it is unsatisfying to label it a classifier language given the limited number of cases. She gives the following examples of the English class terms '-berry' and 'tree'.

(18) English Plant-Based Class Terms
   a. *strawberry, blueberry, raspberry, boysenberry, gooseberry, marionberry,* etc.
   b. *apple tree, banana tree, orange tree, cherry tree, olive tree, palm tree,* etc.
   (Grinevald 2000:59–60)

Another common semantic field is that of occupations, using class terms such as 'man', 'woman', or the gender-neutral 'person' or 'member.'

(19) English Occupation-Based Class Terms
   a. *milkman, clergyman, chairman*
   b. *business woman, cleaning woman, chairwoman*
   c. *spokesperson, salesperson, band member, service member*

Similar class terms may be found in Ojibwe with compounds formed using *inini* 'man' and *ikwe* 'woman'.

(20) Ojibwe Class Terms
   a. *mandaag**nini*** 'gentleman'
   b. *mandaag**kwe*** 'lady'
   (called "compound sets" by Valentine 2001:521–522)

The relation between class terms and classifiers is a close one, as class terms may serve as a source for new classifiers in a language. In the Tai family of languages, class terms and noun classifiers coexist (DeLancey 1986). Class terms are described as being halfway between classifiers and nouns based on their syntactic and semantic behavior (DeLancey 1986:438–440).[8] Further complicating the distinction between classifiers and class terms is the fact that, like classifiers, class terms may occasionally be omitted.

(21) a. duaŋ-taa
round/light.source.CT-eye
'eye'
(Thai; DeLancey 1986:441)

b. taa
eye
'eye'

Recall the earlier comparison in Figure 1 between gender/noun classes and classifiers—gender and noun classes are more grammaticalized systems of noun categorization, while classifiers are more lexicalized. Class terms are even more lexical in nature. This is illustrated in Figure 1.

FIGURE 1. Lexico-grammatical scale of noun categorization systems

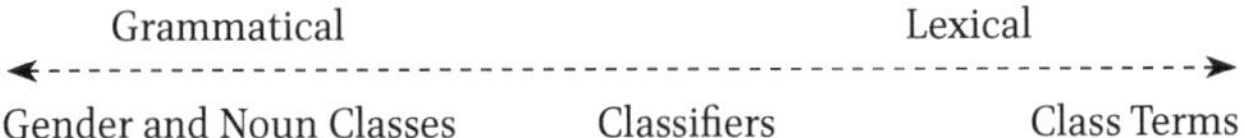

Adapted from Grinevald 2000:61.

Our next potential label for classifying morphemes in Ojibwe nouns is lexical morphemes. They are so far to the lexical end of this continuum that they do not appear on it, since their semantic and syntactic principles of organization are too broad to allow any useful characterization.

Lexical Morphemes

Lexical morphemes, also called content morphemes, are free or bound morphemes that have concrete, semantic content. In languages with lower morpheme-per-word ratios, such as English, many lexical morphemes are free, but in polysynthetic languages, the same lexical concepts may be represented as bound morphemes. For illustration, several concrete noun finals from Ojibwe are given in (22), along with their counterpart free morpheme English translations.

(22) /-gamigw/ 'building'

a. *aakozii-wigamig*
be.sick.VAI-building
'hospital'

b. *odaabanii-wigamig*
vehicle-building
'garage'

TABLE 2. Comparison of classifying morphemes' characteristics in Ojibwe nouns with class terms and lexical morphemes

CHARACTERISTIC	OJIBWE	LEXICAL MORPHEME	CLASS TERM	MATCH
free morpheme	no	yes/no	no	LM/CT
obligatory	yes	yes	no	LM
cover large semantic inventory	yes	yes	no	LM
always head of compound noun	no	no	yes	LM

(23) /-aboo/ 'liquid'

a. *mandaamin-aaboo*
corn-liquid
'corn soup'

b. *giziibiig-inaagan-e-waaboo*
wash-dish-VAI-liquid
'dish soap'

Having previously eliminated noun classifiers as a potential label for classifying morphemes in nouns of Ojibwe, the next section compares the remaining labels of class term and lexical morpheme.

Comparison

The first column of Table 2 offers several diagnostics for comparing the behavior of classifying morphemes in Ojibwe nouns to lexical morphemes and class terms. The last column identifies which label matches the given characteristic in Ojibwe.

In Ojibwe nouns, the classifying morphemes are bound, obligatory, cover a large semantic inventory, and do not always serve as the head of the noun. Concerning the second diagnostic of obligatoriness, it can be demonstrated that the meaning of a noun changes when the classifying morpheme is omitted, if the omission results in an acceptable noun. Consider again the noun given in (12a), repeated here as (24a). If the classifying morpheme /-iig/ is removed, as in (24b), the outcome is a noun with a different meaning. This is unlike the behavior shown by class terms in Thai in (21).

(24) a. waasechgan-**iig**-in
window-cloth-NOM
'curtain'

b. waasechgan
window
'window'

Likewise, recall that class terms always serve as heads of the compound nouns in which they occur. Example (15), repeated here as (25), is a compound noun for a type of boat, not a type of wood. Thus, the classifying morpheme *isag* 'wood' is not the head of the compound, and its behavior is unlike that of class terms.

(25) naba**gisag**-o-jiimaan
board-linking.vowel-boat
'wooden boat'

Conclusion

It appears that "lexical morpheme," or the more commonly used "classifying morpheme," is the most appropriate label for morphemes occurring in Ojibwe nouns that serve as classifiers proper in numerals and verbs. However, care should be taken in the description to avoid confusion with noun classifiers by language teachers, learners, and linguists alike. More work is needed to understand the diachronic relationship between these morphemes as they occur in different parts of the clause. Additionally, more knowledge about the classifier system of Ojibwe as a whole may help inform the shape of classifier typology going forward, as it still a relatively new area of study within noun categorization.

NOTES

1. I would like to thank my adviser, Amy Dahlstrom, for her guidance on this project. All remaining errors are my own.
2. Abbreviations: CL = classifier, CT = class term, IND = independent order, PST = past, VTA = transitive animate verb, VTI = transitive inanimate verb, VII = inanimate intransitive verb, VAI = animate intransitive verb, IN = inanimate noun, AN= animate noun, SG = singular, PL= plural, 2 = second person, 3 = third person, 3' = third person obviative, 0 = inanimate, IMP = imperative, NOM = nominalizer.
3. Algonquian languages allow constituents to be discontinuous around the verb, following certain constraints. See Kathol and Rhodes (1999) for further details.
4. It seems that mensural classifiers of quantity, when functioning as verbal classifiers, appear only in verbs of counting.
5. See Rhodes (1981) for further examples of suppletive classificatory verbs of breaking.

6. Valentine (2000:440) translates *bookbidoon* as 'break in two using the hands', but Rhodes (1981:52) notes that the additional meaning of 'in two' does not necessarily apply when used with inflexible, one-dimensional objects such as sticks.
7. The first component of the compound, *nabagisag*, can be further broken down into the initial *nabag* 'flat', the medial *isag*, and an abstract final /-w/.
8. In Thai, class terms may be distinguished from classifiers based on the word order Class Term–Noun–Classifier–Numeral. The same strategy is possible in Nung with the order Numeral–Classifier–Class Term–Noun (DeLancey 1986:442–443).

REFERENCES

Aikhenvald, Alexandra. 2000. *Classifiers: A Typology of Noun Categorization Devices*. New York: Oxford University Press.

Baraga, Frederic. 1878. *A Theoretical and Practical Grammar of the Otchipwe Language for the Use of Missionaries and Other Persons Living Among the Indians*. Detroit: Jabez Fox.

Conathan, Lisa. 2004. Classifiers in Yurok, Wiyot, and Algonquian. *Annual Meeting of the Berkeley Linguistics Society* 30(2):22–33.

Craig, Colette G. 1986. Jacaltec Noun Classifiers: A Study in Language and Culture. *Noun Classes and Categorization: Proceedings of a Symposium on Categorization and Noun Classification, Eugene, Oregon, October 1983*, ed. by Colette G. Craig, pp. 263–294. Amsterdam: John Benjamins.

———. 1992. Classifiers in a Functional Perspective. *Layered Structure and Reference in a Functional Perspective*, ed. by Michael Fortescue, Peter Harder, and Lars Kristoffersen, pp. 277–301. Amsterdam: John Benjamins.

DeLancey, Scott. 1986. Toward a History of Tai Classifier Systems. *Noun Classes and Categorization* 7:437–452.

Denny, Peter. 1978. The Semantic Roles of Medials within Algonquian Verbs. *International Journal of American Linguistics* 44(2):153–155.

———. 1979. The "Extendedness" Variable in Classifier Semantics: Universal Semantic Features and Cultural Variation. *Ethnolinguistics: Boas, Sapir and Whorf Revisited*, ed. by Madeleine Mathiot, pp. 97–119. The Hague: Mouton.

Dik, Simon. 1989. *The Theory of Functional Grammar, Part 1: The Structure of the Clause*. New York: Foris Publications.

Dixon, Robert. 1982. *Where Have All the Adjectives Gone? And Other Essays in Semantics and Syntax*. Berlin: Mouton.

Grinevald, Colette. 2000. A Morphosyntactic Typology of Classifiers. *Systems of Nominal*

Classification 4:50–92.

Haas, Mary. 1964. *Thai-English Student's Dictionary*. Stanford, CA: Stanford University Press.

Kathol, Andreas and Richard A. Rhodes. 1999. Constituency and Linearization of Ojibwe Nominals. *Proceedings of WSCLA 4*, ed. by Marion Gerda Caldecott, Suzanne C. Gessner, and Eun-Sook Kim, pp 75–91. Vancouver: University of British Columbia.

Lucy, John. 2000. Systems of Nominal Classification: A Concluding Discussion. *Systems of Nominal Classification*, ed. by Gunter Senft, pp. 326–341. Cambridge: Cambridge University Press.

Nichols, John. 1988. *An Ojibwe Text Anthology.* Centre for Research and Teaching of Canadian Native Languages. London, ON: University of Western Ontario.

———. (ed.). 2015. *Ojibwe People's Dictionary.* http://ojibwe.lib.umn.edu/.

Nichols, John D. and Earl Nyholm. 1995. *A Concise Dictionary of Minnesota Ojibwe.* Minneapolis: University of Minnesota Press.

Rijkhoff, Jan. 1991. Nominal Aspect. *Journal of Semantics* 8(4):291–309.

———. 2010. On Flexible and Rigid Nouns. *Parts of Speech: Empirical and Theoretical Advances*, ed. by Umberto Ansaldo, Jan Don, and Roland Pfau, pp. 227–252. Amsterdam: John Benjamins.

Rhodes, Richard A. 1981. On the Semantics of the Ojibwa Verbs of Breaking. *Papers of the Twelfth Algonquian Conference*, ed. by William Cowan, pp. 47–56. Ottawa: Carleton University.

———. 1985. *Eastern Ojibwa-Chippewa-Ottawa Dictionary*, vol. 3. Berlin: Walter de Gruyter.

Valentine, J. Randolph. 2001. *Nishnaabemwin Reference Grammar*. Toronto: University of Toronto Press.

Walsh, Michael. 1997. Noun Classes, Nominal Classification and Generics in Murrinh-Patha. *Nominal Classification in Aboriginal Australia*, ed. by Mark Harvey and Nicholas Reid, pp. 225–292. Amsterdam: John Benjamin.

Pitch and Intensity of Lexical Accent in Blackfoot

Mizuki Miyashita

This article examines the role of the acoustic elements pitch and intensity in Blackfoot word prominence with respect to lexically specified accent.[1] Blackfoot has been called a pitch accent language, and this notion is widely adopted by linguists in general and those who do research on Blackfoot and other Algonquian languages in particular. Though the notion of pitch accent remains controversial (Hyman 2009), I set that aside for present purposes. Blackfoot pitch accent is lexically specified, causing the contrastive status of two identical sound strings at the surface. For example, as shown in (1), the sequences of phonemes in the words 'it is an arrow' and 'it is a fig' are the same, and the only difference is the accent location.[2] This is assumed to result from lexical accent, which is inherently marked (Taylor 1969; Van Der Mark 2003; Kaneko 1999). However, minimal pairs with only an accent location difference, such as those in (1), are extremely rare.[3]

(1) a. ápssi-wa
arrow-3SG 'It is an arrow.'

b. apssí-wa
fig-3SG 'It is a fig.' (Frantz 2009:3)

There are a small number of studies that deal with the prosodic structure in Blackfoot with respect to pitch accents. Kaneko (1999) examines compound words with two lexical stresses in the Optimality Theory framework (Prince and Smolensky 1993; McCarthy and Prince 1993). Weber (2012) looks at accents in nonextensively inflected or derived verbs, also in terms of Optimality Theory. These studies suggest that Blackfoot accent has some predictability. However, there are a number of examples that demonstrate that accents are indeed unpredictable. As shown in (2a–f), an accent often occurs on a light syllable even when a long vowel appears in the same word, indicating that the accents occur regardless of syllable weight. ([2g–i] show that heavy syllables may also be accented.) Also, comparing (2b and 2c) with (2d) or (2a and 2i) with (2f–h) shows that accents occur regardless of position.

(2) a. káyiis — 'dry meat'
b. skinítsimaan — 'bag'
c. saahkómaapi — 'boy'
d. issitsímaan — 'infant'
e. kákanottsstookii — 'horned owl'
f. kiipó — 'ten'
g. poyíí — 'oil'
h. naamóó — 'bee'
i. náámaa — 'gun' (Frantz and Russell 1995)

The current study focuses on how this lexically specified accent is realized in terms of acoustic signals rather than how the accent may be phonologically predicted. This question is motivated by the fact that acoustic study regarding Blackfoot pitch accent is currently minimal and largely based on the impressionistic description provided by Frantz (2009:3) that it consists primarily of a relatively higher pitch than that of contiguous syllables. However, other impressionistic studies make different claims: that it is observed as "a strong expiratory accent" (Uhlenbeck 1938:9) or is indicated by intensity and often co-occurring with higher pitch (Taylor 1969). Thus, there are multiple claims regarding the acoustic status of accent in Blackfoot, and it is unclear whether the lexically marked accent surfaces with higher pitch, intensity, or both.

A response to this question has been attempted by Van Der Mark (2002, 2003), reporting that it is acoustically manifested in higher pitch (perceived F0) and amplitude (or intensity). While her results support the popular view of Blackfoot accent as manifested by pitch, the intensity correlation of prominence is left unexamined. An essential question addressed in this study, thus, is whether both pitch and intensity correlate with accented vowels and, if not, which better represents lexical accent. Under the assumption that pitch accent is an inherent property of a word, it should consistently surface. If intensity also correlates with accent, then this, too, should surface consistently. To pursue an answer to this question, I look for the stability of acoustic correlates in repeated utterances of the same words. If both pitch and intensity consistently appear in repeated utterances of the same word, then both are lexically important factors. If, on the other hand, only one of them shows consistency, then this one may be considered primarily lexical and the other nonlexical. Based on the study presented here, I claim that pitch is the acoustic factor that better represents Blackfoot lexically marked accent.

Methods

The data source I used for this study consists of recordings of two native speakers collected during my phoneme documentation fieldwork in 2013. One speaker is a female from the Kainai Nation in Alberta, Canada, who was in her sixties at the time of the recording session. Her recording was conducted in August in Lethbridge, Alberta, Canada. The other speaker is a male from the Blackfeet nation in Montana who was in his eighties. His recording was made in October in Browning, Montana. The reliability of the speakers' speech was judged by my observation regarding their language experiences. At the time of the recording session, the female speaker was teaching at an elementary school on the Kainai reserve, where she used Blackfoot regularly with students outside of her English writing classes. Prior to this position she had taught the language at a Blackfoot immersion program in Montana for several years. She also uses the language regularly with her family. The male speaker is currently considered the most fluent Blackfoot speaker on the Blackfeet reservation in Montana. He is knowledgeable about the culture and history of the tribe and is a storyteller and traditional singer. Although he does not converse in Blackfoot regularly, as there are very few proficient speakers in Montana, having the knowledge and skills of special styles of speech such as storytelling is a sign of high fluency and proficiency (Tsunoda 2005).

A list of 176 Blackfoot words was prepared for the recording project. The word list included nouns and inflected verbs and was compiled for the purpose of capturing a phoneme inventory, with no intention of conducting a lexical accent study; therefore, there was no bias toward building samples to support either argument examined in this study. The speakers were asked to pronounce given Blackfoot words in isolation, repeating them three times. The female speaker is literate in Blackfoot and gave forms for those written Blackfoot words she felt confident and comfortable about being recorded. As a result, 162 words were recorded from the female speaker. On the other hand, the male speaker is not literate in Blackfoot, and thus English equivalents for the target words were given by the author. As one English expression can be translated in multiple ways in Blackfoot, depending on context, various forms were given for several target words. Due to the speaker's time constraints, 157 words from the prepared list were elicited. However, because the speaker gave multiple forms for several expressions, a total of 175 words were recorded during the session.

Based on the studies by Van Der Mark (2002, 2003) that report that pitch peak and average intensity were acoustic correlates of word prominence, these features were measured for all vowels in all utterances using Praat (Boersma and Weenink 2013). In order to record pitch peak measurements, I also used my own perceptual judgments. This was necessary when Praat indicated the highest pitch on a consonant or the transition point from a consonant to a vowel with no perceived F0. In this case, I played multiple parts of the vowel separately and selected the highest pitch that matched the perceptually highest part of the entire vowel.

Procedure

Recordings of 33 words (13 from the female speaker; 20 from the male speaker) were excluded for observation based on the words not being repeated three times, the presence of glottal fry, or language mixing with English.[4] Therefore, the set of words examined included 149 from the female speaker's speech and 155 from the male speaker's.

I looked at the STABILITY of acoustic correlates in pitch and intensity by examining whether the highest pitch and highest intensity marked the same vowel in repeated utterances of a word. Stability, in this study, is defined as the situation when the highest acoustic correlate (i.e., pitch or intensity) occurs on the same vowel in all three utterances of a word. If both pitch and intensity correlate with accented vowels, then both of them are likely to be lexically important factors. If not, one of them may be primarily lexical and the other nonlexical. Most of examples in the dictionary (Frantz and Russell 1995) and the grammar (Frantz 2009) indicate accents with an acute sign; I used these materials for reference. This method significantly differs from the study previously reported by Van Der Mark (2002, 2003) in which she examined only one utterance per word, meaning that accent stability has not been previously examined. The schematic illustrations in Figure 1 represent this distinction. Each diagram depicts three utterances of the same word containing three vowels. For each utterance, the accented vowel is in bold and the vowel with the highest pitch and/or intensity is circled. The highest pitch is indicated by an association line labeled P and intensity by I. In (A), the highest measured pitch and intensity are both on the accented initial vowel in all three utterances of the word. Therefore, in this case both acoustic correlates are stable. On the other hand, the illustration in (B) describes a case where the highest pitch is repeatedly observed on the initial vowel of the word, but the highest intensity does not consistently show up on the same vowel. In this case, only pitch is stable and intensity is flexible.

FIGURE 1. Schematic illustration of the highest pitch and intensity in a word.

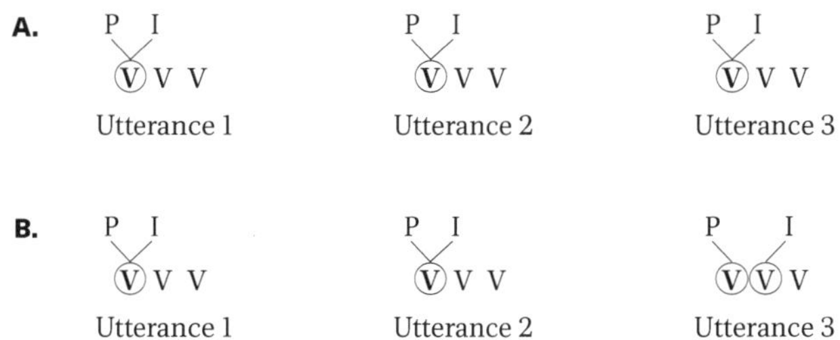

Figure 2 shows tracking lines of pitch (dark) and intensity (gray) of the word áakokaawa 'he will rope,' pronounced by the female speaker. This is an example of both highest pitch and intensity being stable. The last vowel is devoiced, hence this is treated as a word with three vowels (Bliss and Gick 2009). Table 1 provides the values of the same word's pitch and intensity of all vowels in three repeated utterances (U). The highest measurements are in bold; the highest pitch and intensity of the word in all three utterances are both on the first accented vowel.

TABLE 1. Value of pitch and intensity in *áakokaawa* 'he will rope' (female speaker)

PITCH (Hz)				INTENSITY (dB)			
U	V1	V2	V3	U	V1	V2	V3
1	**159.2**	134.9	119.9	1	**66.6**	62.5	60.9
2	**152.8**	129.1	123.2	2	**65.1**	59.1	57.8
3	**147.5**	138.5	106.1	3	**63.2**	61.5	56.2

FIGURE 2. Pitch and intensity of *áakokaawa* 'he will rope' (female speaker).

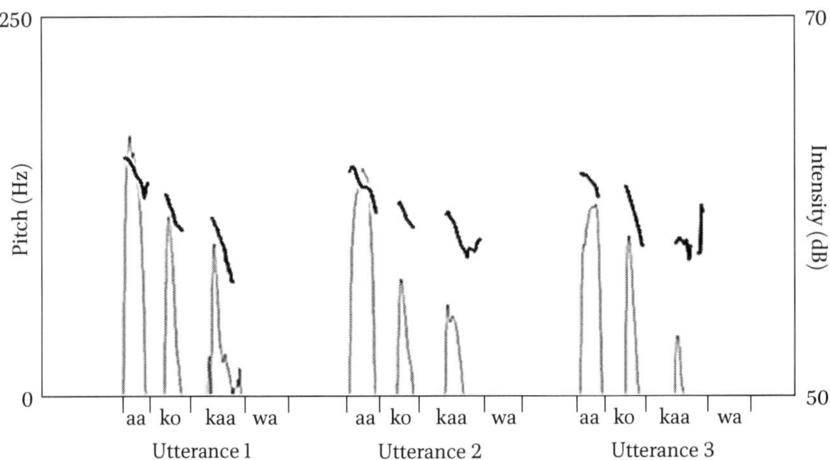

If pitch is the only lexically contributing element, then we would expect to find instances where pitch is observed on the same vowel, but intensity is not. Figure 3 shows this pattern. The highest pitch is observed on the first vowel in all three utterances, while the highest intensity is observed on the first vowel in the first and third utterances and on the second vowel on the second utterance. Table 2 gives the values from the measurements.

TABLE 2. Value of pitch and intensity of *áakaapihkaiwa* 'she will sell it'

PITCH (Hz)				INTENSITY (dB)			
U	V1	V2	V3	U	V1	V2	V3
1	**160.5**	149.2	129.9	1	**68.9**	68.3	60.2
2	**157.5**	145.1	121	2	65.3	**65.6**	57.8
3	**153.2**	139.1	112.6	3	**67.2**	66.8	57.3

FIGURE 3. Pitch and intensity of *áakaapihkaiwa* 'she will sell it' (female speaker).

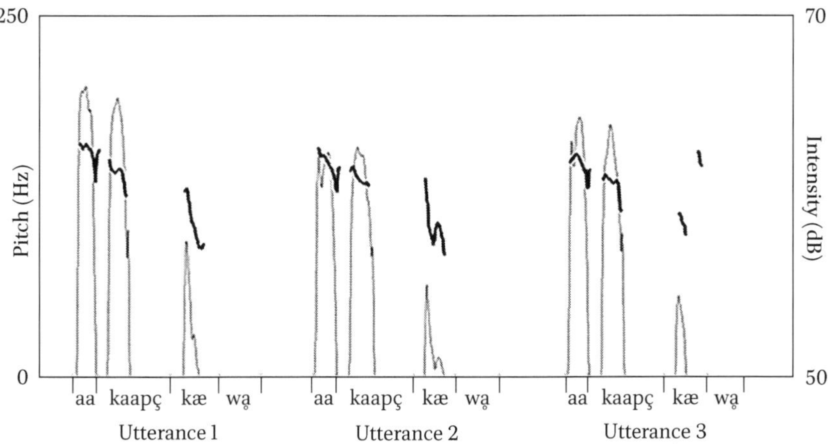

TABLE 3. Ratio of pitch and intensity together matching lexical accent

	WORDS EXAMINED	PITCH & INTENSITY	%
Female	149	97	65.1
Male	155	96	61.9
Total	304	193	63.4

Results

As shown in Table 3, pitch and intensity were both stable in 65.1 percent of words in the female speaker's speech and 61.9 percent in the male speaker's speech.

The correlation between pitch and intensity does not look very strong,

TABLE 4. Ratio of words with pitch matching accented vowel

	WORDS EXAMINED	PITCH	%
Female	149	141	94.6
Male	155	145	93.5
Total	304	286	94

TABLE 5. Ratio of words with intensity matching accented vowel

	WORDS EXAMINED	INTENSITY	%
Female	149	102	68.4
Male	155	99	63.8
Total	304	201	66

suggesting that pitch and intensity do not behave the same way. This fact motivates separate examinations of these acoustic correlates of accented vowels.

Table 4 shows the number of words occurring with stable pitch, regardless of intensity stability. There were 94.6 percent of words with this pattern in the female speaker's pronunciations and 93.5 percent in the male speaker's speech. The converse is shown in Table 5: 68.4 percent of words in the female speaker's speech and 63.8 percent from the male speaker's speech were found to have stable intensity, regardless of pitch stability.

Similar results were found in both speakers' utterances. The highest pitch is considerably more stable than the highest intensity for both speakers. Based on this, pitch seems to better represent lexical accent than intensity.

Discussion

The results showed that pitch is an acoustic correlate of accented vowels. Considering the general assumption that a phonetic element must surface if it is lexically specified (assuming there is no further phonology), it is intriguing that 18 words in the data did not show stability in their highest pitch. If pitch is indeed an authentic lexically marked element, it would be expected to surface at a rate of or close to 100 percent. Though the exceptions in these data are not extensive, they are hard to ignore as they indicate that highest pitch and intensity are sometimes correlated

TABLE 6. Words not demonstrating stable pitch (female speaker)

CITATION FORM	IPA	VOWELS	GLOSS
tsimá	[tsim**á**]	vv́	'where?'
saipohtóót	[sejpxw**tóót**]	vvv́	'take it out!'
ippotóóhtsi	[ippo**tóx**wts]	vvv́	'in the direction of the door'
siksiká	[siksik**á**]	vvv́	'Blackfoot'
napayíni	[napa**jíí**n]	vvv́	'bread'
nottoksííksi	[nottok**síí**ks]	vvv́	'my knees'
ksiksináttsiiwa	[ksiksin**á**ttsiiw]	vvv́v	'white'
iisokóttatsiiwa	[iiso**kó**ttatsiiw]	vvv́vv	'he spit at him'

TABLE 7. Words not demonstrating stable pitch (male speaker)

CITATION FORM	IPA	VOWELS	GLOSS
tsimá	[t^{s}im**á**]	vv́	'where?'
sa'áí	[sa'j**éé**]	vv́	'goose'
oyík	[ʊj**í**k]	vv́	'eat! (pl.)'
oyít	[ʊj**í**t]	vv́	'eat! (sg.)'
saipohtóót	[sejpx^{w}**tóó**t]	vvv́	'take it out!'
napayíni	[napaj**í**n]	vvv́	'bread'
iisowóowa	[iisow**ó**o]	vvv́	'my son ran'
ksiksináttsiiwa	[k^{s}ik^{s}in**áá**tt^{s}ii]	vvv́v	'white'
sopoyáá'paniit	[sopoj**áá**panit]	vvv́vv	'say it correctly!'

and sometimes not correlated. In order to understand this discrepancy, I suggest that there is something else phonological or morphological that is interacting with pitch accent in these 18 examples. Based only on these examples, I propose two interacting factors as possible accounts: pitch contour type and the involvement of an accented affix.

Pitch Contour Type

The list in Table 6 shows all eight words with flexible, or unstable, highest pitch from the female speaker's recording. Likewise, the list in Table 7 shows nine of the ten examples from the male speaker's utterances with unstable pitch. (The remaining word is discussed later.) The 'Vowels' columns show the number of vowels in each word using the symbol "v," with the lexical accent indicated by the acute sign.

None of these examples has a lexical accent on the first vowel. If a word contains only two vowels, the last vowel is accented; if longer, the third vowel is accented. Thus, based on these facts, it appears that when a word has a lexical accent later than the first vowel, there is a tendency to find less stability in the highest pitch.

I suggest that this relates to general differences in pitch ranges among words depending on accent locations. Such differences are shown in the pitch tracks of the two example words in Figure 4: *napayín* 'bread', which showed unstable pitch in both speakers' utterances; and *áakokaawa* 'she will sell it', which had stable pitch in both speakers' utterances.[5] Both words contain three vowels. The pitch peaks of all vowels are indicated by circles. The two horizontal lines over the pitch tracking indicate the range between the highest and the lowest pitch values. The F0 range from the lowest (136.5Hz) to the highest (143.5Hz) pitch in *napayín* is narrow: only 7Hz. Its perceptual distance would be something close to a half musical note apart, with the closest being notes C#3 (138.59Hz) and D3 (146.38Hz), respectively. On the other hand, the F0 range in *áakokaawa* is wider (119.9Hz to 159.2Hz, for a difference of 12.82Hz), similar to two and a half notes apart, from somewhere between the notes A#2 (116.54Hz) and B2 (123.47Hz) to between the notes D#3 (155.56Hz) and E3 (164.81Hz).

FIGURE 4. Pitch ranges of words *napayín* 'bread' and *áakokaawa* 'she will sell it'.

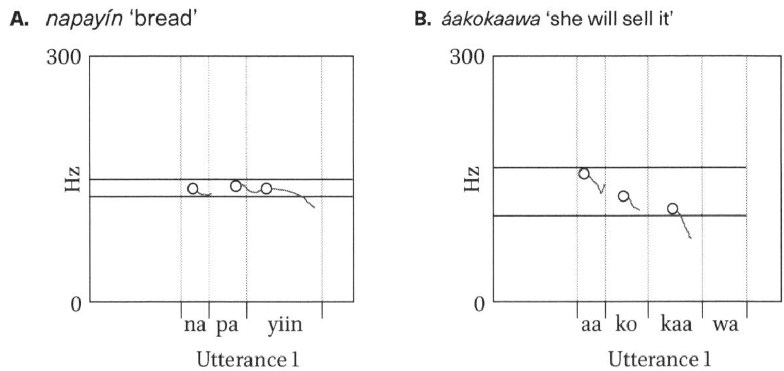

This difference in range—a wider range for words with accent on the initial vowel, a narrower range for words with accent on a later vowel—is pervasive in the data. Table 8 shows an examination of the F0 range in words with three vowels

TABLE 8. F0 distance within trisyllabic words

	ACCENT ON V1	AVE F0 DIFFERENCE	ACCENT ON V3	AVE F0 DIFFERENCE
	n	Hz	*n*	Hz
Female	66	36.79	18	8.27
Male	45	40.19	15	9.46

with these two accent patterns. (Words with multiple accents are excluded.) In the female speaker's speech, the average F0 distance in words with accent on the first vowel is 36.79Hz, while in words with accent on the third vowel it is 8.27Hz. A similar result was found in the male speaker's speech: the F0 distance in the words with the initial syllable accented is 40.19Hz, while in words with final vowel accented it is 9.46Hz.

A similar observation is reported in Fish and Miyashita (2017), which claims that Blackfoot word melody may be realized by the interaction between pitch accent and declination. Blackfoot has a tendency to begin a word at a midpoint in the pitch range, and a declination occurs throughout the word. For example, as shown in Figure 5, in the case of a three-syllable word, when the accent is located on the first vowel the initial pitch is very high and followed by pitch declination (A); when the accent is on the second vowel, there is a relatively steep rising pitch, and the declination occurs from this point (B); and when the accent is located at the end of a word, the pitch movement from the beginning to the accented vowel is almost flat (C).

FIGURE 5. Schematics of observed word melodies

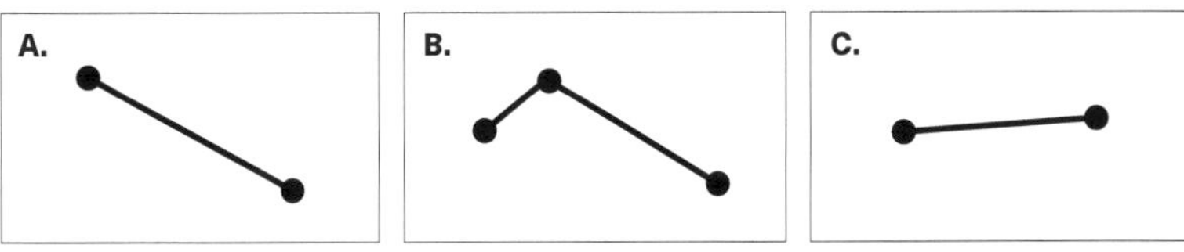

Fish and Miyashita 2017.

The last case is the pattern of *napayín* 'bread', where the pitch values of the three vowels are close. This may be related to the inconsistent occurrence of the highest pitch. Interestingly, the lists in Tables 6 and 7 have three words in common besides *napayín* 'bread': *tsimá* 'where,' *saipohtóót* 'Take it out!', and *ksiksináttsiiwa* 'white'. This fact could also imply that the effect of the interaction between pitch and declination on the realization of highest pitch may not be totally random.

Accented Affix Involvement

In the male speaker's speech, there was one additional word with unstable highest pitch: *áínnisí'* 'he falls off,' with two lexically marked accents. In this word, the highest pitch was observed on the first vowel twice and the third vowel once. This instability may be accounted for by the involvement of an accented affix. As shown in (3), this word contains the durative prefix *á-*, which is described as an inherently accented affix (Frantz 2009). The third person singular suffix *-wa* is not detected because the Blackfoot proximate and obviative suffixes *-wa* and *-yi* are often not fully pronounced, though they may be articulatorily present (Bliss and Gick 2009).

(3) Morphology of *áínnisí'* [ɛ́nnisíʔ]
á-innisi'-(wa)
DUR-fall.off-3SG 'He falls off.'

Although there is an accented affix at the beginning of the word, the lexically specified accent on the verb seems to stay high, as shown in Figure 6. The pitch movement throughout the word is close to flat, though showing a slight falling and rising contour. The pitch values of the first and last vowels are very close, and consequently either vowel's pitch may show up as the highest.

FIGURE 6. Three utterances of *áínnisí'wa* [ɛ́nnisíʔ] by the male speaker (U = utterance).

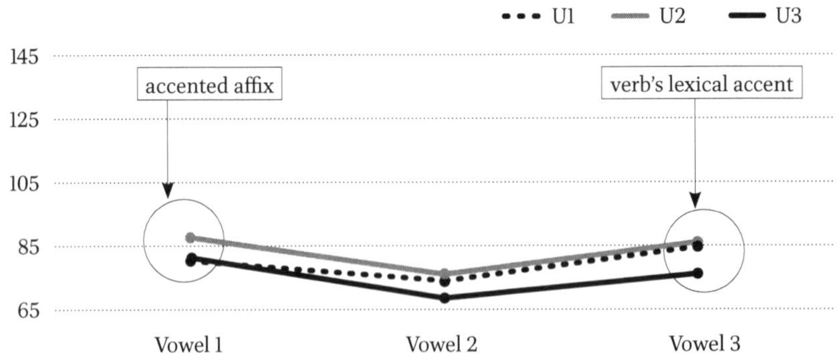

In comparison, Figure 7 shows the pitch movement of the same word produced by the female speaker. The female speaker had the highest pitch on the first vowel, the accented prefix *á-*, in all three utterances. The last vowel has the lowest pitch in all three utterances, as though the initial accented affix is canceling the lexical accent on the verb.

FIGURE 7. Three utterances of *áínnisí'wa* [ɛ́nnisíʔ] by the female speaker (U = utterance).

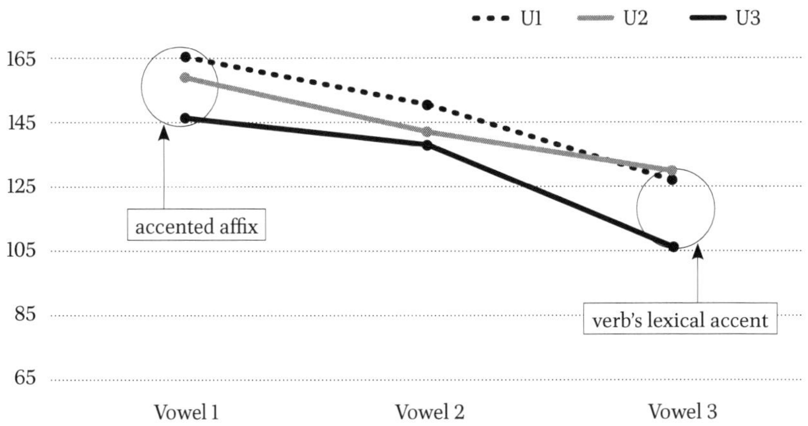

Thus, there seem to be different treatments of the word with multiple lexically specified accents depending on the speaker. It is possible that this difference between the two speakers is due to a dialectal variation, as they are from geographically different Blackfoot speaking bands, or a type of language change, as they are from different generations.[6] Although the speakers are of different genders, it is unlikely that this accounts for the difference; assuming that the pitch movement of the word *áínnisí'* is interacting with the accented affix, the difference must relate to something grammatical rather than stylistic. Either way, an extended study with more speakers is necessary to address these issues.

Conclusion

This study has provided a first investigation of Blackfoot prominence with respect to lexically specified accents. The sample recordings were obtained from two speakers from different geographic bands, different generations, and different genders.

Similar results were found in both speakers' utterances. The stability of pitch was approximately 94 percent; the stability of intensity was 64–68 percent. Based on the result that the highest pitch is more stable than the highest intensity, it is likely that pitch better represents lexical accent than intensity. Conversely, intensity is not a required acoustic element at the surface level, due to its flexibility.

This study has several implications. First, the study adds instrumentally analyzed data on Blackfoot word prominence, which is still rare. Phonetic study in the language is also important for language documentation (Whalen and McDonough 2015). Although both speakers in this study show similar results, it is essential to include samples from more speakers if possible so that the data can be statistically analyzed.

Second, as a result, this study addresses a remaining question raised by Van Der Mark (2003) from her experiment showing that average amplitude is a correlate of pitch accent in addition to pitch. Among the four possible accounts she provided, two can be evaluated by the results of the present study.[7] One is that "intensity is deliberately manipulated to mark a prominent syllable" (2003:29), which suggests that intensity marks the lexically specified accent. The current study shows that intensity does not mark lexical accent, because it is not as stable as pitch. The other account is that "an increase in intensity results from an increase in F0" (2003:29), which would indicate that pitch and intensity are inseparable factors—or, at least, that they significantly correlate. Again, this study suggests that such a correlation does not exist, because pitch and intensity seem to hold their independence, as is common cross-linguistically (Hayes 1995).

A third implication comes from the fact that the results were not parallel to the previous study's outcome. The previous study showed a correlation between pitch and amplitude, but this study did not. This calls for more comparable instrumental research. Also, since the possible accounts for unstable highest pitch are here suggested to be interaction with pitch contour type and involvement of an accented affix, this implies that detecting the highest pitch peak may not be the only factor in how the accent is perceived. Consequently, this invites a perception study, which might give us new insights in terms of Blackfoot prominence, especially because existing prosodic studies have been conducted by nonnative scholars only.

Furthermore, this study contributes to the understanding of second language acquisition of Blackfoot prosody. The notion of a second language transfer effect (Saville-Troike 2006) predicts that second language learners may incorrectly perceive and produce Blackfoot words with respect to pitch accent. For example, based on the experiment by Fry (1958) showing that duration, intensity, and frequency all played a role in listeners' prominence perception in English, speakers of English learning Blackfoot might perceive and produce words using a combination of these acoustic factors as the prominence cue, rather than primarily pitch. Consequently, this study provides Blackfoot language educators with information about authentic Blackfoot pronunciation, which is usually considered very important by elderly members of the community. This outcome is of special importance because many community members who are not native speakers are showing an interest in not only learning their ancestral language but also sounding like their elders.

NOTES

1. This study was supported by an NSF DEL grant [BCS 1251684] and the Phillips Fund of the American Philosophical Society. I would like to acknowledge my appreciation of the late Darrell R. Kipp for having supported the ongoing Blackfoot research; Rosella Many Bears and Earl Old Person for serving as native speaker language consultants; Donald G. Frantz for his mentorship; and Naatosi Fish, Amanda Belcourt, and Caroline Allen for their work as research assistants. I also thank the audiences at the Forty-Eighth Algonquian Conference in Milwaukee, Wisconsin, and at the annual meeting of the Society for the Study of the Indigenous Languages of the Americas in Austin, Texas; the editors, Monica Macaulay and Margaret Noodin; as well as the anonymous reviewer. All errors are of course mine.
2. Abbreviations: 3SG = third person singular, DUR = durative, pl. = plural, sg. = singular.
3. There are four Blackfoot-speaking bands that belong to the Blackfoot Confederacy—Siksiká, Kainai, and Aapátohsipikani in Alberta, Canada, and Aamskáápipikani (also known as Blackfeet nation) in Montana. The data come from Kainai and Aamskáápipikani (see Methods section).
4. Language mixing occurred mostly from the male speaker, who was excited to share his knowledge of the words' cultural backgrounds. Though instructed to repeat each word three times, he often started to talk about a word without repeating it. As he was explaining these words to me in English, the recording resulted in mixed prosody.
5. The word *napayín* 'bread' is also pronounced *napayíín*, with the last vowel long, depending on the speaker (Frantz and Russell 1995).
6. Generational variations are briefly discussed in Chatsis et al. (2013) and Miyashita and Chatsis (2013).
7. The other two possibilities are that "intensity is related to phrasal intonation" (Van Der

Mark 2003:29) and that "a process of vowel devoicing interfered with the measurements of intensity" (Van Der Mark 2003:29).

REFERENCES

Bliss, Heather and Bryan Gick. 2009. Articulation without Acoustics: "Soundless" Vowels in Blackfoot. *Proceedings of the 2009 Canadian Linguistics Association Annual Conference*, ed. by Frédéric Mailhot, pp. 1–15. http://homes.chass.utoronto.ca/~cla-acl/actes2009/actes2009.html.

Boersma, Paul and David Weenink. 2013. *Praat: Doing Phonetics by Computer*. Version 5.3.51. http://www.praat.org.

Chatsis, Annabelle, Mizuki Miyashita, and Deborah Cole. 2013. A Documentary Ethnography of a Blackfoot Language Course: Patterns of Variationism and Standard in the Organization of Diversity. *The Persistence of Language: Constructing and Confronting the Past and Present in the Voices of Jane H. Hill*, ed. by Shannon T. Bischoff, Deborah Cole, Amy V. Fountain, and Mizuki Miyashita, pp. 257–290. Amsterdam: John Benjamins.

Fish, Naatosi and Mizuki Miyashita. 2017. Guiding Pronunciation of Blackfoot Melody. *Honoring Our Teachers*, ed. by Jon Reyhner, Joseph Martin, Louise Lockard, and Willard Sakiestewa Gilbert, pp. 203–210. Flagstaff: Northern Arizona University.

Frantz, Donald G. 2009 [1991]. *Blackfoot Grammar*. Toronto: University of Toronto Press.

Frantz, Donald G. and Norma Jean Russell. 1995. *Blackfoot Dictionary of Stems, Roots, and Affixes*. Toronto: University of Toronto Press.

Fry, Dennis B. 1958. Experiments in the Perception of Stress. *Language and Speech* 1:126–152.

Hayes, Bruce. 1995. *Metrical Stress Theory: Principles and Case Studies*. Chicago: University of Chicago Press.

Hyman, Larry. 2009. How (Not) to Do Phonological Typology: The Case of Pitch Accent. *Language Sciences* 31:213–238.

Kaneko, Ikuyo. 1999. A Metrical Analysis of Blackfoot Nominal Accent in Optimality Theory. MA thesis, University of British Columbia.

McCarthy, John and Alan Prince. 1993. Prosodic Morphology I: Constraint Interaction and Satisfaction. Unpublished manuscript, University of Massachusetts–Amherst and Rutgers University.

Miyashita, Mizuki and Annabelle Chatsis. 2013. Respecting Dialectal Variations in a Blackfoot Language Class. *Honoring Our Elders: Culturally Appropriate Approaches for Teaching Indigenous Students*, ed. by Jon Reyhner, Joseph Martin, Louise Lockard, and Willard Sakiestewa Gilbert, pp. 109–116. Flagstaff: Northern Arizona University.

Prince, A. and P. Smolensky. 1993. Optimality Theory: Constraint Interaction in Generative Grammar. Unpublished manuscript, Rutgers University and University of Colorado, Boulder.

Saville-Troike, Muriel. 2006. *Introducing Second Language Acquisition*. Cambridge: Cambridge University Press.

Taylor, Allan R. 1969. A Grammar of Blackfoot. PhD thesis, University of California, Berkeley.

Tsunoda, Tasaku. 2005. *Language Endangerment and Language Revitalization: An Introduction*. Berlin: Mouton de Gruyter.

Uhlenbeck, C.C. 1938. *A Concise Blackfoot Grammar, Based on Material from the Southern Peigans*. Verhandelingen der Koninklijke Nederlandsche Akademie van Wetenschappen te Amsterdam, Afdeeling Letterkunde, n.s., part 41.

Van Der Mark, Sheena. 2002. The Acoustic Correlates of Blackfoot Prominence. *Calgary Working Papers in Linguistics* 24:169–216.

———. 2003. The Phonetics of the Blackfoot Pitch Accent. MA thesis, University of Calgary.

Weber, Natalie. 2012. Accent and Prosody in Blackfoot Verbs. *Papers of the Forty-Fourth Algonquian Conference,* ed. by Monica Macaulay, Margaret Noodin, and J. Randolph Valentine, pp. 348–369. Albany, NY: SUNY Press.

Whalen, Doug H. and Joyce McDonough. 2015. Taking the Laboratory into the Field. *Annual Review of Linguistics* 1(1):395–415.

Revisiting the Historical Context of Some Menominee Morphophonological Rules

Campbell Nilsen

A glance at the morphophonology of any Algonquian language will reveal traces of old sound shifts and the remnants of processes operational in Proto-Algonquian, such as vowel contraction or coronal obstruent palatalization.[1] More broadly, "morphophonology generally but not always comes from patterns of sound change," as an anonymous reviewer noted, and the Algonquian family is replete with examples, such as the *b*~*w* alternation in Arapaho (both *b* and *w* deriving ultimately from Proto-Algonquian *m in different environments) and the alternation between *n* and *s* or *š* found in many of the languages surrounding the Great Lakes, such as the Meskwaki group and Ojibwe.

The relationship between synchronic and diachronic (morpho)phonology is a particularly thorny one in Algonquian, a point recently and thoroughly made in Macaulay and Salmons (2016). Macaulay and Salmons's central question, one that this article will also attempt to answer within its own domain, was,

> in essence, how much of an analysis of components should be synchronic and how much diachronic? That is, to what extent are the components and formatives being assembled by some operation in the speaker's mind and to what extent are the similarities across elements just "a residual diachronic pattern", as an anonymous

> reviewer puts it, still visible in the synchronic grammar? (Macaulay and Salmons 2016:181)

That article dissented from many morphological theories (particularly of the generative school) in analyzing Menominee derivational morphology as a product of the language's historical development as well as of its synchronic structure.

This article argues that a similar analysis holds for Menominee morphophonology. It is clear that many (indeed, most) Menominee morphophonological rules, such as the palatalization of underlying |t| to /c/ before the vowels |e e·| and the glide |y| (Bloomfield 1962:81), are historical processes that still have a synchronic presence in the modern language. Indeed, I think that in the case of morphophonology Blevins's statement that "principled diachronic explanations for sound patterns have priority over competing synchronic explanations unless independent evidence demonstrates, beyond reasonable doubt, that a synchronic account is warranted" (2004:23, quoted in Macaulay and Salmons 2016:181) holds water insofar as the synchronic reality of a proposed morphophonological rule should, if at all possible, be explicable in diachronic terms. As a corollary, a morphophonological rule without a clear diachronic pedigree is suspicious, particularly in a language such as Menominee in which many historical developments have been retained as transparent synchronic rules (cf. Macaulay and Salmons 2016:213).

Bloomfield proposes two such rules for Menominee in *The Menomini Language* (1962:80–82). The first, which I term the 'consonant deletion rule', proposes that certain clusters of the form |hC| reduce to /h/ before a morpheme beginning with a consonant. The second, the 'double-*a·* rule', proposes that two contiguous instances of underlying |a·| over a morpheme boundary reduce to a single one. While Bloomfield proposes in *The Menomini Language* that these are true synchronic processes, it is clear that they are historically rather anomalous, and that understanding their synchronic reality requires a closer look be given to their diachronic development.

The Consonant Deletion Rule

In a list of exceptions to the usual insertion of connective /e/ between two consonants over a morpheme boundary, Bloomfield gives a rule by which the second consonant of some clusters is deleted before another consonant (bolding mine): "Irregularly, in certain forms, connective <u>-e-</u> is not used. A prior consonant <u>N</u>, <u>m</u>, t, n(?) **or cluster ht, hk** before subsequent consonant p, k, or s is replaced by h” (Bloomfield 1962:80–81). The replacement of underlying |N|, |m|, |t|, and |n| by /h/ before obstruents in morphophonemic combination is historically unsurprising. The morphophoneme |N| represents a merger (Hockett 1981:56, 57) of PA *θ and *r, which became /h/ preconsonantally at an early date; the replacement of preconsonantal |m| and |n| dates back to a later shift (Hockett 1981:60). It seems reasonably well-established (Pentland 1979:380–382) that many instances of Proto-Algonquian *t became *ʔ (usually written *x) before the stops *p and *k, though some seem to have given *θ (Pentland 1979:387), and the details have not been fully worked out. The clusters *xp, *xk respectively became /hp/ and /hk/ in the phonological history of Menominee (Hockett 1981:57), and this shift adequately explains the change of |t| to /h/ before obstruents in contemporary Menominee.[2]

More puzzling, however, is the simplification of |ht| and |hk| before an obstruent in a following morpheme; there is no clear precedent for such a morphophonemic rule in Proto-Algonquian as reconstructed, and it is not present in Menominee's close relatives. Further investigation reveals that Bloomfield posits the rule based on the behavior of four roots (1962:435–436), in a list of roots that combine with suffixes without the insertion of connective *-e-*: “Suffixes are added to roots without connective -e- in the following cases: kɛhk-: before AI -pesi, II -petɛ·, TA -peN, TI -peto·. ke·hk-: before AI -pi. mo·hk-: before AI -pokosi, II -pokwat. oht-: before AI -pwa·, -pya·” (Bloomfield 1962:435–436).

By considering each root and its formations in turn, I show that—since Bloomfield's consonant deletion rule has no historical precedent and all formations in question can be easily explained by established processes—no synchronic rule of consonant deletion should be proposed for Menominee's system of morphophonology.

Formations in kɛhk-

Bloomfield (1962:436) claims that *kɛhk-* loses its final *-k* before four finals, differing only in transitivity and animacy and all relating to the meaning ‘tie’ (cf. Bloomfield 1962:286). A footnote in Goddard (1982) provides a solution for the TA verb *kɛhpe·nɛ·w* ‘he ties him up’. An exact cognate of Munsee Delaware *koxpí·le·w*, *kɛhpe·nɛ·w* is derived from a Proto-Algonquian preform *keθ-piθ-e·wa, with initial *keθ- ‘held firmly’ (Goddard 1982:28). All four of the finals AI *-pesi,* II *-petɛ·*, TA *-peN,* and TI *-peto·* are derived synchronically from the prefinal element *-p-* ‘tie’

TABLE 1. Preforms of Menominee verbs in *kɛhp-*

MENOMINEE LEMMA	PA PREFORM
kɛhpe·sow (AI)	**keθ-piso-wa*
kɛhpe·tɛ·w (II)	**keθ-pi·t-e·wa*
kɛhpe·nɛ·w (TA)	**keθ-pi·θ-e·wa*
kɛhpe·ta·w[4] (TI)	**keθ-pi·ta·-wa*

(Bloomfield 1962:420),[3] with extensions marking animacy and transitivity; as these are transparently related, preforms in *keθ-* can be reconstructed for all four Menominee verbs.[4] See Table 1.

Analyzing Menominee verbs of tying as deriving from *keθ- also explains their semantic distance from other verbs in *kɛhk-*, which generally have to do with knowing, learning, teaching, and so on; these derive from PA *kexk- 'know, learn, teach', e.g., *kɛhke·nawɛw* 'he knows him', from *kexk-inaw-e·wa. It can thus be safely concluded that no process of consonant deletion took place in the history of the Menominee verb *kɛhpe·sow* and its derivational siblings. In synchronic terms, I propose that Menominee possesses, alongside the initial *kɛhk-* 'learn, know, teach', a defective root *kɛh-* 'hold, tie', which only appears before the 'hand' finals in *-p-*.

Formations in ke·hk-

Bloomfield cites a single verb *ke·hpow* 'he has indigestion, a stomach-ache' as an irregular derivation from the root *ke·hk-* 'spite, insult, berate' (from PA *ki·hk-; cf. Hewson 2014:92), with the AI final *-pi-*, a middle reflexive deriving from TA *-pw-* 'by mouth' (Bloomfield 1962:295).[5] An alternative derivation, albeit one for which I can find no exact cognates, is from *ki·t- 'sore'; the -t- of *ki·t- would have reduced regularly to a glottal stop before PA *p, giving a preform *ki·xpwiwa for which *ke·hpow* is the expected Menominee reflex.[6] As most reflexes of *ki·t- across the family show an epenthetic vowel when the initial is followed by a consonant in morphophonemic combination (e.g., Cree *ki·tiskawe·w* 'he hurts his sore place by stepping on him', from *ki·t- and the TA final *-škaw- 'foot or body'; see Hewson 2014a:224), Menominee *ke·hpow* appears to be an archaism. Synchronically, however, the revised analysis is unexceptional: modern Menominee possesses an initial *ke·t-* 'sore, hurt' which is the direct descendent of PA *ki·t-, appearing in words such as *ke·tanamowɛw* 'he hurts his sore place by touching' (Hewson 2014b:103). Since the reduction of the final |t| of this initial to /h/ before finals in |p| is an already established rule of synchronic morphophonology dating back to Proto-Algonquian, no additional synchronic or diachronic process needs to be invoked to explain it.

Formations in mo·hk-

Bloomfield cites a pair of intransitives, differing only in animacy—*mo·hpokosew* 'he (as, onion) appears in the taste of something' and its inanimate counterpart *mu·hpokwat*—as examples of consonant deletion in the stem *mo·hk-* (Bloomfield 1962:436).[7] Based on the reanalyses posited for *kεhk-* and *ke·hk-*, it is reasonable to hypothesize that some smaller root *mo·h-* underlies both *mo·hpokosew/mu·hpokwat* and forms in *mo·hk-*. The Menominee root *mo·hk-* appears to go back to a PA root *mo·θk(w)- 'attack, appear' (Hewson 2014b:168), and it seems possible that an original root *mo·θ- may underlie it. A similar root *mo·r- is reconstructed meaning 'suspect' (Hewson 2014b:165), and it is tempting to connect it with *mo·θk(w)-, both on semantic grounds and because in the majority of Algonquian languages, including Menominee, there would be no way to distinguish reflexes of *mo·r- from those of *mo·θ-. Ives Goddard (personal communication) points out that similar *θ~*r alternation within a single root is already attested in existing reconstructions, such as in the root *mya·θ/*mya·r- 'bad'. Also belonging to this root would be words reconstructed with *mo·š- 'sense, perceive' (Hewson 2014b:166), reflecting the PA *θ~*š alternation before *i(·) and *y. The existence of Cree reflexes such as *mo·siho·w* 'he feels something is coming' suggests that *mo·θ-, not *mo·r-, was the original form of this root, as Cree reflexes of the palatalized variant *mo·š- could only derive from *mo·θ- unless borrowing was involved. The source of the post-root accretion *-k- of forms from *mo·θk- remains unclear, but there is no reason to believe it was ever present in the root underlying *mu·hpokwat* and *mo·hpokosew* in Menominee, for which I posit the preforms *mo·θ-pw-ekw-atwi and *mo·θ-pw-ekw-esi-wa.

Formations in oht-

Bloomfield proposes that the root *oht-* reduces to *oh-* before the two AI finals *pwa·* and *-pya·* (Bloomfield 1962:436); these words have the homophonous third person citation form *ohpi·w* in the *Menominee Lexicon*, but differing first person singular forms *netu·hpwam* 'I smoke tobacco' and *netu·hpyam* 'I come from there' (Bloomfield

1975:170). It is quite likely on comparative grounds that these two verbs do not share the same initial root. While Hewson (2014b:323–325) reconstructs a PA root *ont- 'from there' underlying Menominee words in *oht-*, this seems to derive from a combination of the root *om- 'up' with the TI final *-t- (Ives Goddard, personal communication). *Ohpi·w* 'he comes from there' thus appears to be an archaism without *t-, deriving from a preform *om-pye·-wa.

The verb *ohpi·w/netu·hpwam* 'he, I smoke tobacco', however, likely has nothing to do with Menominee words in *oht-*.[8] A solution is again found in Goddard's 1982 paper on the historical phonology of Munsee Delaware, in which Munsee *óhpwe·w* 'he smokes' and, by extension, Menominee *ohpi·w* are derived from *wexpwe·wa (*oxpwe·wa) (Goddard 1982:28). This stem *oxpw- is likely to be a secondary derivation from PA *ot- 'draw, drag, pull' and the AI final *-pw- 'by mouth', with the normal change of *t to *ʔ/*x before *p (Pentland 1979:380–381); the consonant of the root is preserved in Meskwaki *atame·wa* 'smokes a pipe' (Goddard and Thomason 2014:28). There is thus no reason to believe that the history of either meaning of Menominee *ohpi·w* shows evidence of historical consonant deletion.

Conclusion

The highly restricted scope of Bloomfield's consonant deletion rule (only occurring before four finals) and its lack of a historical or comparative parallel elsewhere in Algonquian suggests that the forms in question may simply be the remnants of earlier diachronic processes, rather than the result of a synchronic morphophonological process. Careful historical analysis of the words Bloomfield cites bears this out: in all cases, an etymology that cleanly gives the contemporary Menominee form is possible, though the synchronic formation of some words requires reanalysis (such as *kɛhpe·sow*, which preserves an initial *keθ-, which is no longer productive in Menominee). There seems no good reason to believe that consonant deletion along the lines Bloomfield suggests operates, or has ever operated, as a synchronic rule in Menominee.

The Double-*a·* Rule

Bloomfield proposes a rule by which two instances of long *a·* merge into one over a morpheme boundary: "The only other combination of successive long vowels appears to be that of a· and a·; this is replaced by a·: anwa·-a·nɛm- ~ anwa·nɛm-: anuanemat 'the wind subsides'" (Bloomfield 1962:82).

The historical context of this morphophonemic rule is difficult to discern, partially because morphophonemic combination of |a·-a·| is rare in Menominee and seems to have been so in Proto-Algonquian as well. The only other example of |a·-a·| that I have been able to find in Bloomfield's extensive Menominee writings is *naka·pi·naʔsow* 'he brings his horses to a stop', derived from |naka·-a·pyɛ·-| (Bloomfield 1939:248), and here the synchronic contraction rule holds as well.[9]

It is difficult to determine, due to the rarity of the combination, how the underlying sequence |a·-a·| was treated in morphophonological combination in Proto-Algonquian. Both Meskwaki and Cree, however, insert an epenthetic *y* in combination: thus, Meskwaki shows *akwa·ya·šo·wi·wa* 'he comes to land after fording' from *akwa·-* 'out from water' and *-a·šo·wi·-* 'ford' (Bloomfield 1925:231), while Cree has *ki·sika·ya·pan* 'it is day-break' from *ki·sika·-* 'be day' and *-a·pan-* 'be dawn' (Wolfart 1970:256). It seems reasonable to propose that this rule is archaic, but for Menominee this would predict ***anuaya·nemat* and ***naka·ya·pi·naʔsow*, which are not attested.

Because in both *anuanemat* and *naka·pi·naʔsow* the contraction in question is between an initial and a medial, and because the contraction seems to be unique to Menominee, it seems possible that a morphological solution may be at work. A number of Menominee initials have both short and long forms, the latter with the abstract postradical *a·* (Bloomfield 1962:430). The only other words cited from the root *anwa·-* (PA *arwa·-) are *anuakawew* 'it runs as the last flow', with the AI final *-kawe-* 'flow' (Bloomfield 1962:319–320), and *anuapi·ʔnan* 'the rain or snow ceases', with the AI final *-ɛpi·-* 'liquid' (Bloomfield 1962:326–327). There is a somewhat longer list of derivations from *naka·-*, shown in Table 2 along with the immediately following suffix.[10]

If the root extension *-a·-* dates back to the PA period, as suggested by Ives Goddard (personal communication), it may have disappeared before following *-a·-* by haplology or merely the simple coalescence of identical segments. While a historical process of coalescence may seem at first to be somewhat ad hoc as a possible explanation, the rarity of |a·-a·| sequences over a morpheme boundary, along with the phonological prohibition on a surface sequence **/a·a·/, means that a simplification might have happened at any time in the history of the words in question as a repair process. Moreover, because |a·-a·| seems to have been a rare underlying sequence in Proto-Algonquian as well as Menominee, it would be

TABLE 2. Derivations of initial *naka-*

MENOMINEE LEMMA	GLOSS (LEXICON)	FOLLOWING SUFFIX
naka·hkiskam	'he comes to a stop hitting the ground'	|-ahky-| (< PA *-axky-)
naka·nɛ·w	'he brings him to a stop by hand'	|-ɛn-| (< *-en-)
naka·pi·nɛ·w	'he brings him to a stop by pulling a line'	|-a·pyɛ·-| (< *-a·pye·-)
naka·ʔtaw	'he stops in his actions or movement'	|-ʔta·-| (< *-ʔta·-)
naka·skaw	'he comes to a halt, stops going'	|-ɛska·-| (< *-ešk-)

unsurprising to find that different descendent languages developed different ways of turning the underlying sequence into a permissible surface sequence.

Before underlying sequences other than |a·|, the development of the Menominee reflexes of words formed from the initials *naka·- and *arwa·- is fairly straightforward. When followed by a short vowel, as with *-en- 'by hand', the following short vowel would have disappeared by a well-established rule of vowel contraction (Pentland 1979:406). If protoforms are constructed for all forms in *anwa·-* and *naka·-*, it can be seen that the root extension *-a·-* can be projected back to the protolanguage in all cases except those where it is followed by *-a·-*.[11] As the root extension is absent before only two suffixes, both medials—*-a·pye·- and *-a·nem-—it seems reasonable to propose that its disappearance was likely due to a repair process of haplology or simplification, whose generalization may have been helped along by the fact that all other words containing the roots possessed a single **-a·-*. In Table 3 I give protoforms for derivations of the two roots in question; preforms showing double-*a·* simplification are marked with a following asterisk, while those showing contractive loss of a short vowel are marked with a dagger.

It should additionally be noted that at least one other solution has been proposed for the behavior of these roots that I have seen: a root extension *-aw- that appeared in some forms of an initial, but not others, contracting with a following epenthetic *-e- to give a surface *a· (examples in Hewson 2014b). However, Ives Goddard notes (personal communication) that this *-aw- does not seem to be attested except as an underlying input to the contractive process, and proposes (e.g.) *arwa·- as a revised reconstruction. I conclude that, as the *y*-insertion rule seen in Meskwaki and Cree seems to be archaic,[12] Bloomfield's rule for the contraction of |a·-a·| in Menominee is the reflection of a process of coalescence that arose at some

TABLE 3. Preforms of Menominee verbs in *anwa··* and *naka··*

MENOMINEE LEMMA	SUFFIX FOLLOWING INITIAL	PA PREFORM
anuanemat	|-a·nɛm-|	**arwa··a·nem-atwi**
anuakawew	|-kawe-|	**arwa··kawi-wa*
anuapi·ʔnen	|-ɛpi··|	**arwa··epye·ʔθ-enwi*†
naka·hkiskam	|-ahky-|	**naka··axky-ešk-amwa*†
naka·nɛ·w	|-ɛn-|	**naka··en-e·wa*†
naka·pi·nɛ·w	|-a·pyɛ··|	**naka··a·pye··θe·wa**
naka·ʔtaw	|-ʔta··|	**naka··ʔta··wa*
naka·skaw	|-ɛska·|	**naka··ešk-a·wa*†

point in the history of the language to create a valid surface form for a phonologically difficult underlying sequence.

Synchronically speaking, however, since the underlying sequence |a··a·| found in words formed with the initials in question must be underlyingly real but is clearly forbidden as a surface realization, a morphophonological process is probably at work, even if only as an exception to the *y*-insertion rule otherwise used between two long vowels. It is clear that the underlying form of (e.g.) the initial for 'cease' is |anwa··|, and that of the medial 'wind' |-a·nɛm-|; but, as ***anuaa·nemat* is phonologically forbidden, some rule must exist that gives the phonologically valid *anuanemat*. While it is true that (as an anonymous reviewer points out) very strong evidence needs to be presented to postulate a synchronic morphophonological rule, it seems quite clear that a contemporary Menominee speaker (or at least one at the time of Bloomfield's fieldwork) would intuitively know that *anuanemat* was formed from the existing morphemes |anwa··| and |a·nɛm-|, and so would possess a morphophonological rule giving the correct surface form. While this rule would have few opportunities for application, the transparency of its application seems to guarantee that it must have existed in some form; since the comparative evidence suggests that it historically originated in a repair process somewhere in the history of Menominee, it also fits the existing pattern of old sound changes being preserved as morphophonological rules.

Conclusion

Although most Menominee morphophonology has a clear historical origin and can provide clues to the language's phonological and morphological history, some rules of morphophonology as stated by Bloomfield seem to be historically anomalous and therefore invite a close historical analysis. In some cases, such as the consonant deletion rule postulated for forms such as *kɛhpo·w*, the rule's application appears to be irregular and on a word-by-word basis, which raises doubts as to its status as a true synchronic process. A close historical analysis of instances in which this rule applies shows that the words in question are remnants of known diachronic processes, and that no synchronic rule need be postulated. For other synchronic rules, such as the double-*a·* rule, there does seem to have been a historical process at work behind the forms found in modern Menominee. Although this process seems to have been a limited morphological repair process, not a true sound shift, the morphological transparency of the forms showing the rule indicates that it probably is synchronically present in some form.

More broadly, Menominee (and Algonquian as a whole) provides an interesting case study in how knowledge of a language's diachronic development can inform synchronic understanding. As demonstrated by Macaulay and Salmons in the context of Menominee derivational morphology, attempting to describe a language purely in synchronic terms may lead the linguist to misinterpret features that derive from historical processes. In the case of morphophonology, which for the most part (but not always) echoes historical phonology, checking postulated morphophonological rules against the known history allows the linguist to check historically anomalous rules and, where necessary, provide solutions to problematic forms (such as apparent reduction of consonant clusters) within the framework of established processes without having to postulate a synchronic rule that may not exist for speakers. Historical analysis thus provides a basis for distinguishing between productive synchronic processes and the detritus of diachronic linguistic change.

NOTES

1. I would like to thank Ives Goddard, David Pentland, Marcia Haag, Dylan Herrick, Monica Macaulay, Ollie Sayeed, and an anonymous reviewer for their comments. Any errors remaining are of course my own. The following abbreviations are used in this paper,

following standard Algonquianist practice: PA = Proto-Algonquian, TA = transitive animate, TI = transitive inanimate, AI = animate transitive, II = inanimate intransitive.

2. A few notes on reconstructions may be warranted. I follow Goddard in reconstructing *o-, *i- word-initially for Bloomfield's (1946) *we-, *e-, and *r for Bloomfield's *l. However, I find it likely that the clusters *xk and *xp likely began with a glottal stop, as proposed in Pentland (1979). In citing roots from Hewson I write *r for *l and *o *i for word-initial *we *e, so as to maintain congruence with the rest of the paper.
3. This set of finals is clearly related to the nearly semantically identical set *ahpesi*, *-ahpetε·*, *-ahpeN*, *-ahpeto·* (Bloomfield 1962:287), which, however, is probably a combination of the original 'tie' finals with the suffix *-ah-* 'by tool' (Goddard 1990:456, ex. 29).
4. While Bloomfield cites Menominee Class 2 TI finals as ending in *-o·-*, this is replaced by *-a·-* in the third person of the independent paradigm (Bloomfield 1962:159). This alternation appears to be an archaism shared with Cree (Goddard 1979:72–73).
5. One might expect the meaning of *ke·hpow* to mean 'he has a sore mouth'; but Bloomfield makes clear (1962:295) that *-pi-* has a rather broad semantic range, covering nourishment and eating as well.
6. Hewson reconstructs a root **ki·xpw-* 'eating, stomach' (2014b:107), but this is likely to be a secondary derivation. Since its main derivations have to do not with stomach aches but with satiation and fullness, it is probably not ultimately from **ki·t-*; my suspicion is that it may derive from **ki·p-* 'fall over, topple' (Hewson 2014b:95), with the semantic shift of 'falling over, falling asleep from fullness', with normal reduction of **p* to **ʔ/*x* before a stop.
7. Note that *mu·hpokwat* 'it appears in the taste of something' is only cited in its full form in Bloomfield's *Lexicon* (1975:138), whence also the seemingly strange definition of *mo·hpokosew* 'he (as, onion) appears in the taste of something' (1975:136), whose subject is understood to be a grammatically animate foodstuff.
8. It may be noted that Bloomfield (1962:313) derives *ohpi·w* 'he smokes' not only from *oht-* but also from *oN-* (< PA **or-* 'arrange'); the Meskwaki evidence counters this derivation as well, at least historically.
9. The rule also applies unmentioned in *naka·pi·nε·w* 'he brings him to a stop by pulling a line', of which *naka·pi·naʔsow* is a derivative, and whose *-a·-* is the result of an identical contraction.
10. For space, I have only cited one form per following suffix, although there are verbs differing in transitivity and animacy not listed, as well as transparent derivatives. For instance, TA *naka·nε·w* 'he brings him to a stop by hand' has an unlisted TI pair *naka·nam* and a derived passive reflexive *naka·nekasow* 'he gets stopped'. In all cases, however,

exactly the same processes of contraction have applied to variants of the listed verb.

11. It should be emphasized that the root extension can, to my knowledge, be generalized for the history of Menominee and only Menominee; **nak-*, at least, produced forms elsewhere with no extension at all, such as Meskwaki *nakeške·wa* 'he stops walking' (Goddard and Thomason 2014:96).
12. Whether it is of Proto-Algonquian date, however, remains an open question. Blackfoot, which seems to be a sister language to the ancestor of all the rest (Goddard 2015), inserts /w/ between two instances of long |a·| (Taylor 1969:84–85), and there may be traces of *w*-epenthesis in "Core Algonquian," though the details are not clear (Pentland 1979:406). However, both Meskwaki and Cree are relatively conservative languages and do not form a subgroup, so it seems reasonable to think that *y*-epenthesis, whatever the exact details, is probably old.

REFERENCES

Blevins, James. 2004. *Evolutionary Phonology*. Oxford: Oxford University Press.

Bloomfield, Leonard. 1925. Notes on the Fox Language [Part 1]. *International Journal of American Linguistics* 3:219–232.

———. 1939. [1970.] Menomini Morphophonemics. *A Leonard Bloomfield Anthology*, ed. by Charles F. Hockett, pp. 351–362, Bloomington: Indiana University Press.

———. 1946. Algonquian. *Linguistic Structures of Native America*, ed. by Cornelius Osgood and Harry Hoijer, pp. 85–129. Viking Fund Publications in Anthropology, vol. 6. New York.

———. 1962. *The Menomini Language*. New Haven, CT: Yale University Press.

———. 1975. *Menominee Lexicon*, ed. by Charles F. Hockett. Milwaukee Public Museum Publications in Anthropology and History, vol. 3. Milwaukee.

Goddard, Ives. 1979. *Delaware Verbal Morphology: A Descriptive and Comparative Study*. New York: Garland.

———. 1982. The Historical Phonology of Munsee. *International Journal of American Linguistics* 48:16–48.

———. 1990. Primary and Secondary Stem Derivation in Algonquian. *International Journal of American Linguistics* 56:449–483.

———. 2018. Blackfoot and Core Algonquian Inflectional Morphology: Archaisms and Innovations. *Papers of the Forty-Seventh Algonquian Conference*, ed. by Monica Macaulay and Margaret Noodin, pp. 87–110. East Lansing: Michigan State University Press.

Goddard, Ives and Lucy Thomason. 2014. *A Meskwaki-English and English-Meskwaki Dictionary: Based on Early Twentieth-Century Writings by Native Speakers*. Petoskey, MI:

Mundart Press.

Hewson, John. 2014a. Proto-Algonkian Formatives. http://www.mun.ca/linguistics/people/faculty/protoalgonkian.php.

———. 2014b. Proto-Algonkian Roots. http://www.mun.ca/linguistics/people/faculty/protoalgonkian.php.

Hockett, Charles F. 1981. The Phonological History of Menominee. *Anthropological Linguistics* 23:51–87.

Macaulay, Monica and Joseph Salmons. 2016. Synchrony and Diachrony in Menominee Derivational Morphology. *Morphology* 27:179–215.

Pentland, David. 1979. Algonquian Historical Phonology. PhD thesis, University of Toronto.

Taylor, Allan. 1969. A Grammar of Blackfoot. PhD thesis, University of California, Berkeley.

Wolfart, Hans. 1970. An Outline of Plains Cree Morphology. PhD thesis, Yale University.

Giiwosebinesiwag maamawi ningikendamamin: A Raptor Collaboration Centered on Language and Culture

Margaret Noodin

Gaa maawanji'idiyaang Minowakiing dagwaagig dash migizi gii agawaatesed akiing miinawaa mazina'iganing. Ezhi-gii-ganawaabamangid giizhigong mii bagidaa'endamoyang. Maada'oonidiyaang gaa miizhangidwaa. Aanawi dbaajimotawangid, ganoozhangid, nagamotawangid, mazinibii'angid . . . apane igo oma ayaayaang imaa ayaad gaawiin gashki'osiiwaang bakaaniziyaang mii ezhi-nisidotaadiyaang.

Algonquian language speakers and allies met in Milwaukee at the Forty-Eighth Algonquian Conference, and the eagle cast a shadow on the earth and on the page. Observations and ideas became networks of knowing. We acknowledged that we share the same space, and while we may speak of the eagle, speak to the eagle, sing songs of eagle beings, and trace eagle images with our lines, we are present in a way that is different.

The language and art we create to articulate networks of knowing signify the ways our lone and together selves perceive others: *manidoog, aanikoobijiganag, aadizookaanag*, and *bawaaganag* (spirits, ancestors, living stories, and visions). Our communications trace Anishinaabe phenomenology, cosmology, and the "poetics of dwelling" some have called *ezhi-bagosendamo*, which translates as the way one embodies hope as the expression of desire (Ingold 2000; Matthews et al. 2010). Using a holistic framework (Absolom 2010) based on recent studies of indigenous epistemologies that recognize knowledge exchanged between human and nonhuman forms of life (Graveline 2004; Hart 2002; Geniusz 2009; Kimmerer 2013; Nabigon 2006; Thomas 2005; Simpson 2001), as well as the understanding that language is an efficient means for passing on this knowledge (McCarty and Zepeda 2010; Whalen et al. 2016), this essay recounts the raptor collaboration that took place in Milwaukee, Wisconsin, between June and October 2016 in order to advance two hypotheses related to Anishinaabemowin, phenomenology, cosmology, and language revitalization.

The first hypothesis is that individual language use and individual identity intersect with communal language use and communal identity to produce more clearly defined epistemologies and more holistic linguistic and cultural revitalization. When speakers use ancestral languages connected with their personal and collective identity they are able to articulate shared phenomenological and cosmological perspectives in the transnational transtemporal present. Indigenous cosmology has been explored in a range of communities (Blommaert 2008; Hornberger and Swinehart 2012; Hymes 2003) and should be a consideration in language revitalization efforts. Related to this trend is the need for more exploration of indigenous phenomenology and the ways that indigenous languages articulate the nature of being and perception of consciousness across a broad spectrum of animate beings. The epistemologies, or theories of discourse, that evolve around these shared ways of perceiving should be based in indigenous languages, not translations with imposed limitations. Fundamental ways of knowing can be found in the etymology, syntax, and rhetorical options for narrative construction passed down between speakers over generations. It is important to acknowledge an indigenous framework in order to arrive at an indigenous interpretation. *Giishpin bwaanisidotamaang ziibiwan, zaaga'iganan gaye ezhi-asabkeyaang mii apii bagida'waayaang mii igo gaawiin debisiniisiiyaang* (Without understanding the rivers, the lakes, and the way nets are made, we cannot be satisfied by the nets we set). Without an understanding of the systems we use and create, there is no hope that we can remember their past applications and adapt them for continued use into the future.

The second hypothesis is that collaborative revitalization projects foster lasting theoretical, methodological, and philosophical alliances and can result in linguistic, cultural, and ontological lessons. These new directions in revitalization are essential for continued linguistic and cultural vitality (Mihas et al. 2013) and should be part of the dialogue on nonhuman agency and global intellectual evolution (Horton and Berlo 2013). *Apii Animikiig bizindawangidwaa awashime nitaanisidotaadiyaang gaye nisidotamaang ayaayaang naawayi'ii giizhigong miinawaa akiing* (When we listen to Thunderbeings we can better understand our own existence between the sky and earth). Listening to the full dimensions of the conversations around us helps all speakers understand the dialogue of the universe and form an indigenous ontology, or frame of reference, for the ways in which we understand reality and our own invented categories of being. Indigenous philosophy, phenomenology, cosmology, and ontology are found, and will continue to reflect lived experience, through the use of diverse languages.

The conclusions drawn here stem from a creative collaboration that came to be known as *Giiwosebinesiwag: Raptors*. The primary language engaged in the project was Anishinaabemowin, but this essay includes a summary of ways in which the experience broadened to include other Algonquian languages and identities including Maliseet, Menominee (also referred to as Omāēqnomenēw), and Blackfoot (also known as Siksika). The project began as a conversation centered on curriculum, moved to an interactive digital series of images combined with audio, and culminated in the appearance of two raptors at the Forty-Eighth Annual Algonquian Conference.

The search for curriculum centered on raptors began when the Anishinaabemowin language instructors at the Milwaukee Indian Community School and the University of Wisconsin–Milwaukee were introduced to the community of birds who live at the Schlitz Audubon Nature Center. The 16 residents of the Raptor Program are not releasable to the wild for a variety of reasons and remain in the permanent care of humans. They have become "feathered ambassadors" who educate the public about the ecosystem (Schlitz Audubon 2017). In some cases, these birds of prey are physically unable to provide for themselves; in other cases they have bonded too intensely with humans and are not able to live away from human society. The teachers were struck by the similarities between the raptors and students of Anishinaabemowin who often felt stranded in an English-only environment with no ability to experience immersion in the language of their ancestors. Both students and raptors have been forced to adapt to a modern, irreversible urban reality. For animals, the phenomenon of adaptability had both social and cognitive side-effects (Proulx et al. 2016), and for the children, the impact of assimilation, both voluntary and involuntary, is part of a well-documented body of work on language loss and identity (Ambler 2004; Dauenhauer and Dauenhauer 1998; Emberley 2014; McCarty et al. 2006).

Knowing that most modern educational practices are not adequate to address issues of identity loss and cultural dissonance, the teachers considered ways to move beyond the classroom to explore connections between raptors and people in order to improve communication between all beings and to also foster positive perceptions of identity. While visiting the birds, students considered the *debweta-agwadoon* (true facts) and *ezhi-dibaajimangidwaa* (narrative traditions) focused on the *giiwosebinesiwag ningikenimaanaanig*, the hunter-birds we know.

Some of the facts were *bineshiinyag indaajimaanaanig*, Anishinaabe ornithology. The initial conversation, led by Michael Zimmerman Jr., centered on *ezhi-ginisidawaabamaanaanig*, the way we recognize the birds and understand them by observing their behavior. Some of the statements illustrated the reason for the bird's name. Throughout the experience, students gained an appreciation for language diversity and came to understand how morphology is connected to epistemology, which reinforces the reasoning behind revitalization (Harrison 2007). Examples of this include the following sentences:

> *Migizi babaamigiziige ishpiming.* (The eagle flies around surveying high in the sky.)
>
> *Boodawidoombe boodawidombi apii dibishigiishkaag.* (The barn owl makes a blowing sound while sitting when it is dark.)

In other instances, the statements described a key part of the bird's identity, telling the story of the bird, which is considered a useful technique with affective learners especially in middle school when "young adolescents begin to notice the 'otherness' of the world and they are inspired by adventure and drama" (Shrum and Glisan 2005:156). This project indicates that the indigenous language classroom fosters affective learning and would suggest use of storytelling at all levels. Students were encouraged to observe the birds and then illustrate the following sentences:

> *Migiziwag zidan aabajitoonaawaan miijim ji-debibidoowaad.* (They use their feet to grab food.)
>
> *Miskonaniisi odamawaan ginebigoon.* (The red-tailed hawk can eat a snake.)

> *Wenjida-gookookoo'oo naaningodinong odebinaan giigoonan.* (The barred owl sometimes grabs a fish.)
>
> *Okoonzh aabajitoonaawaan wiiyaas ji-biigobidoowaad.* (They use their beak to tear meat.)
>
> *Biipiigwe nisaan gichibineshiiyan.* (The kestrel kills big birds.)
>
> *Aanind goshkoziwag gabe-giizhig gaye nibaawag gabe-dibik.* (Some are awake all day and sleep all night.)
>
> *Waabi-gookookoo'oo odebaabamaan nenaapaajinikesiyan apii mookinid.* (The snowy owl will watch for the mole to rise up.)
>
> *Zhiibingo-naniisi gizhiibizo apii bakaded.* (The peregrine flies fast when hungry.)
>
> *Migizi, Giniw gaye Zhiibingo-naniisi nandawenjigewag awasaakwaa.* (Eagle, golden eagle, and peregrine falcon hunt for food beyond the woods.)

Beyond visual observation, students were asked to consider other ways of knowing including *ezhi-ginisidotoonaanig*, aural recognition. Birds can be identified by the sounds they make for various reasons, and students discussed ways they might be engaged in communicating with one another.

> *Wenjiganooshiin jiichiigwaadaanan waabiganoojii-kanan.* (The great horned owl crunches on mouse bones.)
>
> *Aangodinong bineshiinh nagamo mii gaye aangodinong nandonged.* (Sometimes a bird sings and sometimes calls out to others.)
>
> *Apii gikinabizidan oshki-nagamowin anaaminagamowinked.* (When learning by listening to a new song, a bird creates a subsong.)

Moving beyond observation for the purpose of classification, students were invited to think about the life of the birds in a fully dimensional way, considering their traditional behavior as well as their adaptive behavior. They discovered that subsongs are the sounds made when birds are learning a song or the warm-up sounds made by adult birds that precede their regular songs. They researched the ways a bird's call changes throughout the day, across the seasons, and during its life as it grows and learns more about its own environment. This pushed the limits not only of the students' understanding of the birds, challenging them to describe a postindustrial landscape; it also required students to use Anishinaabemowin to describe the modern world, which now includes plastic and other manufactured items. For instance, students thought about the fact that: *Noongom apii wadiswankewaad waabishki-zhaabwaate'iigini aabajitoowaad ji-wiindamaadiwaad minik mashkoziwaad* (Today when making nests with white plastic they tell each other how strong they are) (Canal et al. 2016).

The most complex information about the birds was in references to entire narratives. When students learned "*gaakaabishiiwag zegaajimowag apii enwewaad* (screech owls tell a scary story when making a sound)" and "*gibwanisi babaamose ingo biitoosin giizhigong* (the hawk walks about on the first level of the sky)" they needed to reference particular *aadizookaanag*, or teaching legends, about the messages of owls and hierarchies of the clan system (Gibbs 2010; Jones 2011; Whipple 2015).

The experience with the birds extended to an interactive digital series of images combined with audio hosted by the community-based site www.ojibwe.net. On the website, phrases used as curriculum are posted with interactive images based on bird activities. These resources are available for students, their families, and learners from the general public to enjoy. Adding the perspective of another Algonquian culture, Maliseet artist and linguist Bernard Perley created line drawings of the *migizi* (bald eagle), *boodawidoombe* (barn owl), *biipiigwe* (kestrel), *zhiibingo-naniisi* (peregrine falcon), and *gaakaabeshii* (saw-whet owl). As viewers hover over an image with their mouse, it flips over to reveal a phrase with an audio button. The extent to which Perley represented the motion of the birds is impressive. In his drawings, the eagle faces east, low on the page with dark wings taking up the full horizon, and is shown at multiple points in time. The immediate past is represented on the same page by a smaller image of the bird facing forward just below the main image, and a full time-lapse effect is achieved with an arc of three shadows representing the full multidirectional flight forward in space and time as *migizi* flies west and then north. Similarly, the peregrine falcon image is multifaceted with an upper drawing featuring outspread wings navigating the wind and a lower drawing on the same page showing *zhiibingo-naniisi* diving to the ground, wings tucked tightly together.

Through these images viewers are given an illustration of indigenous philosophical eternalism and scientific relativity. Students can be invited to consider theories of relativity, gravity, and the way the curve of a bird's wing finds a space between high and low pressure to create lift and escape the pull of the earth.

An interactive learning experience that can lead to more complex discussions is increasingly common with endangered languages now available on many websites. One of the best examples for Anishinaabemowin is the *Ojibwe People's Dictionary* (2015), which includes definitions, grammar information, sample sentences, and sometimes audio and images. The page for *migizi* includes three forms of the word, seven audio files, an image, and the following two sentences:

> *Gichi-mindido a'awe migizi o'omaa ge-gizhibaayaashid.* (That bald eagle who is soaring around in the air is huge.)

> *Ishpiming niizh gizhibaayaashiwag migiziwag.* (There are two eagles circling up in the sky.)

Learners today have come to expect a multimodal experience, and teachers are increasingly able to insist that serious learners take advantage of these tools so that the conversations in the classroom can be richer and more interdisciplinary.

The final component on the raptor web page is a *giiwosebinesiwag nagamowin*, a raptor song written by Margaret Noodin and her daughters, Shannon and Fionnan, and then posted online by web designer Stacie Sheldon (Noodin and Sheldon 2016). It is intended to be sung with a rattle by male or female singers and echoes the call of the red-tailed hawk. The lyrics focus on lessons human observers can learn from raptors. Visitors to the website are given the history of the song, which can be shared by anyone who sings it. Enabling this protocol to continue is an important part of revitalizing Anishinaabe lyric traditions. Visitors can also read all of the words in Anishinaabemowin and English as well as listen to an audio file to help them learn the song. Like the curriculum, the song moves beyond basic naming to invoke messages of cosmology and philosophy. The birds are located beyond the realm of existence easily accessed by humans. From this position they foster connections to what is real but not visible; what is known but not perceived by physical sensations; and the way the self is shaped through attention and contemplation as an element in the world. It also includes a traditional Anishinaabe metaphor comparing *zagaakwaang* (the dense woods) to difficult life experiences.

Giiwosebinesiwag (Raptors)
gidishpaashim (you soar)
zagaakwaang. (above the woods and the hard times.)
Gikinoo'amawiyaang (You teach us)
ji-debibidoomaang (to grab tight)
bawajiganan. (our dreams.)
Gego zegiziken (Don't be afraid)
wiindamawiyaang (you tell us)
ji-dakwanjigen. (take a bite.)
Nitaawaziswanken (Make your nest well)
mii mikwendaan (and remember)
azhegiiwen. (to return home.)

Together, all of the tools and information on the page seek to provide visitors the opportunity to learn and then use the language. By providing full sentences, images, and a song, the editors of the site hope to inspire Anishinaabemowin speakers to carry the language forward creatively into the future.

The *giiwosebinesiwag nagamowin* also became a part of a collaborative presentation. For the first time in 48 years, raptors attended the Annual Algonquian Conference. Skywalker, a red-tailed hawk, and Glory, a bald eagle, arrived with their friends Lindsay Obermeier and Sara Sloan from the Audubon Raptor Program. The goal was simply to use Algonquian languages while getting to know the birds. The outcome was that all participants invoked or explored their own and others' individual and relational identities while also strengthening alliances between Algonquian language communities and between humans and birds of prey.

The presentation began as Margaret Noodin and four students from the University of Wisconsin–Milwaukee Anishinaabemowin classes (Monea Warrington, Nathon Breu, Nicole Rice, and Kai Pyle) shared the curriculum, images, and song. This was followed by an open invitation to the audience to speak to, or for, the birds. Glory, the bald eagle, began with three chatter calls as humans were approaching his space. Studies of chatter calls have shown that they are the most common form of communication for eagles, and individuals can be recognized by their own distinct variation of the call, which also changes across seasons and over a lifetime (Eakle et al. 1989). In his own way, Glory offered a reminder that every speech act is both individual and part of a shared system of communication.

The first to speak was Jarrid Baldwin, who introduced himself: "*Aya ceeki, ciinkwia weenswiaani niila myaamiaataweenki neepwaankia.*" (Hello everyone, my name is Jarrid Baldwin [ciinkwia] and I am a Myaamia language teacher.) He then went on to say, "I can give you how we would call both of these: *oonaana mikicia neehi-hsa* (bald eagle) *oonaana meemihkwihkicia* (red-tailed hawk)." Jarrid has been using Myaamia all of his life and works with his father, Daryl Baldwin, and other speakers at The Myaamia Center, a cross-cultural effort supported by the Miami Tribe of Oklahoma and Miami University to continue the recovery of the language (Myaamia Center 2016).

The next participant to speak was Joey Awonohopay, the director of the Menominee Language and Culture Commission, which promotes the revitalization of Menominee language, history, traditions, and culture. Members of the Menominee community believe: "Menominee Language is a gift from the Creator to the Menominee people and should be treated with respect" (Menominee Indian Tribe 2016). Joey shared the following:

> *Pōsōh māwaw new weyak.* (Hello everyone.) *Pakāhcekaew netāēkāēm.* (I'm called Pakāhcekaew.) *Omāēqnomenēw netāwem.* (I'm Menominee.) *Ēh-ayom ohpēqtaw nayāēnekotoken keckīwak eneq āētuaq penāēhsiw kāēmāw men new kenēw* (About this raptor, sometimes what the old people used to say was the bald eagle or the golden eagle)*, mesek taeh enoh wēc-ohpēqtaw mēqsenekāēhkaeh, kāēmāw men new māēskwananīw* (also his fellow raptor, the big hawk, or red-tail hawk)*, red-sitter and messenger, and nayīs new* (both of them)*, both of these birds are in our origin story, our origin of our Menominee people. He, he māēc-ohpēqtawak* (big birds)*, these big sitters, to us they're little relatives to the enāēmaehkiwak* (Thunderers)*, the Thunders. And so that's what they serve in our clan system, is they represent the enāēmaehkiwak* (Thunderers)*, the Thunderbirds, the mythical spiritual beings to our people. Eneq* (That's all).

Joey was followed by Michael Sullivan, the resident linguist for Waadookodaading Ojibwe Immersion School. As a parent, teacher, and member of the local community, he is committed to language revitalization. He is also known for his skill as a storyteller and singer. He not only uses the language in a classroom setting, he carries it with him at all times making connections between people, stories, songs, and the environment that sustains them. He had the following to share with the audience:

Ahaw boozhoo indinawemaaganidog. (Hello my relatives.) *Mii go omaa gaye niin wii-wiindamaageyaan endazhimangwaa ogow binesiwag.* (So I too will tell how we talk about these great birds.) *Nashke wa'aw migizi mii indapinikaazowin, mii ezhinikaazoyaan gaye niin mii niwiinzowin gaa-pi-miizhid a'aw niiyawe'enyiban mewinzha.* (See I'm named after this one, the eagle, that is how I am known too, my name that was given to me by namesake a long time ago.) *Miinawaa aw migizi indoodem gaawiin wiin indedeyiban gii-Anishinaabewisiin. Nashke dash ekidowaad iwidi ishkoniganing wenjibaayaan, giishpin chimookomaaniwid a'aw gidede giwaangoomigoo imaa migizi-doodeming. Mii gaa-inakamigiziyaan ge niin.* (And I am eagle clan. My father wasn't Anishinaabe. But you see, they say on my reservation where I am from if your dad is White, you are adopted spiritually into eagle clan and that is what happened with me.) *Geget manidoowaadiziwag agiw binesiwag ogow niizh. Aanind agiw chi-aya'aag gaa-pizindawagig dazhimaawaad iniw migiziwan, "waabamad aw migizi mii go dibishkoo go waabamad aw binesi, mii enaabishkawaad aniw binesiwan".* (Definitely these are spiritual birds these two. Some of the elders I have listened to talking about eagles say "When you see an eagle, it's like you're seeing a thunderbird, that is who represents the thunderbirds.") *Awedi dash kekek izhi-wiinaa. Manidoowaadizi gaye wiin aabajichigaazod imaa midewigaaning ezhi-niizho-midewid a'aw Anishinaabe, mii iw dinowa midewayaan aabajichigaazod.* (That other one is named '*Kekek.*' He too is sacred when they use him in the midewiwin lodge when the Anishinaabe becomes second degree mide.) *Niwii-shaaganaashiim bangii da-nisidotameg gaawiin akina omaa nitaa-ojibwemo-siiwag.* (So I will speak English now a little for those who don't speak Ojibwe so well.) So, my name coincidentally, my Ojibwe name is Migizi, which is the same name as that first guy there. He is also my clan. So we have a teaching in my community of Lac Courte Oreilles, Wisconsin, that if you are born to a white father and Ojibwe mother then you are adopted into the eagle clan. One of the roles that our eagle clan has is a leadership role and also public speaking, singing, and caretakers of our language. So real good to see, *indapinikaazowin,* the one I'm named after. A lot of elders who taught me talk about the *migizi* serving as a spiritual representation of the *animikiig* just as Joey was talking about with the Menominee, sort of little brothers to the thunderbirds. The other one *kekek* that's what we call a hawk. And he's kind of a special bird to us too. He is used in our Midewiwin lodge and in our spiritual practices. So his hide is used when a person goes through the lodge for the second time . . . at least that's the teaching in our community in the lodges that we attend. *Mi iw.*

To balance the Menominee and Ojibwe, Ron Corn followed Michael Sullivan. Ron is equally well known in the Great Lakes region as a language expert whose passion for revitalization has been sustained over many years. Like Joey Awonohopay, Ron works to sustain the Menominee language.

> *Nahāw, pōsōh māwaw new weyak.* (Well, hello everyone.) *Nenaeq ayāweyan Muqsāhkwat.* (I'm Muqsāhkwat.) *Omāēqnomenēw netāwem.* (I'm Menominee.) *Nemāēnīnehtan yōq 's kew-īyan.* (I'm glad to be here.) *Taq enoh, nēmatak, ayāh penāēhsiw, kāēhkāēh.* (My brothers, that eagle, hawk.) *Nekāēhkenan enoh nēmat kayēs-kīketit wāēkiq new eneh 's aw-esēkemakat, āēs-wēhcekatāēk, kāēyas ācemowan kayēs-ūkuaq.* (I know that my friend who talked before me [talked] about what might happen, what it means, how the old stories were used.) *Eneq taeh maeqsēh new kew-enāēnehtaman.* (And I think highly of them.) *Taq enoh, nahāēneseyan kan mānāēwak nenāēwāwak.* (Well, when I was small, there weren't a lot of them that I would see.) *Yōq-peh taeh men new nenāēwāwak, eneq wāēkiq new kāēqc-esāweyan āēs-nāēwāw.* (And today I see them, it makes me proud to see one of them.) *Nemāq taeh enoh penāēhsiw, kenēwak, kāēhkāēh mēkonan kew-ōkuaq, kēspen kāēkōh esēkemakat kepāēmātesewan, kapaq weyak kenaw-mēnek.* (And wow, the bald eagle, golden eagles, hawk—they use their feathers, depending on what happens in your life, someone might give you one.) *Nemāq, nemāēnīnehtan wenaeq new 's kew-mēneh eneh mēkwan.* (I really like it when they give a feather.) *Wāēwāēnen ketāēnenemuaw kēs-nawāc-paehtāwekeyan.* (Thank you for listening to me.)

The last person to offer a comment was Heather Bliss, a linguist who works with Blackfoot, also known as Siksika, an Algonquian language located north of the Rocky Mountains and the Great Plains.

> I thought I would stand up quickly to pay tribute to my dear friend Tootsinam Beatrice Bullshields. She was my good friend and my Siksika teacher and we lost her about a year and a half ago. And when we did our work together, eagles featured really large. We often talked about eagles and when we'd seen eagles together and even where we worked at the University of British Columbia the vantage point we had looking out to the forest—there was a tree where eagles often sat and flew away. She always told me seeing eagles flying over top was a good omen. So now I carry that with me and when I see eagles I think of Beatrice.

Each of the people who spoke in the presence of the birds identified themselves from an indigenous linguistic perspective. They shared their own identity and shared what they had learned humans should know about the raptors. By doing this, these speakers and keepers of Algonquian languages wove a network of understanding based upon individual and collective identity and experience. Their comments included names but quickly moved beyond names to stories of how the birds and humans share a social space and enrich one another's lives.

Between the presentation of raptor images and stories in a digital environment to the appearance of raptors at the conference, the entire event affirms the two hypotheses suggested at the outset of planning. Individual language use and individual identity definitely intersect with communal language use and communal identity to produce more clearly defined individual and communal epistemologies and more holistic linguistic and cultural revitalization. When speakers fully understand and use languages connected with their personal and collective identities, they construct shared phenomenological and cosmological perspectives in the transnational transtemporal present; the central reality is found in the mode of articulation, not the historical situation. Use of indigenous languages ensures indigenous philosophical perspectives are part of the global understanding of human experience. Language can become a methodology when modern thinkers work to describe their own and others' states of being. This collaborative revitalization project provided an opportunity for language learning and archival documentation as well as the advancement of philosophical theories fundamentally related to identity. Although the audio was not ideal, it was unobtrusive and, with the help of numerous collaborators, was transcribed and translated so that second language speakers' voices from several Algonquian languages became part of the conference summary. Each speaker offered their own statement on human and nonhuman relations, and together all of the speakers contributed to a cross-cultural indigenous perspective that could either be considered a non-Western, non-Eastern indigenous viewpoint; or entirely beyond cardinal geolocation and better defined as evidence of a dialogue between layers of being. Creative and unconventional events like this one, which combine documentation, linguistics, pedagogy, and lived experiences, forge new theoretical, methodological, and philosophical alliances. Children can mark new ancestral territory for future generations as they process lived urban and rural dialogic, and the birds invite us to begin a subsong between species as together we continue to understand differences. When we understand our ecosystem and the network we inhabit we can remember and revitalize Anishinaabemowin. Languages not only define and describe ancient alliances, they call our attention to the fact that communication is fundamentally the echo of our being. *Ezhi-enweweyaang mii bimaadiziyaang,* the way we speak is inherently the way we move through existence.

REFERENCES

Absolon, Kathy. 2010. Indigenous Wholistic Theory: A Knowledge Set for Practice. *First Peoples Child and Family Review* 5(2):74–87.

Ambler, Marjane. 2004. Native Languages: A Question of Life or Death. *Tribal College Journal* 15(3):8–9.

Blommaert, Jan. 2008. Bernstein and Poetics Revisited: Voice, Globalization and Education. *Discourse and Society* 19:425–451.

Canal, David, Margarita Mulero-Pazmany, Juan Jose Negro, and Fabrizio Sergio. 2016. Decoration Increases the Conspicuousness of Raptor Nests. PLoS ONE 11(7):e0157440. doi:10.1371/journal.pone.0157440.

Dauenhauer, Nora Marks and Richard Dauenhauer. 1998. Technical, Emotional, and Ideological Issues in Reversing Language Shift: Examples from Southeast Alaska. *Endangered Languages: Language Loss and Community Response*, ed. by Lenore A. Grenoble and Lindsay J. Whaley, pp. 57–98. Cambridge: Cambridge University Press.

Eakle, Wade, R. William Mannan, and Teryl Grubb. 1989. Identification of Individual Breeding Bald Eagles by Voice Analysis. *Journal of Wildlife Management* 53(2):450–455. doi:10.2307/3801149.

Emberley, Julia. 2014. *The Testimonial Uncanny: Indigenous Storytelling, Knowledge, and Reparative Practices*. Albany, NY: SUNY Press.

Genuisz, Wendy Makoons. 2009. *Our Knowledge Is Not Primitive: Decolonizing Botanical Anishinaabe Teachings*. Syracuse, NY: Syracuse University Press.

Gibbs, Anna. 2010. Wenji-beshizhid agongos: How the Chipmunk Got Its Stripes. *Oshkaabewis Native Journal* 7(2):78–81.

Graveline, Fyre Jean. 2004. *Healing Wounded Hearts*. Halifax: Fernwood Publishing.

Harrison, K. 2007. *When Languages Die: The Extinction of the World's Languages and the Erosion of Human Knowledge*. New York: Oxford University Press.

Hart, Michael. 2002. *Seeking mino-pimatisiwin*. Halifax: Fernwood Publishing.

Hornberger, Nancy and Karl Swinehart. 2012. Bilingual Intercultural Education and Andean Hip Hop: Transnational Sites for Indigenous Language and Identity. *Language in Society* 41(4):499–525.

Horton, Jessica and Janet Berlo. 2013. Beyond the Mirror. *Third Text* 27(1):17–28.

Hymes, Dell. 2003. *Now I Know Only So Much: Essays in Ethnopoetics*. Lincoln: University of Nebraska Press.

Ingold, Tim. 2000. *The Perception of the Environment: Essays on Livelihood, Dwelling and Skill.* London: Routledge.

Jones, WIlliam. 2011. Gaa-ozhichigaadeg, wenjibaamagak nibowin. *Oshkaabewis Native Journal* 8(1):43–48.

Kimmerer, Robin Wall. 2013. *Braiding Sweetgrass.* Minneapolis: Milkweed Editions.

Matthews, Maureen, Roger Roulette, and Rand Valentine. 2010. Anishinaabemowin: The Language of Pimachiowin Aki. Discussion paper written for the Pimachiowin Aki UNESCO World Heritage site proposal.

McCarty, Teresa, Mary Eunice Romero, and Ofelia Zepeda. 2006. Reclaiming the Gift: Indigenous Youth Counter-Narratives on Native Language Loss and Revitalization. *American Indian Quarterly* 30(1):28–48.

McCarty, Teresa and Ofelia Zepeda. 2010. Native Americans. *Handbook of Language and Ethnic Identity*, 2nd ed., ed. by J.A. Fishman and O. García, pp. 323–339. New York: Oxford University Press.

Menominee Indian Tribe. 2016. http://www.menominee-nsn.gov/GovernmentPages.

Mihas, Elena, Bernard Perley, Gabriel Rei Doval, Kathleen Wheatley, and Michael Noonan. 2013. *Responses to Language Endangerment: In Honor of Mickey Noonan: New Directions in Language Documentation and Language Revitalization.* University of Wisconsin–Milwaukee. *Studies in Language Companion*, n.s., vol. 142. Amsterdam.

Myaamia Center. 2016. http://myaamiacenter.org/statement-of-purpose/.

Nabigon, Herb. 2006. *The Hollow Tree: Fighting Addiction with Traditional Native Healing.* Montreal and Kingston: McGill-Queen's University Press.

Nichols, John D. (ed.). 2015. *Ojibwe People's Dictionary.* http://ojibwe.lib.umn.edu/.

Noodin, Margaret and Stacie Sheldon. 2016. Raptors: Giiwosebinesiwag. http://ojibwe.net/projects/raptors/.

Proulx, Michael, Orlin Todorov, Amanda Taylor Aiken, and Alexandra de Sousa. 2016. Where Am I? Who Am I? The Relation Between Spatial Cognition, Social Cognition and Individual Differences in the Built Environment. *Frontiers in Psychology* 7(64). doi: 10.3389/fpsyg.2016.00064.

Schlitz Audubon. 2017. Raptor Program. http://www.schlitzaudubon.org/education/raptor-program.

Shrum, Judith and Eileen Glisan. 2005. *Teacher's Handbook: Contextualized Language Instruction.* Boston: Thomson/Heinle.

Simpson, Leanne. 2001. Aboriginal Peoples and Knowledge: Decolonizing Our Processes.

Canadian Journal of Native Studies 21(1):137–148.

Thomas, Robina (Qwul'sih'yah'maht). 2005. Honouring the Oral Traditions of My Ancestors through Storytelling. *Research as Resistance: Critical, Indigenous, and Anti-Oppressive Approaches*, ed. by L. Brown and S. Strega, pp. 237–254. Toronto: Canadian Scholars' Press.

Whalen, D.H., Margaret Moss, and Daryl Baldwin. 2016. Healing through Language: Positive Physical Health Effects of Indigenous Language Use. *F1000Research 2016* 5:852. doi: 10.12688/f1000research.8656.1.

Whipple, Dorothy Dora. 2015. *Chi-mewinzha: Ojibwe Stories from Leech Lake.* Minneapolis: University of Minnesota Press.

Alford's Shawnee Translation of the Gospels

Carl Schaefer

With more than 3,700 verses—some 65,000 words in the current normalization—Thomas Wildcat Alford's translation of the four Gospels (Alford 1929) is a large text in Absentee Shawnee, produced by a bilingual speaker who was also a professional educator.[1] While the translation's Shawnee word order often follows the English word order closely, it is clear that Alford did not disregard obligatory word order rules of Shawnee; an example is his consistent placement of direct quotation tags such as *hotelahi* 'he said to them' after the quote, even when this puts the tag in the following verse. Regardless of the possible nonidiomatic word order in his translation, the text provides much information about the language. This report focuses mainly on Alford's transcription and what it tells us not just about his pronunciation of Shawnee but also about his thinking as a linguist. It also notes several features of Alford's morphology: archaic forms and forms not reported in Voegelin (1936) or Parks (1975).[2]

Transcription

This section discusses four aspects of Alford's transcription: representation of vowel length; variation in representation of the syllable /ki/; treatment of final /-h/ in preverbs; and introduction of "ghost" vowels in certain consonant clusters.[3]

Alford's text is not a direct, phonetic transcription of how his Shawnee translation would have sounded if read aloud. It is closer to a phonemic rendering; indeed, in some respects it is more abstract than a phonemic transcription. The final pages of his work contain a brief English description of equivalences between the Latin letters of his transcription and the sounds of Shawnee, but little beyond these equivalences. He does not cite previous work that may have influenced his transcription.

Alford uses all letters in the Latin alphabet except for *z*. He uses the apostrophe, generally to indicate a loss of phonetic material; but in cases of contraction, the apostrophe can alter the general rules of Latin-letter-to-Shawnee-pronunciation equivalences. For example, Alford would probably have pronounced the sequences <k'uci>, <k' uci>, and <ki uci> all as if he had written <koci> (*kooci*, prefixed form of preverb *hoci*). Hyphenation, like word-space, is generally used to indicate morphology, not phonetics. For example, in nouns with stems ending in /n/, Alford regularly writes the locative as <-nagi>. However, his use of the hyphen is not consistent; thus *neepekiki* 'the dead' appears six times as <na-pagiki> and four times as <napagiki>.[4]

Aside from the hyphen, Alford's translation appears to have many other inconsistencies in spelling. Some of these are undoubtedly proofreading oversights—more than 145 can be identified with a high level of confidence.[5] However, some are likely the result of indecision or a change in Alford's practice as his understanding of the relation between Shawnee phonology and a standardized orthography deepened. Indeed, a significant number of apparent inconsistencies can, on further examination, be shown to result from the consistent application of sophisticated, though complex, spelling rules.

Alford makes no use of diacritics. At the same time, it appears that he intended to represent the distinction between long and short vowels using only one letter per vowel sound. By repurposing the otherwise unneeded Latin letters *r* and *v*, he can accommodate all the distinctions except for the distinction between /e/ and /ee/ (Table 1).

He does have a partial, and sophisticated, workaround for the ambiguity of <a>.

TABLE 1. Original-normalized equivalences

ORIGINAL	NORMALIZED	ORIGINAL	NORMALIZED
<l>	l	<i>	i, y
<m>	m	<e>	ii
<n>	n	<u>	o, w
<b>, <p>	p	<o>	oo
<d>, <t>	t	<a>	e, ee
<g>, <k>	k	<v>	a
<c>, <j>	c [č]	<r>	aa
<f>	θ	<w>	w
<s>	s [š]	<y>	y
<q>	kw	<h>	h
<x>	ks		

TABLE 2. Vowel length (normalized equivalents in intersection cells)

	<e>	<o>	<r>	<a>	<i>	<u>	<v>
<b>	pii	poo	paa	pee			
<d>	tii	too	taa	tee			
<j>	cii	coo	caa	cee			
<g>	kii	koo	kaa	kee, ke	ki		
<p>				pe	pi	po	pa
<t>				te	ti	to	ta
<c>				ce	ci	co	ca
<k>					ki	ko	ka

Since he does not need to represent the distinction between voiceless and voiced stops, he uses grapheme distinctions <b>~<p>, <d>~<t>, <j>~<c> to indicate the length of a following <a>. Thus, <pa> represents /pe/ while <ba> represents /pee/ (Table 2). He also notes that <i> is used in place of <y> before short vowels and that <h>, when followed by a consonant, seems to "cut short the vowel that precedes it" (Alford 1929:200). In other contexts, <a> remains ambiguous in length: after resonants <l>, <m>, <n>; after <h>; after fricatives <f>, <s>; to some extent after semivowel <w>; and, exceptionally, after letter <g>. Alford notes, "G is sounded as *g* in English word give (always hard), and is followed by all vowels, excepting u and v" (1929:200). Thus, <g> occurs not only before long vowel letters <e>, <o>, <r>, and the length-ambiguous <a>, but also before the short vowel letter <i>, while <k> occurs only before the unambiguously short vowel letters <i>, <u>, <v>. The asymmetry of Alford's treatment of <g> and <k>, on the one hand, and the non-velar stops on the other, is apparent in Table 2. This asymmetry results not only in <a> being ambiguous in post-velar position, but also in a redundancy: there are two ways to spell the syllable /ki/.

Alford's rule for <g> vs. <k> is not as unmotivated as it might seem at first glance. For one thing, because of a historical raising (in most contexts) of short /e/ to /i/ after the velar stop, syllable /ke/ (with short vowel) should be found only in predictable contexts, namely before /h/ and when in word-final position. On the other hand, the redundant spellings for /ki/ might be expected to result in free variation in the spelling of this syllable. Alford constrains this variation with another condition, this one an explicitly morphological condition: "The syllable ki in most Shawnee words occurring at the end of a word is a sign of a plural as s in English" (1929:200). With this constraint, all plural nouns ending in syllable /ki/ would be spelled <ki>. However, the vast number of occurrences of syllable /ki/ should still have two possible spellings. Indeed, reading the original text can leave one with the impression of random variation. In fact, however, his practice is far from random.

While Alford's statement implies that the spelling <ki> is restricted to the suffix of noun plurals, his rule for <gi> ~ <ki> is more general. Whenever the syllable /ki/ is part of an inflectional prefix or suffix and the inflected form is plural, the spelling is <ki>; otherwise, the spelling is <gi> (1–8):[6]

(1) Initial <gi> if part of the verb stem, even if the form is plural:
<macimi bami gifinvmuwrci ud rqvsqhrwanwv>
mecimi peemi kiθinamowaaci hotaakwaskwhaawenwa
and PROG.IC wash.TI.CONJ.3P net.NI.POSS.3P
'and were washing their nets.' (Luke 5:2)

(2) NA.3P: <ilaneki> *hileniiki* 'men'

(3) AI.3P: <iwvki> *hiwaki* 'they say'

(4) TI.PART_AG.3P: <ma-mecicki> *meemiicicki* 'that which they eat' (Mark 6:44)

(5) Personal preverb prefix /ki/: *kimehci* PERF is <gimahci> when the verb is singular, and <kimahci> when the verb is plural:

a. <ki mahci nodrgapwv>

kimehci nootaakeepwa

PERF hear.AI.2P

'You have heard it said' (Matt. 5:21)

b. <gi mahci tapvsvwafi>

kimehci tepasaweθi

PERF faithful.AI.2S

'Thou hast been faithful' (Matt. 25:21)

(6) Personal possessor prefix /ki/: <gi sgesaku> *kiskiiseko* eye.NI.POSS.2S.P 'thine eyes' (Luke 19:42), since the possessor is singular (while the noun itself is plural).

(7) II.CONJ/PART: <gi> for a semantically singular subject and <ki> for a semantically plural subject:

a. <chena ini yrtafvgi iah biayrgi>

chiine hini yaateθaki yeh pyeeyaaki

and DEM.INAN.S hour when come.II.CONJ

'And when the hour was come' (Mark 15:33)

b. <xvga qelvhi ini yagi wvhsi nili biayrki>

ksake kwiilahi hini yeeki wahsi nili pyeeyaaki

for necessarily DEM be.SO.II.PART PURP DEM.INAN.P come.II.CONJ

'For it must needs be that the occasions come;' (Matt. 18:7)

(8) TA.1/2.2/1 forms: the spelling of the prefix follows the number of the agent. Thus a TA.1S.2P will have a prefix spelled <gi> while a TA.2.1X form (paradigmatically ambiguous for agent number) will be spelled <gi> for a semantically singular second person agent and <ki> for a semantically plural second person agent:

a. <ni grmrnelafewa gi melalapwv>

nikaamaaniileθiiwe kimiilelepwa

peace.NI.POSS.1S.S give.TA.1S.2P

'My peace I give unto you;' (John 14:27)

b. <gi mvci-mipa nahfrpi>

kimacimipe	nehθaapi
reproach.TA.2.1X	also

'Thou reproachest us also.' (Luke 11:45)

Alford also extends the <gi> ~ <ki> rule to cases where the underlying /i/ has been lost in contraction; thus the preverb *kooci* (*ki+hoci*) is spelled <g'uci> when the agent is singular and <k'uci> when the agent is plural (9–10).

(9) <nahiwa g'uci rnwahsa>

nehiwe	kooci	haanwehse
what	WHY	doubt.AI.2S

'Wherefore didst thou doubt?' (Matt. 14:31)

(10) <nahiwa gawvgi k'uci skvtv la-lamrpa dabwawa-nvki>

nehiwe	keewaki	kooci	skata	leelemaape	teepweewenaki
what	still	WHY	further	need.TA.1I.3	witness.NA.3P

'What further need have we of witnesses?' (Matt. 26:65)

Another spelling convention, one based on phonetic rather than grammatical or morphological context, results in variation in the spelling of the preverbs that normally end in <h>: the independent future (*-eh*), the irrealis (*-ih*), the dependent future (*wah*), the locational (*tah*), and the *teh*-preverb (*teh*). Each of these has a variant spelling without the final <h>. The underlying pattern here is not hard to uncover, given that Alford's normal practice is to NOT explicitly represent the predictable phonetic initial /h/ before words that would otherwise begin with a vowel. In contrast, when one of these preverbs precedes a word with the predictable /h/ onset, the final <h> in the preverb's spelling is moved to initial position in the spelling of the following word (11–12). If the following word begins with a single consonant, then the preverb retains its final <h> spelling (13). When the following word begins not with a single consonant but with a consonant cluster, the final <h> is again omitted from the preverb (14–16).

(11) <ki mahci utfaku-nrwv>

kimehci	hotθekonaawa
PERF	receive.TA.INAN_SUBJ.3.2P

'Ye have received.' (Luke 6:24)

(12) <wa hutfakunrwv>
we hotθekonaawa
FUT receive.TA.INAN_SUBJ.3.3P
'shall receive' (Luke 20:47)

(13) <nvmahfvli wah nvtumrli>
namehθali weh natomaali
fish.NA.4S FUT ask.for.3S.4S
'shall ask for a fish' (Matt. 7:10)

(14) <wa nfr-wrli>
we nhθaawaali
FUT kill.TA.3P.4S (Matt. 17:23)

(15) <wa pgah-whrli>
we pkehwaali
FUT set.apart.TA.3S.4S (Matt. 19:9)

(16) <wa sfv-hvhi>
we sθahahi
FUT send.TA.3S.4P (Matt. 21:3)

To this relatively simple set of spelling rules there are a few exceptions that are probably due to oversight; thus the text has nine occurrences of *weh wanhto* 'will lose'. In seven instances the spelling conforms to the rule (with the preverb-final <h> explicit, <wah wvntu>), while in two instances the final <h> is omitted (<wa wvntu>). Other apparent exceptions have a more interesting explanation. Consider these examples in Alford's original text (17–18):

(17) <wa gijepita>
FUT be.bound.II (Matt. 16:19)

(18) <wa kufaqa>
FUT fear.TA.PART_OB.2P.3 (Luke 12:5)

Given that the verbs in these examples appear to begin with a single consonant, we would expect the preverb to be spelled <wah>. In these and other cases, the

TABLE 3. Ghost vowels inferred from internal variation

VOEGELIN 1938–1940	ALFORD NORMALIZED STEM	ALFORD ORIGINAL
θaKky- 'crinkled, crumpled'	θakkehkaw- 'press, crowd'	fvggahgr-goki fvgigahgr-goki
kt-, kc- 'big'	ktikaan- 'field'	gtikv gitikv
	ppaktehw- 'beat'	ppvgta-whvhi p'pvgtahugo-pwa pipvgtawhr-wvhi
	hott- 'enter'	uttv-maqa utitv-maqa uttv uttitv
kwakw- 'detach'	kwakwkot- (*possibly* kwakwt- *or* kwakkot-)	qvkkutvnu qvkukutvnu

apparent exceptional spelling actually conforms to Alford's rules if we take into account his use of a "ghost vowel," the insertion of an orthographic vowel letter in a context that, in all likelihood, did not include a phonetic vowel. In (17) and (18) it appears that Alford has inserted an orthographic ghost vowel but has been consistent in representing the phonetics; thus the proper normalizations for (17) and (18) are *we kciipite* and *we kwθeekwe*, respectively.

Alford consistently spells words related to Voegelin's (1938–1940) *kk-* 'old' stem with the doubled <gg>: <ggvtwi>, <ggvtu>, <ggvdowi>, <ggvdoweyv>. While this shows that the Shawnee double stop sequences attested elsewhere were present in Alford's speech, this consistency is not the rule in Alford's text. For words related to other stems with doubled stops or stop clusters, it is more common to find variation in the spelling. In Table 3 we see spelling variants in the doubled /kk/ as well as in /pp/, /tt/, /kt/, and possibly /kwt/: in each case, one variant has the orthographic doubled stop (or unbroken consonant cluster), while the other variant has the two consonant letters separated, in a few cases, by an apostrophe, but more commonly by an intervening vowel letter, most frequently <i> but sometimes <u>. Apparently Alford felt that the orthographic doubled stop (or consonant cluster) was not an appropriate representation for his speech.

In addition to relying solely on comparative evidence and internal variation in the presence/absence of the ghost vowel itself, there is a third kind of evidence, the variation in the immediately preceding orthographic context. As already noted,

TABLE 4. Ghost vowel inferred from preceding context

VOEGELIN 1938–1940	ALFORD NORMALIZED STEM	ALFORD ORIGINAL
ckw- 'preserving part'	ckonooθo- 'be kept, be left'	wa cikunofu
Ppe?t-, pet- 'sustain, support weakness'	ppehim- 'speak against'	wa pipahcimrli
kk- 'conceal'	kkit- 'hide'	u ta gigitu
kkwit-, Kkwit- 'higher, up'	kwkwicsin- 'go up'	ki ta kuqicsi-napa
kw- 'fear'	kwtel- 'rebuke'	u ta kutalrli

TABLE 5. Ghost vowel before hp-, hk-

VOEGELIN 1938–1940	ALFORD NORMALIZED STEM	ALFORD ORIGINAL
(-)hpapi 'sitting on something'	hpapi- 'sit'	wa ipvpi
?pena- 'way of treatment'	hpenal- 'do to/for'	git panvlakurwv (/ki+hp-/) git ipanvlaqv (/ki+hp-/) wa ipanvlrli (vs. <wa hipanvlrli>)
	hpenat- 'do to/with'	ya-ipanvdo-daki (/yee+hp-/) ya-panvdo-dagi (/yee+hp-/)
hkw- 'farthest point possible'	hkwinamo- 'perish' hkwineh- 'destroy'	ihqi-nvmo-ivqa wa iqinahvhi (vs. <wa hiqinahvhi>)
hkwee-, y?kwee 'female, sister, woman'	yhkwee- 'woman'	iqawv

Alford's practice is to write preverbs normally ending in <h> (<-eh>, <-ih>, <wah>, <tah>, <teh>) without the final <h> in only two cases: when the following word would begin with a vowel, in which case the final <h> of the preverb is positioned as an initial <h> on the following word; and when the following word begins with a consonant cluster. As noted earlier, there are apparent exceptions to these rules, at least some of which are explained by the fact that Alford's use of a ghost vowel obscures the presence of a phonetic consonant cluster (Table 4). In these cases, the conclusion that Alford's orthographic vowel is actually a ghost vowel is also supported by comparative evidence and, in some cases, internal variation in the presence/absence of the orthographic vowel itself.[7] Alford's ghost vowels appear in another context: in words where we would expect, on historical/comparative grounds, an initial /h/ followed by a stop (Table 5). In Alford's orthography, word-initial <h> is never followed by a consonant. With respect to the last row of Table 5, *yhkwee-*,

Alford always writes <iqawv> for the uncompounded stem, with no indication that his <i> is a ghost vowel. However, the form <sasgihqa> 'virgin' in Matt. 12:42 lends some support for the /hkw/ cluster that Voegelin (1938–1940) assumes.[8]

We can only speculate why Alford introduced these ghost vowels into his orthography. His hesitation to write the doubled stops—<pp>, <tt>, <gg>—may have to do with the conventional pronunciation of these letter sequences in English, where the orthographic double indicates quality or length of the preceding vowel, not a doubly released sequence of stops, as in Shawnee. Perhaps Alford thought of the Shawnee pronunciation as actually having an intervening but UNVOICED short vowel. Whatever his logic, the persistence of internal variation suggests indecision or a change of mind in the course of his work.

Morphology

This section discusses several aspects of morphology: use of the old passive conjugation; the marking of initial change with the older stem-internal variation instead of with reduplication; and inflectional forms (subjunctive and various obviative forms) not described in two general treatments of twentieth-century Shawnee, Voegelin (1936) and Parks (1975). Why these sources did not cover the subjunctive and obviative inanimate forms is not clear; perhaps these forms, like the old passives and stem-internal initial change, represented an older mode of speech, or perhaps they did not occur with sufficient frequency in their informants' speech to be included in productive paradigms.

While derived stems in *-ooθoo* for AI and *-ootee* for II are far more common passive forms, there are a number of examples of the older inflectional passive (Table 6). For some roots, both the derived passive and the inflectional passive are found, with no apparent difference in connotation (19–20).

(19)	ksake	hina	peepoonaka	hina	weh	miilekwi
	for	DEM	have.TI.PART_AG.3S	DEM	FUT	give.TA.PASS.3S

'For he that hath, to him shall be given.' (Mark 4.25)

(20)	ksake	kookwe-neeθa-kaci	hopoona	hina	weh	miilooθo
	for	whoever	have.TI.3S.S	DEM	FUT	be.given.AI.3S

'For whosoever hath, to him shall be given;' (Luke 8:18)

TABLE 6. Inflectional passive

FORM	ENDING	FREQUENCY (DISTINCT VERB FORMS IN ALFORD)
TA.3P	-ekwiiki	6
TA.3S	-ekwi	19
TA.4P	-ekwihi	1
TA.PART_OB.3	-eci	4
TA.CONJ.3	-eci	7
TA.SUBJ.1S	-ike	2
TA.SUBJ.2S	-akwate	1
TA.SUBJ.3	-ete	1

TABLE 7. Examples of old initial change

VARIATION	FORM	GLOSS	STEM
aya(a)~aa	layaapitepeelecikeeta	inherit.AI.PART.3S	laapitepeelecike
	wayaakotamaake	know.TI.PART_OB.1X.3	waakot-
aye(e)~ee	mayecθetawaata	prepare.TA.PART_AG.3S.4	mecθetaw-
	nayeekasiweeyaaki	follow.II.PART	neekasiweeya
ee~i	keenwaaki	long.II.PART	kinwi
kehc~kc	kehcimeciloo θicki	least.AI.PART.3P	kcimeciloo θi
	kehcitawahaacki	guard.TA.PART_AG.3P.4	kcitawah-
aa~ii	saakeelemelakwe	hate.TA.PART_AG.3.1I	siikeelem-
	waasikatowicki	strong.AI.PART.3P	wiisikatowi
aa~oo	paaθkwahki	cloudy.II.PART	pooθkwatwi

Initial change is most frequently marked by reduplication, but there are examples of the older stem-internal change (Table 7). For some stems, Alford uses both older initial change and the newer reduplicated initial change, perhaps intending a different stylistic effect. For example, both *wayaakotamaake* ('know'. TI.part_ob.1x.3) and *weewaakotaka* ('know'. TI.part_ag.3s.3) occur in the text (21–22):

(21) tepilo tepilo kitele niila nikalawipe hini wayaakotamaake
truly truly say.TA.1s.2s PRO speak.AI.1X DEM know.TI.PART_OB.1X.3
'Verily, verily, I say unto thee, We speak that we do know.' (John 3:11)

(22) mecimi hina haloolaaka weewaakotaka
and DEM servant.NA.S know.TI.PART_AG.3S.3

yeesiteheewenilici teepeelemekoci
want.NI.POSS.4 rule.TA.PART_AG.INV.4.3S
'And that servant, which knew his lord's will . . . ' (Luke 12:47)

While Voegelin (1936) does not describe any subjunctive forms, the subjunctive is well represented in Alford's text (Table 8). The most common use of the subjunctive is to translate conditional clauses, either with an explicit Shawnee conditional conjunction (*kwehkwi* 'if', *weeciwephi* 'unless') or without the conjunction, as in (23). *kwehkwi* can also be used without the subjunctive, as when *kwehkwi* introduces a clause with the future or irrealis preverb.

(23) hiinawiyane hokwihθali maneto, hini yaasitehθeki hoci
be.that.AI.SUBJ.2S son.NA.4S god.NA.3S DEM cross.NI.LOC from

kwasθaalo
come.down.AI.IMP.2S
'If thou art the Son of God, come down from the cross.' (Matt. 27:40)

There are several obviative forms not described in Voegelin (1936) or Parks (1975). Alford has 45 examples of nouns with obviative possessor. The inflection is *-ilici* in all cases, for both singular and plural possessed nouns (24–26). For the obviative AI participle, Alford has *-lici* for both singular and plural, in contrast to Voegelin's forms, *-lita* for singular and *-licki* for plural.[9] Finally, Alford has a number of obviative-inflected inanimate intransitive forms, with all verb modes represented (Table 9 and examples 27–31).[10] The II.IND.4 forms are identical to the corresponding AI.IND.4 forms, but with *-li* serving for both singular and plural adjuncts in the II.IND (31). Most instances have a possessed noun as subject, either explicitly as in (27) or implicitly as in (28). (29) and (31) are exceptions, lacking even an implicit possessor.

(24) mecimi nili hotpapiiwenilici nihi maamyeekinelici myaasipawiiθhi
and DEM seat.NI.POSS.4P.P DEM sell.AI.PART.4P dove.NA.4P
'And the seats of them that sold doves' (Mark 11:15)

TABLE 8. Subjunctive forms (not in Voegelin 1936)

VERB CLASS	FORM	ENDING	FREQUENCY (DISTINCT VERB FORMS IN ALFORD)
AI	AI.2S	-yane	23
	AI.3	-ke	10
	AI.3P	-waate	12
	AI.3S	-te	37
	AI.4S	-lite	7
II	II.3	-ke	33
	II.4S	-lite	1
TA	TA.1S.3	-ake	4
	TA.1X.3	-akite	1
	TA.2S.1S	-iyane	1
	TA.2S.3	-ate	1
	TA.3P.1S	-iwaate	2
	TA.3S.4	-aate	14
	TA.3P.4	-aawaate	3
	TA.3S.1S	-ite	5
	TA.3S.2S	-ehke	5
	TA.INAN_SUBJ.3.2S	-ekoyane	1
	TA.INV.4.3S	-ekote	3
	TA.PASS.1S	-ike	2
	TA.PASS.2S	-akwate	1
	TA.PASS.3	-ete	1
TI	TI.2S.3	-ane	6
	TI.3S.3	-ake	17
	TI.3P.3	-waate	1

TABLE 9. Obviative inanimate intransitive forms

MODE	ENDING	FREQUENCY (DISTINCT VERB FORMS IN ALFORD)
independent	-li	33
conjunct	-lici	7
participle	-lici	5
	-lita	1
subjunctive	-lite	1

(25) hini hokimaawi hotpapiiwenilici hohθali teepitiili
DEM king seat.NI.POSS.4S.S father.NA.4S David.NA.4S
'And the throne of his father David' (Luke 1:32)

(26) chiine nili hoteleskaakooli hoktikaanilici
and DEM send.TA.3S.4S field.NI.POSS.4S.P
'And he sent him into his fields' (Luke 15:15)

(27) nehiwe howe weh si niipawiiyaali hookimaawiiwe?
what then FUT MAN stand.II.4 kingdom.NI.POSS.3S.S
'How then shall his kingdom stand?' (Matt. 12:26)

(28) payeekwa hini teepweewe peepoonama halika hinwi
but DEM witness.NI.3S have.TI.PART_OB.1S.3 more be.SO.II.3S

yeenwilici caanii
be.SO.II.PART.4 John.NA.3S
'But the witness which I have is greater than that of John:' (John 5:36)

(29) mecimi kiisenaacinamoowe weelaa naanohkaachetiiwe yeh
and tribulation.NI.S or persecution.NI.S when

paθekwiiyaalici ksake hini kalawiiwe hoci, weelena
arise.II.CONJ.4 for DEM word from immediately

hotakikahsinwa hina.
stumble.AI.3S DEM.ANIM
'and when tribulation or persecution ariseth because of the word, straightaway he stumbleth.' (Matt. 13:21)

(30) kwehkwi yooma hotawakaaki pyeeyaalite hina kapenali
if DEM ear.NI.LOC come.II.SUBJ.4 DEM governor.NA.3S
'if this come to the governor's ears' (Matt. 28:14)

(31) payeekwa nihki hokwihθenili wiyakoweewe
but DEM full.II.4 anger.NI.S
'But they were filled with madness.' (Luke 6:11)

Conclusion

Alford's transcription offers insights into his thinking as a linguist. He understood the principle of phonemic distinction, even if failing to represent the phonemic vowel length of /e/~/ee/ in all contexts. Further, he understood that the presence of a phoneme is predictable in some contexts and therefore dispensable, in these contexts, to an orthography that values economy. For example, he never represents the predictable /h/ between resonant and obstruent or the prevocalic word-initial /h/; and, as already noted, he recognized that long /ee/ does not occur after /k/, before /h/, or in word-final position. He approached his language analytically, always separating the personal prefix as a separate word and—with less consistency—introducing hyphens to separate reduplicated syllables and inflectional suffixes. He also used his orthography to make explicit a basic morphological distinction—singular/plural—albeit limited to inflectional affixes with the syllable /ki/. Thus he recognized that he could supplement the more concrete function of a grapheme (representing the voiceless velar stop) with an abstract function (conveying the singular/plural distinction). Similarly, he used graphemes <b>, <d>, and <j> not only as autonomous phonetic segments but also as abstract units specifying the phonetic value of the following vowel. Finally, his "ghost vowels" are purely abstract units whose function is to clarify the pronunciation of the preceding consonant.

The presence of some uncommon morphological forms in Alford's text points to a different appreciation of language. Given Alford's embrace of Christianity (discussed at length in Fear 1983) and his profession as educator, his main motivation for translating the Gospels may have been to make the content of the Gospels more accessible to Shawnee speakers. However, in his autobiography he cites another motivation: "The more that I read and studied the English language, the more my admiration grew for my own Shawnee language, and I was anxious to preserve it in all its purity and beauty. In the description of nature and things natural, and in the idea of things intangible, the inner man, the soul, the Spirit and God, the Shawnee language is peculiarly sweet and full, and seems to stand alone" (Alford 1936:166). Alford was conscious of creating a work of literature whose literary merit was not less than that of the English Revised Version. This may have influenced him to make greater use of linguistic features—like the inflectional passive and stem-internal initial change—that conveyed a sense of archaic dignity, as the English Revised Version does to contemporary English speakers. With respect to the conservatism of Alford's language, Costa (2002:159) notes that "The most plausible conclusion seems to be that in translating the Gospels into Shawnee, Alford was intentionally evoking an older style of oratorical or narrative speech he remembered from his youth, and which he felt was appropriate for the job of translating the Bible." It is possible that his use of the subjunctive and inanimate intransitive obviatives also represents an attempt to evoke an older style of speech; but it may also be that Voegelin simply did not include these forms in his productive paradigms because he did not encounter them frequently.

Beyond phonology and inflectional morphology, other aspects of Alford's translation are of interest. One area deserving attention is vocabulary. Alford's effort involved considered word choices, extensions of meaning, and inventive use of the word-building resources of his language. The repetition of semantic content across the Gospels—sometimes with identical phrasing, sometimes with variation—could prove fruitful for a study of Alford's usage.

NOTES

1. The work reported here is based on an extensive revision and expansion of earlier, unpublished work by David Costa and Ives Goddard. The revision has benefited from a new scan and optical character recognition (OCR) of Alford's text, available at archive.org/details/fourgospelsofour00alfo. As is the case with many OCR products, this newer OCR of Alford's text contains many misinterpretations. A manually verified, fully digital version of Alford's original text is included in the supplementary materials for this paper, which can be found at https://algonquianconference.atlas-ling.ca/eng/supplementary-materials/. In addition to a plain-text, verified version of Alford's original text, the supplementary materials accompanying this paper include the following: a list of approximately 145 probable typographical errors in the original; verse-by-verse interlinear version with the original spelling, normalized spelling, morphological annotations, English glosses, and the original English Revised Version text; concordance (also with original spelling, normalized spelling, morphological annotations, and English gloss); lexicon; and cross-references between Alford's lexical entries and entries in Voegelin (1938–1940).
2. For information about Alford's life, see his autobiography (Alford 1936). Fear's (1983) discussion of Alford's autobiography focuses on Alford's attempt to personally reconcile Shawnee and Western cultures.
3. Alford's original spelling is given in angle brackets (< >) except in tables when the column header specifies "original." Unbracketed Shawnee forms, or phonemes between

slashes (/ /), are in normalized spelling. The normalized spelling generally follows Costa's (2001, 2002) practice in avoiding the use of diacritics. With respect to word breaks, Alford's practice is to always separate preverbs from a following verb by a space and always separate the personal prefixes from a following preverb, verb, or possessed noun with a space. The normalization retains the space after a preverb but always joins the personal prefix to the following word. In the normalization, the use of hyphens is minimized, mainly for certain compounds.

4. For single-word examples, verse citations are given for infrequently occurring forms but not for common forms. Citations are given for multiword examples. If a verse citation for a Shawnee example is given, the English translation is the text of the English Revised Version. Alford's (1929) title page cites "the Version [of the Gospels] set forth A.D. 1611, compared with the most Ancient Authorities and Revised A.D. 1881." This is the English Revised Version.
5. Some examples of typographical errors: (i) <mrmosigesgatv> (occurring once, Matt. 4:14) should be <mrmosigesqatv>, *maamoosikiiskweeta* 'prophesy.AI.PART.3S' (occurring 41 times); (ii) <macmi> (occurring 15 times, e.g., Matt. 9:23) should be <macimi> *mecimi* 'and' (occurring 2,933 times); (iii) <kvtvwici> (occurring once, Matt. 12:22) should be <kvlvwici> *kalawici* 'speak.AI.CONJ.3S' (occurring 17 times); (iv) <u qifvli> (occurring once, Mark 1:19) should be <u qihfvli> *hokwihθali* 'son.NA.POSS.3S.4S' (occurring 239 times). In the supplementary materials, the probable proofreading oversights are identified in a separate file (suggested_corrections.pdf); they are retained as is in the original text but are corrected in the normalization.
6. Abbreviations: TA = transitive animate verb class, TI = transitive inanimate verb class, AI = animate intransitive verb class, II = intransitive inanimate verb class, INV = inverse, INAN_SUBJ = inanimate subject, PASS = passive, IND = independent, CONJ = conjunct, SUBJ = subjunctive, IMP = imperative, PART = participle, PART_AG = agent-headed participle, PART_OB = object-headed participle, 1I = first person inclusive, 1X = first person exclusive, 4 = obviative, IC = initial change FUT = future preverb, PROG = progressive preverb, PERF = perfective preverb, PURP = purposive preverb, MAN = manner preverb, WHY = reason preverb, DEM = demonstrative, PRO = personal pronoun, NI = inanimate noun, NA = animate noun, INAN = inanimate, ANIM = animate, POSS = possessed, S = singular, P = plural, LOC = locative. For glosses of transitive verbs, the person/number of the agent or subject precedes the person/number of the object. For glosses of the possessed nouns, the person/number of the possessor precedes the person/number of the possessed noun. If a form is not formally distinguished for number, the number annotation may be omitted.

7. In contrast to word-initial /ck-/, which can show a ghost vowel, as in <wa cikunofu> in Table 4, the post-vocalic participle ending *-cki* (AI.PART.3P; TA.PART_AG.3P.4; TA.PART_OB.2S.3P; TI.PART_AG.3P.3) is consistently spelled without the ghost vowel. Of the 339 occurrences of this ending, all but one are spelled <cki>, the one exception being <ma-cilofi-ciki> *meciloo θicki* 'little.AI.PART.3P' (Matt. 18:10).
8. Voegelin's representation of the stem varies; in Voegelin (1934), he prefers *ykweewa*.
9. The ending *-licki* does not appear in Alford's text; the ending *-lita* is used once, but for the inanimate form *hahteelita* exist.II.PART (John 8:7). All other cases of II.PART end in *-lici*.
10. While inanimate intransitive obviative forms have not been previously reported for Shawnee, they have been described in Meskwaki (Thomason 2003).

REFERENCES

Alford, Thomas Wildcat. 1929. *The Four Gospels of Our Lord Jesus Christ in Shawnee Indian Language*. Xenia, OH: W.A. Galloway.

———. 1936. *Civilization*. Norman: University of Oklahoma Press.

Costa, David J. 2001. Shawnee Noun Plurals. *Anthropological Linguistics* 43:255–287.

———. 2002. Preverb Usage in Shawnee Narratives. *Papers of the Thirty-Third Algonquian Conference*, ed. by H.C. Wolfart, pp. 120–161. Winnipeg: University of Manitoba.

Fear, Jacquelin. 1983. The "Civilization" of Thomas Wildcat Alford. *Revue française d'études américaines* 17:295–310.

Parks, Douglas R. 1975. Shawnee Noun Inflection. *Studies in Southeastern Indian Languages*, ed. by James M. Crawford, pp. 135–161. Athens: University of Georgia Press.

Thomason, Lucy. 2003. The Proximate and Obviative Contrast in Meskwaki. PhD thesis, University of Texas at Austin.

Voegelin, Carl F. 1934. Shawnee Laws. Unpublished manuscript, Library of the American Philosophical Society, Philadelphia.

———. 1936. Productive Paradigms in Shawnee. *Essays in Anthropology Presented to A.L. Kroeber*, ed. by Robert Lowie, pp. 301–403. Berkeley: University of California Press.

———. 1938–1940. Shawnee Stems and the Jacob P. Dunn Miami Dictionary, Parts I–V. Indiana Historical Society Prehistory Research Series, vol. 1, pp. 63–108, 135–167, 289–323, 345–406, 409–478. Indianapolis.

Plains Cree Verbal Derivational Morphology: A Corpus Investigation

Katherine Schmirler, Atticus G. Harrigan, Antti Arppe, and Arok Wolvengrey

The complex morphosyntax of Plains Cree and related languages has long been the focus of Algonquian research. Verbs in particular offer a wealth of morphological issues to be investigated. For Plains Cree, verbal templates have been constructed containing up to seventeen slots for preverbs and inflectional affixes. For preverbs, up to eight slots are allotted for various functions, which may be either grammatical or inflectional. Derivational templates for Plains Cree verb stems also allow for several layers of secondary derivation, and extreme examples of Plains Cree verb stems contain seven or more morphemes (Bakker 2006; Wolfart 1973, 1996; Wolvengrey 2012). Our goal is to investigate the derivational morphological complexity of Plains Cree verbs in actual language use compared to the complexity demonstrated in theoretical templates; furthermore, we consider both lexical preverbs and stem derivational morphemes (i.e., those used in primary and secondary derivation), due to their considerable influence on semantics and lexeme formation, to constitute derivational morphology in the present study.

Previous investigations (e.g., Wolvengrey 2015) of Plains Cree have found restrictions on the number of preverbs before disfluencies (false starts, hesitations, etc.) begin to consistently occur; including both grammatical and lexical preverbs, up to five are seen to occur before such disfluencies consistently appear. Thus, when lexical preverbs are combined with extreme examples of secondary derivation, we might expect up to fourteen derivational morphemes in the most complex of verbs. However, cursory corpus searches indicate that this kind of complexity is not the norm in Plains Cree. Here, we undertake a quantitative corpus investigation of Plains Cree derivational morphology, in which we investigate the overall derivational complexity of Plains Cree verbs and how stem and preverbal morphology co-occur. Some semantic and functional patterns become evident. Additionally, while extreme complexity might in principle be possible in Plains Cree verbs, actual language use demonstrates considerably fewer derivational morphemes than the theoretical maximum.

Background

Plains Cree

Plains Cree is a member of the Algonquian language family and the westernmost member of the Cree-Montagnais-Naskapi language continuum, spoken across Canada from Alberta to Labrador. Plains Cree has several thousands of speakers, mostly in Alberta and Saskatchewan. Still spoken and written in many contexts today, such as in online communication, radio and television broadcasts, and published books, Plains Cree offers an excellent opportunity for corpus investigations of a native North American language. The corpus used here is further discussed later.

While the focus of this paper is derivational morphology, several features common to Algonquian languages are referenced. These include primarily the noun classification system of animacy and verbal classification by animacy and transitivity. The animacy system includes the grammatical categories of animate and inanimate that are pervasive in Plains Cree through pragmatics, semantics, and morphosyntax. Verbs are categorized by the animacy of their participants and by their transitivity, resulting in four classes: inanimate intransitive, animate intransitive, transitive inanimate, and transitive animate. The derivation of verb stems involves different morphemes for different verb classes, and so these are referenced throughout.

Derivational Morphology

Like all Algonquian languages, Plains Cree is a polysynthetic language with complex derivational and inflectional morphology. There are various templates describing how verbal inflection (person, number, tense) and grammatical and lexical preverbs may occur (see Bakker 2006; Wolfart 1973, 1996; Wolvengrey 2012). Furthermore, recursive derivation within verb stems is also described, with extreme examples containing several layers of secondary derivation. For the purposes of our investigation into derivational morphology, we have included under the umbrella of "derivational morphology" stem derivation (both primary and secondary derivation), the subset of preverbs that are deemed to have more lexical rather than grammatical functions, and reduplicative preverbs—unlike clearly inflectional morphology, these morphological elements contribute to the lexical semantics of a word form and so are considered under one category. Stem derivation and preverbs are discussed in the following subsections.

Verb Stem Derivation

Plains Cree verbal derivation involves (1) root or initial, (2) medial, and (3) final morphemes. Primary verb stems are comprised of a root, an optional medial, and a required final, which may be a zero morpheme. A primary stem may then undergo further derivation, again with an optional medial and required final, forming a secondary stem, which may then undergo further derivation, as in the template in Table 1. Verb stems of five morphemes or more, such as those in Table 2 and Table 3, are commonly attested in Cree dictionaries (adapted from Wolfart 1996).[1]

In our analysis, we consider the most common pairs of stem derivational morphemes and the patterns they suggest. We then scrutinize common combinations of derivational morphemes with preverbs.

Preverbs

Preverbs in Plains Cree are prefixed to verb stems and are preceded by person prefixes in the independent order. Preverbs may have grammatical functions, such as marking conjunct or relative clauses (*ê*-, *kâ*-), tense (*kî*-, *ôh-/ohci*- past, *wî*- future intentional), or both (*ta*- conjunct infinitive, *kê*- changed conjunct future). The majority of preverbs, however, have more lexical functions. These occur closer to

TABLE 1. Verb stem derivation template

SECONDARY STEM					
SECONDARY STEM					
PRIMARY STEM			SECONDARY DERIVATION		
ROOT	(MEDIAL)	FINAL	(MEDIAL)	FINAL	ETC.
/wâp-/ 'light, bright' /pim-/ 'along' /mihkw-/ 'red' /it-/ 'thus, so'	/-âskw-/ 'wood' /-âpisk-/ 'metal, stone' /-êk(inw)-/ 'cloth, material'	/-(i)kê/ general object AI /-payi/ 'move' II/AI /-(i)n/ 'by hand' TA			

TABLE 2. Secondary derivation of verb stems

pimipayihcikêstamâso- 'manage for oneself' (TA)					
pimipayihcikêstamaw- 'manage for s.o' (TA)					
pimipayihcikê- 'manage things' (AI)					
pimipayihtâ- 'manage, run s.t.' (TI)					
pimipayi- 'work, function' (II)					
ROOT	FINAL	FINAL	FINAL	FINAL	FINAL
/pim-/ 'along'	/-payi/ 'move'	/-htâ/ TI	/-(i)kê/ AI	/-stamaw/ BENEF	/-iso/ REFL

TABLE 3. Secondary derivation of verb stems

kanawêyimiskwêwêski- 'be a habitual wife-watcher' (AI)					
kanawêyimiskwêwê- 'watch one's wife' (AI)					
kanawêyim- 'watch over s.o.' (TA)					
ROOT	MEDIAL	FINAL	MEDIAL	FINAL	FINAL
/kanaw-/ 'watch'	/-êyi-/ 'by mind'	/-m/ TA	/-iskwêw-/ 'woman'	/-ê/ AI	/-ski/ habitual

TABLE 4. Preverb template for Plains Cree

GRAMMATICAL			LEXICAL		
CONJUNCT CLAUSE	TENSE	PERSPECTIVAL ASPECT	PARTICIPANT-ORIENTED MODALITY	PHASAL ASPECT	MANNER/ DIRECTION
ê- kâ- ta- kê-	kî-	wî- ô(h)-/ohci-	nôhtê- 'want to' kakwê- 'try to' nihtâ- 'be good at'	mâci- 'start' pôni- 'stop' kîsi- 'finish'	nitawi- 'go and' isi- 'thus' pê- 'come and'

Adapted from Wolvengrey 2012

the verb stem than grammatical preverbs and carry various adverbial meanings that modify the verb stem or other lexical preverbs. Some grammatical and lexical preverbs and their identified functions are demonstrated in the preverbal template in Table 4.

While the set of grammatical preverbs is quite small, and the number of grammatical preverbs that can occur in any verb is restricted, lexical preverbs can occur much more freely and constitute a more open class, with well over 200 listed in Wolvengrey (2001); lexical preverbs may be derived from roots or stems using the particle final *-i*, and existing free particles can be co-opted for use as preverbs as well. Also included in dictionaries are verbal compounds, or lexicalized strings of preverbs and verb stems; they are included as lexical entries when they are common or have unpredictable semantics. For example, *miyo-* 'well, good' compounds with *kîsikâw* 'it is day' to form *miyo-kîsikâw* 'it is a nice day', but with *akohpêw* 's/he owns blankets' to form *miyo-akohpêw* 's/he owns good blankets'. Such lexical entries are also taken into account here as a preverb plus the number of stem morphemes.

While different slots for lexical preverbs of different functions are recognized, multiple preverbs of each lexical function may occur, so more than four lexical preverbs can theoretically be present in a verb form. Furthermore, reduplicative preverbal elements may also occur before lexical preverbs and the stem itself, and lend adverbial meaning: *Ca-* indicates an ongoing action and *Câh-* a repeated action. We have also counted these as lexical preverbs as they lend semantic information to the verb form. Wolvengrey (2015) has found in a corpus investigation that the maximum number of preverbs that can occur is five; after five preverbs, disfluencies appear consistently, such as false starts, hesitation markers (e.g., *ê-kî-pê-is*[*i*]*-âya-*. . .), or intrusive syntactic particles (e.g., *kâ-kî-***ita***-***ohci***-mâci-na-* . . .). While false starts or other repairs occur within verb stems, these are much rarer than disfluencies in the preverb complex; this suggests that preverbal derivation falls more toward the syntactic side of the morphosyntactic spectrum of the Plains Cree verbal complex.

The Corpus

The corpus used for the present study is comprised of Plains Cree texts edited by Freda Ahenakew and H. C. Wolfart (Bear et al. 1992; Kâ-Nîpitêhtêw 1998; Masuskapoe 2010; Minde 1997; Vandall and Douquette 1987; Whitecalf 1993). These texts add up to 108,413 tokens (18,649 types), of which 73,189 tokens (15,994 types) are

Plains Cree words (the difference being punctuation and English, French, and other foreign names and words), which, though dwarfed by available corpora for many majority languages, is a sizable corpus for an indigenous language and is sufficient for the quantitative analyses reported here. The corpus has been morphologically analyzed by means of finite state transducer (FST) tools (e.g., Beesley and Karttunen 2003) that provide for each word form its word class, subclass, and features such as number, obviation, person, direction, verbal order, possession, and diminution, and, key to the present investigation, identifies preverbs and presents the lemma form of the word based on Wolvengrey (2001). Furthermore, this corpus has been manually verified and corrected as necessary by two researchers, improving its coverage and accuracy considerably. The majority of errors or missing analyses in the output of the morphological analyzer involved orthographic differences such as vowel length mismatches, missing lemmata in the database, and morphological elements that have not yet been modeled. As the morphological analyzer is still in the development stage (currently described in Harrigan et al. 2017; Snoek et al. 2014), this manual verification not only improves the analyzed corpus but also identifies issues for further development.

After the manual verification, where we did not take sentential context into account, a degree of ambiguity remained among the analyses, with 22.9 percent of the Cree word form types having two or more possible analyses (of which the majority, 16.7 percent, were two-way ambiguities).[2] We applied a simple but straightforward heuristic implementing a preference for morphological simplicity that selected the analysis with the smallest number of morphemes, and these being equal, the smallest number of preverbs. As a result of this, only one morphological analysis remained for each Cree word form in the corpus. The majority of verbal ambiguities involve inverse VTA inflections (e.g., the suffix sequence *-ikoyâhk*, which may be a proximate, obviative, or inanimate actor with a first person plural exclusive goal), forms that may be grammatical preverbs or reduplication (e.g., *ka-*, *tâh-*), and preverbs that are also found in lexicalized preverb-stem entries in the database (e.g., the morphological analyzer returns two analyses for *miyo-atoskêw* 'she works well', as this could be the preverb *miyo-* 'good, well' plus the verb *atoskêw* 's/he works', but it is also a lexicalized compound found in dictionaries). These three patterns represent over one-third of the ambiguity in the corpus, and less frequent patterns are still predominantly inflectional. The latter two of these patterns do involve the verb stem and lexical preverbs and as such affect the present study; we opted to select lexicalized compounds as they are especially representative of derivation. Additionally, though our disambiguation allowed for any potential reduplicative suffix to be represented as such, these were infrequent enough that they do not occur in our results.

Method

For the purposes of our investigation, we have made use of the output of the analyzed corpus in two key ways. First, we do not consider grammatical preverbs. These include preverbs that mark conjunct clauses and tense preverbs. Some preverbs have multiple functions, some grammatical and some lexical; for instance, *ohci-* can indicate past tense in a negative clause or indicate the source or origin of an action. While these were not distinguished before the analyses, where *ohci-* occurs as the first member of a frequent preverb pair, it is apparent from corpus searches that these clauses are negative; these pairs are then ignored in the analysis.

Second, we have taken the lemma form supplied by the analysis and drawn its morphological composition from the database underlying Wolvengrey's (2001) dictionary of Plains Cree. This database gives the root, medial, and final morphemes of each lemma, where they can be identified through synchronic and diachronic analysis. The lexical preverbs identified by the analyzer and the stem morphology drawn from the database are used in the following analyses. For instance, a verb form such as (1) found in the corpus was identified to have four preverbs, *kâ-*, *kî-*, *isi-*, and *miyo-* (of which the last two are lexical, namely *miyo-* and *isi-*), and the lemma *waskawîstamâsow* 's/he works for him/herself' has five derivational morphemes, given in (2).

(1) kâ-kî-isi-miyo-waskawîstamâsot
CNJ-PST-thus-well/good-work.for.oneself.3SG
'thus s/he worked well for him/herself'

(2) waskawîstamâso-

/waskaw-/	/-î/	/-st/	/-amaw/	/-iso/
turn, move	go, move	TRZ	BENEF	REFL
root	VAI final	final	VTA final	AI final

'to work for oneself'

Results

Altogether, the corpus contained 9,983 unique verb form types (representing 16,538 tokens); thus, verbs represent 62.4 percent of all the Cree word form types but only 22.5 percent of the word tokens in the corpus. The verb forms in the corpus exhibited 149 preverbs (of which 18 were grammatical ones) and 1,171 distinct stem morphemes. The most common lexical preverbs, in terms of their occurrences in various verb form types, were *pê-* 'come' (*n* = 541), *isi-* 'thus' (*n* = 277), *nitawi-* 'go' (*n* = 229), *ati-* 'begin to' (*n* = 146), and *kakwê-* 'try' (*n* = 124), and the most common verb stem morphemes were /-ê/ (*n* = 860), /-â/ (*n* = 836), /-h/ (*n* = 808), /-ht/ (*n* = 740), /-m/ (*n* = 716), /-i/ (*n* = 687), and /iT-/[3] (*n* = 628).

Next, co-occurrence frequencies and statistics were calculated, retaining co-occurrence order as apparent in the word forms, though that could in principle vary, yielding in all 303 unique preverb pairings, 4,027 stem morpheme pairings, and 4,788 preverb-stem morpheme pairings. Among the lexical preverbs, the ones that combine the most with others are *pê-* (24), *isi-* (13), and *nitawi-* (12). Of the many co-occurrence statistics, MUTUAL INFORMATION (MI) was selected, since it is fairly easy to understand in representing the strength of a joint occurrence of two features in comparison to the individual frequencies of these two features; the higher the MI value is, the stronger the joint occurrence of a feature pair is in comparison to the frequencies of the individual features. Nevertheless, with a small corpus such as the one at our disposal, the downside of the MI measure is that it is relatively useless when the individual and joint feature frequencies are relatively low (cf. Evert 2004), and thus we do not make much use of it but provide it simply for reference.

In Tables 5 and 6, the last two columns give the morphemes (preverbs or stem derivation elements) in question and their glosses. The first columns indicate the MI value, the second and third columns indicate the individual frequency of the first and second elements respectively, and the fourth column the joint frequency of a feature pair.

Preverbs

In Table 5, we present the twelve most common lexical preverb pair combinations in the corpus. While the most common pair *pê-* . . . *isi-* occurs in thirty-eight word forms in the corpus,[4] the rest of these most frequent pairs drop to less than a

TABLE 5. Most frequent preverb pairs

MI	N_1	N_2	N_{1+2}	PREVERB PAIR	PAIR GLOSSES
0.898483	541	277	38	**pê- isi-**	**'come', 'thus, towards'**
2.566461	541	11	8	**pê- kîwê-**	**'come', 'back, homeward'**
0.120329	124	277	4	***kakwê- isi-***	***'try', 'thus, towards'***
1.251731	277	40	4	isi- miyo-	'thus, toward', 'good, well'
2.038673	52	97	4	nipahi- misi-	'really, extremely', 'large, great'
−0.591184	541	97	3	pê- misi-	'come', 'large, great'
−0.110818	541	40	2	***pê- nihtâ-***	***'come', 'be good at'***
−0.136952	229	97	2	nitawi- misi-	'go', 'large, great'
−0.736143	146	277	2	*ati- isi-*	*'begin to', 'thus, towards'*
−1.242220	124	541	2	***kakwê- pê-***	***'try', 'come'***
−1.710206	541	198	2	**pê- ohci-**	**'come', 'from'**
1.093155	541	12	2	**pê- sipwê-**	**'come', 'leave'**

dozen. Compared to the individual counts for each preverb, we see that the pairs are not particularly common; while common combinations do exist, they are much less frequent than their individual members. This further reinforces the idea that preverbs combine quite freely and behave more as syntactic elements, with greater combinatory freedom, than the morphological elements within verb stems.

However, among these common preverb pairs, some function combination patterns do arise. First, in black boldface, are combinations of manner/direction preverbs; *pê-* 'come', *isi-* 'thus, thither', *ohci-* 'by means of, thence', *kîwê-* 'back, homeward', *sipwê-* 'leaving' are seen here. Second, in italicized boldface, are combinations of manner/direction preverbs and participant-oriented modality preverbs (*kakwê-* 'try', *nihtâ-* 'be good at'). However, due to the order of manner followed by modality, which contradicts the order given in the template in Table 2, further investigation into the context of the forms is required. Finally, there is one instance of a phasal aspect preverb *ati-* 'begin to' followed by a manner/direction preverb (italicized), which is in line with the aforementioned templates. As there is only one instance here, however, no further comment can be made. The remaining preverbs, *misi-* 'big', *nipahi-* 'extremely', and *miyo-* 'good, well', are qualitative adverbs and are not included in the available templates.

TABLE 6. Most frequent stem morpheme pairs

MI	N_1	N_2	N_{1+2}	STEM COMBINATIONS	PAIR GLOSSES
1.922021	540	740	282	**/-êýi-/ /-ht/**	**‘think’, TI**
1.434042	740	836	268	**/-ht/ /-â/**	**causative, TI**
2.170965	325	860	253	***/-oht-/ /-ê/***	***‘walk’, AI***
2.423391	256	808	241	*/wît-/ /-h/*	*‘fellow’, causative TA*
1.781144	540	716	237	**/-êýi-/ /-m/**	**‘think’, TA**
2.225492	234	836	187	/ay-/ /-â/	‘thing’, TI
1.013962	687	716	140	/-i/ /-m/	AI, TA
2.947364	148	443	129	*/wîht-/ /-amaw/*	*‘tell about’, benefactive TA*
1.654565	716	331	128	/-m/ /-o/	TA, AI
2.645999	114	687	114	/w-/ /-i/	3, AI
1.670467	628	325	112	***/iT-/ /-oht-/***	***‘thus, towards’, ‘walk’***
2.453104	128	716	110	/ât-/ /-m/	‘tell about’, TA
2.645999	108	687	108	/-îk-/ /-i/	‘dwelling’, AI
4.432833	114	108	107	/w-/ /-îk-/	3, ‘dwelling’
0.471248	687	836	95	/-i/ /-â/	AI, TI

Stem Morphology

In Table 6, we present the fifteen most common pairs of derivational morphemes found in stems in the corpus. Compared to the preverbs above, we see much more frequent pairs occurring throughout the words found in the corpus, though the individual occurrences still number in the hundreds. While these indicate pairs that co-occur in a stem regardless of whether they are adjacent, most still represent sequences of morphemes. For instance, *-êyi-ht* and *-êyi-m*, which derive ‘thought processes’ (VTI and VTA respectively, e.g., *itêyihtam* ‘he thinks thus (of s.t.)’, *itêyimêw* ‘he thinks thus of s.o.’), are often considered extended finals and written without hyphens (Wolfart 1973:74).

While many of the pairs in this table contain more abstract grammatical morphemes for which concrete meanings are not discernable (e.g., *-i*, *-a*, *-m*), some patterns are seen in finals. For instance, we see considerable number of occurrences of the ‘thought process’ morphemes mentioned above (*-êyiht*, *-êyim*) which indicate the use of many VTI and VTA verbs formed with these morphemes. Similarly, the sequence *-ht-â*, which commonly forms VAI+O verb stems (Wolfart 1973:74), indicates that many frequent VTIs have been formed using these morphemes. Forms with more specific semantics are also evident, given in italicized boldface.

The sequence *-oht-ê* forms an extended VAI final meaning 'walk' (e.g., *pimohtê-* 'to walk', from the root *pim-* 'along'), and *-oht-* is also seen in the pair *iT-oht,* which occurs in the frequent VAI *itohtêw* 's/he goes (there)'.[5] Finally, common root-final combinations are seen here, given in italics in Table 6. The frequency of /wîht-/ /-amaw/ matches the occurrences of the VTA stem *wîhtamaw-* 'to tell someone about it/him' in the corpus, indicating that this is not only a common sequence but in fact is only realized in one common verb stem. The pair /wît-/ /-h/ is seen in the similarly common VTA stem *wîcih-* 'to help someone', but is also seen in secondary derivations based on this stem, such as the VAI *wîcihiwê-* 'to help people'.

Unlike the preverb pairs above, these morpheme pairs not only occur more commonly together but also form common verb stems or extended finals. Though the MI measures may not fully reliable in such a small data set, a cursory comparison of Tables 5 and 6 reveals a stark difference between the numbers: the stem morpheme pairs occur together more often than preverb pairs.

Co-occurrences

In Table 7, we present the fifteen most common pairs of preverbs and stem morphemes. The common manner and direction preverbs are once again apparent, especially *pê-*, though these generally occur with short, abstract verb finals. There are two pairs that suggest a semantic pattern and one that is indicative of a common preverb-verb stem combination, all given in boldface. The pairs *pê- -oht* and *pê- -iT* indicate combinations of manner, direction, and motion, similar to preverb combinations; they are combined in *pê-itohtêw* 's/he comes walking', a lexicalized compound found in dictionaries of Cree (e.g., Wolvengrey 2001). The root *pimât-*, found in the frequent VAI stems *pimâtisi-* 'to be alive' and *pimâciho-* 'to live, travel, make living', frequently occurs with *isi-* 'thus', indicating frequent comment on the ways in which people live or make a living in the corpus. Though these are not yet included in dictionaries as lexicalized compounds, this is the most strongly correlated preverb-stem morpheme in the corpus.

Overall Derivational Complexity

While preverbs and stem morphemes can co-occur quite freely with little discernable patterning, of greater interest is the overall numbers of derivational morphemes, both preverbs and stems, that may occur. In our corpus, we have found

TABLE 7. Most frequent preverb-stem morpheme combinations

MI	N_1	N_2	N_{1+2}	PREVERB-STEM COMBINATIONS	PAIR GLOSSES
0.302369	541	860	65	pê- /-ê/	'come', AI
0.317487	541	808	62	pê- /-h/	'come', causative TA
0.902805	277	808	57	isi- /-h/	'thus, towards', TA
0.907752	541	325	45	**pê- /-oht-/**	**'come', 'walk'**
0.053292	541	628	37	**pê- /iT-/**	**'come', 'thus, towards'**
0.660967	229	808	37	nitawi- /-h/	'go', TA
–0.150912	541	687	33	pê- /-i/	'come', AI
0.773724	541	256	31	pê- /wît-/	'come', 'fellow'
–0.139707	541	597	29	pê- /-n/	'come', 'by hand'
0.158640	541	443	29	pê- /-amaw/	'come', benefactive TA
1.030786	124	808	29	kakwê- /-h/	'try', causative TA
–0.356561	541	716	28	pê- /-m/	'come', TA
–0.511510	541	836	28	pê- /-â/	'come', TI
1.606040	541	97	27	pê- /takw-/	'come', 'join'
2.033289	277	119	26	**isi- /pimât-/**	**'thus, towards', 'life'**

that up to three lexical preverbs occur (e.g., string *kâ-kî-**pê-isi-kanâci**-pimâtisit* 's/he has been living such a clean life'), excluding grammatical preverbs and the hesitation preverbal element *aya-*,[6] and that lexemes with up to seven morphemes occur (e.g., ***kâ-kî-wîci-kiskinohamâkosîmakik*** ← wîci- +/kiskinw-/+/-h/+/-amaw/+/-ikw-/+/-isi/+/-m/ 'the ones with whom I went to school').[7] Moreover, the maximum number of preverbs plus stem morphemes that we have observed to occur is nine, as in the form *ê-kî-pê-isi-postayiwinisahisocik* 'they clothe themselves such', (*pê-*, *isi-*, and stem /post-/+/ay-/+/-iwi/+/-n/+/-is/+/-ah/+/-iso/). Furthermore, we observed a weak but clearly significant inverse correlation $r_{pearson} = 0.040$, $p(t = -3.9498, df = 9981) = 7.874e^{-5}$, including both the number of lexical preverbs (including reduplicative elements) and the number of stem morphemes. The more lexical preverbs there are in a form, the slightly fewer stem morphemes one might expect to observe, and vice versa. This suggests, as predicted, an upper limit to the derivational complexity found in a verb form, and that the theoretical maximally complex verb in Plains Cree may be a relatively rare occurrence.

Discussion

Overall, the patterns seen in preverb and stem morpheme combinations align well with semantic descriptions of individual morphemes and with preverbal templates. For preverbs, the most prevalent pattern is the frequent co-occurrence of manner and direction preverbs with each other: to come toward or away from, to leave or go home. For derivational morphology, the most frequent co-occurrences create familiar verb classes and subtypes, as well as frequent stems themselves. Perhaps unsurprisingly, the only striking pattern among the preverb-stem morphology co-occurrences are between manner/direction and motion morphemes. Overall, preverbs demonstrate considerably more combinatory freedom than stem derivational morphemes, with fewer discernible patterns, highlighting their more syntactic nature.

Finally, looking beyond combinations, we investigated the total numbers for preverbs and stem morphology, both separately and together, with respect to derivational complexity. We found that lexical preverbs reach upper limits of three in a string, and that lexemes contain as many as seven morphemes, but when lexical preverbs appear, we see as many as nine derivational morphemes in total (divided into two preverbs and seven stem morphemes). Furthermore, the weak though significant inverse correlation between the number of preverbs and the number of morphemes in the stem serves to illustrate that Plains Cree verbs in everyday language use rarely, if ever, display the maximum complexity made possible by the rich morphological system of the language. Further investigation into this relationship is needed, and a larger corpus, especially including different registers, or field experimentation with native speakers, may also offer more data that will reveal stronger effects or different patterns entirely.

Conclusion

The complexity of Cree morphosyntax, in both inflection and derivation, has been extensively studied in the literature. Now, with the use of an analyzed corpus, quantitative investigations of previously described phenomena are possible. We have presented a preliminary quantitative investigation into derivational complexity in Cree verbs, including both lexical preverbs and stem derivation under the umbrella of derivation, in opposition to inflectional categories such as person, number, and tense, among others. We have found some patterns, generally in line with previous preverbal templates, of direction and motion preverbs, and semantic links with motion medials and finals. However, the counts predominantly only reflect the overall frequencies of certain preverbs and stems containing certain morphemes; while perhaps not of great theoretical interest, such counts may be useful in classrooms, where more frequent elements may be taught before those less frequent, and more frequent sequences or combinations before those less frequent.

Our findings do, however, suggest an upper limit to derivational complexity in Cree verbs not reflected in typical theoretical templates; in the corpus, the maximum total found was nine morphemes, though theoretical descriptions allow for upward of fifteen morphemes including preverbs and the roots, medials, and finals of stem derivation (e.g., Bakker 2006; Wolvengrey 2012). Further data collection and analysis may shed light on the actual complexity of verbal derivation in spoken Plains Cree. Finally, though lexical preverbs and stem morphology both carry semantic information and contribute to lexeme formation, and these similarities have motivated the present study, lexical preverbs occur more freely. Thus, lexical preverbs and stem morphology are functionally distinct; these categories found in descriptive literature have been confirmed using quantitative methods.

NOTES

1. Abbreviations: II = inanimate intransitive verb, AI = animate intransitive verb, TI = transitive inanimate verb, TA = transitive animate verb, BENEF = benefactive, REFL = reflexive, TRZ = transitivizer, 3SG = third person singular, 3 = third person.
2. Though this degree of ambiguity is considerable, it has little bearing on the results presented here, and more sophisticated disambiguation methods are under development.
3. This is the initial morpheme in *itêw* 's/he says thus to someone' and *itwêw* 's/he says so'. This form is known as a relative root, in that it requires an antecedent (e.g., to go to a specified place, say a certain thing). This form is also in the particle *isi* and its preverb counterpart *isi-*, and as such is very common in our corpus.
4. The actual token frequency is often much higher, but we are using here form types as the basis of our co-occurrence stats (to focus rather on possible forms and to rule out the undue influence of a single form that has a high frequency). For example, there are 67 word tokens with the combination *pê-* . . . *-isi*, nearly twice the type frequency.
5. There is overlap here: *iT-oht-ê* (in, e.g., *itohtêw* '(s)he goes') is a common sequence of

three derivational morphemes.

6. We have included *aya* 'um' as a preverb in our computational model to increase recognition rates, as it commonly occurs among preverbs. However, it is not included among our counts.
7. This is counted as a single lexeme, *wîci-kiskinohamâkosîm-*, which is a lexicalized compound. The preverb *wîci-* and the suffix *-m* form the comitative VTA derivation 'to do something with someone'.

REFERENCES

Ahenakew, Alice. 2000. âh-âyîtaw isi ê-kî-kiskêyihtahkik maskihkiy / They Knew Both Sides of Medicine: Cree Tales of Curing and Cursing Told by Alice Ahenakew, ed. by H. Christoph Wolfart. Winnipeg: University of Manitoba Press.

Bakker, Peter. 2006. Algonquian Verb Structure: Plains Cree. *What's in a Verb? Studies in the Verbal Morphology of the Languages of the Americas*, ed. by E.B. Carlin and C.J. Rowicak, pp. 3–28. Utrecht: LOT.

Bear, Glecia, Minnie Fraser, Irene Calliou, Mary Wells, Alpha Lafond, and Rita Longneck. 1992. *kôhkominawak otâcimowiniwâwa / Our Grandmothers' Lives as Told in Their Own Words*, ed. by Freda Ahenakew and H. Christoph Wolfart. Regina: Canadian Plains Research Center.

Beesley, Kenneth R. and Lauri Karttunen. 2003. *Finite State Morphology*. Stanford, CA: CSLI Publications.

Evert, Stefan. 2004. The Statistics of Word Co-occurrences: Word Pairs and Collocations. PhD thesis, University of Stuttgart.

Harrigan, Atticus, Katherine Schmirler, Antti Arppe, Lene Antonsen, Sjur Moshagen, and Trond Trosterud. 2017. Learning from the computational modeling of the Plains Cree Verb. *Morphology* 27(4):565–598.

Kâ-Nîpitêhtêw, Jim. 1998. *ana kâ-pimwêwêhahk okakêskihkêmowina / The Counselling Speeches of Jim Kâ-Nîpitêhtêw*, ed. by Freda Ahenakew and H. Christoph Wolfart. Winnipeg: University of Manitoba Press.

Masuskapoe, Cecilia. 2010. *piko kîkway ê-nakacihtât: kêkêk otâcimowina ê-nêhiawastêki*, ed. by H. Christoph Wolfart and Freda Ahenakew. Winnipeg: Algonquian and Iroquoian Linguistics.

Minde, Emma. 1997. *kwayask ê-kî-pê-kiskinowâpatihicik / Their Example Showed Me the Way: A Cree Woman's Life Shaped by Two Cultures*, ed. by Freda Ahenakew and H. Christoph Wolfart. Edmonton: University of Alberta Press.

Snoek, Connor, Dorothy Thunder, Kaidi Lõo, Antti Arppe, Jordan Lachler, Sjur Moshagen, and Trond Trosterud. 2014. Modeling the Noun Morphology of Plains Cree. Paper read at ComputEL: Workshop on the Use of Computational Methods in the Study of Endangered Languages, Fifty-Second Annual Meeting of the ACL, Baltimore, June 26.

Vandall, Peter and Joe Douquette. 1987. *wâskahikaniwiyiniw-âcimowina / Stories of the House People, Told by Peter Vandall and Joe Douquette*, ed. by Freda Ahenakew. Winnipeg: University of Manitoba Press.

Whitecalf, Sarah. 1993. *kinêhiyawiwininaw nêhiyawêwin / The Cree Language Is Our Identity: The La Ronge Lectures of Sarah Whitecalf*, ed. by H. Christoph Wolfart and Freda Ahenakew. Winnipeg: University of Manitoba Press.

Wolfart, H. Christoph. 1973. *Plains Cree: A Grammatical Study*. Transactions of the American Philosophical Society, n.s., vol. 63, part 5. Philadelphia.

———. 1996. Sketch of Cree, an Algonquian Language. *Handbook of North American Indians*, vol. 17: *Languages*, ed. by Ives Goddard, pp. 390–439. Washington, DC: Smithsonian Institution.

Wolvengrey, Arok. 2001. *nêhiyawêwin: itwêwina / Cree: Words*. Regina: University of Regina Press.

———. 2012. The Verbal Morphosyntax of Aspect-Tense-Modality in Dialects of Cree. Paper read at the 2012 International Conference on Functional Discourse Grammar, Ghent, June 8.

———. 2015. Preverb Combinations, Co-occurrences, and Sequences: Preliminary Findings from a Preliminary Plains Cree Corpus. Paper read at the Forty-Seventh Algonquian Conference, Winnipeg, October 22–25.

The Light Verb *-eke* in Mi'kmaq

Barbara Sylliboy, Elizabeth Paul, Serge Paul, Arlene Stevens, and Dianne Friesen

This paper describes and analyzes the Mi'kmaq morpheme *-eke*, based on data from the Cape Breton dialect, the first language of the first four authors of this paper.[1] We found that, in contrast to previous work, *-eke* allows referential direct objects. We analyze *-eke* as a semantically transitive light verb, part of a set of light verbs in Mi'kmaq.

Wider Context

Mi'kmaq are an East Coast tribe in the Algonquian family.[2] Traditionally the Mi'kmaq territory covered Nova Scotia, Prince Edward Island, parts of New Brunswick, Newfoundland, and Quebec, and extended into northeastern Maine. They called their homeland *Mi'kma'ki*. Mi'kma'ki was divided into seven districts: *Unama'ki* (Cape Breton), *Eskikewa'kik* (Antigonish and Guysborough area), *Piktuk* and *Epekwit* (Pictou area and Prince Edward Island), *Sipekne'katik* (Amherst and New Brunswick area), *Kespukwitk* (Yarmouth area), and *Kespe'k* (Gaspé region of Quebec and New Brunswick). Each region spoke a different dialect of Mi'kmaq. The three main dialects are in New Brunswick, Quebec, and Nova Scotia, but there are subdialects within each region. Within Cape Breton, for example, the dialects of Eskasoni, Wagmatcook, and We'koqma'q vary in pronunciation, vocabulary, and speed of utterance.

Prior to European contact, Mi'kmaq did not have a written script, but they did record some history in petroglyphs, which can still be seen today in historic sites such as Kejimukujik Park, McGowan Lake, Bedford Barrens, and Klu'skap Caves. History, legends, and teachings were passed down orally by the elders. Children learned them from an early age. In addition, Mi'kmaq treaties were preserved in wampum belts, which the Putu's of the Sante' Mawiomi (wampum keeper of the Grand Council) would reiterate each year at the annual gathering on Chapel Island. These wampum belts were mnemonic cues to assist in remembering the peace and friendship agreement between two tribes. One wampum belt was read annually until the mid-1900s, when the last reader of the wampum belt (Isaac Alex) passed away. That wampum belt disappeared after this and has never been found.

It was with the first European contact in the 1600s that Mi'kmaq language began to be written down, first in the Hieroglyphic Prayer Book of Father Maillard (Kauder 1866). Then, at around the same time in the 1700s, Reverend Silas T. Rand, a Protestant missionary, and Father Pacifique, a Catholic missionary, each developed an orthography to assist them in teaching prayers and religion. Reverend Rand wrote a lexicon of English to Mi'kmaq words (Rand 1888) and also transcribed legends from Mi'kmaq to English (Rand 1894). He also produced a small Mi'kmaq grammar book (Rand 1875). Father Pacifique published several prayer books as well as catechisms (Pacifique 1921) and a grammar. The grammar has been recently revised to the Smith-Francis orthography and released in 2016 (Francis and Hewson 2016). The Pacifique writing system was used extensively until the 1950s. Then it started to be written and read only by elders. The Union of Nova Scotia Indians and Mi'kmaq Association of Cultural Studies decided in the mid-1970s to hire a linguist to create an easier orthography. This is the Smith-Francis orthography, which is used primarily in Nova Scotia, Prince Edward Island, and parts of Newfoundland and New Brunswick.

The Mi'kmaq language is in danger, as are many native languages across Canada. Eskasoni is the largest Mi'kmaq community, with a population of a little over 4,000 people. Many Mi'kmaq communities consider Eskasoni to be the strongest Mi'kmaq-speaking community. However, in reality only about 25 to 30 percent of the population in Eskasoni speak the language fluently. The majority of speakers are adults and elders, as well as several families who believe it is important to teach

Mi'kmaq to their children. To offset this reduction in speakers, the Eskasoni Band put into operation a Mi'kmaq immersion program. This program has been in effect for about 16 years and is in its second year as a separate education facility called "E.S.K." Through the immersion program, many more young people understand and can carry on conversations in Mi'kmaq. Much more work still needs to be done, however.

The provincial organization Mi'kmaw Kina'matnewey is also making strides in promoting and preserving Mi'kmaq language. It has created Mi'kmaq language apps to use with iPhone and Mac computers. It has published children's books in the Mi'kmaq language and included CD recordings of these books being narrated by Mi'kmaq speakers. In addition, the organization is in the process of implementing a Master-Apprentice Mi'kmaq language program for those communities where the language has dwindled to several speakers.

Transitivity and the Morpheme *-eke*

The structure of the Mi'kmaq verb is well studied (Inglis 1986; McCulloch 2013; Hamilton 2015), but the function of some of the morphemes remains elusive. One of the less well defined morphemes, *-eke*, is involved in transitivity.[3] *-Eke* is reported in the literature as being a verb final (a non-inflectional suffix) marking an intransitive verb where an animate subject acts on an indefinite object, and is generally found in intransitive clauses (Inglis 1986:15; McCulloch 2013).[4] McCulloch (2013:21) gives two examples as evidence that *-eke* "reduces the valency of a transitive verb," noting that the verb with *-eke* is ungrammatical with an overt object (1), but, "where the verb does not have *-ege*, the overt object is fine" (2). (McCulloch's examples use the Restigouche orthography where some stops are written as voiced, e.g., *k* is written as *g*.)[5]

(1) gesisp-a't-ege-i (*msaqtaqt)
wash-VTI-NONSP-1 (floor)
'I'm washing stuff (*the floor)' (McCulloch 2013:21)

(2) gesisp-a't-u (msaqtaqt)
wash-VTI-1 (floor)
'I'm washing it (the floor)' (McCulloch 2013:21)

Based on these properties, Inglis (1986) proposes that *-eke* functions to indicate an indefinite object, and McCulloch asks whether the morpheme *-eke* "introduces a non-specific internal argument (like an incorporated noun) or deletes/absorbs the internal argument" (2013:21). Inglis (1986) and McCulloch (2013) are primarily morphological studies; most or all of the examples in these works are single words. Hamilton (2015) does not discuss *-eke* as a separate morpheme. Our paper considers more extensive syntactic data as well as a clear definition of transitivity to further define this morpheme and determine some of its distinctive features and functions.

Methodology

The research focuses on the dialect of Mi'kmaq spoken in Cape Breton. All data in this paper were generated and tested by the first four authors, except those identified as originating in other works. We studied 108 verb stems selected to cover a range of verbs using two criteria. First, we selected verb stems that preliminary studies of the charts in Sylliboy (n.d.) indicate are found with different sets of transitivity morphemes. Second, we selected verb stems that cross-linguistically are known to be different in terms of transitivity. The authors discussed each of the verb stems, judging the grammaticality of clauses using each verb stem with and without *-eke*. If speakers judged that the verb could carry *-eke*, we determined whether the verbs/clauses were transitive or intransitive using morphological, syntactic, and semantic criteria. These criteria are explained later. Our examples are written in the Smith-Francis orthography as described in Francis and Hewson (2016). Some examples may not be completely interlinearized since not all morphemes have established glosses and functions.

-Eke as a Light Verb

We propose that *-eke* be analyzed as a light verb (LV), following Manyakina's (2015) analysis of the morpheme *-e'ke* in verb stems with noun incorporation. Note that the morpheme *-eke* is not the same as *-e'ke*. *-E'ke* occurs in specialized verbs with noun incorporation (3–4), and Manyakina glosses it as 'get'; we find that verbs with *-eke* do not exhibit noun incorporation and cannot be glossed as 'get'. Manyakina's examples, like McCulloch's, use the Restigouche orthography.

(3) tia'm-u-e'ge-t
moose-DER-get.VAI-3
'S/he hunts moose.' (Manyakina 2015:1)

(4) e's-e'ge-t
clam-get.VAI-3
'S/he digs for clams.' (Manyakina 2015:4)

A light verb is a semantically minimal functional core of a verb. It does not contain the "semantic elements which characterize full verbal entries, especially manner" (Johns 2007:3). The root provides the lexical content for the verb. The complexity involved in the structure of verbs with LVs has been demonstrated by Larson (1988), Kratzer (1996), and Harley (2013), who argued for expansion of the verb phrase to include other layers because of evidence from ditransitive verbs, causatives, passives, and applicatives. LVs are the functional elements in these layers.

An LV analysis of some abstract finals has been discussed in several Algonquian languages including Naskapi (Brittain 2003), Penobscot (Quinn 2006), Ojibwe (Mathieu 2008), Blackfoot (Ritter and Rosen 2010), and Northern East Cree (Brittain and Acton 2014). 'Light verbs' are "instantiations of little-v" (Brittain and Acton 2014:478; see also Quinn 2006; Mathieu 2008) and are functional elements that can formally license a DP object, determine whether there is an external argument, and theta-mark the external argument DP (Ritter and Rosen 2010). Brittain (2003:29) classifies "at least some abstract finals as light verbs, i.e., category-defining f-morphemes." Branigan et al. (2005:76) propose that in Algonquian in general, "all 'final' morphemes (probably) originate in *v*." Quinn (2006:9) notes that "verbal argument structure is built up in the syntax by 'light' predicate heads that introduce arguments individually." Our investigation clarifies some of the implications an LV analysis has on interpretation of *-eke*. A full investigation into LVs in Mi'kmaq is one subject in our continuing studies.

We propose that verbs are not built around the root/initial as illustrated in Figure 1 (depicting the analysis of Inglis 1986 and McCulloch 2013, who have followed the Algonquianist literature); rather light verbs (which include at least some 'verb finals' or 'theme signs') are the head of the verb (Figure 2). In Figures 1 and 2, the central morpheme is bolded (in Figure 1 it is the root and in Figure 2 the LV).

FIGURE 1. Traditional analysis of Mi'kmaq verb word.

(preverb-) | root | (-medial) -final -inflection

FIGURE 2. LV analysis of Mi'kmaq verb word.

(preverb-) root (-medial) | LV | -final -inflection

Note that the verb word can be much more complex, with the addition of other optional morphemes, including other preverbs, medials, finals, and markers for existential, absentative, obviate, negative, and plurality (see Inglis 1986; McCulloch 2013; Hamilton 2015).

Defining Transitivity

Mi'kmaq is like other Algonquian languages in that the syntax does not always reflect the morphological transitivity of a verb. In Algonquian languages, verbs are classified by their inflections as being II (intransitive verb with inanimate subject), AI (intransitive verb with animate subject), TI (transitive verb with inanimate object), and TA (transitive verb with animate object). However, it has long been noted that there are various types of non-correspondence between the morphology and the syntax. For example, 'intransitive' verbs can sometimes take direct objects (AI+O), and 'transitive' verbs can sometimes take two objects (TI+O; Goddard 1974:319; see also Oxford 2014; Hamilton 2015).

In order to do this study, we find it necessary to carefully distinguish transitivity in terms of morphology, syntax, and semantics, as follows:

> Morphological transitivity is determined in the Algonquianist tradition by the verbal inflections. In this paper, we broaden the scope to include any morpheme within the verb word that gives information about any participant (including morphemes such as LVs, inflections and incorporated nouns). We do not discuss the applicative morpheme (Hamilton 2015).
>
> Semantic valence is defined by the number of semantic roles associated with a particular verb in context (Comrie 1989), as determined by native speaker judgment.
>
> Syntactic transitivity is defined in terms of the number of DP complements or pronominal clitics that can appear in a clause; e.g., Kemmer 2003. We do

not discuss examples where there are multiple objects or objects with differing semantic roles.

One reason that transitivity needs to be defined in these terms is exemplified by (5–6) (both from our data). Both *-m* (5) and *-eke* (6) are known to be verb morphemes that indicate a transitive verb where an animate subject acts on an inanimate object. However, these morphemes are not the same in terms of syntactic transitivity. The root *ewi'k* 'write' and the transitive morpheme *-m* are shown in (5); the clause requires an object DP (*wi'katikn* 'letter'/'paper'/'book') or an object referent in the immediate context; cf. (7a, b) which shows a question-answer pair. In the absence of such a context, **ewi'k-m-Ø* 'I write' is ungrammatical. In contrast, (6) shows the same root *ewi'k* but with *-eke*.[6] This time an object DP is ungrammatical; cf. (8). Note that the 1S subject inflection for *-eke* (*-y*) is different than that for *-m* (-Ø, see Francis and Hewson 2016).

(5) ewi'k-m-Ø wi'katikn
write-LV-1s paper
'I write a letter.'

(6) ewi'k-ike-y
write-LV-1s
'I write (something).'

(7) a. nut-a-y wi'katikn
want-LV-1s letter
'I need a letter.'
b. ewi'k-m-Ø
write-LV-1s
'I am writing it.'

(8) *ewi'k-ike-y wi'katikn
write-LV-1s letter
'I write a letter.'

When (5) and (6) are described morphologically, semantically, and syntactically

TABLE 1. Transitivity criteria exemplified

EXAMPLE	MORPHOLOGICAL TRANSITIVITY	SEMANTIC VALENCE	SYNTACTIC TRANSITIVITY
(5)	Transitive with inanimate object (indicated by *-m*) Subject only inflection	Two participants	Transitive (object DP is required in immediate context)
(6)	Transitive with inanimate object (indicated by *-eke*) Subject only inflection	Two participants	Intransitive (object DP is ungrammatical)

(Table 1), their similarities (in morphology and semantics) and difference (only in syntactic transitivity) are made clear.

Distinguishing the morphological, semantic, and syntactic transitivity of a particular Mi'kmaq verb clarifies the picture when there are mismatches. For example, there are some verbs that carry transitive morphology that are syntactically intransitive (TI minus O). The morpheme *-m* is a verb morpheme that indicates an animate subject and inanimate object. The expected transitive syntax is seen in (9–10).

(9) wikt-**m**-Ø pipnaqn
taste.good-LV-1s bread
'I like the taste of bread.'

(10) ewi'k-**m**-Ø wi'katikn
write-LV-1s paper
'I write a letter.'

In contrast, (11–12) show the same morpheme but with intransitive syntax.[7] Bloomfield (1946:95) says these intransitive verbs have "a merely *formal* goal" (emphasis his). Inglis (1986:8) calls them "pseudo-intransitive," i.e., verbs that "have the morphology of TI verbs, but meanings which are intransitive" (Inglis 1986:18).

(11) pem-tukwi'-**m**-Ø
along-run-LV-1s
'I run along.'

TABLE 2. Transitive morphology with differing syntax and semantics

EXAMPLE	MORPHOLOGICAL TRANSITIVITY	SEMANTIC VALENCE	SYNTACTIC TRANSITIVITY
(9)	Transitive with inanimate object (indicated by *-m*) Subject only inflection	Two participants	Transitive (object DP is required)
(11)	Transitive with inanimate object (indicated by *-m*) Subject only inflection	One participant	Intransitive (object DP is ungrammatical)

(12) ey-**m**-Ø
be-LV-1s
'I am here.'

Table 2 illustrates (9) and (11); their similarity is only in their morphology since their semantic valence and morphological transitivity are different.

Results and Discussion

This study revealed four main findings, each discussed in subsequent subsections. First, *-eke* can occur in transitive clauses, contrary to expectations from the literature. Second, syntactically transitive/intransitive alternations are due to the presence of another set of LVs (called LV2). Next, *-eke* as part of a set of semantically transitive LVs is discussed. Finally, some features of *-eke* are discussed.

-Eke Is Not Detransitivizing

We find that *-eke* can occur in syntactically transitive clauses.[8] The light verb *-eke* and the object DP are bolded in (13–17).

(13) menu-**eke**-y **pipnaqn**
stem-LV-1s bread
'I want bread.'

(14) kesisp-**eke**-y **lassiet**
stem-LV-1s plate
'I wash the plate.'

(15) el-**eke**-y **tu'aqn**
DIR-LV-1S ball
'I throw the ball.'

(16) tew-**eke**-y **tu'aqn**
out-LV-1s ball
'I throw the ball outside.'

(17) pem-**eke**-y **tu'aqn**
along-LV-1s ball
'I am walking along throwing a ball.'

Since *-eke* can occur in a transitive clause, its primary function is not to delete or absorb the internal object, as hypothesized in the literature. The DPs are referential and can be modified, specified, or possessed, as (18–20) show.

(18) pem-**eke**-y mekw-e:-k **tu'aqn**
along-LV-1s red-LV-1s ball
'I am walking along throwing a red ball.'

(19) tew-**eke**-y ula **tu'aqn**
out-LV-1s DEM ball
'I am throwing this ball outside.'

(20) ejikl-**eke**-y n-**tu'aqn**-m
away-LV-1s 1s -ball-POSS
'I am throwing away my ball.'

Syntactic Transitivity Due to Another Proposed LV Set

We found that *-eke* is in fact unrelated to the syntactic transitivity of a clause. Compare (21) and (22). Both clauses contain *-eke*; (21) is syntactically transitive and

TABLE 3. Transitive semantics and morphology with differing syntax

EXAMPLE	MORPHOLOGICAL TRANSITIVITY	SEMANTIC VALENCE	SYNTACTIC TRANSITIVITY
(21)	Transitive morpheme *-eke* Subject only inflection	Two participants	Transitive (object DP is required in context)
(22)	Transitive morphemes *-eke* and *-ut* Subject only inflection	Two participants	Intransitive (object DP is ungrammatical)

(22) intransitive. The only difference in verb morphology is that the syntactically intransitive clause contains the morpheme *ut-*. This morpheme is bolded and glossed as LV2 (a second LV).[9] *-Eke* is now glossed as LV1.

(21) kaqam-eke-y aptu'n
stand-LV-1s cane
'I stood up the cane.' (leaned it against the wall)

(22) kaqam-**ut**-eke-y
stand-LV2-LV1–1s
'I am tolerant.' (lit. I withstand stuff)

In both examples, the verbs/clauses are morphologically and semantically transitive. When *ut-* is absent, the clause with *-eke* is syntactically transitive; when *ut-* is present, the clause is syntactically intransitive but semantically has a nonspecific object (**kaqam-ut-eke-y aptu'n* is ungrammatical). This is illustrated in Table 3.

Table 4 shows more examples of syntactically transitive and intransitive clauses with *-eke*. The presence (left column) or absence (right column) of a DP (and whether its object is referential) depends on another verb final—*o't-*, *a't-*, or *ut-*, bolded in these examples.

The examples in (22) and Table 4 contain the morphemes *o't-*, *a't-*, or *ut-*, all glossed as LV2 (precise meanings are the subject of future research). We propose that these morphemes are part of a set of light verbs (cf. Quinn 2006; Brittain and Acton 2014, whose analyses support the view that some if not all verb finals are light verbs). This LV set including *o't-*, *a't-*, or *ut-* is not of the same type as *-eke* since the distribution and syntactic function of each are different.

TABLE 4. *-Eke* and LV2

VERB ROOT	*-EKE* WITHOUT LV2 (OBJECT DP IS REQUIRED)	*-EKE* WITH LV2 (OBJECT DP IS UNGRAMMATICAL)
tew- 'out'	tew-eke-y tu'aqn out-LV1-1s ball 'I throw the ball outside.'	tew-**o't**-eke-y out-LV2-LV1-1s 'I am buying stuff on credit.'
el- DIR	el-eke-y tu'aqn DIR-LV1-1s ball 'I throw the ball.'	el-**o't**-eke-y DIR-LV2-LV1-1S 'I am throwing hints around.'
kesisp- 'wash'	kesisp-eke-y n-unji wash-LV1-1s 1S-head 'I give my head a quick wash.'	kesisp-**a't**-eke-y wash-LV2-LV1-1s 'I am washing the floor.'
nis- 'down'	nis-eke-y kuntew down-LV1-1s rock 'I throw down/drop the rock.'	nis-**a't**-eke-y down-LV2-LV1-1s 'I put cards down (play them in a game)' / 'I wager.'

-eke Is Part of a Set of LVs

We have interpreted *-eke* as an LV; the distribution of other morphemes indicates that *-eke* is part of a set of LVs in Mi'kmaq (glossed as LV1). Future study will further explore this hypothesis and look at the entire sets of LV1s and LV2s. Table 5 shows a partial list of proposed LV1 morphemes, with examples. We propose that there is a set of semantically intransitive LV1s (including *-i*, *-e*, *-a*, and *-ie*) and another set of semantically transitive LV1s (including *-m*, *-u*, *-eke*, and -Ø). Note that there is a zero morpheme in the list, which indicates a verb that is semantically transitive with an animate object. Wiltschko (2014) indicates that only morphemes that are at functional heads can have a zero form, meaning that the LVs are functional heads. The LV1s are bolded in the examples.

Features of -eke

Table 5 shows that that *-m*, *-u*, and *-eke* are three LV1s that are semantically transitive with an inanimate object as well as -Ø, an LV that is semantically transitive with an animate object. Three features of *-eke* as compared with the other transitive LVs are outlined here.

First, Little (2016) notes objects with *-eke* can only be third person; first and second person objects are ungrammatical. We note further that the object must also

TABLE 5. Light verbs in Mi'kmaq

	LV1	EXAMPLE	GLOSS
SEMANTICALLY INTRANSITIVE	*-i*	tek-**i**-t tek-**i**-k	'S/he is cold.' 'It is cold.'
	-e	elukw-**e**-t elukw-**e**-k	'S/he works.' 'It works.'
	-a	pew-**a**-t melk-atp-**a**-t	'S/he is dreaming.' 'S/he is hard-headed.'
	-ie	pem-**ie**-t	'S/he is going along.'
SEMANTICALLY TRANSITIVE	*-m*	ewi'k-**m**-Ø nest-**m**-Ø	'I write it.' 'I understand it.'
	-u	tep-a't-**u**-Ø pew-it-**u**-Ø	'I put it on.' 'I dream about it.'
	-eke	tep-**eke**-y ewi'k-**ike**-y	'I throw something on.' 'I write something.'
	-Ø	tep-a'l-**Ø**-ɨk pew-i'-**Ø**-k	'I put him/her on.' 'I dream about him/her.'

be singular. While *-eke* with a 3S object is grammatical (23), a 3P is not **tew-eke-y kutputi'l* or **tew-a't-eke-y kutputi'l*. Rather, the LV2-LV1 combination *a't-u* must be employed (24).

(23) tew-eke-y kutputi
out-LV1–1S chair
'I throw the chair outside.'

(24) tew-a't-u-Ø-ann kutputi-'l
out-LV2-LV1–1S-3P chair-P(in.)
'I take the chairs outside.'

Second, the LV2 that occurs with *-eke* indicates that the semantic object is inanimate, even when the referent is animate. It has long been noted that the verb finals we have renamed as LV2 morphemes occur in pairs (Inglis 1986), with one indicating an inanimate object; e.g., *o't-* in (25) and the other an animate; e.g., *ey-* in (26). While it is beyond the scope of this paper to explore the allomorphy in these pairings, we do note that when an LV2 collocates with *-eke*, it is always from the set that indicates that the object is morphologically inanimate, regardless of the semantic animacy of the actual semantic referent. To illustrate, (25–27) all have the same root *ank-* 'care' but different LV2-LV1 combinations. In the verb with the LV1 *-m* (25), the animacy of the direct object *wasuek* 'flower' matches that indicated by the LV2 *o't-* (both indicate inanimate).

(25) ank-**o't-m**-Ø wasuek
care-LV2-LV1–1s flower
'I take care of a flower.'

Likewise, in the case of the LV1 *-Ø* (26), the animacy of the direct object *Pie'l* 'Peter' matches that indicated by the LV2 *ey-* (both indicate animate).

(26) ankw-**ey-Ø**-aq Pie'l
care-LV2-LV1–1s>3s Peter
'I take care of Peter.'

For *-eke*, the LV2 is the same as that in (25), indicating an inanimate object, even though the semantic object referent is animate (people).

(27) ank-**o't-eke**-y
care-LV2-LV1–1s
'I take care of others.'

Table 6 illustrates more examples with the LV2-LV1 combinations bolded. Column 1 shows three verb roots. Column 2 illustrates each verb root with the LV1s *-m* or *-u*. These LV1s collocate with *o't-*, *at-*, and *it-*—LV2 morphemes that indicate an inanimate object. Column 3 illustrates each verb root with the LV1 -Ø. The LV2 morphemes found in these verbs all indicate that the object is animate: *ey-*, *e'-*, *i'-*, and *al-*. Column 4 shows each verb root with the LV1 *-eke*. The LV2 morphemes that collocate with *-eke* are the same as those with *-m*, all indicating inanimate object. It thus appears that one way that *-eke* functions is to give inanimate status to a semantically animate object referent, perhaps taking it out of focus for discourse reasons. This discourse function of *-eke* has also been noted with respect to a similar morpheme in Nishnaabemwin. Valentine considers the morpheme *-ge* a "detransitivizing suffix" that causes focus on the actor by making it the only role (Valentine 2001:403).

TABLE 6. *-Eke* has morphologically inanimate object

ROOT	LV *-M/-U* (MORPHOLOGICALLY INANIMATE OBJECT)	LV *-Ø* (MORPHOLOGICALLY ANIMATE OBJECT)	LV *-EKE* (MORPHOLOGICALLY INANIMATE OBJECT)
ne'p- 'kill'	ne'p-**at-u**-Ø suliewey kill-LV2-LV1-1s money 'I earn money.' (lit. I kill money)	ne'p-**e'**-Ø-k Pie'l kill-LV2-LV1-1s>3s Peter 'I kill Peter.'	ne'p-**at-eke**-y kill-LV2-LV1-1s 'I am a murderer.' (lit. I kill things)
pew- 'dream about'	pew-**it-u**-Ø wasuek dream-LV2-LV1-1s flower 'I dream about a flower.'	pew-**i'**-Ø-k Pie'l dream-LV2-LV1-1s>3s Peter 'I dream about Peter.'	pew-**it-eke**-y dream-LV2-LV1-1s 'I am having dreams.'
kes- 'like/ love'	kes-**at-m**-Ø n-t-a'kwesn like-LV2-LV1-1s 1s-EP-hat 'I like my hat'	kes-**al**-Ø-k Pie'l like-LV2-LV1-1s>3s Peter 'I like Peter.'	kes-**at-eke**-y like-LV2-LV1-1s 'I fool around (have affairs).' (lit. I love things)

Third, preliminary investigation illustrates some distinguishing features between LV2–LV1 combinations with *-eke* and *-u*.[10] One aspectual feature Ø*-eke* (28) seems to carry as compared with *a't-u* (29) is that Ø*-eke* implies a brief contact, less hands-on type of action as compared with *a't-u,* where the action is more deliberate throughout the duration of the action. The difference is not volitional vs. nonvolitional, as has been noted in other languages (Hopper and Thomson 1980; Rice 1989; Jacobs 2011).

(28) ejikl-Ø-eke-y lisqeikn
away-LV2-LV1-1s box
'I throw out the box.'

(29) ejikl-**a't-u**-Ø lisqeikn
away-LV2-LV1-1s box
'I remove the box.'

Table 7 provides more examples.

TABLE 7. *-Eke* vs. *-u*

ROOT	*A'T- + -U*	*Ø- + -EKE*
tep- 'on'	tep-a't-u-Ø lisqeikn on-LV2-LV1-1s box 'I put the box on.'	tep-Ø-*eke*-y lisqeikn out-LV2-LV1-1s box 'I throw the box on.'
ilt- 'close'	ilt-a't-u-Ø lisqeikn close-LV2-LV1-1s box 'I close the box.'	ilt-Ø-*eke*-y lisqeikn close-LV2-LV1-1s box 'I slam the box shut.'
kut- 'pour'	kut-a't-u-Ø sam'qwan pour-LV2-LV1-1s water 'I pour the water.'	kut-Ø-*eke*-y sam'qwan pour-LV2-LV1-1s water 'I spill the water.'

Conclusions and Further Issues

-Eke as a light verb appears to be part of a set of semantically transitive light verbs in Mi'kmaq; we propose that there is another set of semantically intransitive light verbs as well. Syntactic transitivity in clauses with *-eke* depends on the presence or absence of a second set of proposed LV morphemes (the *a't/o't* set). Without the second LV morpheme, the clause with *-eke* must have an object DP, and it indicates an aspectual situation where there is a brief contact between the subject and object. A more continuous contact between subject and object is indicated by the LV combination *a't-* plus *-u*.

It appears that all constructions with *-eke* require third person objects; these objects must also be singular in syntactically transitive clauses. In intransitive clauses, it appears that *-eke* selects a second LV that indicates an inanimate object, even when the semantic object is animate.

Questions that are raised concerning the nature of *-eke* as an LV include: what are the characteristics of the various proposed LV sets in Mi'kmaq and, when there is a choice, why would a speaker choose one combination of LVs over another? For example, Inglis (1986:96) says the distinction between *o't-* and *a't-* is that *o't-* represents an actor doing something bit by bit and *a't-* represents an actor performing an action in one continuous motion. What is the relationship between transitivity and animacy in Mi'kmaq?[11] Do morphemes similar to *-eke* exist in other Algonquian languages, and, if so, do they function in the same way as *-eke* does in Mi'kmaq? For example, Quinn (2006:101–102) shows that in Penobscot (a language closely related to Mi'kmaq), the cognate verb stem *-əlahke* 'throw (thus),' although normally classified as intransitive, can in some situations take a syntactic object DP. Our intentions are to concentrate efforts first on the LV2 morpheme set, looking at a large list of verbs in context to further explore the relation between the proposed LV combinations and the internal object.

NOTES

1. This research was supported by SSHRC and University of Victoria doctoral research grants and carried out under the supervision of Leslie Saxon and Heather Bliss. We gratefully acknowledge their input.
2. We use the spelling 'Mi'kmaq'. 'Mi'kmaq' and 'Mi'gmaq' represent different dialects and orthographies of the same language found in different regions. Mi'kmaq is an Eastern Algonquian language spoken by some 8,500 speakers according to the 2011 census (Lewis et. al. 2014). This oral history and background information is given by the first author of this paper.
3. This morpheme is written -*ege* in other orthographies. In the examples in this paper we write *k* (and voiceless variants for all stops).
4. A reviewer noted that Bloomfield (1962:278–280) uses the term "verb of indefinite action" for a similar derivational morpheme in Menominee.
5. Abbreviations used in this paper include: AB = absentative, AI, VAI = intransitive verb with animate subject, AN = animate, CL = classifier, DEM = demonstrative, DER = derivational, DIR = directional, DO = direct object, DP = demonstrative phrase, EP = epenthesis, II = intransitive verb with inanimate subject, IN = inanimate, LV = light verb, NONSP = non-specific object, POSS = possessive, TA = transitive verb with animate object, TI, VTI = transitive verb with inanimate object, 1s = first person singular, 3s = third person singular, 1s>3s = first person singular subject acts on third person singular object. In the orthography, the letters *q*, *y*, *j*, and *ɨ* correspond to phonetic [χ], [j], [ʧ], and [ə], respectively, and apostrophe indicates vowel length. Abbreviations used in examples from other works are noted with the example.
6. We assume that -*ike* is a phonological variant of -*eke*.
7. There is no evidence to suggest that -*m* has TI and AI homophones.
8. Carol Rose Little (2016) has noted the occurrence of -*eke* with an object DP in Mi'gmaq. One of Hamilton's examples (2015:29) also shows the morpheme -*ege* in a transitive clause (although -*ege* is not parsed as a separate morpheme from the root).
9. In the Algonquianist literature, the addition of a second verb final is called a case of secondary derivation (cf. Inglis 1986:96–98 for Mi'kmaq). Quinn (2006:10) notes that

"the stacking of light verbs is possible and indeed common." We make no judgment as to structure at this point.

10. Matthewson (2004:389) reminds us that "translations should always be treated as a clue rather than a result."
11. Little (2018) discusses the relationship of animacy to syntax in Mi'gmaq.

REFERENCES

Bloomfield, Leonard. 1946. Algonquian. *Linguistic Structures of Native America*, ed. by Cornelius Osgood and Harry Hoijer, pp. 85–129. Viking Fund Publications in Anthropology, vol. 6. New York.

———. 1962. *The Menomini Language*. New Haven, CT: Yale University Press.

Branigan, Phil, Julie Brittain, and Carrie Dyck. 2005. Balancing Syntax and Prosody in the Algonquian Verb Complex. *Papers of the Thirty-Sixth Algonquian Conference*, ed. by H. Christoph Wolfart, pp. 75–93. Winnipeg: University of Manitoba.

Brittain, Julie. 2003. A Distributed Morphology Account of the Syntax of the Algonquian Verb. *Proceedings of the 2003 Annual Conference of the Canadian Linguistic Association*, ed. by Sophie Burelle and Stanca Somesfalean, pp. 26–41. Montreal: Université du Québec à Montréal.

Brittain, Julie and Sara Acton. 2014. The Lexicon–Syntax Interface: Root Semantics as an Indirect Determinant of Intransitive Verb Syntax in Cree. *International Journal of American Linguistics* 80(4):475–506.

Comrie, Bernard. 1989. *Language Universals and Linguistic Typology: Syntax and Morphology*. Chicago: University of Chicago Press.

Francis, Bernie and John Hewson 2016. *The Mi'kmaw Grammar of Father Pacifique*, 2nd ed. Sydney: Cape Breton University Press.

Goddard, Ives. 1974. Remarks on the Algonquian Independent Indicative. *International Journal of American Linguistics* 40(4):317–327.

Hamilton, Michael D. 2015. The Syntax of Mi'gmaq: A Configurational Account. PhD thesis, McGill University.

Harley, Heidi. 2013. External Arguments and the Mirror Principle: On the Distinctness of Voice and v. *Lingua* 125:34–57.

Hopper, Paul J. and Sandra A. Thompson. 1980. Transitivity in Grammar and Discourse. *Language* 56(2):251–299.

Inglis, Stephanie. 1986. The Fundamentals of Micmac Word Formation. MA thesis, Memorial University of Newfoundland.

Jacobs, Peter W. 2011. Control in Skwxwu7mesh. PhD thesis, University of British Columbia.

Johns, Alana. 2007. Restricting Noun Incorporation: Root Movement. *Natural Language and Linguistic Theory* 25(3):535–576.

Kauder, Rev. Christian. 1866. *Das Gut Buch, enhaltend den Katechismus, Betrachtung, Gesang*, (The Good Book, Containing the Catechism, Meditations, Hymns). Vienna: The Imperial and Royal Printing Press.

Kemmer, Suzanne. 2003. Transitivity and Voice. *International Encyclopedia of Linguistics*, vol. 4, ed. by William J. Frawley, pp. 277–279. Oxford: Oxford University Press.

Kratzer, Angelika. 1996. Severing the External Argument from Its Verb. *Phrase Structure and the Lexicon*, ed. by Johan Rooryck, and Laurie Zaring, pp. 109–137. Dordrecht: Springer Netherlands.

Larson, Richard K. 1988. On the Double Object Construction. *Linguistic Inquiry* 19(3):335–391.

Lewis, M. Paul, Gary F. Simons, and Charles D. Fennig. 2014. *Ethnologue: Languages of the Americas and the Pacific*, 17th ed. Dallas: SIL International.

Little, Carol Rose. 2018. Inanimate Nouns as Subjects in Mi'gmaq: Consequences for Agreement Morphology. *Proceedings of the Workshop on the Structure and Constituency of Languages of the Americas 21*, ed. by Megan Keough et al., pp. 127–141. Vancouver: University of British Columbia Working Papers in Linguistics.

———. 2016. Notes on AI+Os in Mi'gmaq. Unpublished manuscript, Cornell University, Ithaca, NY.

Manyakina, Yuliya. 2015. Two Types of "Incorporation" in Mi'gmaq. MA. thesis, McGill University.

Mathieu, Eric. 2008. The Syntax of Abstract and Concrete Finals in Ojibwe. *Proceedings of the North East Linguistic Society*, vol. 37, no. 2, ed. by Emily Elfner and Marin Walkow, pp. 101–114. Amherst: University of Massachusetts.

Matthewson, Lisa. 2004. On the Methodology of Semantic Fieldwork 1. *International Journal of American Linguistics* 70(4):369–415.

McCulloch, Gretchen. 2013. Verb Stem Composition in Mi'gmaq. MA thesis, McGill University.

Oxford, William R. 2014. Microparameters of Agreement: A Diachronic Perspective on Algonquian Verb Inflection. PhD thesis, University of Toronto.

Pacifique, Father (ed.). 1921. *Sapeoig Oigatigen Gômgoetjoigasigel, Alasotmaganel, Ginamatineoel ag Getapegiemgeo*el (Manual of Prayers, Instructions, Psalms & Hymns in Micmac Ideograms). Ristigouche, QC: Micmac Messenger Press.

Quinn, Conor M. 2006. Referential-Access Dependency in Penobscot. PhD thesis, Harvard University.

Rand, Silas T. 1875. *A First Reading Book in the Micmac Language*. Halifax: Nova Scotia Printing.

———. 1888. *Mi'kmaw Dictionary*. Halifax: Nova Scotia Printing.

———. 1894. *Legends of the Micmacs*. New York: Longmans, Green.

Rice, Keren. 1989. *A Grammar of Slave*. Berlin: Walter de Gruyter.

Ritter, Elizabeth and Sara Thomas Rosen. 2010. Animacy in Blackfoot: Implications for Event Structure and Clause Structure. *Syntax, Lexical Semantics and Event Structure*, ed. by Malka Rappaport-Hovav, Ivy Sichel, and Edit Doron, pp. 124–152. Oxford: Oxford University Press.

Sylliboy, Helen. [n.d.] Mi'kmaw Verb Conjugations. Unpublished manuscript, Ta'n L'nuey-Etl-mawlukwatmumk, Eskasoni, Nova Scotia.

Valentine, J. Randolph. 2001. *Nishnaabemwin Reference Grammar*. Toronto: University of Toronto Press.

Wiltschko, Martina. 2014. *The Universal Structure of Categories: Towards a Formal Typology*. Cambridge: Cambridge University Press.

A Pedagogical Grammar of Moose Cree for Second Language Learners

Jimena Terraza

The Moose Cree dialect is an L-dialect spoken on Moose Factory Island and in Moosonee, Ontario. Contrary to other Cree dialects, mostly those spoken in Quebec, it is no longer used by children and young adults as the language of communication. Faced with this situation, the Moose Cree First Nation Band Council has undertaken actions to develop pedagogical materials for those interested in learning the language as a second language. The published materials include a dictionary (Brousseau and Collette 2014) and a grammatical outline, and to these will soon be added an online talking dictionary. Since last year, I have been developing a pedagogical grammar as part of this language learning project. The pedagogical grammar employs user-friendly, nontechnical terminology and narrative form to teach the main aspects of the grammar of Moose Cree (obviation, animacy, verb classes, conjugations, orders, word formation, etc.). The purpose of this article is to share the process of writing this pedagogical grammar and to discuss the challenges it posed, along with some questions that arose during the process.

The Context for Creating the Pedagogical Grammar

The positive reception of the first edition of the Moose Cree-English dictionary (Brousseau et al. 2014) convinced our team to undertake a more sustained effort at promoting and documenting the language. The Department of Language and Culture of the Moose Cree First Nation Band Council decided that something in the way of a grammar ought to be included in the subsequent edition of the dictionary. To this end, Brousseau et al. (2015) produced a grammatical outline to accompany the second edition of the dictionary. One of the goals of this grammatical outline was to complement the information contained in the dictionary and to explain concepts such as verb type, animacy, possession, and person (first, second, etc.). It included a short section on phonology, nominal inflection (gender, number, obviation, possession), and demonstratives, and another on verbal inflection (verb classes, orders, modes, tenses, and the relational paradigm). While of great interest to linguists and teachers, the outline was overly technical for use by language learners. This is the main reason why the Department of Language and Culture of the Moose Cree First Nation Band Council asked me to write a user-friendly version of the grammatical outline. This version is aimed at adults whose first language is English.

Methodology

The main challenge in making a user-friendly version of the grammatical outline was to find a way to present the grammatical concepts without using specialized terminology: How does one talk about gender, obviation, and orders, without using those terms? To address this issue in the grammatical outline, I reverse the way in which grammatical notions are conventionally introduced to language learners, asking them first to identify the grammatical features within a STORY, before explaining the function of those features. This approach has the advantage of showing the grammar in its contexts of usage, rather than in sample sentences composed to illustrate a particular grammatical feature. By grasping the grammatical features in context, learners will better comprehend their function and usage than if these notions are only explained conceptually with isolated sentences.

The narratives used in this pedagogical grammar are of different types and come from different sources. Two come from the book *Cree Legends and Narratives* by Douglas Ellis:[1] *E waškwayi-cîmânihkâniwahk* ('Making birch bark canoes') told by

Willie Frenchman in 1964 and *Nîšťam kâ pâpalik kâ pimihlâmakahk môsonîwî-ministikohk* ('The first airplane comes to Moose Factory') told by Andrew Faries in 1958. Another narrative included in the book is an âtalôhkân (traditional myth) called "The Roc,"[2] which is perhaps one of the earliest examples of a genuine Cree language *âtalôhkân*. It was originally written by a native Moose Cree speaker in the late 1800s and was published in 1881 in Horden's *A Grammar of the Cree Language* under the name "An Indian's Adventure." Finally, I included an excerpt from a story, told by an elder of the community, narrating the bad relationship between a man and his son-in-law, and the latter's transformation into a caribou. The narratives are all transcribed in the standard Roman orthography and followed by English translation.

Where to Start?

The first lesson starts with the introduction of the *âtalôhkân*, "The Roc." I begin with a discussion of Cree nouns and their equivalents in English by singling out the first sentence, circling the nouns, and drawing an arrow to the corresponding nouns in English.[3] I decided to start with nominal inflection because it is simpler than verbal inflection.

EXAMPLE 1.

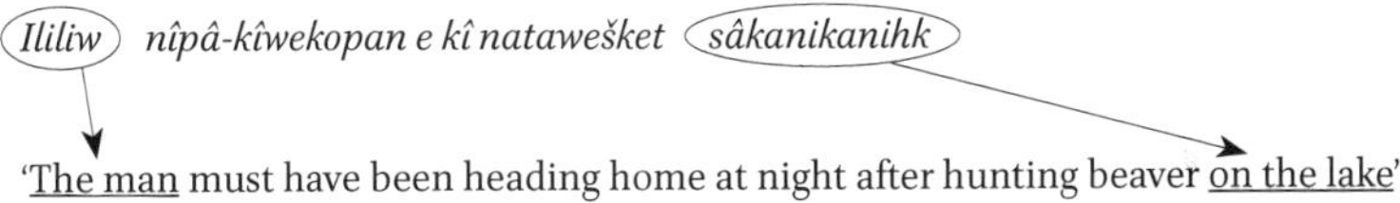

Ililiw *nîpâ-kîwekopan e kî natawešket* *sâkanikanihk*
'The man must have been heading home at night after hunting beaver on the lake'

I used this sentence to discuss the notion of bare nouns by simply saying that—in this context—the noun can appear without a determiner and still refer to a definite referent. To exploit the nominal inflection in this sentence, I also explained the notion of locative case and provided a list of other nouns followed by this suffix to illustrate phonological variation and the range of possible meanings and translations into English. The term 'suffix' is replaced here by 'ending' and the term 'morpheme' by 'part of a word'. I also included a discussion about the fact that fewer nouns are used in Cree than in English to express the same idea.

After exploring all possible explanations for nominal features in the first sentences, I turn to verbal features. The same sentences are used to introduce the lexical category of verbs, which are identified with a rectangle:

EXAMPLE 2.

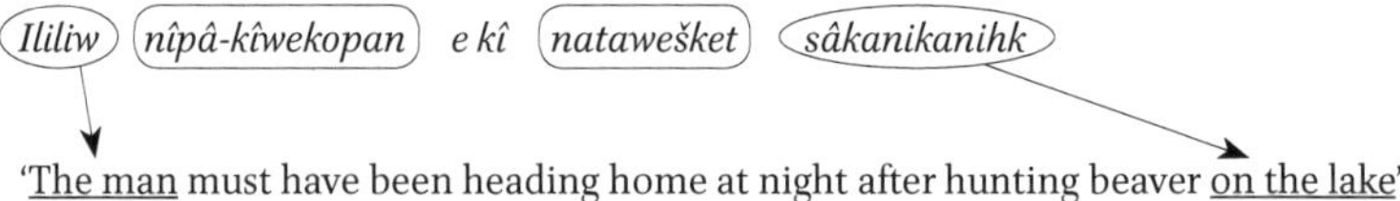

This sentence is interesting because of the dubitative tense employed in the first verb (*-kopan*). This tense is not widely used and would not normally be included in a beginner's grammar. However, as the story contains many such occurrences, I decided to explain its function briefly, based on James (1984). Besides the dubitative tense, I used this sentence to present the initial *kîwe-* 's/he returns' and the notion of preverb (*nipa-*). In the next section, I discuss how to take advantage of this example to develop morphological awareness.

The last lexical category I introduce is what Algonquianists call *particles*, following the label used in the dictionary (Brousseau et al. 2015). As in the dictionary, particles are surrounded by a rectangle (remember that nouns are circles and verbs are rounded rectangles). Here is an example of a sentence in which the particle has been highlighted:

EXAMPLE 3.

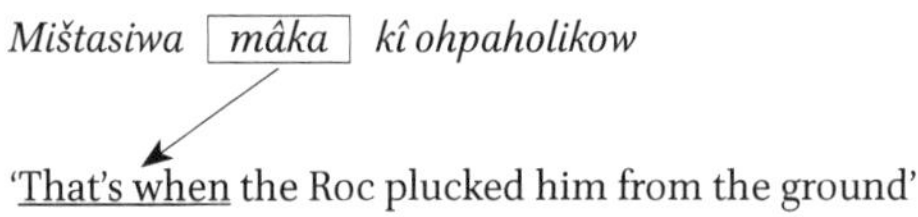

Mištasiwa
mâka
kî ohpaholikow
'That's when the Roc plucked him from the ground'

The important point about particles here is that they are pervasive and recurrent in stories. These particles need to be memorized to be learned, and there is little to be said about their morphology.

For the rest of the story I proceed according to the same principle, extracting the sentences that contain an instance of one of the grammatical concepts I want to discuss, and pinpointing the item in the sentence that best illustrates the concept (see Grammatical Concepts).

Developing Morphological Awareness

Central to the literature on polysynthetic language acquisition is the claim that "learning the morphology of a language is a difficult task even for languages with small amounts of morphology" (Kelly et al. 2014:51). The authors hypothesize that the learning task in languages with rich morphology must be substantially more challenging. Even if these claims refer to first language acquisition, we find the same conclusions in Kell (2014:24): "A command of word-building patterns frees learners from having to simply memorize long lists of vocabulary. Memorization and rote learning can play a substantial role in learning isolating languages, but may be less helpful for polysynthetic languages, due to their vast numbers of roots and affixes which can combine in multiple ways."

Following this line of thought, throughout this pedagogical grammar I promote morphological awareness. For example, going back to sentence (2), we can recall the meaning of the verb *kîwew* ('s/he goes home') and show that there are other verbs that share the first part with this verb:

- ***Kîwe**tišaham*: 's/he sends it back'
- ***Kîwe**how*: 's/he goes back by boat'
- ***Kîwe**paliw*: 's/he or she drives back'

Later in the grammar I use another example:

EXAMPLE 4.

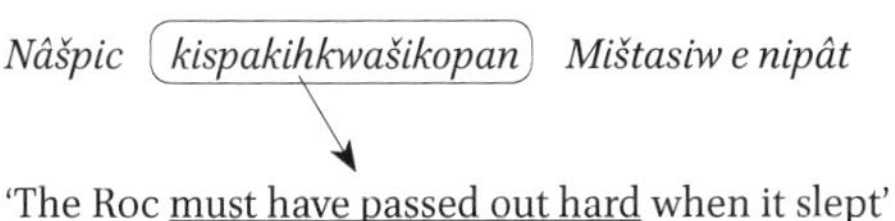

Nâšpic *kispakihkwašikopan* *Mištasiw e nipât*
'The Roc must have passed out hard when it slept'

Here I highlight the initial (called 'the first part of this word') and show other verbs that contain it:

- ***kispak**âw* 'it is thick'
- ***kispak**atin*: 'the ice is thick'
- ***kispak**âlihkwew*: 's/he has thick hair'

I do the same with the medial *-ihkwaši-*:

- *kawihkwašiw* 's/he falls asleep'
- *koštâcihkwašiw* 's/he has a nightmare'
- šâkot*ihkwašiw* 's/he is overcome by sleepiness'

The reader is then asked to figure out the meaning of these two 'parts of words'.

Noun incorporation poses one of the greatest challenges to learners of polysynthetic languages. Rosborough (2012:206) relates her own belated grasp of lexical suffixes in Kwak'wala (a Wakashan language spoken in British Columbia): "Until tonight, I couldn't understand why the phrase *didaxt'sana*—wiping hands—doesn't have the word *a'ya'su* [hand] in it." Noun incorporation is a very productive device in Cree, and learners need to be aware of the fact that some nouns have a different form when incorporated as medials. In the pedagogical grammar, I remind learners of the fact that bound morphemes, such as medials, are not listed in the dictionary and that they may refer to the same concept or entity as an independent word. For example, if the reader looks up the word for 'hair' in the dictionary, s/he will find the noun *oštikwânipîwaya,* which is very different from the medial *-âlihkwe-* found in *kispakâlihkwew:* 's/he has thick hair'.

Grammatical Concepts

In this project, most of the grammatical concepts were determined prior to story and narrative selection, although some notions (such as the dubitative tense) were added later, given their appearance in the stories.

The narratives introduce readers to the following grammatical notions: some basic distinctions between English and Cree (determiners, person, and gender); obviation in nouns; possession of singular persons; diminutive; locative case; nominal number; the animate-inanimate distinction; personal pronouns; the use of the dubitative tense in stories (*-kopan*); basic notions about word order; the notion of verb orders (independent, conjunct, imperative); a selection of conjugations (neutral, preterite, past dubitative); verb and noun formation; verb types (VII, VAI, VTI, VTA); negation; passives; and question words.

There are many other grammatical concepts that could have been introduced based on the stories and narratives. However, after reviewing the content of two Cree textbooks, *Beginning Cree* (Ratt and Martin 2016) and *Spoken Cree, Level I* (Ellis 2000), I concluded that there was already sufficient material for beginners.

Using Applied Cognitive Linguistics to Explain Specific Grammatical Concepts

In the search for user-friendly ways of explaining complex notions, I drew upon a Cognitive Linguistics framework applied to second language learning and teaching (Littlemore 2009). Croft and Cruse (2004:1) identify the major hypotheses of cognitive linguistics:

- language is not an autonomous cognitive faculty
- grammar is conceptualization
- knowledge of language emerges from language use

The first hypothesis, which is the one most relevant to the explanation of specific grammatical concepts in Moose Cree, implies that fundamental cognitive abilities have direct and pervasive linguistic manifestations. I will illustrate this point through Langacker's theory of cognitive "reference points," which he describes as "the ability to invoke the conception of one entity for purposes of establishing mental contact with another, i.e., to single it out for individual conscious awareness" (1993:5). We can engage reference points as a strategy of orientation (e.g., with the purpose of locating the North Star in the sky), but for the most part, cognitive reference points remain below the threshold of explicit attention. For instance, we use it when we recite the alphabet, but we do not necessarily consider the letters as 'reference points'. The important aspect of this comparison is that the reference point has a certain cognitive salience, which is either inherent or contextually determined. The essential aspects of the reference-point ability as proposed by Langacker (1993:6) are sketched in Figure 1. Figure 1 contains C, which is the conceptualizer/speaker; R, the reference point; and T, the target, or "the entity that the conceptualizer uses the reference point to establish mental contact with" (Langacker 1993:6). The dashed arrows represent the mental path toward the target. Finally, D represents the dominion. The dominion is an abstract entity, a conceptual region that contains both the reference point and the target. The heavy-line circle is used to indicate the reference point's cognitive salience.

FIGURE 1. Reference-point ability based on Langacker (1993:6).

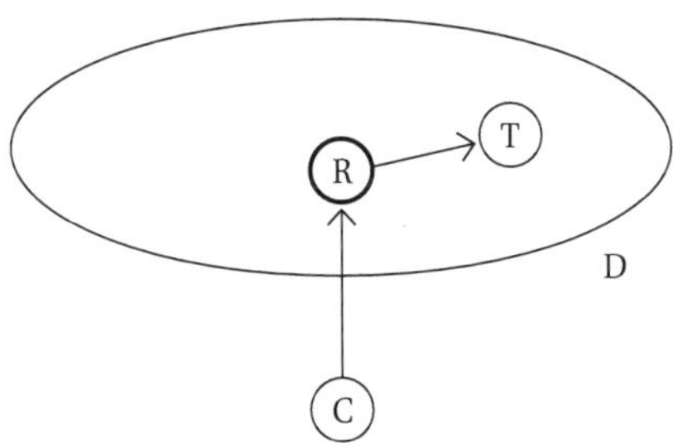

As suggested by Machado Estevam and Terraza (2017), the relationship of a reference point with the target can be equated with the relationship between a proximate and an obviative participant. In Algonquian languages, protypically, the proximate participant is always more salient than the obviative. Here it is important to emphasize prototypical cases, grammatical constraints, and the asymmetrical relationship between the proximate and the obviative. On the one hand, obviation reflects the inherent salience of animates over inanimates, since only animates can trigger obviation. On the other hand, obviation can be used in discourse to mark a conceptual ranking of participants. With this background in mind, the proximate is equated with the reference point and the obviative with the target.

Next, we see how this notion can be transposed in an example. Here is the first instance of obviation (*Mištasiwa*) in the story "The Roc":

> *Ililiw nîpâ-kîwekopan e kî natawešket sâkahikanihk. Nimitâwakâm pimâtakâskôpan. Ot eškan piminikâtahamokopan. Mištasiwa mâka kî ohpaholikow.*
>
> The man must have been heading home at night after hunting beaver on the lake. He was walking out on the ice and must have been carrying his chisel over his shoulder. That's when the Roc plucked him from the ground.

The reader has already encountered *ililiw* 'man' in the story. In this sentence, another participant suddenly enters the scene and interacts with him. The important point is that this other participant, the Roc, is here WITH RESPECT TO the man:

FIGURE 2. Reference point and target equate proximate and obviative.

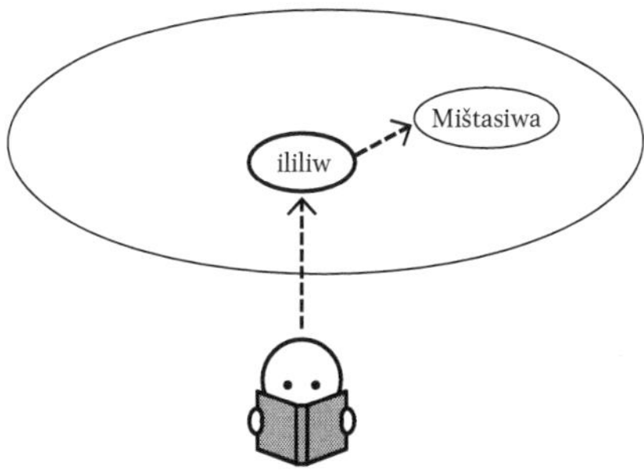

In Figure 2 we can see the proximate participant *ililiw* acting as a reference point with respect to the obviative participant *Mištasiwa*. This same diagram can be used to explain other contexts in which obviation takes place, such as in the prototypical and asymmetrical relationships between: possessor-possessum, actor-goal, human-nonhuman, animate-inanimate, and topic-nontopic. It can also be used to explain proximate shifts. The following paragraph from the same story contains an instance of this:

> *Môšak mâka kihcihlâw Mištasiw e natawahot. Misiwe mâka tôwihkâna petaholew, ašici* ***atihkwa*** *nešta* ***môswa****.*

> Now, the Roc would constantly fly off to hunt. It would bring back all kinds of animals, including **caribou** and **moose**.

As Langacker notes, reference points have a dynamic aspect: "even as it fulfills its reference-point function, R recedes into the background in favor of T, which may itself then be invoked as a reference point for reaching another target" (1993:6). In this context again, we see the parallel that can be drawn between proximate shifts and the dynamic aspect of reference points, illustrated in Figure 3.

FIGURE 3. Proximate shifts.

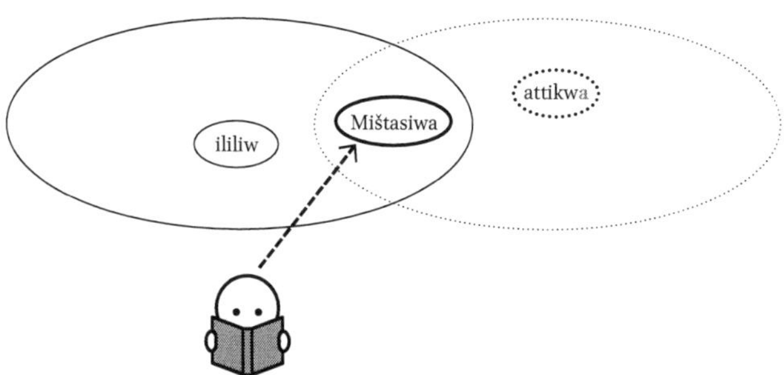

As proposed by Machado Estevam and Terraza (2017), using the framework of reference points to explain obviation is an attempt to unify the different linguistic levels at which this grammatical phenomenon operates. By unifying the explanation, the authors propose a useful tool to teach obviation.

Another contribution of the Cognitive Linguistics approach to language can be found in the work of Talmy (2000), who offers a framework to explain lexicalization patterns. I follow this author's analysis to show the elements that may be present in some VAI verbs lexicalizing a motion event. In broad terms, a motion event consists of (1) a **figure** moving or located with respect to another object, (2) a **ground**: a reference object, (3) the **path** followed or site occupied by the figure object with respect to the ground object, and (4) the **motion and/or manner**: the presence per se of motion or locatedness in the event (Talmy 2000:25). Following this analysis, York (2010) proposes that motion verbs in Innu lexicalize the four elements mentioned earlier as follows: the initial encodes the path (3), the medial the ground (2), the final the movement/manner (4), and the person marker the figure (1). This analysis of the Innu verb—easily transposable into the Cree data—holds important educational value and can be used for teaching purposes.

Based on Table 1, I propose activities such as 'fill in the blank with a manner of motion', or 'circle a motion verb in a story'. These kinds of activities foster morphological awareness and offer a simple way of learning a special category of verbs that share the same structure. Here is an excerpt of a statement made in 2015 by Hilda Jeffries in Moose Factory containing a few motion verbs that can be used to discuss these notions:

TABLE 1. Motion verbs

PATH	GROUND	MANNER OF MOTION	VERB
patote . . . 'aside'		. . . *pahtâ* 'running'	*patote**pahtâ**w* 's/he runs aside'
patote . . . 'aside'		. . . *pali* 'by gliding, driving'	*patote**pali**w* 's/he glides, drives aside'
lâl i . . . 'alongside'	. . . *aške* . . . 'muskeg'	. . . *pahtâ* 'running'	*lâlaške**pahtâ**w* 's/he runs alongside the muskeg'
kihci . . . 'off'		. . . *pic i* . . . 'hauling camp'	*kihci**pici**w* 's/he takes off hauling camp'

"Eliwehk manâ oti mišikitiliw [pâhce . . .] ***pimipahtâw, lâlewepahtwâw*** *anihi e*

it was ever very big, **it ran, it ran besides him,**

pimipahtât. *Kekwân manâ oti mâka ana . . ."môla kata ihkin" itikow,*

it ran. "It is not going to work" I guess he said

nawac nakipalihow ana atihkw patote . . . ***wî kihcipahtâw.***

The caribou also stopped suddenly and **ran off side.**

Discussion

The production of this pedagogical grammar of Moose Cree posed several challenges and raises several questions. First, do we need to follow a logical progression of the concepts as taught in textbooks and grammars? For instance, is it important to learn VII verbs before VTIs and VAIs before VTAs? Is obviation a necessary category that beginners must learn from the start? Do learners need to understand the notion of the animacy hierarchy to grasp the direct-inverse system? And finally, how much grammar does one need to learn a polysynthetic language as a second language? Does one need any grammatical concepts at all?

I am not able to answer all these questions, but I will share some reflections on using grammar to learn an Algonquian language. Some authors, such as Hermes (2007:67), discuss the importance of teaching grammatical concepts in the context of language immersion, claiming that "just speaking to the children in the language is not enough." Other authors (e.g., McInnes 2014) suggest that language learning always implies more than the mastery of lexicon and grammar. 'More than' in this case still implies that some grammar is necessary. Grammatical notions even play an important role in a more communicative method based on images on flashcards (Sarkar et al. 2011).

As for the challenges that writing this pedagogical grammar poses, there is one concrete limitation to using a text-based approach. Narratives and stories represent one specific linguistic register and style. Some structures, particular to other registers, such as conversations or procedurals, are necessarily missing. Also, some typical features, such as indirect discourse, are more pervasive in narratives than in other registers. In some cases, narratives recorded many decades ago might pose a challenge to learners, as certain lexical items in them may have fallen out of use. However, and this is mentioned in the book, the grammar of the language remains essentially unchanged.

Beyond these limitation and challenges, I believe it is important to use narratives, stories, legends, myths, etc. for educational purposes not only because they are invaluable tools linguistically speaking, but because they also give a sense of value to the local culture. These narratives need to take center stage in language maintenance and revitalization.

NOTES

1. The author has given permission to reproduce the narration.
2. The Roc is an enormous legendary bird of prey. The story is published in Kevin Brousseau's blog as "The Roc," available at https://creelanguage.wordpress.com/2015/06/24/the-roc/.
3. One of the reviewers alerted me to the possibility that focusing on nouns first might permit an Indo-European subject-verb perspective to dominate. I think this is a real danger and will take this into consideration in future work. I am aware that Algonquian languages are verb-centered, and it is important to prioritize the learning of verbs over nouns; however, the reason why I decided to start with nouns is because they are simpler than verbs, morphologically speaking, and I sensed that they would be easier for

beginners to analyze. Proving this hypothesis would require experimental data, and to my knowledge, this data is unavailable.

REFERENCES

Brousseau, Kevin and Vincent Collette. 2014. *Ililîmowin Wemištikôšîmowin: A Dictionary of Moose Cree*. Moose Factory: Aanischaaukamikw Cree Cultural Institute & Moose Cree First Nation.

Brousseau, Kevin, Susan Cheechoo, Vincent Collette, and Jimena Terraza. 2015. *Dictionary of Moose Cree: Including an Introduction to Cree Grammar*. Moose Factory: Aanischaaukamikw Cree Cultural Institute & Moose Cree First Nation.

Croft, William and Allan Cruse. 2004. *Cognitive Linguistics*. Cambridge: Cambridge University Press.

Ellis, Douglas (ed). 1995. *Cree Legends and Narratives from the West Coast of James Bay: âtalôhkâna nêsta tipâcimôwina*. Winnipeg, MB: University of Manitoba Press.

———. 2000. *Spoken Cree, Level I, West Coast of James Bay*. Alberta: University of Alberta Press.

Hermes, Mary. 2007. Moving Toward the Language: Reflections on Teaching in an Indigenous-Immersion School. *Journal of American Indian Education* 46(3):54–71.

Horden, John. 1881. *A Grammar of the Cree Language, as Spoken by the Cree Indians of North America*. London: Society for Promoting Christian Knowledge.

James, Deborah. 1984. The Dubitative in Moose Cree. *Papers of the Fifteenth Algonquian Conference*, ed. by William Cowan and José Mailhot, pp. 287–302. Ottawa: Carleton University.

Kell, Sarah. 2014. *Polysynthetic Language Structures and Their Role in Pedagogy and Curriculum for BC Indigenous Languages*. Final Report. Aboriginal Education Team, BC Ministry of Education.

Kelly, Barbara, Gillian Wigglesworth, Rachel Nordingler, and Joseph Blythes. 2014. The Acquisition of Polysynthetic Languages. *Language and Linguistics Compass* 8(2):51–64.

Langacker, Ronald. 1993. Reference-Point Constructions. *Cognitive Linguistics* 4(1):1–38.

Littlemore, Jeannette. 2009. *Applying Cognitive Linguistics to Second Language Learning and Teaching*. London: Palgrave Macmillan UK.

Machado Estevam, Adriana and Jimena Terraza. 2017. Applying Cognitive Linguistics to Algonquian Languages: Understanding and Teaching Obviation. *Online Proceedings of the UK-CLA Meetings*, vol. 4, pp. 69–87. http://www.uk-cla.org.uk/proceedings/volume_4_37.

McInnes, Brian. 2014. Teaching and Learning Ojibwe as a Second Language: Considerations for a Sustainable Future. *Journal of Language Teaching and Research* 5(4):751–758.

Ratt, Solomon and Holly Martin. 2016. *Mâci-nêhiyawêwin* (*Beginning Cree*). Regina: University of Regina Press.

Rosborough, Patricia Christine. 2012. K'angextola Sewn-on-Top: Kwak'wala Revitalization and Being Indigenous. PhD thesis, University of British Columbia.

Sarkar, Mela, Janine Metallic, Mary Ann Metallic, and Janice Vicaire. 2011. Listugujg nemitueg tli'suti napui'gnigtug: apprendre le mi'gmaq à l'âge adulte à Listuguj. *Les langues autochtones du Québec: un patrimoine en danger*, ed. by Lynn Drapeau, pp. 87–106. Montréal: Les presses de l'Université du Québec.

Talmy, Leonard. 2000. *Towards a Cognitive Semantics*. Cambridge, MA: MIT Press.

York, Fanny. 2010. La sémantique des verbes de déplacement en innu. MA thesis, Université du Québec à Montréal.

CONTRIBUTORS

Antti Arppe received his PhD in general linguistics from the University of Helsinki in 2009 and has been assistant professor of quantitative linguistics at the University of Alberta since 2012 and the founding director of Alberta Language Technology Laboratory (ALTLab) since 2013. His research interests include lexical semantics, corpus linguistics, and computational and statistical methods, as well as exploiting multiple methods and sources of evidence. More recently he has started work in language documentation and developing language technological tools and applications for Indigenous languages to support their revitalization, in particular for Cree but also other Canadian Indigenous languages.

After completing her bachelor's in linguistics and anthropology at the universities of Lausanne and Neuchâtel in Switzerland, **Aubrée Boissard** is continuing her studies at the Université Laval in Quebec City, Canada. There, she wrote her master's thesis on Innu-aimun. Her main interests are aspectuality, passive voice, and semantics.

Vincent Collette is sessional in linguistics at First Nations University of Canada. He holds a degree in anthropology and a PhD in linguistics from Laval University.

He works on the morphology and semantics of East Cree (Algonquian) and Nakota (Siouan), as well as on a grammar of Southern Auvernhat (Romance). He is also interested in historical semantics and the ethnohistory of the Indigenous populations of Canada.

David J. Costa is the program director for the Language Research Office at the Myaamia Center at Miami University of Ohio. He grew up in northern California and completed his PhD in linguistics at the University of California, Berkeley in 1994. He has been studying the Miami-Illinois language since 1988.

Amy Dahlstrom is associate professor of linguistics at the University of Chicago. Her research deals with issues of morphology, syntax, and information structure in Meskwaki and Plains Cree.

Dianne Friesen lives in Sydney, Cape Breton, Nova Scotia, where she studies the Mi'kmaq language and grammar. She is a PhD student in linguistics at the University of Victoria.

Ives Goddard is Senior Linguist, Emeritus, in the Department of Anthropology in the National Museum of Natural History, Smithsonian Institution. He has conducted fieldwork on Munsee, Unami, and Meskwaki and has written extensively on Native North American languages, cultures, and ethnohistory, particularly of the speakers of Algonquian languages.

Atticus G. Harrigan is a graduate student in the Department of Linguistics at the University of Alberta studying corpus and computational linguistics of North American indigenous languages. His research focuses on morphosyntax, phonetics, and semantics, as well as endangered language sustainability.

Mans Hulden is an assistant professor in linguistics at the University of Colorado Boulder, where he also holds an affiliation with the Institute of Cognitive Science. His research focuses on developing computational methods to model linguistic structure, particularly in the domains of phonology and morphology. Much of this work involves development of language resources, particularly for minority and low-resource languages.

Philip S. LeSourd is an associate professor of anthropology and second language studies at Indiana University, Bloomington. He has worked with the Maliseet and Passamaquoddy communities in New Brunswick and Maine since the 1970s.

Robert E. Lewis Jr. is a graduate student in linguistics at the University of Chicago.

Hunter Thompson Lockwood received his PhD from the University of Wisconsin–Madison in 2017. His research focuses on Algonquian language documentation; he helped produce the first authoritative dictionary of Potawatomi and wrote a descriptive grammar of the language for his dissertation.

Cherry Meyer is currently a doctoral candidate in linguistics at the University of Chicago with a focus on Anishinaabemowin. She has worked on topics such as discontinuous constituents, word order, information structure, and, most recently, gender and classifiers.

Mizuki Miyashita is a professor of linguistics at the University of Montana. Her research focus is Blackfoot prosody. She is also interested in documentary linguistics and has recorded Blackfoot lullabies, narratives, and conversations.

Campbell Nilsen is a graduate of the University of Oklahoma with a strong interest in historical linguistics, linguistic typology, and the languages of North America. He currently teaches English in Sichuan and is working on an extended study in the historical development of the Menominee inflectional complex prior to a return to linguistics on the postgraduate level.

Margaret Noodin is director of the Electa Quinney Institute for American Indian Education and associate professor of English at the University of Wisconsin–Milwaukee. She is the author of *Bawaajimo: A Dialect of Dreams in Anishinaabe Language and Literature* and *Weweni*, a collection of bilingual poems in Ojibwe and English. She also serves as editor of www.ojibwe.net.

Elizabeth Paul and her late husband were married for forty-five years. They have five grown children and nineteen grandchildren. She has worked more than forty years teaching Mi'kmaq language and writing. She has taught in schools, in universities, and at the community level. She works in curriculum development for the Mi'kmaq Immersion School, translating and editing documents into Mi'kmaq, and teaches Mi'kmaw language at the university. She is also an orthography consultant.

Serge Paul is married with four children and three grandchildren. Known as an *etawaqa'teket*—a jack-of-all-trades—he works for the Eskasoni School Board. He is also recognized by the community as a good speaker of Mi'kmaq.

Carl Schaefer is a volunteer at the Smithsonian Institution. He holds a PhD in general linguistics from Cornell University.

Katherine Schmirler received her MA in linguistics from the University of Toronto and is currently pursuing a PhD in linguistics at the University of Alberta. She is involved with the Alberta Language Technology Laboratory's Plains Cree dictionary collaboration with Maskwacîs Education and Schools Commission (MESC, formerly Miyo Wahkohtowin Education) located in Maskwacîs, Alberta.

Miikka Silfverberg is a postdoctoral researcher at the University of Colorado Boulder. His work falls within the fields of natural language processing (NLP) and computational linguistics. His primary research interests include NLP for morphologically complex and underserved languages, computational semantics, morphological tagging, parsing, as well as computational phonology and morphology.

Arlene Stevens is married to Spencer Stevens, is the mother of three adult children, and has ten grandchildren. She worked as a teacher and vice principal in the Eskasoni School and now does translating for the Eskasoni School Board. She has also taught adult education and courses for McGill University and has done translation for government contracts. She has also been involved in transcribing old Mi'kmaq language and song into the modern writing system. She has been involved in the church choir, in prayer ministries, and in the translation of Bible stories (both written and oral) into Mi'kmaq and the Lectionary. She has a Bachelor of Education and certificate in Mi'kmaw immersion.

Barbara Sylliboy is a Mi'kmaq from Nova Scotia with two daughters and several grandchildren. She has a Bachelor of Arts and a Bachelor of Education. She has taught in the Mi'kmaw Language Program at the school in Eskasoni, helped to organize and facilitate the Mi'kmaw Immersion certificate program at St. Francis Xavier University, and mentored students at Cape Breton University. She works as a translator to develop curriculum for the Mi'kmaw immersion program at Eskasoni school, and does translation contracts for the government and various people. She is also involved in translation of oral and written Bible stories in Mi'kmaq and translation of the Lectionary.

Jimena Terraza holds a PhD in linguistics and specializes in an indigenous language of South America called Wichi, for which she wrote a reference grammar. Aside from her expertise in grammar, she has completed postdoctoral studies on animacy hierarchies in Anishinabemowin (Ojibwe). She was a member of a research team for the Cree dialects spoken along the North Shore in Quebec and currently works as a consultant for Moose Cree First Nation in language revitalization. She is the author of *Moose Cree: A Learner's Grammar.*

Arok Wolvengrey is professor of linguistics and coordinator for the Indigenous Languages and Linguistics programs at First Nations University of Canada (FNUniv) and the University of Regina. He specializes in Cree language studies, particularly syntax, and Algonquian linguistics in general. He has been active in Cree revitalization efforts, in addition to his descriptive and theoretical linguistic research, and he serves as the series editor for the University of Regina Press's First Nations Language Reader series.